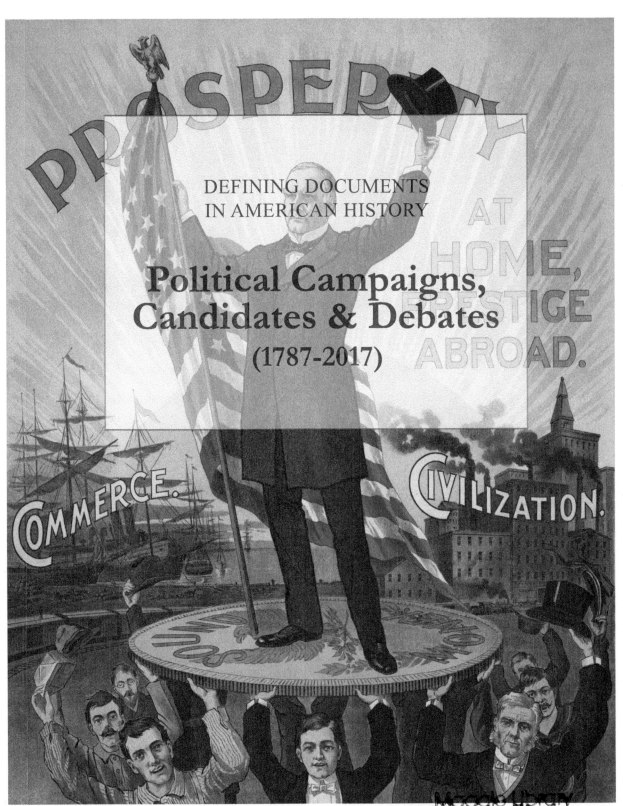

DEFINING DOCUMENTS
IN AMERICAN HISTORY

Political Campaigns, Candidates & Debates

(1787-2017)

DEFINING DOCUMENTS
IN AMERICAN HISTORY

Political Campaigns, Candidates & Debates

(1787-2017)

Volume 2

Editor

Michael Shally-Jensen, PhD

SALEM PRESS
A Division of EBSCO Information Services, Inc.
Ipswich, Massachusetts

GREY HOUSE PUBLISHING

Publisher's Cataloging-In-Publication Data
(Prepared by The Donohue Group, Inc.)

Names: Shally-Jensen, Michael, editor.
Title: Political campaigns, candidates & debates (1787-2017) / editor, Michael Shally-Jensen, PhD.
Other Titles: Political campaigns, candidates and debates (1787-2017) | Defining documents in American history (Salem Press)
Description: [First edition]. | Ipswich, Massachusetts : Salem Press, a division of EBSCO Information Services ; [Amenia, New York] : Grey House Publishing, [2018] | Includes bibliographical references and index.
Identifiers: ISBN 9781682177006 (set) | ISBN 9781682172995 (v.1) | ISBN 9781682173008 (v.2)
Subjects: LCSH: Political campaigns--United States--Sources. | Campaign debates--United States--Sources. | Speeches, addresses, etc., American--Sources. | United States--Politics and government--Sources. | Political oratory--United States--Sources.
Classification: LCC JK2281 .P65 2018 | DDC 324.70973--dc23

FIRST PRINTING
PRINTED IN THE UNITED STATES OF AMERICA

Contents

THE SEVENTH PARTY SYSTEM? 2016-

APPENDIXES

Chronology

Web Resources

Bibliography

Index

Complete List of Contents

Volume 1

THE FIRST AND SECOND PARTY SYSTEMS, 1787–1854

THE THIRD PARTY SYSTEM, 1854-96

THE FOURTH PARTY SYSTEM, 1896-1932

Volume 2

THE FIFTH PARTY SYSTEM, 1932-60

THE SIXTH PARTY SYSTEM, PART I, 1960-1974

The Sixth Party System, Part II, 1974-2016

The Seventh Party System? 2016-

Appendixes

DEFINING DOCUMENTS
IN AMERICAN HISTORY

Political Campaigns, Candidates & Debates (1787-2017)

THE FIFTH PARTY SYSTEM, 1932-60

The fifth party system began with FDR and the New Deal and encompassed World War II, the start of the Cold War, the Korean War, and the age of Eisenhower, the last of which some observers point to as the height of American power and stability. (Others are less sanguine about that.) As noted in the Introduction, some scholars believe that the fifth party system lasted into the 1960s or even into the 1980s or beyond. But for our purposes, here, we prefer the shorter time period, from 1932 to 1960.

Although control of the executive was split into a long period of Democratic control (1933-53) and two terms of Republican control (1953-61), rivalry between the two parties was persistent and the control of government was not one-sided—in fact, often it was divided between the two. The Democratic constituency was made up labor unions, urban machines, agrarian populists, Southerners, disenfranchised African Americans, Catholics, and liberal intellectuals. (A strange brew, indeed.) The Republican constituency was made up of economic and cultural conservatives, business owners, old-line Protestants, law-and-order voters, and nativist/anti-immigration elements. Most came together to one degree or another during the war years, but for much of the rest of the period the social and political landscapes were turbulent.

Although no major party realignments took place between the time of Eisenhower and the election, in 1960, of John F. Kennedy, the latter event can serve as the close of the fifth phase of U.S. political history and the start of the sixth because of disruptions (Civil Rights) and realignments that would soon take place.

■ FDR's Fireside Chat on "The Forgotten Man" Speech

Date: April 7, 1932
Author: Franklin D. Roosevelt
Genre: Speech

Summary Overview

In 1932, New York governor and presidential candidate Franklin D. Roosevelt delivered a radio address to the American people regarding the economic crisis. Following the stock market crash in 1929, the Great Depression hit the United States, leading to widespread unemployment, home and farm foreclosures, and financial loss. In his address, Roosevelt stated that any permanent solution must be built from the "bottom up," and he outlined three steps he believed were necessary to secure economic recovery: first, purchasing power had to be restored to American farmers; second, the federal government had to provide financial relief to small banks in order to prevent further foreclosures; and third, tariff policies had to be revised to ensure that the United States could sell its excess consumer goods on the global market.

Defining Moment

The United States experienced an economic boom during the 1920s. Europe had suffered significant infrastructure damage during World War I, placing the United States in a relatively strong financial position with its abundant raw materials and available investment funds. Technological developments such as mass-production assembly lines allowed more goods to be manufactured quickly and cheaply. Newly imposed import tariffs encouraged citizens to buy American-made goods, and favorable tax laws encouraged businessmen to invest in the manufacturing sector.

This changed abruptly on October 24, 1929, when the U.S. stock market began a rapid, steady decline. By the following week, panic was in full swing as stock prices across all economic sectors plummeted. Banks of all sizes were in danger of closing their doors, and many demanded immediate repayment of loans and mortgages in an attempt to save their businesses. However, few borrowers—either personal or corporate— had cash available for immediate repayment. By November 1929, the value of the stock market decreased by $30 billion; many companies closed, leading to widespread unemployment.

By the end of the 1920s, numerous countries around the world with free-market economies experienced similar financial decline. Some were hit harder than others, and the situation was especially dire in the United States. By 1932, the stock market had dropped to about 20 percent of its 1929 value. By the time the Great Depression reached its official peak in 1933, 25 percent of workers were unemployed, and thousands of U.S. banks had collapsed. The increased unemployment led to decreased spending and lower demand for consumer goods, which led to fewer manufacturing jobs and ultimately even more unemployment. The failure of so many banks—including many large ones—led to further foreclosures and restricted access to the credit many believed was necessary to boost the depressed economy.

In the immediate aftermath of the 1929 crash, President Herbert Hoover and his administration established or expanded several government programs designed to help destitute Americans. However, the public criticized his approach as spending too heavily on corporate subsidies while ordinary Americans literally starved. For example, Hoover established the Reconstruction Finance Corporation, which lent $2 billion in government funds to banks, insurance companies, building and loan associations, agricultural credit organizations, and railroads. By contrast, Hoover declined to support a bill that would have provided additional payments to World War I veterans for their time in the service, claiming the $4 billion price tag was too high.

By 1932, Roosevelt, then the New York state governor, was campaigning in earnest to become the next president of the United States. His platform focused on establishing federal programs designed to provide immediate relief to the starving and homeless and to put Americans back to work through government-funded works projects such as environmental conservation initiatives and improvements to government buildings and other public infrastructure.

Author Biography

Franklin D. Roosevelt was born on January 30, 1882, in Hyde Park, New York. He attended Groton School in Massachusetts and received his bachelor's degree in history from Harvard University. He studied law at Columbia University in New York, but, upon passing the bar examination, left school without completing his degree in 1907. He practiced law in New York City for three years, before being elected to the New York State Senate in 1910.

President Woodrow Wilson appointed Roosevelt assistant secretary of the Navy from 1913 until 1920. Following an unsuccessful run for U.S. vice president as the running mate of James M. Cox, Roosevelt briefly withdrew from politics. After a partial recovery from polio he contracted in 1921, Roosevelt was elected governor of New York State in 1928. In 1932, Roosevelt was elected president of the United States. He was inaugurated during the height of the Great Depression and saw the country through World War II. He died while still in office on April 12, 1945.

HISTORICAL DOCUMENT

Although I understand that I am talking under the auspices of the Democratic National Committee, I do not want to limit myself to politics. I do not want to feel that I am addressing an audience of Democrats or that I speak merely as a Democrat myself. The present condition of our national affairs is too serious to be viewed through partisan eyes for partisan purposes.

Fifteen years ago my public duty called me to an active part in a great national emergency, the World War. Success then was due to a leadership whose vision carried beyond the timorous and futile gesture of sending a tiny army of 150,000 trained soldiers and the regular navy to the aid of our allies. The generalship of that moment conceived of a whole Nation mobilized for war, economic, industrial, social and military resources gathered into a vast unit capable of and actually in the process of throwing into the scales ten million men equipped with physical needs and sustained by the realization that behind them were the united efforts of 110,000,000 human beings. It was a great plan because it was built from bottom to top and not from top to bottom. In my calm judgment, the Nation faces today a more grave emergency than in 1917.

It is said that Napoleon lost the battle of Waterloo because he forgot his infantry—he staked too much upon the more spectacular but less substantial cavalry. The present administration in Washington provides a close parallel. It has either forgotten or it does not want to remember the infantry of our economic army. These

unhappy times call for the building of plans that rest upon the forgotten, the unorganized but the indispensable units of economic power, for plans like those of 1917 that build from the bottom up and not from the top down, that put their faith once more in the forgotten man at the bottom of the economic pyramid. Obviously, these few minutes tonight permit no opportunity to lay down the ten or a dozen closely related objectives of a plan to meet our present emergency, but I can draw a few essentials, a beginning in fact, of a planned program.

It is the habit of the unthinking to turn in times like this to the illusions of economic magic. People suggest that a huge expenditure of public funds by the Federal Government and by State and local governments will completely solve the unemployment problem. But it is clear that even if we could raise many billions of dollars and find definitely useful public works to spend these billions on, even all that money would not give employment to the seven million or ten million people who are out of work. Let us admit frankly that it would be only a stopgap. A real economic cure must go to the killing of the bacteria in the system rather than to the treatment of external symptoms.

How much do the shallow thinkers realize, for example, that approximately one-half of our whole population, fifty or sixty million people, earn their living by farming or in small towns whose existence immediately depends on farms. They have today lost their purchasing power. Why? They are receiving for farm products less than the cost to them of growing these farm products. The result of this loss of purchasing power is that many other millions of people engaged in industry in the cities cannot sell industrial products to the farming half of the Nation. This brings home to every city worker that his own employment is directly tied up with the farmer's dollar. No Nation can long endure half bankrupt. Main Street, Broadway, the mills, the mines will close if half the buyers are broke.

I cannot escape the conclusion that one of the essential parts of a national program of restoration must be to restore purchasing power to the farming half of the country. Without this the wheels of railroads and of factories will not turn.

Closely associated with this first objective is the problem of keeping the home-owner and the farm-owner where he is, without being dispossessed through the foreclosure of his mortgage. His relationship to the great banks of Chicago and New York is pretty remote. The two billion dollar fund which President Hoover and the Congress have put at the disposal of the big banks, the railroads and the corporations of the Nation is not for him.

His is a relationship to his little local bank or local loan company. It is a sad fact that even though the local lender in many cases does not want to evict the farmer or home-owner by foreclosure proceedings, he is forced to do so in order to keep his bank or company solvent. Here should be an objective of Government itself, to provide at least as much assistance to the little fellow as it is now giving to the large banks and corporations. That is another example of building from the bottom up.

One other objective closely related to the problem of selling American products is to provide a tariff policy based upon economic common sense rather than upon politics, hot-air, and pull. This country during the past few years, culminating with the Hawley-Smoot Tariff in 1929, has compelled the world to build tariff fences so high that world trade is decreasing to the vanishing point. The value of goods internationally exchanged is today less than half of what it was three or four years ago. Every man and woman who gives any thought to the subject knows that if our factories run even 80 percent of capacity, they will turn out more products than we as a Nation can possibly use ourselves. The answer is that if they run on 80 percent of capacity, we must sell some goods abroad. How can we do that if the outside Nations cannot pay us in cash? And we know by sad experience that they cannot do that. The only way they can pay us is in their own goods or raw materials, but this foolish tariff of ours makes that impossible.

What we must do is this: revise our tariff on the basis of a reciprocal exchange of goods, allowing other Nations to buy and to pay for our goods by sending us such of their goods as will not seriously throw any of our industries out of balance, and incidentally making impossible in this country the continuance of pure monopolies which cause us to pay excessive prices for many of the necessities of life.

Such objectives as these three, restoring farmers' buying power, relief to the small banks and home-owners and a reconstructed tariff policy, are only a part of ten or a dozen vital factors. But they seem to be beyond the concern of a national administration which can think in terms only of the top of the social and economic structure. It has sought temporary relief from the top down rather than permanent relief from the bottom up. It has totally failed to plan ahead in a comprehensive way. It has waited until something has cracked and then at the last moment has sought to prevent total collapse. It is high time to get back to fundamentals. It is high time to admit with courage that we are in the midst of an emergency at least equal to that of war. Let us mobilize to meet it.

Document Analysis

Roosevelt begins his radio address by recounting the Allied forces' success in World War I. He observes that success came from a "bottom-up" approach that rallied support, from not only trained military personnel, but also from more than 100 million ordinary people across the globe. He offers this story to demonstrate his position that building from the "bottom up" is the best approach to resolving the economic crisis.

Many factors contributed to the Great Depression, but Roosevelt says the main cause is relatively straightforward: Farmers—nearly half of the country's population—lost a significant amount of purchasing power when prices dropped because of overproduction. Because of this loss, families could no longer afford to purchase manufactured goods, which led to job loss in the industrial sectors. In turn, this further eroded the purchasing power of the American public and created a cycle of economic loss.

Roosevelt believes that the country must once again use a bottom-up approach in order to improve the economy. He says that large expenditures of public funds for creating government works-related jobs are only a stopgap measure, and it is necessary to address the root of the problem. The federal government must provide financial assistance to smaller banks to help them maintain solvency and prevent them from foreclosing on houses and farms. Additionally, the 1930 Hawley-Smoot Tariff Act compounds the overproduction problem: with the decline of the American consumer's purchasing power, too many excess goods exist in the domestic market, thus driving down prices. But with the high tariff rates and the prohibition on international exchange of goods in favor of cash-only transactions, companies have no viable way of selling these excesses on the global market.

Roosevelt concludes by identifying three steps necessary to bring the economy back into balance: farmers' purchasing power must be restored; the federal government must provide financial relief to small banks and homeowners; and the tariff policy must be revised to give American goods an outlet in the global market. Roosevelt closes by saying that "it is high time to get back to fundamentals," and encourages the American public to mobilize to meet the challenges presented by the state of the economy.

Essential Themes

A significant theme throughout Roosevelt's campaign and presidency was his attention to the plight of everyday Americans. Many believe that his bottom-up approach to economic recovery was a major contributing factor to his victory over Herbert Hoover in the 1932 election. Contrary to Hoover's approach, Roosevelt believed that first restoring financial security to the farmers and workers would lead to increased spending and ultimately strengthen corporate financial positions. Additionally, Roosevelt frequently addressed the impact of global trade barriers on the domestic economy.

He explained how the European and U.S. economies were interconnected, especially in light of American investments in Europe's post– World War I rebuilding efforts. As economies softened across the globe in the early 1930s, the United States and many other countries enacted or raised tariffs to protect their domestic production from global competition. But the combination of overproduction and high export barriers created a surplus of goods that drove down prices across the manufacturing sector, thus decreasing the purchasing power of both industrial workers and farmers. Restoring a proper balance of international trade, Roosevelt believed, was another key factor to economic recovery.

Despite Roosevelt's new ideas and significant financial investment from the federal government, recovery from the Great Depression was slow. The economy showed signs of improving in 1933, but it stalled during 1934 and 1935 before picking up again between 1935 and 1937. A second wave of economic depression hit in 1937, however, from which the United States did not fully recover until entering World War II in 1941.

—*Tracey M. DiLascio, JD*

Bibliography and Additional Reading

"The Great Depression (1929–1939)." *Eleanor Roosevelt Papers Project*. George Washington U, n.d. Web. 18 May 2014.

McElvaine, Robert S. *The Great Depression: America, 1929–1941*. 25th anniversary ed. New York: Three Rivers, 2009. Print.

Smith, Jean Edward. *FDR*. New York: Random, 2007. Print.

■ FDR on Government's Role in the Economy

Date: September 23, 1932
Author: Franklin D. Roosevelt
Genre: Speech

Summary Overview

In this speech, given during his 1932 presidential campaign, Franklin D. Roosevelt laid out his reasons for believing that a new relationship or "social contract" between the American people and its government was needed. As economic conditions worsened during the Great Depression, Roosevelt proposed that the government needed to be involved in a new way to protect individual rights, this time not against political tyranny, but against the economic power of corporations. Roosevelt argued that this new relationship between individual Americans and their government could preserve the core values of democracy—such as the ability of individuals to succeed through hard work—against the threat of industries that had a stranglehold on labor, resources, and finances. This new relationship became the basis for Roosevelt's New Deal policies and programs after he won the 1932 election. New Deal programs were designed to reform the financial system, stabilize the economy, and provide employment using unprecedented government regulation and intervention. The philosophical basis for Roosevelt's activist agenda was articulated clearly in this speech.

Defining Moment

On October 29, 1929, a day that came to be known as Black Tuesday, the United States stock market crashed, sending the nation into the worst economic depression it had ever seen. The 1920s had seen unprecedented growth in finance and industry, as politicians loosened regulations and unapologetically pursued pro-business policies. There was no federal deposit insurance system for banks and no unemployment insurance. Labor unions, which traditionally offered a measure of protection for working people, were weakened by anti-immigrant and anti- Socialist sentiment, internal divisions, and economic prosperity, which lessened public support for labor activism. In the fallout from the stock market crash, corporations went bankrupt, banks failed, and by 1932, approximately

one-quarter of the nation's workforce was unemployed. In industrial cities and major ports, unemployment rates reached even higher than the national average. Farm prices fell by more than 50 percent. President Herbert Hoover and many others in government saw the crash as part of a recession that would quickly right itself, and Hoover urged patience and private charitable assistance to the poor, believing that it was not the government's job to interfere with business and the economy.

By the election of 1932, many Americans were destitute, and it was clear that the Great Depression was not a short-lived economic downturn. The election pitted the incumbent Hoover, a Republican, against the popular Democratic governor of New York, Franklin Delano Roosevelt. Hoover argued that Roosevelt's belief in an activist, interventionist government might help in the short term, but would ultimately lead to Socialism. Hoover opposed direct government aid to individuals, believing it to be against the spirit of American individualism. Hoover failed to see that the nation had lost all faith in the ability of corporations and industry to help put the economy right, and people in bread lines were no longer interested in the philosophical underpinnings of the Hoover administration's refusal to intervene. Roosevelt spoke of the government's responsibility to protect the individual and blamed Hoover and the Republicans for the disastrous economic situation.

Roosevelt won the 1932 election by a landslide, extending Democratic control over the House and Senate as well. An era of Republican leadership ended, as Republicans had largely dominated the presidency since 1860, with the exception of Grover Cleveland and Woodrow Wilson. Roosevelt's election signaled the beginning of twenty years of Democratic leadership in the White House.

When Roosevelt took office in March 1933, he acted quickly to bring relief to the poor and unemployed and to stabilize the economy. In the first months of his administration, he closed banks that were insolvent and reorganized those that remained, urging the American people to return their money to savings and promising to protect their investments. Roosevelt oversaw the repeal of Prohibition, initiated several major public works projects, and supported subsidies for farmers. Roosevelt encouraged organized labor, as he saw unions as a way to protect workers. In his first one hundred days in office, Roosevelt made major regulatory and domestic reforms and had clearly kept his promise to offer a "New Deal" to the American people.

Author Biography

Franklin Delano Roosevelt was born on January 30, 1882, in Hyde Park, New York, to a wealthy family. He was a distant cousin of President Theodore Roosevelt. Roosevelt attended the prestigious Groton School and then Harvard University, where he graduated with a degree in history. Roosevelt met his fifth cousin and future wife, Eleanor, in 1902, and they married in 1905. Roosevelt passed the New York State bar exam in 1907 and worked as a corporate lawyer. Roosevelt won election to the New York state senate in 1910, and he worked to end the control of the Tammany Hall branch of the Democratic Party in New York. He was appointed assistant secretary of the Navy by President Woodrow Wilson in 1913, serving until he was selected as the vice presidential running mate of James M. Cox for the 1920 presidential election. Cox was ultimately defeated by Warren G. Harding.

Roosevelt was stricken with polio in 1921 and lost the use of his legs. Roosevelt served as the governor of New York from 1929 until 1932, when he ran for and won the presidency of the United States. His first term as president coincided with the lowest point of the Great Depression, and he immediately turned his attention to the relief of the unemployed. Roosevelt implemented the New Deal, a series of domestic programs designed to return the nation to prosperity. He was reelected by a wide margin in 1936 and then won an unprecedented third term in 1940 during World War II. He was elected to a fourth term in 1944, but he died in office on April 12, 1945. He was buried in Hyde Park, New York.

HISTORICAL DOCUMENT

My Friends:

I count it a privilege to be invited to address the Commonwealth Club. It has stood in the life of this city and State, and it is perhaps accurate to add, the Nation, as a group of citizen leaders interested in fundamental problems of Government, and chiefly concerned with achievement of progress in Government through non-partisan means. The privilege of addressing you, therefore, in the heat of a political campaign, is great. I want to respond to your courtesy in terms consistent with your policy.

I want to speak not of politics but of Government. I want to speak not of parties, but of universal principles. They are not political, except in that larger sense in which a great American once expressed a definition of politics, that nothing in all of human life is foreign to the science of politics.

I do want to give you, however, a recollection of a long life spent for a large part in public office. Some of my conclusions and observations have been deeply accentuated in these past few weeks. I have traveled far—from Albany to the Golden Gate. I have seen many people, and heard many things, and today, when in a sense my journey has reached the half-way mark, I am glad of the opportunity to discuss with you what it all means to me. Sometimes, my friends, particularly in years such as these, the hand of discouragement falls upon us. It seems that things are in a rut, fixed, settled, that the world has grown old and tired and very much out of joint. This is the mood of depression, of dire and weary depression. But then we look around us in America, and everything tells us that we are wrong. America is new. It is in the process of change and development. It has the great potentialities of youth, and particularly is this true of the great West, and of this coast, and of California.

I would not have you feel that I regard this as in any sense a new community. I have traveled in many parts of the world, but never have I felt the arresting thought of the change and development more than here, where the old, mystic East would seem to be near to us, where the currents of life and thought and commerce of the whole world meet us. This factor alone is sufficient to cause man to stop and think of the deeper meaning of things,

2232. 78th Street
Brooklyn, N.Y.
March 13th 1933.

Secretary to the President
The White House
Washington. D.C.

Dear Sir:

Being a citizen of little or no consequence I feel the utter futility of writing to the President at a time such as this, but I trust you will accept this letter in the spirit in which it was written.

For me to sit down to write to any public official, whoever he may be, it must be prompted by a very special and appealing occasion or personality. That happened last evening, as I listened to the President's broadcast. I felt that he walked into my home, sat down and in plain and forceful language explained to me how he was tackling the job I and my fellow citizens gave him. I thought what a splendid thing it would be if he could find time to do that occasionally.

Needless to say, such forceful, direct and honest action commands the respect of all Americans, it is certainly deserving of it.

My humble and sincere gratitude to a great leader. May God protect him.

Respectfully

J. F. Bambo

Letter to the White House following the first fireside chat on the Banking Crisis, eight days after taking office (March 12, 1933) 2232. 78th Street Brooklyn, N.Y. March 13, 1933. (U.S. National Archives and Records Administration) when he stands in this community.

But more than that, I appreciate that the membership of this club consists of men who are thinking in terms beyond the immediate present, beyond their own immediate tasks, beyond their own individual interests. I want to invite you, therefore, to consider with me in the large, some of the relationships of government and economic life that go deeply into our daily lives, our happiness, our future and our security.

The issue of Government has always been whether individual men and women will have to serve some system of Government or economics, or whether a system of Government and economics exists to serve individual men and women. This question has persistently dominated the discussion of government for many generations. On questions relating to these things men have differed, and for time immemorial it is probable that honest men will continue to differ.

The final word belongs to no man; yet we can still believe in change and in progress. Democracy, as a dear old friend of mine in Indiana, Meredith Nicholson, has called it, is a quest, a never-ending seeking for better things, and in the seeking for these things and the striving for them, there are many roads to follow. But, if we map the course of these roads, we find that there are only two general directions.

When we look about us, we are likely to forget how hard people have worked to win the privilege of government. The growth of the national Governments of Europe was a struggle for the development of a centralized force in the Nation, strong enough to impose peace upon ruling barons. In many instances the victory of the central Government, the creation of a strong central Government, was a haven of refuge to the individual.

The people preferred the master far away to the exploitation and cruelty of the smaller master near at hand. But the creators of national Government were perforce ruthless men. They were often cruel in their methods, but they did strive steadily toward something that society needed and very much wanted, a strong central State able to keep the peace, to stamp out civil war, to put the unruly nobleman in his place, and to permit the bulk of individuals to live safely. The man of ruthless force had his place in developing a pioneer country, just as he did in fixing the power of the central Government in the development of Nations. Society paid him well for his services and its development. When the development among the Nations of Europe, however, had been completed, ambition and ruthlessness, having served their term, tended to overstep their mark.

There came a growing feeling that Government was conducted for the benefit of a few who thrived unduly at the expense of all. The people sought a balancing—a limiting force. There came gradually, through town councils, trade guilds, national parliaments, by constitution and by popular participation and control, limitations on arbitrary power.

Another factor that tended to limit the power of those who ruled, was the rise of the ethical conception that a ruler bore a responsibility for the welfare of his subjects. The American colonies were born in this struggle. The American Revolution was a turning point in it. After the Revolution the struggle continued and shaped itself in the public life of the country. There were those who because they had seen the confusion which attended the years of war for American independence surrendered to the belief that popular Government was essentially dangerous and essentially unworkable. They were honest people, my friends, and we cannot deny that their experience had warranted some measure of fear. The most brilliant, honest and able exponent of this point of view was Hamilton. He was too impatient of slow-moving methods. Fundamentally he believed that the safety of the republic lay in the autocratic strength of its Government, that the destiny of individuals was to serve that Government, and that fundamentally a great and strong group of central institutions, guided by a small group of able and public spirited citizens, could best direct all Government.

But Mr. Jefferson, in the summer of 1776, after drafting the Declaration of Independence turned his mind to the same problem and took a different view. He did not deceive himself with outward forms. Government to him was a means to an end, not an end in itself; it might be either a refuge and a help or a threat and a danger, depending on the circumstances. We find him carefully analyzing the society for which he was to organize a Government. "We have no paupers. The great mass of our population is of laborers, our rich who cannot live without labor, either manual or professional, being few and of moderate wealth. Most of the laboring class possess property, cultivate their own lands, have families and from the demand for their labor, are enabled to exact from the rich and the competent such prices as enable them to feed abundantly, clothe above mere decency, to labor moderately and raise their families."

These people, he considered, had two sets of rights, those of "personal competency" and those involved in acquiring and possessing property. By "personal competency" he meant the right of free thinking, freedom of forming and expressing opinions, and freedom of personal living, each man according to his own Rights. To insure the first set of rights, a Government must so order its functions as not to interfere with the individual. But even Jefferson realized that the exercise of the property rights might so interfere with the rights of the individual that the Government, without whose assistance the property rights could not exist, must intervene, not to destroy individualism, but to protect it.

You are familiar with the great political duel which followed; and how Hamilton, and his friends, building toward a dominant centralized power were at length defeated in the great election of 1800, by Mr. Jefferson's party. Out of that duel came the two parties, Republican and Democratic, as we know them today.

So began, in American political life, the new day, the day of the individual against the system, the day in which individualism was made the great watchword of American life. The happiest of economic conditions made that day long and splendid. On the Western frontier, land was substantially free. No one, who did not shirk the task of earning a living, was entirely without opportunity to do so. Depressions could, and did, come and go; but they could not alter the fundamental fact that most of the people lived partly by selling their labor and partly by extracting their livelihood from the soil, so that starvation and dislocation were practically impossible. At the very worst there was always the possibility of climbing into a covered wagon and moving west where the untilled prairies afforded a haven for men to whom the East did not provide a place. So great were our natural resources that we could offer this relief not only to our own people, but to the distressed of all the world; we could invite immigration from Europe, and welcome it with open arms.

Traditionally, when a depression came a new section

of land was opened in the West; and even our temporary misfortune served our manifest destiny. It was in the middle of the nineteenth century that a new force was released and a new dream created. The force was what is called the industrial revolution, the advance of steam and machinery and the rise of the forerunners of the modern industrial plant. The dream was the dream of an economic machine, able to raise the standard of living for everyone; to bring luxury within the reach of the humblest; to annihilate distance by steam power and later by electricity, and to release everyone from the drudgery of the heaviest manual toil. It was to be expected that this would necessarily affect Government.

Heretofore, Government had merely been called upon to produce conditions within which people could live happily, labor peacefully, and rest secure. Now it was called upon to aid in the consummation of this new dream. There was, however, a shadow over the dream. To be made real, it required use of the talents of men of tremendous will and tremendous ambition, since by no other force could the problems of financing and engineering and new developments be brought to a consummation. So manifest were the advantages of the machine age, however, that the United States fearlessly, cheerfully, and, I think, rightly, accepted the bitter with the sweet. It was thought that no price was too high to pay for the advantages which we could draw from a finished industrial system. This history of the last half century is accordingly in large measure a history of a group of financial Titans, whose methods were not scrutinized with too much care and who were honored in proportion as they produced the results, irrespective of the means they used. The financiers who pushed the railroads to the Pacific were always ruthless, often wasteful, and frequently corrupt; but they did build railroads, and we have them today. It has been estimated that the American investor paid for the American railway system more than three times over in the process; but despite this fact the net advantage was to the United States. As long as we had free land; as long as population was growing by leaps and bounds; as long as our industrial plants were insufficient to supply our own needs, society chose to give the ambitious man free play and unlimited reward provided only that he produced the economic plant so much desired.

During this period of expansion, there was equal opportunity for all and the business of Government was not to interfere but to assist in the development of industry. This was done at the request of business men themselves. The tariff was originally imposed for the purpose of "fostering our infant industry," a phrase I think the older among you will remember as a political issue not so long ago. The railroads were subsidized, sometimes by grants of money, oftener by grants of land; some of the most valuable oil lands in the United States were granted to assist the financing of the railroad which pushed through the Southwest. A nascent merchant marine was assisted by grants of money, or by mail subsidies, so that our steam shipping might ply the seven seas. Some of my friends tell me that they do not want the Government in business. With this I agree; but I wonder whether they realize the implications of the past. For while it has been American doctrine that the Government must not go into business in competition with private enterprises, still it has been traditional, particularly in Republican administrations, for business urgently to ask the Government to put at private disposal all kinds of Government assistance. The same man who tells you that he does not want to see the Government interfere in business — and he means it, and has plenty of good reasons for saying so—is the first to go to Washington and ask the Government for a prohibitory tariff on his product. When things get just bad enough as they did two years ago, he will go with equal speed to the United States Government and ask for a loan; and the Reconstruction Finance Corporation is the outcome of it. Each group has sought protection from the Government for its own special interests, without realizing that the function of Government must be to favor no small group at the expense of its duty to protect the rights of personal freedom and of private property of all its citizens.

In retrospect we can now see that the turn of the tide came with the turn of the century. We were reaching our last frontier; there was no more free land and our industrial combinations had become great uncontrolled and irresponsible units of power within the State. Clear-sighted men saw with fear the danger that opportunity would no longer be equal; that the growing corporation, like the feudal baron of old, might threaten the economic freedom of individuals to earn a living. In that hour, our antitrust laws were born. The cry was raised against the great corporations. Theodore Roosevelt, the first great Republican Progressive, fought a Presidential campaign on the issue of "trust busting" and talked freely about malefactors of great wealth. If the government had a policy it was rather to turn the clock back, to destroy the large combinations and to return to the time when every man owned his individual small business.

This was impossible; Theodore Roosevelt, abandoning the idea of "trust busting," was forced to work out a difference between "good" trusts and "bad" trusts. The Supreme Court set forth the famous "rule of reason" by which it seems to have meant that a concentration of industrial power was permissible if the method by which it got its power, and the use it made of that power, were reasonable.

Woodrow Wilson, elected in 1912, saw the situation more clearly. Where Jefferson had feared the encroachment of political power on the lives of individuals, Wilson knew that the new power was financial. He saw, in the highly centralized economic system, the despot of the twentieth century, on whom great masses of individuals relied for their safety and their livelihood, and whose irresponsibility and greed (if they were not controlled) would reduce them to starvation and penury. The concentration of financial power had not proceeded so far in 1912 as it has today; but it had grown far enough for Mr. Wilson to realize fully its implications. It is interesting, now, to read his speeches. What is called "radical" today (and I have reason to know whereof I speak) is mild compared to the campaign of Mr. Wilson. "No man can deny," he said, "that the lines of endeavor have more and more narrowed and stiffened; no man who knows anything about the development of industry in this country can have failed to observe that the larger kinds of credit are more and more difficult to obtain unless you obtain them upon terms of uniting your efforts with those who already control the industry of the country, and nobody can fail to observe that every man who tries to set himself up in competition with any process of manufacture which has taken place under the control of large combinations of capital will presently find himself either squeezed out or obliged to sell and allow himself to be absorbed." Had there been no World War—had Mr. Wilson been able to devote eight years to domestic instead of to international affairs—we might have had a wholly different situation at the present time. However, the then distant roar of European cannon, growing ever louder, forced him to abandon the study of this issue. The problem he saw so clearly is left with us as a legacy; and no one of us on either side of the political controversy can deny that it is a matter of grave concern to the Government.

A glance at the situation today only too clearly indicates that equality of opportunity as we have known it no longer exists. Our industrial plant is built; the problem just now is whether under existing conditions it is not overbuilt. Our last frontier has long since been reached, and there is practically no more free land. More than half of our people do not live on the farms or on lands and cannot derive a living by cultivating their own property. There is no safety valve in the form of a Western prairie to which those thrown out of work by the Eastern economic machines can go for a new start. We are not able to invite the immigration from Europe to share our endless plenty. We are now providing a drab living for our own people.

Our system of constantly rising tariffs has at last reacted against us to the point of closing our Canadian frontier on the north, our European markets on the east, many of our Latin-American markets to the south, and a goodly proportion of our Pacific markets on the west, through the retaliatory tariffs of those countries. It has forced many of our great industrial institutions which exported their surplus production to such countries, to establish plants in such countries, within the tariff walls. This has resulted in the reduction of the operation of their American plants, and opportunity for employment. Just as freedom to farm has ceased, so also the opportunity in business has narrowed. It still is true that men can start small enterprises, trusting to native shrewdness and ability to keep abreast of competitors; but area after area has been pre-empted altogether by the great corporations, and even in the fields which still have no great concerns, the small man starts under a handicap. The unfeeling statistics of the past three decades show that the independent business man is running a losing race.

Perhaps he is forced to the wall; perhaps he cannot command credit; perhaps he is "squeezed out," in Mr. Wilson's words, by highly organized corporate competitors, as your corner grocery man can tell you. Recently a careful study was made of the concentration of business in the United States. It showed that our economic life was dominated by some six hundred odd corporations who controlled two-thirds of American industry. Ten million small business men divided the other third. More striking still, it appeared that if the process of concentration goes on at the same rate, at the end of another century we shall have all American industry controlled by a dozen corporations, and run by perhaps a hundred men. Put plainly, we are steering a steady course toward economic oligarchy, if we are not there already.

Clearly, all this calls for a re-appraisal of values. A mere builder of more industrial plants, a creator of more railroad systems, an organizer of more corporations, is as likely to be a danger as a help. The day of the great promoter or the financial Titan, to whom we granted anything if only he would build, or develop, is over. Our task now is not discovery or exploitation of natural resources, or necessarily producing more goods. It is the soberer, less dramatic business of administering resources and plants already in hand, of seeking to reestablish foreign markets for our surplus production, of meeting the problem of under-consumption, of adjusting production to consumption, of distributing wealth and products more equitably, of adapting existing economic organizations to the service of the people. The day of enlightened administration has come.

Just as in older times the central Government was first a haven of refuge, and then a threat, so now in a closer economic system the central and ambitious financial unit is no longer a servant of national desire, but a danger. I would draw the parallel one step farther. We did not think because national Government had become a threat in the eighteenth century that therefore we should abandon the principle of national Government. Nor today should we abandon the principle of strong economic units called corporations, merely because their power is susceptible of easy abuse. In other times we dealt with the problem of an unduly ambitious central Government by modifying it gradually into a constitutional democratic Government. So today we are modifying and controlling our economic units.

As I see it, the task of Government in its relation to business is to assist the development of an economic declaration of rights, an economic constitutional order. This is the common task of statesman and business man.

It is the minimum requirement of a more permanently safe order of things.

Happily, the times indicate that to create such an order not only is the proper policy of Government, but it is the only line of safety for our economic structures as well. We know, now, that these economic units cannot exist unless prosperity is uniform, that is, unless purchasing power is well distributed throughout every group in the Nation. That is why even the most selfish of corporations for its own interest would be glad to see wages restored and unemployment ended and to bring the Western farmer back to his accustomed level of prosperity and to assure a permanent safety to both groups. That is why some enlightened industries themselves endeavor to limit the freedom of action of each man and business group within the industry in the common interest of all; why business men everywhere are asking a form of organization which will bring the scheme into balance, even though it may in some measure qualify the freedom of action of individual units within the business. The exposition need not further be elaborated. It is brief and incomplete, but you will be able to expand it in terms of your own business or occupation without difficulty. I think everyone who has actually entered the economic struggle — which means everyone who was not born to safe wealth — knows in his own experience and his own life that we have now to apply the earlier concepts of American Government to the conditions of today.

The Declaration of Independence discusses the problem of Government in terms of a contract. Government is a relation of give and take, a contract, perforce, if we would follow the thinking out of which it grew. Under such a contract rulers were accorded power, and the people consented to that power on consideration that they be accorded certain rights. The task of statesmanship has always been the re-definition of these rights in terms of a changing and growing social order. New conditions impose new requirements upon Government and those who conduct Government.

I held, for example, in proceedings before me as Governor, the purpose of which was the removal of the Sheriff of New York, that under modern conditions it was not enough for a public official merely to evade the legal terms of official wrongdoing. He owned a positive duty as well. I said in substance that if he had acquired large sums of money, he was when accused required to explain the sources of such wealth. To that extent this wealth was colored with a public interest. I said that in financial matters, public servants should, even beyond private citizens, be held to a stern and uncompromising rectitude. I feel that we are coming to a view through the drift of our legislation and our public thinking in the past quarter century that private economic power is, to enlarge an old phrase, a public trust as well. I hold that continued enjoyment of that power by any individual or group must depend upon the fulfillment of that trust. The men who have reached the summit of American business life know this best; happily, many of these urge the binding quality of this greater social contract.

The terms of that contract are as old as the Republic, and as new as the new economic order. Every man has a right to life; and this means that he has also a right to make a comfortable living. He may by sloth or crime decline to exercise that right; but it may not be denied him. We have no actual famine or dearth; our industrial and agricultural mechanism can produce enough and to spare. Our Government formal and informal, political and economic, owes to everyone an avenue to possess himself of a portion of that plenty sufficient for his needs, through his own work.

Every man has a right to his own property; which means a right to be assured, to the fullest extent attainable, in the safety of his savings. By no other means can men carry the burdens of those parts of life which, in the nature of things, afford no chance of labor; childhood, sickness, old age. In all thought of property, this right is paramount; all other property rights must yield to it. If, in accord with this principle, we must restrict the operations of the speculator, the manipulator, even the financier, I believe we must accept the restriction as needful, not to hamper individualism but to protect it.

These two requirements must be satisfied, in the main, by the individuals who claim and hold control of the great industrial and financial combinations which dominate so large a part of our industrial life. They have undertaken to be, not business men, but princes of property. I am not prepared to say that the system which produces them is wrong. I am very clear that they must fearlessly and competently assume the responsibility which goes with the power. So many enlightened business men know this that the statement would be little more than a platitude, were it not for an added implication. This implication is, briefly, that the responsible heads of finance and industry instead of acting each for himself, must work together to achieve the common end.

They must, where necessary, sacrifice this or that private advantage; and in reciprocal self-denial must seek a general advantage. It is here that formal Government—political Government, if you choose—comes in. Whenever in the pursuit of this objective the lone wolf, the unethical competitor, the reckless promoter, the Ishmael or Insull whose hand is against every man's, declines to join in achieving an end recognized as being for the public welfare, and threatens to drag the industry back to a state of anarchy, the Government may properly be asked to apply restraint. Likewise, should the group ever use its collective power contrary to the public welfare, the Government must be swift to enter and protect the public interest.

The Government should assume the function of economic regulation only as a last resort, to be tried only when private initiative, inspired by high responsibility, with such assistance and balance as Government can give, has finally failed. As yet there has been no final failure, because there has been no attempt; and I decline to assume that this Nation is unable to meet the situation. The final term of the high contract was for liberty and the pursuit of happiness. We have learned a great deal of both in the past century. We know that individual liberty and individual happiness mean nothing unless both are ordered in the sense that one man's meat is not another man's poison. We know that the old "rights of personal competency," the right to read, to think, to speak, to choose and live a mode of life, must be respected at all hazards. We know that liberty to do anything which deprives others of those elemental rights is outside the protection of any compact; and that Government in this regard is the maintenance of a balance, within which every individual may have a place if he will take it; in which every individual may find safety if he wishes it; in which every individual may attain such power as his ability permits, consistent with his assuming the accompanying responsibility.

All this is a long, slow talk. Nothing is more striking than the simple innocence of the men who insist, whenever an objective is present, on the prompt production of a patent scheme guaranteed to produce a result. Human endeavor is not so simple as that. Government includes the art of formulating a policy, and using the political technique to attain so much of that policy as will receive general support; persuading, leading, sacrificing, teaching always, because the greatest duty of the a statesman is to educate. But in the matters of which I have spoken, we are learning rapidly, in a severe school. The lessons so learned must not be forgotten, even in the mental lethargy of a speculative upturn. We must build toward the time when a major depression cannot occur again; and if this means sacrificing the easy profits of inflationist booms, then let them go; and good riddance. Faith in America, faith in our tradition of personal responsibility, faith in our institutions, faith in ourselves demand that we recognize the new terms of the old social contract. We shall fulfill them, as we fulfilled the obligation of the apparent Utopia which Jefferson imagined for us in 1776, and which Jefferson, Roosevelt and Wilson sought to bring to realization. We must do so, lest a rising tide of misery, engendered by our common failure, engulf us all. But failure is not an American habit; and in the strength of great hope we must all shoulder our common load.

Document Analysis

Roosevelt begins this speech by providing some historical background from before the American Revolution. Throughout history, he argues, people have formed centralized governments in order to limit the power of the aristocracy and to protect the interests of the general public. When these centralized governments became too powerful, Roosevelt asserts, "popular participation and control" have coordinated to establish "limitations on arbitrary power." Roosevelt compares American statesmen Alexander Hamilton and Thomas Jefferson and their differing visions of the role of government. Hamilton "believed that the safety of the republic lay in the autocratic strength of its Government, that the destiny of individuals was to serve that Government."

Jefferson, on the other hand, saw government as "a means to an end, not an end in itself" and believed that the government was created to serve the people and to protect their individual rights. Roosevelt argues that the protection of individual rights is not ensured by a total absence of regulation but rather through government policies that enable individuals to thrive and prosper. This idea is fundamental to Roosevelt's theory of government. Since its founding, he argues, the U.S. government has understood that it "must intervene, not to destroy individualism, but to protect it."

Most Americans prospered with minimal interference from the government in the first century following the country's founding. "So began, in American political life, the new day, the day of the individual against the system, the day in which individualism was made the great watchword of American life. The happiest of economic conditions made that day long and splendid." In other words, while there were abundant natural resources, free land in the West, and nearly limitless opportunities for expansion, individual Americans could be left alone to make their way. People who worked hard were rewarded with success without the government's help.

Roosevelt draws a hard line between the preindustrial and postindustrial United States. He describes the Industrial Revolution as a "dream of an economic machine, able to raise the standard of living for everyone . . . to release everyone from the drudgery of the heaviest manual toil," and he describes how the government, long accustomed to leaving individuals alone to make their way, found itself called upon to support industry so all Americans could benefit from the advances of the industrial age. Throughout the unprecedented industrial and financial growth of the nineteenth century, "the business of Government was not to interfere but to assist in the development of industry," and government policies protected industries, such as railroads and shipping with tariffs, land grants, and other regulatory protections. Roosevelt describes this as a circumstantial shift from a government whose purpose was the protection of the individual to one whose primary goal was the support of business, with the theory that this would benefit all.

Roosevelt concludes with a call for a new role for the government, a return to Jeffersonian principles of the protection of individual rights and government in service to the people. Unfettered industry has failed to protect these rights, Roosevelt asserts, and "equality of opportunity as we have known it no longer exists." It is time for the "soberer, less dramatic business of administering resources . . . of distributing wealth and products more equitably, of adapting existing economic organizations to the service of the people." Roosevelt asserts that if he is elected, he will provide "enlightened administration" and will use government resources to help individuals protect their rights to a fair chance of success and security.

Essential Themes

This speech was a call to consider a new, activist role for government. Roosevelt wished to convince his listeners that the protection of individual rights, a foundational belief of American democracy, now required government intervention in a way that was not needed in a preindustrial society. Roosevelt positions himself as the candidate who will protect these rights by intervening and regulating private industry, and he introduces terms that indicated a radical departure from the free-market capitalism of his predecessor. The idea that the government had a role in limiting corporate power so that wealth could be more fairly distributed set the stage for the New Deal policies and programs of his presidency.

—Bethany Groff, MA

Bibliography and Additional Reading

Katznelson, Ira. *Fear Itself: The New Deal and the Origins of Our Time*. New York: Liveright, 2013. Print.

Parrish, Michael E. *Anxious Decades: American in Prosperity and Depression 1920–1941*. New York: Norton, 1992. Print.

Shlaes, Amity. *The Forgotten Man: A New History of the Great Depression*. New York: HarperCollins, 2007. Print.

■ Herbert Hoover Speaks Against the New Deal

Date: October 31, 1932
Author: Herbert Hoover
Genre: Speech

Summary Overview

In one of his last campaign speeches during the 1932 presidential election, incumbent Herbert Hoover offered an analysis of the New Deal proposed by his opponent, Democratic New York governor Franklin Delano Roosevelt. Hoover cautioned his audience to see the benefits of the proposed New Deal as little more than rhetorical. He also warned that the New Deal would represent a dramatic shift away from the traditional social and governmental mechanisms that had been in place for generations. Hoover said that the government's current infrastructure was already proving effective in addressing the Depression's impact; Roosevelt's proposals were, therefore, not only ineffective, but obsolete when compared to the activity of the federal government to date. The government, Hoover determined, must remain ready to intervene when needed, but keep its distance from fostering a new "family."

Defining Moment

In 1929, the "Roaring Twenties"—distinctive because of the tremendous economic boom that occurred in the United States during this period—came to a dramatic halt. Stock markets crashed, banks folded, industries faltered, and countless jobs disappeared in what would come to be called the Great Depression.

Economists, social scientists, and other scholars have not come to a firm agreement on the specific causes of the Depression. Generally, however, experts point to citizens' inability to repay loans and credit debt, a lack of government regulation of businesses and markets, and a lack of sustainability in the country's leading industries as some of the leading causes of this event. Many scholars point to the sharp divide between the nation's wealthy and poor (including the large percentage of immigrants, who came to the country during the early twentieth century to work in the energy and manufacturing industries) as a contributing factor as well, as the latter group represented a majority of the population that would be ad-versely affected by any fluctuations in the economy.

Herbert Hoover, the incumbent president in 1929, had only been in office for nine months when the stock market crashed in October of that year. Hoover believed that government's role in private, economic affairs should be minimal, and he argued repeatedly that the nation's economic infrastructure was still solid and healthy despite the tumult of the Black Thursday stock market crash and other events leading to the Depression's onset. After Black Thursday, Hoover did not look to implement any major reforms or pass emergency legislation. Rather, he convened a meeting of leaders in finance, construction, labor, the Federal Reserve, and other relevant economic interest groups. As the Depression continued, he eventually acceded to ongoing pressure for federal relief and signed the Emergency Relief Construction Act, providing $2 billion for public works and $300 million for state-level direct relief programs.

Despite these actions, Hoover largely clung to his philosophy that the economy would right itself through the actions of private business and the altruism of the citizens (upon whom Hoover called to help the people most affected by the Depression). Congress, which largely disagreed with Hoover on this point, was more proactive in its efforts to pass reforms and aid packages, although few of these initiatives passed and fewer still proved effective; indeed, some (such as the Smoot-Hawley Tariff Act, which raised import and export taxes) may have aggravated the situation.

Hoover, whom many historians suggest would have enjoyed a second term if not for the Depression, found his presidency in jeopardy during the 1932 campaign. The Democratic Party, held down by Republicans throughout the 1920s, found new life because of the Depression and Hoover's perceived inaction. They nominated New York governor Franklin Delano Roosevelt as their candidate. Roosevelt called for a New Deal for Americans, a campaign promise that included major regulatory reforms, direct aid packages, and new initiatives designed to help bring the country out of the economic doldrums for good. Hoover spoke against the program in Madison Square Garden, New York City, on October 31, 1932.

Author Biography

Herbert Clark Hoover was born on August 10, 1874, in West Branch, Iowa. Orphaned at the age of nine, he worked for a while on an uncle's farm in Oregon and, in 1891, attended the newly opened Stanford University, from which he graduated four years later with a degree in geology. During World War I, Hoover established the Committee for Relief of Belgium, an organization dedicated to providing food and other forms of aid for civil-ians trapped in Belgian war zones. Based on his work in this arena, President Woodrow Wilson tapped Hoover to be his food administrator. Hoover later declared his affiliation with the Republican Party and became Warren Harding's secretary of commerce. He would continue to hold this post during Calvin Coolidge's administration.

In 1928, Hoover successfully sought the Republican nomination for president and easily won the election. Victimized politically by the onset of the Great Depression, Hoover lost the 1932 election to Franklin Delano Roosevelt. He remained active in public service after his presidency, including helping President Harry Truman with the post–World War II reconstruction effort. He died on October 20, 1964, while living in Iowa.

HISTORICAL DOCUMENT

My fellow citizens: . . .

This campaign is more than a contest between two men. It is more than a contest between two parties. It is a contest between two philosophies of government. We are told by the opposition that we must have a change, that we must have a new deal. It is not the change that comes from normal development of national life to which I object or you object, but the proposal to alter the whole foundations of our national life which have been builded through generations of testing and struggle, and of the principles upon which we have made this Nation. The expressions of our opponents must refer to important changes in our economic and social system and our system of government; otherwise they would be nothing but vacuous words. And I realize that in this time of distress many of our people are asking whether our social and economic system is incapable of that great primary function of providing security and comfort of life to all of the firesides of 25 million homes in America, whether our social system provides for the fundamental development and progress of our people, and whether our form of government is capable of originating and sustaining that security and progress.

This question is the basis upon which our opponents are appealing to the people in their fear and their distress. They are proposing changes and so-called new deals which would destroy the very foundations of the American system of life.

Our people should consider the primary facts before they come to the judgment—not merely through political agitation, the glitter of promise, and the discouragement of temporary hardships—whether they will support changes which radically affect the whole system which has been builded during these six generations of the toil of our fathers. They should not approach the question in the despair with which our opponents would clothe it. Our economic system has received abnormal shocks during the last three years which have temporarily dislocated its normal functioning. These shocks have in a large sense come from without our borders, and I say to you that our system of government has enabled us to take such strong action as to prevent the disaster which would otherwise have come to this Nation. It has enabled us further to develop measures and programs which are now demonstrating their ability to bring about restoration and progress.

We must go deeper than platitudes and emotional appeals of the public platform in the campaign if we will penetrate to the full significance of the changes which our opponents are attempting to float upon the wave of distress and discontent from the difficulties through which we have passed. We can find what our opponents would do after searching the record of their appeals to discontent, to group and sectional interest. To find that, we must search for them in the legislative acts which they sponsored and passed in the Democratic-controlled

House of Representatives in the last session of Congress. We must look into both the measures for which they voted and in which they were defeated. We must inquire whether or not the Presidential and Vice-Presidential candidates have disavowed those acts. If they have not, we must conclude that they form a portion and are a substantial indication of the profound changes in the new deal which is proposed.

And we must look still further than this as to what revolutionary changes have been proposed by the candidates themselves.

We must look into the type of leaders who are campaigning for the Democratic ticket, whose philosophies have been well known all their lives and whose demands for a change in the American system are frank and forceful. I can respect the sincerity of these men in their desire to change our form of government and our social and our economic system, though I shall do my best tonight to prove they are wrong. I refer particularly to Senator Norris, Senator La Follette, Senator Cutting, Senator Huey Long, Senator Wheeler, William Randolph Hearst, and other exponents of a social philosophy different from the traditional philosophies of the American people. Unless these men have felt assurance of support to their ideas they certainly would not be supporting these candidates and the Democratic Party. The zeal of these men indicates that they must have some sure confidence that they will have a voice in the administration of this Government. I may say at once that the changes proposed from all these Democratic principals and their allies are of the most profound and penetrating character. If they are brought about, this will not be the America which we have known in the past.

Now, I may pause for a moment and examine the American system of government and of social and economic life which it is now proposed that we should alter.

Our system is the product of our race and of our experience in building a Nation to heights unparalleled in the whole history of the world. It is a system peculiar to the American people. It differs essentially from all others in the world. It is an American system. It is rounded on the conception that only through ordered liberty, through freedom to the individual, and equal opportunity to the individual will his initiative and enterprise be summoned to spur the march of national progress.

It is by the maintenance of an equality of opportunity and therefore of a society absolutely fluid in the movement of its human particles that our individualism departs from the individualism of Europe. We resent class distinction because there can be no rise for the individual through the frozen strata of classes, and no stratification of classes can take place in a mass that is livened by the free rise of its human particles. Thus in our ideals the able and ambitious are able to rise constantly from the bottom to leadership in the community. We denounce any attempt to stir class feeling or class antagonisms in the United States.

This freedom of the individual creates of itself the necessity and the cheerful willingness of men to act cooperatively in a thousand ways and for every purpose as the occasion requires, and it permits such voluntary cooperations to be dissolved as soon as it has served its purpose and to be replaced by new voluntary associations for new purposes.

There has thus grown within us, to gigantic importance, a new conception. That is the conception of voluntary cooperation within the community; cooperation to perfect the social organizations; cooperation for the care of those in distress; cooperation for the advancement of knowledge, of scientific research, of education; cooperative action in a thousand directions for the advancement of economic life. This is self-government by the people outside of the Government. It is the most powerful development of individual freedom and equality of opportunity that has taken place in the century and a half since our fundamental institutions were founded.

It is in the further development of this cooperation and in a sense of its responsibility that we should find solution for many of the complex problems, and not by the extension of the Government into our economic and social life. The greatest function a government can perform is to build up that cooperation, and its most resolute action should be to deny the extension of bureaucracy.

We have developed great agencies of cooperation by the assistance of the Government which do promote and protect the interests of individuals and the smaller units of business: the Federal Reserve System, in its strengthening and support of the smaller banks; the Farm Board, in its strengthening and support of the farm cooperatives; the home loan banks, in the mobilizing of building and loan associations and savings banks; the Federal land banks, in giving independence and strength to land mortgage associations; the great mobilization of relief to distress, the mobilization of business and industry in measures of recovery from this depression, and a score of other activities that are not socialism, and they are not the Government in business. They are the essence of protection to the development of free men. I wish to explore this point a little further. The primary conception of this whole American system is not the ordering of men but the cooperation of free men. It is rounded upon the conception of responsibility of the individual to the community, of the responsibility of local government to the State, of the State to the National Government.

I am exploring these questions because I propose to take up definite proposals of the opposition and test them with these realities in a few moments. Now, our American system is rounded on a peculiar conception of self-government designed to maintain an equality of opportunity to the individual, and through decentralization it brings about and maintains these responsibilities. The centralization of government will undermine these responsibilities and will destroy the system itself.

Our Government differs from all previous conceptions, not only in the decentralization but also in the independence of the judicial arm of the Government. Our Government is rounded on a conception that in times of great emergency, when forces are running beyond the control of individuals or cooperative action, beyond the control of local communities or the States, then the great reserve powers of the Federal Government should be brought into action to protect the people. But when these forces have ceased there must be a return to State, local, and individual responsibility.

The implacable march of scientific discovery with its train of new inventions presents every year new problems to government and new problems to the social order. Questions often arise whether, in the face of the growth of these new and gigantic tools, democracy can remain master in its own house and can preserve the fundamentals of our American system. I contend that it can, and I contend that this American system of ours has demonstrated its validity and superiority over any system yet invented by human mind. It has demonstrated it in the face of the greatest test of peacetime history—that is the

emergency which we have passed in the last three years.

When the political and economic weakness of many nations of Europe, the result of the World War and its aftermath, finally culminated in the collapse of their institutions, the delicate adjustments of our economic and social and governmental life received a shock unparalleled in our history. No one knows that better than you of New York. No one knows its causes better than you. That the crisis was so great that many of the leading banks sought directly or indirectly to convert their assets into gold or its equivalent with the result that they practically ceased to function as credit institutions is known to you; that many of our citizens sought flight for their capital to other countries; that many of them attempted to hoard gold in large amounts you know. These were but superficial indications of the flight of confidence and the belief that our Government could not overcome these forces.

Yet these forces were overcome—perhaps by narrow margins—and this demonstrates that our form of government has the capacity. It demonstrates what the courage of a nation can accomplish under the resolute leadership of the Republican Party. And I say the Republican Party because our opponents, before and during the crisis, proposed no constructive program, though some of their members patriotically supported ours for which they deserve on every occasion the applause of patriotism. Later on in the critical period, the Democratic House of Representatives did develop the real thought and ideas of the Democratic Party. They were so destructive that they had to be defeated. They did delay the healing of our wounds for months.

Now, in spite of all these obstructions we did succeed. Our form of government did prove itself equal to the task. We saved this Nation from a generation of chaos and degeneration; we preserved the savings, the insurance policies, gave a fighting chance to men to hold their homes. We saved the integrity of our Government and the honesty of the American dollar. And we installed measures which today are bringing back recovery. Employment, agriculture, and business—all of these show the steady, if slow, healing of an enormous wound. As I left Washington, our Government departments communicated to me the fact that the October statistics on employment show that since the first day of July, the men returned to work in the United States exceed one million.

I therefore contend that the problem of today is to continue these measures and policies to restore the American system to its normal functioning, to repair the wounds it has received, to correct the weaknesses and evils which would defeat that system. To enter upon a series of deep changes now, to embark upon this inchoate new deal which has been propounded in this campaign would not only undermine and destroy our American system but it will delay for months and years the possibility of recovery. ...

Now, to go back to my major thesis—the thesis of the longer view. Before we enter into courses of deep-seated change and of the new deal, I would like you to consider what the results of this American system have been during the last 30 years—that is, a single generation. For if it can be demonstrated that by this means, our unequaled political, social, and economic system, we have secured a lift in the standards of living and the diffusion of comfort and hope to men and women, the growth of equality of opportunity, the widening of all opportunity such as had never been seen in the history of the world, then we should not tamper with it and destroy it, but on the contrary we should restore it and, by its gradual improvement and perfection, foster it into new performance for our country and for our children.

Now, if we look back over the last generation we find that the number of our families and, therefore, our homes, has increased from about 16 to about 25 million, or 62 percent. In that time we have builded for them 15 million new and better homes. We have equipped 20 million out of these 25 million homes with electricity; thereby we have lifted infinite drudgery from women and men.

The barriers of time and space have been swept away in this single generation. Life has been made freer, the intellectual vision of every individual has been expanded by the installation of 20 million telephones, 12 million radios, and the service of 20 million automobiles. Our cities have been made magnificent with beautiful buildings, parks, and playgrounds. Our countryside has been knit together with splendid roads. We have increased by 12 times the use of electrical power and thereby taken sweat from the backs of men. In the broad sweep real

wages and purchasing power of men and women have steadily increased. New comforts have steadily come to them. The hours of labor have decreased, the 12-hour day has disappeared, even the 9-hour day has almost gone. We are now advocating the 5-day week. During this generation the portals of opportunity to our children have ever widened. While our population grew by but 62 percent, yet we have increased the number of children in high schools by 700 percent, and those in institutions of higher learning by 300 percent. With all our spending, we multiplied by six times the savings in our banks and in our building and loan associations. We multiplied by 1,200 percent the amount of our life insurance.

With the enlargement of our leisure we have come to a fuller life; we have gained new visions of hope; we are more nearly realizing our national aspirations and giving increased scope to the creative power of every individual and expansion of every man's mind.

Now, our people in these 30 years have grown in the sense of social responsibility. There is profound progress in the relation of the employer to the employed. We have more nearly met with a full hand the most sacred obligation of man, that is, the responsibility of a man to his neighbor. Support to our schools, hospitals, and institutions for the care of the afflicted surpassed in totals by billions the proportionate service in any period in any nation in the history of the world.

Now, three years ago there came a break in this progress. A break of the same type we have met 15 times in a century and yet have recovered from. But 18 months later came a further blow by the shocks transmitted to us from earthquakes of the collapse of nations throughout the world as the aftermath of the World War. The workings of this system of ours were dislocated. Businessmen and farmers suffered, and millions of men and women are out of jobs. Their distress is bitter. I do not seek to minimize it, but we may thank God that in view of the storm that we have met that 30 million still have jobs, and yet this does not distract our thoughts from the suffering of the 10 million.

But I ask you what has happened. This 30 years of incomparable improvement in the scale of living, of advance of comfort and intellectual life, of security, of inspiration, and ideals did not arise without right principles animating the American system which produced them. Shall that system be discarded because vote-seeking men appeal to distress and say that the machinery is all wrong and that it must be abandoned or tampered with? Is it not more sensible to realize the simple fact that some extraordinary force has been thrown into the mechanism which has temporarily deranged its operation? Is it not wiser to believe that the difficulty is not with the principles upon which our American system is founded and designed through all these generations of inheritance? Should not our purpose be to restore the normal working of that system which has brought to us such immeasurable gifts, and not to destroy it?

Now, in order to indicate to you that the proposals of our opponents will endanger or destroy our system, I propose to analyze a few of them in their relation to these fundamentals which I have stated.

First: A proposal of our opponents that would break down the American system is the expansion of governmental expenditure by yielding to sectional and group raids on the Public Treasury. The extension of governmental expenditures beyond the minimum limit necessary to conduct the proper functions of the Government enslaves men to work for the Government. If we combine the whole governmental expenditures—national, State, and municipal—we will find that before the World War each citizen worked, theoretically, 25 days out of each year for the Government. In 1924, he worked 46 days out of the year for the Government. Today he works, theoretically, for the support of all forms of Government 61 days out of the year.

No nation can conscript its citizens for this proportion of men's and women's time without national impoverishment and without the destruction of their liberties.

Our Nation cannot do it without destruction to our whole conception of the American system. The Federal Government has been forced in this emergency to unusual expenditure, but in partial alleviation of these extraordinary and unusual expenditures the Republican administration has made a successful effort to reduce the ordinary running expenses of the Government....

Second: Another proposal of our opponents which would destroy the American system is that of inflation of the currency. The bill which passed the last session of the Democratic House called upon the Treasury of the United States to issue $2,300 million in paper currency that would be unconvertible into solid values. Call it what you will, greenbacks or fiat money. It was the same nightmare which overhung our own country for years after the Civil War....

The use of this expedient by nations in difficulty since the war in Europe has been one of the most tragic disasters to equality of opportunity and the independence of man.

I quote from a revealing speech by Mr. Owen D. Young upon the return of the Dawes Commission from Europe. He stated:

> "The currency of Germany was depreciating so rapidly that the industries paid their wages daily, and sometimes indeed twice a day. Standing with the lines of employees was another line of wives and mothers waiting for these marks. The wife grabbed the paper from her husband's hand and rushed to the nearest provision store to spend it quickly before the rapid depreciation had cut its purchasing power in two."...

Third: In the last session of the Congress, under the personal leadership of the Democratic Vice-Presidential candidate, and their allies in the Senate, they enacted a law to extend the Government into personal banking business. I know it is always difficult to discuss banks. There seems to be much prejudice against some of them, but I was compelled to veto that bill out of fidelity to the whole American system of life and government. I may repeat a part of that veto message, and it remains unchallenged by any Democratic leader. I quote now from that veto message because that statement was not made in the heat of any political campaign. I said: "It would mean loans against security for any conceivable purpose on any conceivable security to anybody who wants money. It would place the Government in private business in such fashion as to violate the very principle of public relations upon which we have builded our Nation, and renders insecure its very foundations. Such action would make the Reconstruction Corporation the greatest banking and money-lending institution of all history. It would constitute a gigantic centralization of banking and finance to which the American people have been properly opposed over a hundred years. The purpose of the expansion is no longer in the spirit of solving a great major emergency but to establish a privilege whether it serves a great national end or not."

I further said:

"It would require the setting up of a huge bureaucracy, to establish branches in every county and town in the United States. Every political pressure would be assembled for particular persons. It would be within the power of these agencies to dictate the welfare of millions of people, to discriminate between competitive business at will, and to deal favor and disaster among them. The organization would be constantly subjected to conspiracies and raids of predatory interests, individuals, and private corporations. Huge losses and great scandals must inevitably result. It would mean the squandering of public credit to be ultimately borne by the taxpayer."

I stated further that:

"This proposal violates every sound principle of public finance and of our Government. Never before has so dangerous a suggestion been made to our country. Never before has so much power for evil been placed at the unlimited discretion of seven individuals."

They failed to pass this bill over my veto. But you must not be deceived. This is still in their purposes as a part of the new deal, and no responsible candidate has yet disavowed it.

Fourth: Another proposal of our opponents which would wholly alter our American system of life is to reduce the protective tariff to a competitive tariff for revenue....

Fifth: Another proposal is that the Government go into the power business....

I have stated unceasingly that I am opposed to the Federal Government going into the power business. I have insisted upon rigid regulation. The Democratic candidate has declared that under the same conditions which may make local action of this character desirable, he is prepared to put the Federal Government into the power business. He is being actively supported by a score of Senators in this campaign, many of whose expenses are being paid by the Democratic National Committee, who are pledged to Federal Government development and operation of electrical power.

I find in the instructions to the campaign speakers issued by the Democratic National Committee that they are instructed to criticize my action in the veto of the bill which would have put the Government permanently into the operation of power at Muscle Shoals.... In that bill was the flat issue of the Federal Government permanently in competitive business. I vetoed it because of principle and not because it was especially applied to electrical power. In that veto I stated that I was firmly opposed to the Federal Government entering into any business, the major purpose of which is competition with our citizens except in major national emergencies.

In that veto message, written long before the emergence of the exigencies of political campaigning, I stated:

"There are national emergencies which require that the Government should temporarily enter the field of business but that they must be emergency actions and in matters where the cost of the project is secondary to much higher consideration. There are many localities where the Federal Government is justified in the construction of great dams and reservoirs, where navigation, flood control, reclamation, or stream regulation are of dominant importance, and where they are beyond the capacity or purpose of private or local government capital to construct. In these cases, power is often a byproduct and should be disposed of by contract or lease. But for the Federal Government to deliberately go out to build up and expand such an occasion to the major purpose of a power and manufacturing business is to break down the initiative and enterprise of the American people; it is destruction of equality of opportunity among our people; it is the negation of the ideals upon which our civilization has been based....

"This bill would launch the Federal Government on a policy of ownership of power utilities upon a basis of competition instead of by the proper

Government function of regulation for the protection of all the people. I hesitate to contemplate the future of our institutions, of our Government, and of our country, if the preoccupation of its officials is to be no longer the promotion of justice and equality of opportunity but is to be devoted to barter in the markets. That is not liberalism; it is degeneration." From their utterances in this campaign and elsewhere, it appears to me that we are justified in the conclusion that our opponents propose to put Federal Government extensively into business."

Sixth: I may cite another instance of absolutely destructive proposals to our American system by our opponents, and I am talking about fundamentals and not superficialities.

Recently there was circulated through the unemployed in this city and other cities, a letter from the Democratic candidate in which he stated that he would support measures for the inauguration of self-liquidating public works such as the utilization of water resources, flood control, land reclamation, to provide employment for all surplus labor at all times.

I especially emphasize that promise to promote "employment for all surplus labor at all times"—by the Government. I at first could not believe that anyone would be so cruel as to hold out a hope so absolutely impossible of realization to those 10 million who are unemployed and suffering. But the authenticity of that promise has been verified. And I protest against such frivolous promises being held out to a suffering people. It is easy to demonstrate that no such employment can be found. But the point that I wish to make here and now is the mental attitude and spirit of the Democratic Party that would lead them to attempt this or to make a promise to attempt it. That is another mark of the character of the new deal and the destructive changes which mean the total abandonment of every principle upon which this Government and this American system are rounded. If it were possible to give this employment to 10 million people by the Government—at the expense of the rest of the people—it would cost upwards of $9 billion a year.

The stages of this destruction would be first the destruction of Government credit, then the destruction of the value of Government securities, the destruction of every fiduciary trust in our country, insurance policies and all. It would pull down the employment of those who are still at work by the high taxes and the demoralization of credit upon which their employment is dependent.

It would mean the pulling and hauling of politics for projects and measures, the favoring of localities and sections and groups. It would mean the growth of a fearful bureaucracy which, once established, could never be dislodged. If it were possible, it would mean one-third of the electorate would have Government jobs, earnest to maintain this bureaucracy and to control the political destinies of the country....

I have said before, and I want to repeat on this occasion, that the only method by which we can stop the suffering and unemployment is by returning our people to their normal jobs in their normal homes, carrying on their normal functions of living. This can be done only by sound processes of protecting and stimulating recovery of the existing system upon which we have builded our progress thus far—preventing distress and giving such sound employment as we can find in the meantime. Seventh: Recently, at Indianapolis, I called attention to the statement made by Governor Roosevelt in his address on October 25 with respect to the Supreme Court of the United States. He said:

> "After March 4, 1929, the Republican Party was in complete control of all branches of the Government— Executive, Senate, and House, and I may add, for good measure, in order to make it complete, the Supreme Court as well."

Now, I am not called upon to defend the Supreme Court of the United States from that slurring reflection. Fortunately for the American people that Court has jealously maintained over the years its high standard of integrity, impartiality, and freedom from influence of either the Executive or Congress, so that the confidence of the people in the Court is sound and unshaken. But is the Democratic candidate really proposing his conception of the relation of the Executive with the Supreme Court? If that is his idea, he is proposing the most revolutionary new deal, the most stupendous breaking of precedent, the most destructive undermining of the very safeguard of our form of government yet proposed by any Presidential candidate.

Eighth: In order that we may get at the philosophical background of the mind which pronounces the necessity for profound change in our economic system and a new deal, I would call your attention to an address delivered by the Democratic candidate in San Francisco early in October.

He said:

"Our industrial plant is built. The problem just now is whether under existing conditions it is not overbuilt. Our last frontier has long since been reached. There is practically no more free land. There is no safety valve in the Western prairies where we can go for a new start.... The mere building of more industrial plants, the organization of more corporations is as likely to be as much a danger as a help.... Our task now is not the discovery of natural resources or necessarily the production of more goods, it is the sober, less dramatic business of administering the resources and plants already in hand ... establishing markets for surplus production, of meeting the problem of under-consumption, distributing the wealth and products more equitably and adopting the economic organization to the service of the people...."

Now, there are many of these expressions with which no one would quarrel. But I do challenge the whole idea that we have ended the advance of America, that this country has reached the zenith of its power and the height of its development. That is the counsel of despair for the future of America. That is not the spirit by which we shall emerge from this depression. That is not the spirit which has made this country. If it is true, every American must abandon the road of countless progress and countless hopes and unlimited opportunity. I deny that the promise of American life has been fulfilled, for that means we have begun the decline and the fall. No nation can cease to move forward without degeneration of spirit.

I could quote from gentlemen who have emitted this same note of profound pessimism in each economic depression going back for 100 years. What the Governor has overlooked is the fact that we are yet but on the frontiers of development of science and of invention. I have only to remind you that discoveries in electricity, the internal-combustion engine, the radio—all of which have sprung into being since our land was settled—have in themselves represented the greatest advances made in America. This philosophy upon which the Governor of New York proposes to conduct the Presidency of the United States is the philosophy of stagnation and of despair. It is the end of hope. The destinies of this country cannot be dominated by that spirit in action. It would be the end of the American system.

I have recited to you some of the items in the progress of this last generation. Progress in that generation was not due to the opening up of new agricultural land; it was due to the scientific research, the opening of new invention, new flashes of light from the intelligence of our people. These brought the improvements in agriculture and in industry. There are a thousand inventions for comfort and the expansion of life yet in the lockers of science that have not yet come to light. We are only upon their frontiers. As for myself, I am confident that if we do not destroy our American system, if we continue to stimulate scientific research, if we continue to give it the impulse of initiative and enterprise, if we continue to build voluntary cooperation instead of financial concentration, if we continue to build into a system of free men, my children will enjoy the same opportunity that has come to me and to the whole 120 million of my countrymen. I wish to see American Government conducted in that faith and hope.

Now, if these sample measures and promises, which I have discussed, or these failures to disavow these projects, this attitude of mind, mean anything, they mean the enormous expansion of the Federal Government; they mean the growth of bureaucracy such as we have never seen in our history. No man who has not occupied my position in Washington can fully realize the constant battle which must be carried on against incompetence, corruption, tyranny of government expanded into business activities. If we first examine the effect on our form of government of such a program, we come at once to the effect of the most gigantic increase in expenditure ever known in history. That alone would break down the savings, the wages, the equality of opportunity among our people. These measures would transfer vast responsibilities to the Federal Government from the States, the local governments, and the individuals. But that is not all; they would break down our form of government. It will crack the timbers of our Constitution. Our legislative bodies cannot delegate their authority to any dictator, but without such delegation every member of these bodies is impelled in representation of the interest of his constituents constantly to seek privilege and demand service in the use of such agencies. Every time the Federal Government extends its arm, 531 Senators and Congressmen become actual boards of directors of that business.

Capable men cannot be chosen by politics for all the various talents that business requires. Even if they were supermen, if there were no politics in the selection of a Government official, if there were no constant pressure for this and for that, so large a number of men would be incapable as a board of directors of any institution. At once when these extensions take place by the Federal Government, the authority and responsibility of State governments and institutions are undermined. Every enterprise of private business is at once halted to know what Federal action is going to be. It destroys initiative and courage....

Now, we have heard a great deal in this campaign about reactionaries, conservatives, progressives, liberals, and radicals. I think I belong to every group. I have not yet heard an attempt by any one of the orators who mouth these phrases to define the principles upon which they base these classifications. There is one thing I can say without any question of doubt—that is, that the spirit of liberalism is to create free men; it is not the regimentation of men under government. It is not the extension of bureaucracy. I have said in this city before now that you cannot extend the mastery of government over the daily life of a people without somewhere making it master of people's souls and thoughts. Expansion of government in business and otherwise means that the government, in order to protect itself from the political consequences of its errors or even its successes, is driven irresistibly without peace to greater and greater control of the Nation's press and platform. Free speech does not live many hours after free industry and free commerce die. It is a false liberalism that interprets itself into Government operation of business. Every step in that direction poisons the very roots of liberalism. It poisons political equality, free speech, free press, and equality of opportunity. It is the road not to liberty but to less liberty. True liberalism is found not in striving to spread bureaucracy, but in striving to set bounds of it. It is found in an endeavor to extend cooperation between men. True liberalism seeks all legitimate freedom first in the confident belief that without such freedom the pursuit of other blessings is vain. Liberalism is a force truly of the spirit proceeding from the deep realization that economic freedom cannot be sacrificed if political freedom is to be preserved.

Even if the Government conduct of business could give us the maximum of efficiency instead of least efficiency, it would be purchased at the cost of freedom. It would increase rather than decrease abuse and corruption, stifle initiative and invention, undermine development of leadership, cripple mental and spiritual energies of our people, extinguish equality of opportunity, and dry up the spirit of liberty and progress. Men who are going about this country announcing that they are liberals because of their promises to extend the Government are not liberals; they are the reactionaries of the United States.

Now, I do not wish to be misquoted or misunderstood. I do not mean that our Government is to part with one iota of its national resources without complete protection to the public interest. I have already stated that democracy must remain master in its own house. I have stated that it is, at times, vitally necessary for the Government to protect the people when forces run against them which they cannot control. I have stated that abuse and wrongdoing must be punished and controlled. Nor do I wish to be interpreted as stating that the United States is a free-for-all and devil-take-the-hindermost society.

The very essence of equality of opportunity in our American system is that there shall be no monopoly or domination by anybody—whether it be a group or section of the country, or whether it be business, or whether it be group interest. On the contrary, our American system demands economic justice as well as political and social justice; it is no system of *laissez faire*.

I am not setting up the contention that our American system is perfect. No human ideal has ever been perfectly attained, since humanity itself is not perfect. But the wisdom of our forefathers and the wisdom of the 30 men who have preceded me in this office hold to the conception that progress can be attained only as the sum of the accomplishments of free individuals, and they have held unalterably to these principles....

My countrymen, the proposals of our opponents represent a profound change in American life—less in concrete proposal, bad as that may be, than by implication and by evasion. Dominantly in their spirit they represent a radical departure from the foundations of 150 years which have made this the greatest Nation in the world. This election is not a mere shift from the ins to the outs. It means the determining of the course of our Nation over a century to come.

Now, my conception of America is a land where men and women may walk in ordered liberty, where they may enjoy the advantages of wealth not concentrated in the hands of a few but diffused through the opportunity of all, where they build and safeguard their homes, give to their children the full opportunities of American life, where every man shall be respected in the faith that his conscience and his heart direct him to follow, and where people secure in their liberty shall have leisure and impulse to seek a fuller life. That leads to the release of the energies of men and women, to the wider vision and higher hope. It leads to opportunity for greater and greater service not alone of man to man in our country but from our country to the world. It leads to health in body and a spirit unfettered, youthful, eager with a vision stretching beyond the farthest horizons with a mind open and sympathetic and generous. But that must be builded upon our experience with the past, upon the foundations which have made this country great. It must be the product of the development of our truly American system.

NEW DEAL LEXICON

1935 cartoon by Vaughn Shoemaker in which he parodied the New Deal as a card game with alphabetical agencies. *Chicago Daily News* 1935.

Document Analysis

President Hoover's speech makes the statement that the country, while certainly under major duress from the Depression, is not at a point at which it needs fundamental changes to its government and financial systems. He cautions citizens that then-candidate Roosevelt's "New Deal" amounts to little more than rhetoric, a series of proposals stemming from panic rather than reason. The country, he says, is not in need of revolutionary changes that would transform traditional American ideals; rather, it needs Americans and the myriad agencies and organizations to cooperate with one another. Reviewing the evidence of the previous three decades, Hoover says that this approach has delivered proven results on many fronts. The principles of the New Deal, he warns, represent a dramatic (and unnecessary) shift away from this proven approach.

Roosevelt's New Deal, Hoover says, is born of panic and reactive rhetoric, when in fact, for decades, the American political and economic system has experienced periods of flux, all of which have been rectified through patience and deliberation. Certainly, the country is understandably anxious at the Depression's impact and length. The Democrats, however, are seizing upon this anxiety and calling for a major overhaul of the American system. Hoover advises his audience—and indeed all Americans—to refrain from embracing such rhetoric.

The alternative, according to Hoover, is to allow traditional American institutions and principles to remedy the economy. Business, finance, and political leaders should work together in a spirit of cooperation to rejuvenate the national economy. Meanwhile, private citizens should work together to help those Americans most adversely affected by the Depression. Hoover cites the tumultuous period following the Great War as an example—in this situation, he says, all aspects of American society came together to reinvigorate the economy and withstand the hardships associated with this period.

Hoover continues by giving his analysis of what would occur if the New Deal provisions became law: government would see an added layer of bureaucracy the likes of which Americans have never before seen. Additionally, the federal government would, in the spirit of a tyranny and not a democratic republic, be free to intrude in business, without any safeguards from state and local government. He argues that the New Deal would impinge on Americans' pursuit of individual liberty, threatening to destroy citizens' "initiative and courage."

To be sure, Hoover says, there are steps to be taken to improve the existing system so that those forces accountable for the Depression cannot continue to operate unchecked; his philosophy is not that the country should be a "free-for-all." Still, he believes the best method for America to successfully reemerge from the Depression is to look to the fundamental systems that have proven effective repeatedly throughout modern American history instead of embracing the un-American proposals offered by Roosevelt and the Democrats.

Essential Themes

This speech illustrated Hoover's political philosophy regarding the handling of the Great Depression. He insisted that the very political, social, and economic institutions that helped the United States survive World War I, an economic downturn in the early 1920s, and other crises would again prove effective in reversing the Great Depression. Throughout this speech, Hoover cited his belief that, with the cooperation of business and industry as well as private citizens, the Depression would not last long.

Hoover also took the opportunity to criticize the New Deal proposed by Democratic presidential candidate Franklin Delano Roosevelt. On one level, Hoover simply dismissed the New Deal concept as mere rhetoric and argued that the Democrats were simply using the fear and anxiety prevalent throughout the country to attempt to give new life to their previously unsuccessful agenda. On another level, however, Hoover viewed the New Deal as a major threat to the liberal, democratic principles on which the United States was founded. In this light, the New Deal was not simply the product of reactionary policy, Hoover said—if made law, the New Deal would move the American political and economic system closer to a tyranny than a democratic republic.

Hoover made an effort, however, to project to his audience an understanding that the nation did indeed face a crisis that warranted action. His approach to the myriad issues arising from the Depression's onset, he argued, was neither to allow business to operate without rules nor to simply allow the issue to resolve itself. He instead advocated a response that suited the American idiom, such as the meetings he had held when the Depression first began. This series of meetings, he said, inspired the participants to strike out and reverse the Depression's effects. He also acknowledged that there were almost certainly reforms to be made to the country's infrastructure in order to both reverse the Depression and prevent such events in the future. However, he saw no cause for changing the very nature of the federal government in such a way that it would potentially endanger the personal liberties of its citizens.

—*Michael P. Auerbach, MA*

Bibliography and Additional Reading

"American President: Herbert Hoover (1874–1964)." *Miller Center.* U of Virginia, n.d. Web. 17 June 2014.

Carroll, Sarah. "Causes of the Great Depression". *OK Economics.* Boston U, 2002. Web. 17 June 2014. Edsforth, Ronald. *The New Deal: America's Response to the Great Depression.* Hoboken: Wiley, 2000. Print.

"The Great Depression (1929–1939)." *Eleanor Roosevelt Papers Project.* George Washington U, n.d. Web. 17 June 2014.

"Herbert Clark Hoover: A Biographical Sketch." *Herbert Hoover Presidential Library and Museum.* National Archives, n.d. Web. 17 June 2014.

McElvaine, Robert S. *The Great Depression: America, 1929–1941.* 25th anniv. ed. New York: Three Rivers, 2009. Print.

Whisenhunt, Donald W. *President Herbert Hoover.* Hauppauge, NY: Nova, 2007. Print.

THE APPOMATTOX OF THE THIRD TERMERS—UNCONDITIONAL SURRENDER.

Ulysses S. Grant is shown surrendering to James A. Garfield after losing the 1880 Republican presidential nomination to him, in this satirical Puck cartoon. (By Joseph Ferdinand Keppler. Library of Congress)

■ Twenty-Second Amendment

Date: March 21, 1947
Author: U.S. Congress
Genre: Government document

Summary Overview

Passed in 1947 and ratified about four years later, the Twenty-Second Amendment to the U.S. Constitution established an official term limit for the nation's presidents. Prior to this amendment's ratification, most U.S. chief executives had adhered to the precedent set by first president George Washington of serving no more than two terms in office. The Constitution lacked any formal guidance on this issue, however, and President Franklin D. Roosevelt had successfully stood for election to four consecutive terms during the 1930s and early 1940s. Although Roosevelt had been fairly elected in each instance and no serious accusations emerged that his long tenure in office had contributed to abuse of power, a federal commission recommended the addition of an amendment establishing the two-term limit as part of a series of suggestions aimed at streamlining government operations. The states ratified the amendment with little fanfare, and it has remained largely uncontroversial.

Defining Moment

The Framers of the U.S. Constitution did not all agree on the best length of time for any given person to serve as the nation's president. Many early American leaders were wary of granting too much power to any one person, fearful that the liberty won by the American Revolution would be endangered by allowing an American monarch to come to power. The nation's first plan for government, the Articles of Confederation, had not allowed for an executive branch at all, assigning the office of "president" to the head of the national Congress. However, by the time of the writing of the Constitution, the weaknesses of the central government had become clear, and the Framers decided to create an office (the presidency) to oversee the implementation of government laws and policies.

As debates over ratification raged in the state legislatures and the press, Federalists and Anti-Federalists clashed over the nature and power of the proposed chief executive. Anti-Federalists argued that a president— especially one not subject to any form of term limits—was akin to the British king. Federalists rejected this claim, and the Constitution was ratified with the office of the presidency intact.

Washington—the first president to serve under the Constitution—declined to run for a third term. This decision set a precedent for a two-term presidency that was strongly endorsed by the nation's third president, Thomas Jefferson, who also refused to seek a third term, but did so on grounds more directly related to political philosophy. Only a few outliers challenged the two-term precedent. For example, Theodore Roosevelt became president upon the assassination of William McKinley in 1901 and served nearly all of McKinley's elected term before winning election in his own right in 1904. After leaving office in 1909, he became frustrated with the policies of his successor William Howard Taft and mounted an unsuccessful campaign at the top of the ticket for the Progressive Party in 1912.

Therefore, not until 1940 did a president successfully attain a third term. During the waning years of his second term in the late 1930s, President Roosevelt kept quiet about his intentions for the election of 1940. Roosevelt may have wished to avoid weakening his position in dealing with Congress to address the economic problems of the Great Depression; he may also have wanted to show strength in the face of the rising Axis threat in Europe. Although historians disagree on Roosevelt's motivations in accepting a nomination for a third term in 1940, voters resoundingly returned Roosevelt to the office at the polls. They did so again in 1944, when Roosevelt ran for a fourth term despite his declining health.

Author Biography

First established in 1947, the Commission on Organization of the Executive Branch of the Government was a nonpartisan committee headed by former Republican president Herbert Hoover, a long-time civil servant who believed in the efficacy of small government. Commonly known as the Hoover Commission, the body studied ways to reduce bureaucracy, increase efficiency, and generally improve the operations of the executive branch to meet the needs of the post–World War II United States. Between 1947 and 1949, the commission made dozens of recommendations to then president Harry S. Truman, another proponent of administrative efficiency. Among the first of these recommendations was the introduction of term limits for the presidency. This idea found favor with the Republican Congress that had been elected in 1946, and the federal legislature sent the amendments to the states for ratification short weeks after its members took office. Ratification was completed in February 1951.

HISTORICAL DOCUMENT

Amendment XXII

Section 1.
No person shall be elected to the office of the President more than twice, and no person who has held the office of President, or acted as President, for more than two years of a term to which some other person was elected President shall be elected to the office of the President more than once. But this article shall not apply to any person holding the office of President when this article was proposed by the Congress, and shall not prevent any person who may be holding the office of President, or acting as President, during the term within which this article becomes operative from holding the office of President or acting as President during the remainder of such term.

Section 2.
This article shall be inoperative unless it shall have been ratified as an amendment to the Constitution by the legislatures of three-fourths of the several states within seven years from the date of its submission to the states by the Congress.

GLOSSARY

inoperative: not operative; not in operation; without effect

ratified: to confirm by expressing consent, approval or formal sanction

Document Analysis
Using clear and simple language, the Twenty-Second Amendment firmly formalizes the traditional two-term cap on the period during which any single person can serve as U.S. president. The heart of the amendment lies in the opening statement of section 1, which stipulates that no one "shall be elected to the office of the President more than twice." Further, section 1 seeks to prevent the creation of loopholes in the amendment's application by establishing a procedure for the relatively uncommon instances in which a vice president ascends to the presidency in the event of the death, resignation, or incapacitation of the elected chief executive. The amendment asserts that "no person who has held the office of President, or acted as President, for more than two years of a term" to which someone else was actually elected can run for office twice, implying that a person who rose to the presidency at the midpoint of an unexpired term could stand for election in his or her own right for a total term in office of ten years. Because vice presidents often act briefly in the capacity of president when the elected chief is unable—for example, during a surgical procedure—this limit allows for needed flexibility in conducting governmental operations, while maintaining the intent of the amendment. The amendment also provides an exemption for the person who was president or acting as president at the time of its proposal and during the presidential term that the amendment becomes ef-

fective.

Section 2 establishes a time limit for full ratification of the amendment. Because the Constitution places no set time limit on the period between which an amendment can be sent for ratification and final approval, the time lapse can be quite significant; the Twenty-Seventh Amendment, for example, was approved by Congress in 1789, but did not garner enough support from the states for ratification until 1992. The Eighteenth, Twentieth, and Twenty-First Amendments contain similar language.

Essential Themes

Likely because of the long-standing U.S. presidential tradition of declining to seek election to any term beyond the second, the Twenty-Second Amendment has been generally accepted by the U.S. electorate and office holders without a great deal of protest. Occasionally, representatives or senators of both political parties have called on the U.S. Congress to introduce a measure repealing the amendment. These efforts, however, have never proceeded to a point of serious consideration. Objections to the amendment rest mostly on its limitation of absolute democracy—voters may not always reelect a popular president whom they otherwise would have—and on its creation of so-called "lame duck" presidents, who find it difficult to garner political support for policies in their second terms. Because such presidents cannot constitutionally stand for reelection, political jockeying within a sitting chief executive's own party to receive support for a presidential nomination in the following election can serve as a distraction from the work of governing.

As of 2014, only a handful of individuals have been directly affected by the amendment's provisions: Dwight D. Eisenhower, the first president elected after ratification; Richard M. Nixon, who resigned in disgrace partway through his second elective term; Ronald Reagan, who served two terms in the 1980s; Bill Clinton, a two-term president who served the following decade; and two twenty-first century presidents, Republican George W. Bush and Democrat Barack Obama. Under the terms of the amendment, incumbent chief executive Truman was exempt from the two-term limit because he was in office when the amendment was proposed as well as when it was enacted. Though Truman had the right to run for a third term in 1952, even after having served most of Roosevelt's elected fourth term and retaining the office in the 1948 election, he declined to run after suffering an early primary defeat. Lyndon B. Johnson would also have been eligible to stand for reelection in 1968 after advancing from the vice presidency to serve part of assassinated president John F. Kennedy's unexpired term in 1963 and winning election in his own right the following year because his total term in office would have remained within the ten-year cap, but Johnson opted not to run in 1968.

The Twenty-Second Amendment has additionally established a constitutional precedent for the usage of term limits that has led to calls for a similar measure to be created for other elected federal officials, particularly U.S. representatives and senators. During the mid-1990s, polls suggested that between two-thirds and three-quarters of Americans would support the passage of a similar amendment placing term limits on members of Congress. Roughly equivalent majorities expressed support for such a measure nearly two decades later. Political gridlock and acrimony, analysts concluded, contributed to the popular belief that term limits helped the government work more effectively—an opinion with which the Hoover Commission would likely have agreed.

—*Vanessa E. Vaughn, MA*

Bibliography and Additional Reading

"Americans Call for Term Limits, End to Electoral College." *Gallup.com.* Gallup, Inc., 18 Jan. 2013. Web. 12 Dec. 2014.

Caress, Stanley M., & Todd T. Kunioka. *Term Limits and Their Consequences: The Aftermath of Legislative Reform.* Albany: State U of New York P, 2012. Print.

Korzi, Michael J. *Presidential Term Limits in American History: Power, Principles, and Politics.* College Station: Texas A&M U Press, 2013. Print.

Dewey during a campaign tour in New York. *New York World-Telegram* and the *Sun* staff photographer (Library of Congress Prints and Photographs Division)

■ "Dewey Defeats Truman"

Date: November 3, 1948
Author: *Chicago Tribune*; National Constitution Center Staff
Genre: Newspaper headline; article

Summary Overview

By 1948, World War II was over but America had certainly been marked by the war and was now facing an election to determine who the postwar U.S. president would be. Harry S. Truman, the Democratic incumbent then running for re-election, was not widely considered to be the most popular candidate in 1948, even though he was viewed as having done a reasonably good job as president when he moved into that role from his position as vice president under Franklin D. Roosevelt. It seemed more likely, however, that Thomas E. Dewey, Republican governor of New York, would rack up the victory. Newspapers were openly supporting Dewey, and in some cases were actively printing poor press on Truman, even resorting to calling him names like "nincompoop." While the public did not necessarily object to Truman, the press generally did not favor him as a candidate. The *Chicago Tribune* was so confident in a Dewey victory that, the morning after Election Day, they erroneously printed a headline touting Dewey as the winner of the race. In a now famous photo taken a few days after the election, Truman holds up the mistaken headline and is shown smiling from ear to ear. In a race troubled by divisions within the Democrat Party, Truman campaigned more diligently than his Republican opponent, thereby securing his position as the 33rd president of the United States.

Defining Moment

Upon the shocking death of FDR in 1945, Vice President Harry S. Truman found himself in the position of acceding to the presidency. Despite his abrupt transition into the highest office in the land, he was perceived by the public as largely successful in this capacity owing to his role in the navigation of the United States through the end of World War II. He was credited with encouraging a positive peacetime economy; however, rising inflation rates and troubled relations with labor ultimately damaged Truman's reputation with the public in the long run. Thus, when it came time for Truman to run for the office in 1948, many questioned the likelihood that he would be successful in his pursuit. Truman, however, felt confident in a victory. Having previously won a U.S. Senate election that he was not expected to win, and possessing a tenacious nature that would not let him accept the idea of a potential defeat even when others thought it inevitable, Truman dug in to the campaign and worked diligently at it.

Harry S. Truman came from an agricultural background and was a farmer with a reputation for being honest and having integrity. He had previously served as a U.S. Senator from Missouri, and vice president of the United States before becoming president. All of these factors combined would normally work to help a candidate advance. However, fractions within the Democratic Party mad it difficult in this case for Truman on the campaign trail. During the Democratic National Convention of 1948, Truman expressed his concern over the lack of progress and action from within Congress, and in particular expressed his concern over the growing civil rights issue in the country. These comments caused a faction of the Democratic Party, known as the Dixiecrats and headed by Governor Strom Thurmond of South Carolina, to walk out of the convention. The splintering of the Democratic Party, and the assumption that Governor Dewey would win the race, made the 1948 campaign a tough one for Truman. In fact, most polling data indicated that Dewey was poised to win the race handily. However, Truman's aggressive campaigning and refusal to give up, combined with the fact that most pollsters did not factor in voters who were waiting until the last minute to make a candidate selection, led to Truman's unexpected victory on November 2, 1948.

Author Biography

The account reproduced in the "Historical Document" section, below, was prepared by the National Constitution Center (NCC), an institution that was established by Congress to provide the public with information about the United States Constitution. The NCC is a nonpartisan organization known as being an international center for civic education. One of the major goals of the center is to increase people's awareness about, and promote in-dividual's understanding of the Constitution. The NCC provides important information about historical American political individuals and events, and aims to make the Constitution more accessible for people everywhere.

HISTORICAL DOCUMENT

In the legacy of presidential history, Harry Truman may be best remembered by one photograph. So how did the 33rd president wind up holding a newspaper that showed him losing an election he had already won?

On Wednesday, November 3, 1948, the Chicago Tribune published the most famous political headline in U.S. history, proclaiming Thomas Dewey as the next President after Tuesday's election. In fact, Truman was the winner, not Dewey.

Earlier in 1948, Truman was running for his first elected term in the White House. A vice president, the little-known Truman replaced Franklin Roosevelt after FDR passed away in April 1945 just after the start of his fourth presidential term.

His presidency was anything but ordinary, and the Democrats had been in the White House for almost 16 years as Truman approached Election Day on November 2, 1948 and a formidable Republican candidate, Thomas Dewey.

Truman was also running against a Democrat faction called the Dixiecrats, who opposed Truman's efforts to integrate the military. The Dixiecrats, led by Strom Thurmond, took 39 electoral votes in the 1948 election to weaken the former "Solid South" controlled by Roosevelt's Democratic Party. And another former Roosevelt vice president, Henry Wallace, ran on the Progressive Party ticket.

And then there was the polling data. Dewey's victory was so expected that the Roper poll had stopped doing surveys in September about the race. The Gallup poll had the race at 45 percent for Dewey and 41 percent for Truman in October.

So the night of November 2, the editors of the Chicago Tribune, based on the advice of their Washington editor and a need for an early first edition, approved a gigantic headline that read, "Dewey Beats Truman."

The Tribune also apparently based its decision on a recent Life magazine cover that called the election for Dewey and a general low regard for Truman, whom it had called a "nincompoop" on its editorial pages. (Only an estimated 15 percent of newspapers nationally supported Truman in the election.)

But when the dust settled, Truman easily defeated Dewey in the Electoral College, by a 303 to 189 margin. Truman also won by a 50-45 percent popular vote.

What the newspapers and pollsters didn't understand was Truman's background as a fighter, and the tendency for voters to wait until closer to Election Day to pick a candidate.

Earlier in his political career, Truman had been written off in the 1940 U.S. Senate election. When Truman's political ally, Tom Pendergrast, was convicted of tax evasion in 1939, few people thought Truman stood a chance of getting re-elected in Missouri. Truman hit the campaign trail hard, spoke about his war record and experience as a common man, and pulled off an upset.

At a raucous 1948 Democratic convention in Philadelphia, Truman made it clear that he would add a campaign against Congress to his set of tactics.

"Congress has still done nothing," Truman pleaded at the deeply divided convention. "With the help of God and the wholehearted push which you can put behind this campaign, we can save this country from a continuation of the 80th Congress, and from misrule from now on."

Truman survived a walkout by the Dixiecrat faction of the Democrats at the convention and successfully used the "do-nothing" Congress as a weapon against the favored Republican candidate, Dewey.

Truman also hit the campaign trail hard after Labor Day, using a presidential train to cross the country making more than 200 campaign speeches. Dewey was known as a dull speaker and campaigned far less. The pollsters also stopped polling before the effect of Truman's whistle-stop campaigning took hold.

Late on November 2, Truman went to sleep in Independence, Missouri, knowing he led by one million votes in early results but was expected to lose. Four hours later, he received a call from the Secret Service – Truman was leading in the election and expected to win.

Dewey conceded the next day, but the famous Tribune photograph was taken two days later, as the Truman family was in Saint Louis and returning to Washington. Life photographer W. Eugene Smith caught Truman in the moment after a staffer handed the President a copy of the Tribune early edition that had been found on a train earlier.

The rest was history, and perhaps the most famous photograph in American politics.

GLOSSARY

Dixiecrat: a splinter party formed in 1948 by Southern Democrats who opposed positive civil rights reform in America

Progressive Party: a political party formed in 1912 by Theodore Roosevelt

whistlestop campaign: a style of campaigning in which a candidate makes a series of brief appearances and/or speeches at a number of towns in a short amount of time

Clifford K. Berryman's editorial cartoon of Oct. 19, 1948, shows the consensus of experts in mid-October: Polls show Dewey ahead so why hold election? (U.S. National Archives)

Document Analysis

No one but Harry Truman foresaw a victory in the 1948 Presidential Election. With Thomas E. Dewey being the favored candidate, news outlets were quick to report high polling numbers in favor of the governor of New York. Under Truman's presidency the nation struggled with rising inflation rates, and combined with the Democrat's loss of the House and the Senate, Truman was not considered a front-runner in the race. Furthermore, the emergence of a third party, the Dixiecrats, threatened Truman's ability to reach Southern voters who were very important for the successful election of a Democrat.

The Dixiecrats were a fragment of the Democratic Party motivated to oppose Truman as a candidate for the presidency mostly because of Truman's stance on civil rights. In 1946, Truman developed a commission to study civil rights in the country, and was sympathetic to the findings which described major injustices directed towards the African American community. Additionally, Truman favored integration of the U.S. military, which Dixiecrats found reprehensible. Strom Thurmond, a former county judge and then governor of South Carolina, ran in opposition to Truman on the Dixiecrat ticket, primarily motivated by Truman's call for civil rights reform. Although Thurmond received only 39 Electoral College votes, his candidacy did weaken Truman's voter base in the South. Another candidate, Henry Wallace, ran on the Progressive Party ticket but was completely unsuccessful, receiving zero Electoral College votes. Truman's most formidable opponent, Thomas Dewey, was expected by most to win the race.

Despite his frontrunner status, Dewey was not a particularly charismatic campaigner; nor did he think "stumping" was necessary to win an election. He was, in fact, a dull, boring public speaker, and he did not spend much time on the campaign trail—especially in comparison to the vigorous campaigning that Truman did. While Truman was engaged in his whirlwind whistlestop campaign, Dewey took comfort in the strong polling numbers showing him at least four points ahead of Truman during the course of the election. Dewey was set to become the youngest president in office since Theodore Roosevelt, and would have been the first Republican in the White House since Hoover was abandoned by voters in the first years of the Great Depression. In the end, Dewey finished the race having secured 189 Electoral College votes, while Truman won 303. The rallying cry "Give 'em hell, Harry!" proved to be an accurate description of what Truman accomplished on Election Day. The polls had failed to take into account the impact of his whistlestop campaign, and what effect those appearances might have on undecided voters. Even though newspapers had predicted a Dewey win, going so far as to print, prematurely, headlines to that effect, Truman, not Dewey, would win the presidency in 1948.

Essential Themes

Observers have come to regard the 1948 election as one of the greatest upsets in American history, as famously demonstrated by the photo of Truman holding up the erroneous *Chicago Tribune* headline naming Dewey the winner. The ramifications of this election, however, go far beyond a wrong headline. The emphasis placed on polling numbers, particularly in modern elections, is enormous. News outlets sometimes report poll numbers that fail to take into account what might happen late in a campaign, or else do not adequately consider what the larger voting population is actually thinking in terms of vote choice. For example, the 2016 race between Hillary Clinton and Donald Trump is a modern-day lesson in polling error. Throughout the election Clinton had been projected to be the winner, yet on Election Day Trump emerged victorious. In addition to occasionally being outright wrong, polling is also used to inform the public which candidate is currently winning a political race. Oftentimes, that coverage can sway a race or even alter its outcome. When people are told that the candidate they support is losing an election based on polling information, they tend to accept it not bother voting. Similarly, polling results showing a candidate to have a commanding lead in a race may cause that candidate's supporters to assume the he or she will win without their votes. Thus do these polls play a much larger role in the election process than simply predicting a winner. They may actually be working to depress voter turnout in the country. In the case of the Truman election, the negative polling numbers clearly did not accurately predict the outcome of the election, and may have worked to push Truman to fight harder than he otherwise might have had the numbers been in his favor.

As a result of Truman's 1948 win, Truman went on to fight communism overseas, help begin the long process of putting an end to racial segregation in America, bring the country into the United Nations, and help in the development of the Central Intelligence Agency, among many other accomplishments. For a man whom news outlets in 1948 had no faith in, he went on to serve his country well. Even though President Truman was eligible to serve for a second term in office, he declined to do so and did not run in 1952. Truman returned home with his wife to write his memoirs and open a library.

—*Amber R. Dickinson, PhD*

Bibliography and Additional Reading

Donaldson, Gary A. *Truman Defeats Dewey*. The University Press of Kentucky, 2015.

Karabell, Zachary. *The Last Campaign: How Harry Truman Won the 1948 Election*. Vintage
Books, 2001.

NCC Staff. "Looking Back at the Truman Beats Dewey Upset." *National Constitution Center –*
Constitutioncenter.org,   constitutioncenter.org/blog/ behind-the-biggest-upset-in-presidential-history-truman-beats-dewey.

"National Constitution Center." *National Constitution Center – Constitutioncenter.org*,
constitutioncenter.org/about.

Nix, Elizabeth. "The Truman-Dewey Election, 65 Years Ago." *History.com*, A&E Television
Networks, 1 Nov. 2013, www.history.com/news/the-truman-dewey-election-65-years-ago.

Sitkoff, Harvard. "Harry Truman and the Election of 1948: The Coming of Age of Civil Rights in American Politics." *The Journal of Southern History*, vol. 37, no. 4, 1971, p. 597., doi:10.2307/2206548.

Democratic party poster 1952 for Adlai Stevenson. A poster from the 1952 campaign: Labor's Committee for Stevenson & Sparkman campaign.

■ Adlai Stevenson's Acceptance Speech at the 1952 Democratic National Convention

Date: July 26, 1952
Author: Adlai Stevenson
Genre: Speech

Summary Overview

The U.S. presidential election of 1952 took place against the backdrop of the Cold War, the stalemate in fighting on the Korean Peninsula, and charges of corruption in the administration of President Harry S. Truman. Though the Twenty-Second Amendment had imposed presidential term limits, Truman was exempt from the restriction because he was in office when the amendment became law; thus, Truman was the presumptive Democratic nominee in 1952. Truman announced that he would not seek reelection after he lost the New Hampshire primary to Estes Kefauver, a senator from Tennessee. As the Democratic National Convention (DNC) approached, Truman tried to persuade Illinois governor Adlai Stevenson to seek the nomination, but Stevenson refused. Party leaders hoped to draft Stevenson into service, as he was the most electable candidate with the least political baggage. His reputation as a gifted orator and cool-headed moderate was solidified during the convention, where he gave the welcoming address and then, after some coaxing, agreed to have his name put forward as a candidate. He gave this speech after winning the Democratic nomination. Stevenson was soundly defeated by Republican Dwight D. Eisenhower in the general election, winning just nine states.

Defining Moment

President Truman's failure to bring the Korean War to a satisfactory conclusion, his replacement of General Douglas McArthur, and accusations that his administration was soft on Communism and rife with corruption had led to a precipitous drop in his popularity. In February 1952, Truman had a 22 percent approval rating, the lowest ever recorded (ratings were first chronicled beginning in the late 1930s). Truman allowed his name to be added to the New Hampshire primary in 1952, later arguing that he had no interest in the position but could not find a suitable candidate to replace him. One of his top choices had been popular Illinois governor Adlai Stevenson, but Stevenson had turned him down. Truman was soundly beaten in the New Hampshire primary and declared publicly that he would not seek a second term. The stage was set for a lively contest for the Democratic nomination.

Stevenson had won the Illinois governorship by a wide margin and was a well-respected and popular governor. He had been mentioned as a possible presidential candidate for several years but always made it clear that he was happy as governor. The early front-runner for the nomination was Tennessee senator Estes Kefauver, who was nationally known as a crusader against corruption and organized crime. However, Kefauver was deeply unpopular with Democratic leadership, some of whom had found themselves named in his investigations of organized crime.

Held in Chicago in July 1952, the Democratic National Convention began with a rousing speech by Stevenson, as the governor of the host state. This speech prompted the delegates to start a "Draft Stevenson" campaign. By the third ballot, Stevenson had won the nomination, though he had steadfastly refused to accept it. He was the first presidential candidate to be drafted since James Garfield in 1880. Finally, he gave in, and his acceptance speech, widely broadcast on both television and radio, had a profound effect on his audience. Though Stevenson's campaign was ultimately a failure, his acceptance speech has been celebrated as an example of elegant political oratory.

Author Biography

Adlai Ewing Stevenson II was born on February 5, 1900, in Los Angeles, California, to a prominent, politically connected Illinois family. He was raised in Bloomington, Illinois, while his father served as Illinois secretary of state. He was the namesake of his grandfather, who had served as vice president under Grover Cleveland, and he recalled meeting Woodrow Wilson in 1912. Stevenson graduated from Princeton University and Northwestern University School of Law. He passed the Illinois bar in 1926 and practiced law in Chicago. During World War II, he was an assistant to the secretary of the Navy, and he was active in the State Department after the war. He was also an advisor to the United Nations delega-tion. In 1948, Stevenson won the governorship of Illinois in a landslide election, which put him on the national political stage. When President Truman decided not to run for office in 1952, Stevenson was his first choice for the Democratic nomination. Stevenson ran unsuccess-fully for president in both 1952 and 1956. He was the U.S. ambassador to the United Nations from 1961 until his death in London on July 14, 1965. He is buried in Bloomington, Illinois.

HISTORICAL DOCUMENT

Mr. President, Ladies and Gentlemen of the Convention, My Fellow Citizens.

I accept your nomination and your program.

I should have preferred to hear those words uttered by a stronger, a wiser, a better man than myself. But, after listening to the President's speech, I even feel bet-ter about myself. None of you, my friends, can wholly appreciate what is in my heart. I can only hope that you understand my words. They will be few.

I have not sought the honor you have done me. I could not seek it, because I aspired to another office, which was the full measure of my ambition, and one does not treat the highest office within the gift of the people of Illinois as an alternative or as a consolation prize.

I would not seek your nomination for the Presidency, because the burdens of that office stagger the imagina-tion. Its potential for good or evil, now and in the years of our lives, smothers exultation and converts vanity to prayer.

I have asked the Merciful Father—the Father of us all—to let this cup pass from me, but from such dreaded responsibility one does not shrink in fear, in self-interest, or in false humility. So, "If this cup may not pass from me, except I drink it, Thy will be done."

That my heart has been troubled, that I have not sought this nomination, that I could not seek it in good conscience, that I would not seek it in honest self-appraisal, is not to say that I value it the less. Rather, it is that I revere the office of the Presidency of the United States. And now, my friends, that you have made your decision, I will fight to win that office with—with all my heart and my soul. And, with your help, I have no doubt that we will win.

You have summoned me to the highest mission within the gift of any people. I could not be more proud. Bet-ter men than I were at hand for this mighty task, and I owe to you and to them every resource of mind and of strength that I possess to make your deed today a good one for our country and for our party. I am confident too, that your selection for—of a candidate for Vice President will strengthen me and our party immeasurably in the hard, the implacable work that lies ahead of all of us.

I know you join me in gratitude and respect for the great Democrats and the leaders of our generation whose names you have considered here in this convention, whose vigor, whose character, whose devotion to the Republic we love so well have won the respect of count-less Americans and have enriched our party. I shall need them; we shall need them, because I have not changed in any respect since yesterday.

Your nomination, awesome as I find it, has not enlarged my capacities, so I am profoundly grateful and emboldened by their comradeship and their fealty, and I have been deeply moved by their expressions of good will and of support. And I cannot, my friends, resist the urge to take the one opportunity that has been afforded me to pay my humble respects to a very great and good American, whom I am proud to call my kinsman, Alben Barkely of Kentucky.

Let me say, too, that I have been heartened by the conduct of this convention. You have argued and dis-agreed, because as Democrats you care and you cared deeply. But you have disagreed and argued without call-ing each other liars and thieves, without despoiling our best traditions—you have not spoiled our best traditions in any naked struggles for power.

And you have written a platform that neither equivocates, contradicts, nor evades. You have restated our party's record, its principles and its purposes, in language that none can mistake, and with a firm confidence in justice, freedom, and peace on earth that will raise the hearts and the hopes of mankind for that distant day when no one rattles a saber and no one drags a chain.

For all things I am grateful to you. But I feel no exultation, no sense of triumph. Our troubles are all ahead of us. Some will call us appeasers; others will say that we are the war party. Some will say we are reactionary; others will say that we stand for socialism. There will be inevitable—the inevitable cries of "throw the rascals out," "it's time for a change," and so on and so on.

We'll hear all those things and many more besides. But we will hear nothing that we have not heard before. I'm not too much concerned with partisan denunciation, with epithets and abuse, because the workingman, the farmer, the thoughtful businessman, all know that they are better off than ever before, and they all know the Great Depression under the hammer blows of the Democratic party.

Nor am I afraid that the precious two-party system is in danger. Certainly the Republican party looked brutally alive a couple of weeks ago—and I mean both Republican parties. Nor am I afraid the Democratic party is old and fat and indolent. After a hundred and fifty years, it has been old for a long time, and it will never be indolent, as long as it looks forward and not back, as long as it commands the allegiance of the young and the hopeful who dream the dreams and see the visions of a better America and a better world.

You will hear many sincere and thoughtful people express concern about the continuation of one party in power for twenty years. I don't belittle this attitude. But change for the sake of change has no absolute merit in itself. If our greatest hazard is preservation of the values of Western civilization, in our self-interest alone, if you please, it is the part—is it the part of wisdom to change for the sake of change to a party with a split personality, to a leader, whom we all respect, but who has been called upon to minister to a hopeless case of political schizophrenia?

If the fear is corruption in official position, do you believe with Charles Evans Hughes that guild is personal and knows no party? Do you doubt the power of any political leader, if he has the will to do so, to set his own house in order without his neighbors having to burn it down?

What does concern me, in common with thinking partisans of both parties, is not just winning this election but how it is won, how well we can take advantage of this great quadrennial opportunity to debate issues sensibly and soberly. I hope and pray that we Democrats, win or lose, can campaign not as a crusade to exterminate the opposing party, as our opponents seem to prefer, but as a great opportunity to educated and elevate a people whose destiny is leadership, not alone of a rich and prosperous, contented country, as in the past, but of a world in ferment.

And, my friends even more important than winning the election is governing the nation. That is the test of a political party, the acid, final test. When the tumult and the shouting die, when the bands are gone and the lights are dimmed, there is the stark reality of responsibility in an hour of history haunted with those gaunt, grim specters of strife, dissension, and materialism at home and ruthless, inscrutable, and hostile power abroad.

The ordeal of the twentieth century, the bloodiest, most turbulent era of the whole Christian age, is far from over. Sacrifice, patience, understanding, and implacable purpose may be our lot of years to come. Let's face it. Let's talk sense to the American people. Let's tell them the truth, that there are no gains without pains, that there—that we are now on the eve of great decisions, not easy decisions, like resistance when you're attacked, but a long, patient, costly struggle which alone can assure triumph over the great enemies of man—war, poverty, and tyranny—and the assaults upon human dignity which are the most grievous consequences of each.

Let's tell them that the victory to be won in the twentieth century, this portal to the Golden Age, mocks the pretensions of individual acumen and ingenuity, for it is a citadel guarded by thick walls of ignorance and of mistrust which do not fall before the trumpets' blast or the politicians' imprecations or even a general's baton. They are, my friends, walls that must be directly stormed by the hosts of courage, of morality, and of vision, standing shoulder to shoulder, unafraid of ugly truth, contemptuous of lies, half truths, circuses, and demagoguery.

The people are wise, wiser than the Republicans think. And the Democratic party is the people's party—not the labor party, not the farmers' party, not the employers' party—it is the party of no one because it is the party of everyone.

That, that, I—I think, is our ancient mission. Where we have deserted it, we have failed. With your help, there will be no desertion now. Better we lose the election than mislead the people, and better we lose than misgovern the people. Help me to do the job in these years of darkness, of doubt, and of crisis which stretch beyond the horizon of tonight's happy vision, and we will justify our glorious past and the loyalty of silent millions who look to us for compassion, for understanding, and for honest purpose. Thus we will serve our great tradition greatly.

I ask of you all you have. I will give you all I have, even as he who came here tonight and honored me, as he has honored you, the Democratic party, by a lifetime of service and bravery that will find him an imperishable page in the history of the Republic and of the Democratic party—President Harry S. Truman.

And finally, my friends, in this staggering task you have assigned me, I shall always try "to do justly, to love mercy, and to walk humbly with my God."

Document Analysis

Stevenson begins his acceptance speech at the 1952 Democratic National Convention with some self-deprecation. He says he would have liked a better man than he to have been the nominee, but he is flattered by the words of Truman, who introduced him. Stevenson publicly refused the candidacy, and he reminds the audience that he has not sought the presidency, "because the burdens of that office stagger the imagination." He sees the presidency as a "dreaded responsibility" and hoped that he would be spared. Despite this, he says he reveres the position. He states that because his nomination is the will of the people and, he implies, the will of God, he will fight to become president of the United States and do his best once he is elected.

Stevenson asks for unity in the Democratic Party and support from all of its members, even the candidates who opposed him mere moments before. He congratulates all of the nominees for a spirited but civil campaign, for they have "not spoiled our best traditions in any naked struggles for power." He urges the American people to remember what party brought them through the Great Depression, when Democratic president Franklin D. Roosevelt set up programs that gave Americans food and work during the country's darkest economic years.

Stevenson asks members of his party to remember that the work of winning an election is secondary to the work of governing a nation, and everything done during a campaign should reflect that. The Democratic Party should see the campaign as an opportunity to "educate and elevate a people whose destiny is leadership . . . of a world in ferment." Stevenson believes that the nation has to be ready to confront the "bloodiest, most turbu-lent era of the whole Christian age"—in doing so, Americans must consider how difficult the work will be and how much patience it will require. Stevenson cautions against easy answers or quick fixes. He says that since the Democratic Party is that of the people, it needs to trust American citizens and to speak to them frankly and openly, "unafraid of ugly truth, contemptuous of lies, half truths, circuses, and demagoguery." Stevenson closes his acceptance speech by thanking President Truman and promising to do his best at the "staggering task" set before him.

Essential Themes

Stevenson began this speech with a lengthy explanation of why he had declined the nomination in the first place: essentially because he had great respect for the office. He found the prospect of the presidency overwhelming, and for good reason. The world was in chaos, he argued, and the responsibility to lead the nation through it was daunting. In his view, the only way to lead was to be honest with Americans about what was going on internationally and to ask for their help and understanding. Stevenson decried political posturing, arguing that it amounted to lying to the people, since the truth was much more subtle and complex than political sound bites or accusations. Stevenson also went to great pains to argue that the Democratic Party was alive and well. Despite being in power for two decades, it was still nimble and best represented the American people.

—*Bethany Groff Dorau, MA*

Bibliography and Additional Reading

Cooke, Alistair. *Six Men*. Rev. ed. New York: Penguin, 2008. Print.

McCullough, David. *Truman*. New York: Simon, 1992. Print.

McKeever, Porter. *Adlai Stevenson: His Life and Legacy*. New York: Quill, 1989. Print.

Walker, Martin. *The Cold War: A History*. New York: Holt, 1993. Print.

THE SIXTH PARTY SYSTEM, PART I, 1960-1974

During the "long 1960s"—that is, from 1960 to 1974—there was both great promise for a new society and great tragedy wrought by war and political division. The decade began with presidential candidate John F. Kennedy promoting the "New Frontier" that he believed lay ahead for the nation. And, indeed, significant expansion was to come in U.S. economic affairs, global influence, and, especially, science and technology. Yet the outgoing president at the time, Dwight Eisenhower, warned in darker tones about what also could lay in store: a rising "military-industrial complex" that stood to outstrip people's ability to contain it.

The first dozen-plus years of the sixth phase of American political history, then, encompass the dawn of Space Age, the hardening of the Cold War, the (actual) Vietnam War, the Civil Rights movement, the Counterculture movement, and the rise of Conservatism.

One thing that is often identified as marking the difference between the 1960s and the previous decade is that, in the 1960s there was a growing willingness to question the government—or, more broadly, the "establishment"—whereas in the 1950s (and earlier) most citizens, including young people, trusted their government. A break with entrenched racialist and sexist attitudes, and the hard realities of the Vietnam War (including government deception regarding it), contributed to this growing unease. A political battle raged, as never before, over the direction that the country should take. Whereas Kennedy's successor, Lyndon Johnson, envisioned a "Great Society" that opened the doors of opportunity for all, funded by progressive taxation and overseen by government agencies, his opponents on the left felt that he failed to address fundamental problems of militarism, imperialism, racism, sexism, and more. In 1968 the Democratic Party split over these issues, fielding a number of left-of-center candidates to challenge the status quo.

Meanwhile, the Republicans had already begun to move to the right. In 1964, the Republican presidential nominee, Barry Goldwater, spoke of "extremism" from the right in positive terms; and, in his first important national political speech, Ronald Reagan endorsed Goldwater and his views. Although the Republicans lost in a landslide that year, four years later, with Richard Nixon at their head, they would take advantage of a divided Democratic Party and win the White House. The 1968 result was especially remarkable in that Nixon, too, faced a challenger on his right—the segregationist George Wallace of Alabama. Nixon, in fact, had managed to win over many southern white voters (former old-line Democrats) through his so-called Southern strategy.

Thus did the country's political climate seem to change from the "promise" of the Kennedy years to the "discontent" of the Johnson years to the hardnosed "realism" of the Nixon years. And through it all, Americans continued to debate the subject of Communist influence in the world—including Vietnam— and what the proper American response should be. Nixon himself had promised to bring peace to Vietnam but instead pursued the war vigorously for four more years. Although he won a second term in 1972, his downfall came soon afterward in the form of the Watergate scandal, which put the entire Republican Party on the defensive for the next several years.

Outgoing President Dwight D. Eisenhower meets with President-elect John F. Kennedy on December 6, 1960

■ JFK's "The New Frontier" Speech

Date: July 15, 1960
Author: John F. Kennedy
Genre: Speech

Summary Overview

John F. Kennedy gave this speech as he accepted the Democratic nomination for president of the United States in 1960. Kennedy was young, only forty-three years old; he was a Roman Catholic, which meant his loyalty to a foreign pope was worrisome to many voters; and he had relatively little foreign-policy experience. This speech assuaged many of those fears, as Kennedy challenged the nation to accept the challenges and opportunities of a "new frontier"—the 1960s, with a new generation of progressive leaders at the helm. He also addressed his religious affiliation, assuring the nation that he believed in the strict separation of church and state, and that his Catholicism was therefore not relevant. Kennedy encouraged the nation to rise to the challenges of its time—to tackle civil rights and economic issues, the nuclear standoff with the Soviet Union, and the possibilities of space exploration and scientific discoveries. This speech was widely broadcast, and Kennedy's eloquence, humor, and youthful energy captured the interest and imagination of a new generation of Americans eager for change.

Defining Moment

The presidential election of 1960 followed eight years of Republican leadership under President Dwight D. Eisenhower. Though Eisenhower himself was popular with the American people, there were some areas of discontent with Republican leadership. The economy was in a slump and many felt that the Eisenhower administration had not done enough to address poverty and civil rights. There were growing Communist threats in Vietnam, Cuba, and the Middle East, and American national pride had taken a hit when the Soviet Union launched *Sputnik*, the first artificial satellite, in 1957. The Cold War was in full swing, with massive nuclear buildup on both sides.

Kennedy, then a senator from Massachusetts, announced his candidacy for president of the United States on January 2, 1960. He had already experienced a meteoric rise through the ranks of the Democratic Party, and had nearly been chosen as Adlai Stevenson's running mate in the 1956 presidential election. Though he was a young, energetic, popular candidate, there were grave concerns in the party that his youth, his Catholicism, and his lack of experience would work against him in the general election. The Republican nominee was almost certain to be Eisenhower's vice president, Richard M. Nixon, who was a less dynamic but far more experienced candidate. It would be an uphill battle for Kennedy to win the Democratic nomination. Senator Hubert H. Humphrey of Minnesota had announced his candidacy on the same day as Kennedy, and there were other strong Democratic contenders, though others had chosen not to publicly announce their candidacy, preferring instead to wait for support they hoped would materialize at the Democratic National Convention in July. Other Democratic candidates included Senate Majority Leader Lyndon B. Johnson of Texas, Senator Stuart Symington of Missouri, and former governor Adlai Stevenson of Illinois, who had run for president unsuccessfully in the previous two elections.

Kennedy campaigned hard across the country, beating out Humphrey to win the Wisconsin and then the West Virginia primaries. His Catholicism was a major issue in the primaries, as anti-Catholic prejudice was still strong in the United States, and many believed that a Catholic's primary loyalty was not to the country, but to the Catholic pope. When Kennedy won West Virginia, it was a turning point in his campaign, proving that he could win in a conservative, primarily Protestant state. By the time of the Democratic National Convention in July, held in Los Angeles, Kennedy was the clear front-runner, and withstood a convention-floor challenge from Johnson. Kennedy won the nomination easily on the first ballot with 806 votes, nearly twice as many as second-place Johnson. Conscious that he was weakest in the

South, where civil rights were a contentious issue, and where his Catholicism seemed to generate the most opposition, Kennedy selected Johnson as his running mate. His televised acceptance speech further galvanized support for Kennedy, as he called on his countrymen to take on the "new frontier," a challenging new era of progress and change in the United States.

Author Biography

John Fitzgerald Kennedy was born in Brookline, Massachusetts, on May 29, 1917. He was the second of nine children in a prominent Irish Catholic family. His father, Joseph Kennedy, was a successful banker who also served as chairman of the Securities and Exchange Commission and as the American ambassador to the United Kingdom. Kennedy attended the Choate School and graduated from Harvard University in 1940, joining the Navy after college, in 1941. Kennedy was seriously injured when his PT boat was sunk by a Japanese destroyer in 1943, though Kennedy famously helped rescue some of his crew. After returning from the war, he served in the U.S. House of Representatives for six years (1947–53) and was elected to the U.S. Senate in 1952. In 1955, he wrote the Pulitzer Prize–winning book *Profiles in Courage*. He was considered a serious contender for the vice presidential nomination in 1956, and was the Democratic nominee for president four years later. He became the first Roman Catholic president of the United States, and the youngest in history to that time. While in office, Kennedy took action on civil rights and combating poverty and founded the Peace Corps. He also narrowly avoided confrontations with the Soviet Union in Berlin and Cuba. Kennedy was assassinated on November 22, 1963, in Dallas, Texas, and was buried at Arlington National Cemetery in Virginia.

HISTORICAL DOCUMENT

Governor Stevenson, Senator Johnson, Mr. Butler, Senator Symington, Senator Humphrey, Speaker Rayburn, fellow Democrats. I want to express my thanks to Governor Stevenson for his generous and heart-warming introduction.

It was my great honor to place his name in nomination at the 1956 Democratic Convention, and I am delighted to have his support and his counsel and his advice in the coming months ahead.

Let me say first that I accept the nomination of the Democratic Party.

I accept it without reservation and with only one obligation, the obligation to devote every effort of my mind and spirit to lead our Party back to victory and our Nation to greatness.

I am grateful, too—I am grateful, too, that you have provided us with such a strong platform to stand on and to run on. Pledges which are made so eloquently are made to be kept. "The Rights of Man"—the civil and economic rights essential to the human dignity of all men—are indeed our goal and are indeed our first principle. This is a Platform on which I can run with enthusiasm and with conviction.

And I am grateful, finally, that I can rely in the coming months on many others: On a distinguished running-mate who brings unity and strength to our Platform and our ticket, Lyndon Johnson; on one of the most articulate spokesmen of modern times, Adlai Stevenson; on a great fighter—on a great fighter for our needs as a Nation and a people, Stuart Symington; on my traveling companion in Wisconsin and West Virginia, Senator Hubert Humphrey; on Paul Butler, our devoted and courageous Chairman; and on that fighting campaigner whose support I now welcome, President Harry Truman.

I feel a lot safer with all of them on my side. And I'm proud of the contrast with our Republican competitors. For their ranks are so thin that not one challenger has dared to put his head up in the last twelve months.

I am fully aware of the fact that the Democratic Party, by nominating someone of my faith, has taken on what many regard as a new and hazardous risk—new, at least since 1928. The Democratic Party has once again placed its confidence in the American people, and in their ability to render a free and fair judgment and in my ability to render a free and fair judgment.

To uphold the Constitution and my oath of office, to reject any kind of religious pressure or obligation that might directly or indirectly interfere with my conduct of the Presidency in the national interest. My record of fourteen years in supporting public education, supporting complete separation of Church and State and resisting pressure from sources of any kind should be clear by now to everyone.

I hope that no American—I hope that no American, considering the really critical issues facing this country, will waste his franchise and throw away his vote by voting either for me or against me because of my religious affiliation. It is not relevant.

I am telling you what you are entitled to know: As I come before you seeking your support for the most powerful office in the free world—I am saying to you that my decisions on every public policy will be my own, as an American, as a Democrat, and as a free man.

I mention all of this only because this country faces so many serious challenges, so many great opportunities, so many burdensome responsibilities that I hope that it is to those great matters that we can address ourselves in the coming months. And if this statement of mine makes it easier to concentrate on our Nation's problems, then I'm glad that I have made it.

Under any circumstances, the victory we seek in November will not be easy. We know that in our hearts. We know that our opponent will invoke the name of Abraham Lincoln on behalf of their candidate, despite the fact that his political career has often seemed to show charity towards none and malice for all.

We know it will not be easy to campaign against a man who has spoken and voted on every side of every issue. Mr. Nixon may feel that it's his turn now, after the New Deal and the Fair Deal—but before he deals, someone's going to cut the cards.

That "someone" may be the millions of Americans who voted for President Eisenhower but would balk at his successor.

For just as historians tell us that Richard the First was not fit to fill the shoes of the bold Henry the Second, and that Richard Cromwell was not fit to wear the mantle of his uncle, they might add in future years that Richard Nixon did not measure up to the footsteps of Dwight D. Eisenhower.

Perhaps he could carry on the party policies, the policies of Nixon and Benson and Dirksen and Goldwater. But this Nation cannot afford such a luxury. Perhaps we could afford a Coolidge following Harding. And perhaps we could afford a Pierce following Fillmore. But after Buchanan this nation needed Lincoln; after Taft we needed Wilson; and after Hoover we needed Franklin Roosevelt.

But we're not merely running against Mr. Nixon. Our task is not merely one of itemizing Republican failures. Nor is that wholly necessary. For the families forced from the farm do not need to tell us of their plight. The unemployed miners and textile workers know that the decision is before them in November. The old people without medical care, the families without a decent home, the parents of children without a decent school: They all know that it's time for a change.

We are not here to curse the darkness; we are here to light a candle. As Winston Churchill said on taking office some twenty years ago: If we open a quarrel between the present and the past, we shall be in danger of losing the future.

Today our concern must be with that future. For the world is changing. The old era is ending. The old ways will not do.

Abroad, the balance of power is shifting. New and more terrible weapons are coming into use.

One-third of the world may be free, but one-third is the victim of a cruel repression, and the other third is rocked by poverty and hunger and disease. Communist influence has penetrated into Asia; it stands in the Middle East; and now festers some ninety miles off the coast of Florida. Friends have slipped into neutrality and neutrals have slipped into hostility. As our keynoter reminded us, the President who began his career by going to Korea ends it by staying away from Japan.

The world has been close to war before, but now man, who's survived all previous threats to his existence, has taken into his mortal hands the power to exterminate his species seven times over.

Here at home the future is equally revolutionary. The New Deal and the Fair Deal were bold measures for their generations, but now this is a new generation.

A technological output and explosion on the farm has led to an output explosion. An urban population revolution has overcrowded our schools and cluttered our cities and crowded our slums.

A peaceful revolution for human rights, demanding

an end to racial discrimination in all parts of our community life, has strained at the leashes imposed by a timid executive leadership.

It is time, in short—It is time, in short, for a new generation of leadership. All over the world, particularly in the newer nations, young men are coming to power, men who are not bound by the traditions of the past, men who are not blinded by the old fears and hates and rivalries—young men who can cast off the old slogans and the old delusions.

The Republican nominee, of course, is a young man. But his approach is as old as McKinley. His party is the party of the past, the party of memory. His speeches are generalities from Poor Richard's Almanac. Their platform—Their platform, made up of old, left-over Democratic planks, has the courage of our old convictions. Their pledge is to the status quo; and today there is no status quo.

For I stand here tonight facing west on what was once the last frontier. From the lands that stretch three thousand miles behind us, the pioneers gave up their safety, their comfort and sometimes their lives to build our new West. They were not the captives of their own doubts, nor the prisoners of their own price tags. They were determined to make the new world strong and free—an example to the world, to overcome its hazards and its hardships, to conquer the enemies that threatened from within and without.

Some would say that those struggles are all over, that all the horizons have been explored, that all the battles have been won, that there is no longer an American frontier. But I trust that no one in this assemblage would agree with that sentiment; for the problems are not all solved and the battles are not all won; and we stand today on the edge of a New Frontier—the frontier of the 1960's, the frontier of unknown opportunities and perils, the frontier of unfilled hopes and unfilled threats.

Woodrow Wilson's New Freedom promised our nation a new political and economic framework. Franklin Roosevelt's New Deal promised security and succor to those in need. But the New Frontier of which I speak is not a set of promises. It is a set of challenges.

It sums up not what I intend to offer to the American people, but what I intend to ask of them. It appeals to their pride—It appeals to our pride, not our security. It holds out the promise of more sacrifice instead of more security.

The New Frontier is here whether we seek it or not.

Beyond that frontier are uncharted areas of science and space, unsolved problems of peace and war, unconquered problems of ignorance and prejudice, unanswered questions of poverty and surplus. It would be easier to shrink from that new frontier, to look to the safe mediocrity of the past, to be lulled by good intentions and high rhetoric—and those who prefer that course should not vote for me or the Democratic Party.

But I believe that the times require imagination and courage and perseverance. I'm asking each of you to be pioneers towards that New Frontier. My call is to the young in heart, regardless of age—to the stout in spirit, regardless of Party, to all who respond to the scriptural call: "Be strong and of a good courage; be not afraid, neither be [thou] dismayed."

For courage, not complacency, is our need today; leadership, not salesmanship. And the only valid test of leadership is the ability to lead, and lead vigorously. A tired nation—A tired nation, said David Lloyd George, is a Tory nation. And the United States today cannot afford to be either tired or Tory.

There may be those who wish to hear more—more promises to this group or that, more harsh rhetoric about the men in the Kremlin as a substitute for policy, more assurances of a golden future, where taxes are always low and the subsidies are always high. But my promises are in the platform that you have adopted. Our ends will not be won by rhetoric, and we can have faith in the future only if we have faith in ourselves.

For the harsh facts of the matter are that we stand at this frontier at a turning-point of history. We must prove all over again to a watching world, as we said on a most conspicuous stage, whether this nation, conceived as it is with its freedom of choice, its breadth of opportunity, its range of alternatives, can compete with the single-minded advance of the Communist system.

Can a nation organized and governed such as ours endure?

That is the real question.

Have we the nerve and the will? Can we carry through in an age where we will witness not only new breakthroughs in weapons of destruction, but also a race for mastery of the sky and the rain, the ocean and the tides, the far side of space, and the inside of men's minds?

That is the question of the New Frontier.

That is the choice our nation must make—a choice that lies not merely between two men or two parties, but between the public interest and private comfort, between national greatness and national decline, between the fresh air of progress and the stale, dank atmosphere of "normalcy," between dedication or mediocrity.

All mankind waits upon our decision. A whole world looks to see what we shall do. And we cannot fail that trust. And we cannot fail to try.

It has been a long road from the first snowy day in New Hampshire many months ago to this crowded convention city. Now begins another long journey, taking me into your cities and homes across the United States.

Give me your help and your hand and your voice.

Recall with me the words of Isaiah that, "They that wait upon the Lord shall renew their strength; they shall mount up with wings as eagles; they shall run and not be weary."

As we face the coming great challenge, we too, shall wait upon the Lord, and ask that He renew our strength.

Then shall we be equal to the test.

Then we shall not be weary.

Then we shall prevail.

Thank you.

Document Analysis

Senator Kennedy begins this speech by thanking the leadership of the Democratic Party, many of whose members opposed him until hours before this speech was given. He thanks them for their support in the tough election ahead, acknowledging their power by saying that "I feel a lot safer with all of them on my side." He also uses this as a way to point out the strength and vigor of the Democratic Party, since the Republicans have only one real candidate, and no one else has dared to "put his head up."

Since his religious affiliation had been such an issue on the campaign trail, Kennedy addresses it directly. A vote for or against him based on his religious beliefs is a wasted vote, he argues, since it is not relevant. He assures Americans that they can trust that his judgment "on every public policy will be my own—as an American, a Democrat and a free man." He states once again his firm belief in the separation of church and state, and his commitment to uphold the Constitution.

Kennedy injects humor into his critique of his Republican challenger, Vice President Nixon. He may believe that is it his turn to lead "after the New Deal and the Fair Deal—but before he deals, someone had better cut the cards." Though Nixon may feel himself Eisenhower's rightful successor, Kennedy uses examples from history to show that the heir of a great leader is often a mediocre or bad one. Kennedy says, Nixon will fail to measure up to Eisenhower, and Republican policies will fail to meet the nation's challenges going forward. He says that he and the Democrats represent the change the nation needs.

Kennedy then lays out the challenges of his time: Communist expansion and aggression threaten the free world. Urbanization has led to slums and collapsing schools. Some Americans are still denied basic human and civil rights. Mechanization and automation are threatening traditional jobs. Though Nixon is himself a young man, his party is obsolete, "the party of the past." Kennedy references the location of the Democratic Convention in Los Angeles, California. Where the West was once the last frontier, explored and settled by brave and fearless pioneers, so too "we stand today on the edge of a New Frontier—the frontier of the 1960s—a frontier of unknown opportunities and perils."

Essential Themes

Following the Democratic National Convention, Kennedy began campaigning hard for the presidency against Republican Richard M. Nixon. The pair engaged in four televised debates, which are widely believed to have significantly boosted Kennedy's campaign. Kennedy appeared poised and relaxed, while Nixon appeared tired, defensive, and stiff. The campaign was not only about appearances, however, with foreign policy dominating the debates. Vice President Nixon was eager to point out that Kennedy was too inexperienced to understand the complexities of Cold War leadership. He argued that his role in the Eisenhower administration had provided him with the experience necessary to contain the Communist threat and keep the nation's defenses strong. On the other hand, Kennedy pointed out that the Eisenhower administration had allowed the Soviet Union to take the lead in dangerous new missile technology, and that they had lost Cuba to the Communists. He portrayed the Eisenhower administration as old-fashioned, conservative, and reactionary, promising to bring new ideas and flexibility to foreign relationships.

On November 8, 1960, John F. Kennedy became the youngest man ever elected to the presidency and the first Catholic president in U.S. history. He won by a narrow margin, less than 0.2 percent of the popular vote, and served for three years until his assassination in 1963.

—*Bethany Groff Dorau, MA*

Bibliography and Additional Reading

Kreitner, Richard. "July 13, 1960: John F. Kennedy Secures the Democratic Presidential Nomination." *Nation*. Nation, 13 July 2015. Web. 11 Feb. 2016.

Rorabaugh, W. J. *The Real Making of the President: Kennedy, Nixon, and the 1960 Election*. Lawrence: UP of Kansas, 2009. Print.

Schlesinger, Arthur M. *A Thousand Days: John F. Kennedy in the White House*. Boston: Houghton, 1965. Print.

◼ Excerpts from the Kennedy-Nixon Debates

Date: September 26, 1960
Authors: John F. Kennedy; Richard M. Nixon
Genre: Political debate; transcript

Summary Overview

In the 1960 presidential campaign, the Republican nominee was the incumbent vice president, Richard M. Nixon. The Democratic candidate was John F. Kennedy, a U.S. Senator from Massachusetts. The two candidates agreed to a series of four, one-hour long televised debates; the document included here is a transcript of part of the first debate, which was broadcast by CBS but ran on all the major television networks on September 26, 1960. This debate, the first televised presidential debate in U.S. history and one of the earliest face-to-face debates of any kind between presidential candidates, drew an audience estimated at 70 million viewers. Many observers at the time, as well as historians writing later, have attached great importance to this first debate, arguing that it was a significant factor in Kennedy's ultimate victory. Nixon, who had been ill in recent days, and who did not have any professional make-up done, looked uncomfortable and ill-at ease. Kennedy, although only four years younger than Nixon, looked youthful and confident. This debate was a foreshadowing of how important image, and the use of television, was going to be in this and future presidential races.

Defining Moment

Although no one during the 1960 presidential election could have foreseen how radically different the 1960s would be from the previous decade, there was a perception at the time that this election was of more than ordinary significance. Democratic presidents Franklin D. Roosevelt and Harry S Truman had occupied the White House for twenty years, from 1933 to 1953. Republican Dwight D. Eisenhower had been elected in 1952 and re-elected in 1956; his vice-presidential candidate in those two elections, Richard M. Nixon, was the Republican presidential candidate in 1960. Eisenhower, one of the key leaders in the Allied victory in Europe in World War II, was a highly-respected and well-liked president, and had presided over a generally prosperous period in

U.S. history. Nevertheless, there was an undercurrent of discontent, and a sense that new directions were needed—many thought the nation was doing well, but could do better. The Democratic candidate, Senator John F. Kennedy, emphasized this theme in this debate and throughout the campaign. Although Kennedy and Nixon had much in common—both being Navy veterans from World War II, who had come to the House of Representatives at the same time, and shared a commitment to fighting communism—they were very different in other ways. Nixon came from a working class background, and Kennedy from a wealthy, prominent Massachusetts family. Nixon, although he had done well in politics, which is perhaps the most public of all careers, was a shy, retiring person at heart—the very opposite of the image that the popular "bon vivant" Kennedy presented. Although only slightly older than Kennedy, to many Nixon represented older times—a perception enhanced by his connection to Eisenhower, who was popular with the public but often perceived as a grandfatherly figure. Many voters seemed to see the contrasts between Kennedy and Nixon as the key factor in the election. In the summer of 1960, political polls continually showed the candidates in a dead heat. Many believed that the four televised debates would decide who would become the next president.

Author Biographies

Both Richard M. Nixon and John F. Kennedy were iconic figures on the American political scene in the twentieth century. Nixon was born in Yorba Linda, California on January 9, 1913. He graduated from Whittier College in California in 1934 and then Duke University Law School in 1937. He enlisted as an officer in the U.S. Navy in 1942 and served until 1946. He was elected to the U.S. House of Representatives in 1946 and to the U.S. Senate in 1950. Dwight D. Eisenhower picked Nixon as his vice-presidential running mate in 1952, in part to placate the conservative wing of the Republican Party. Nixon lost the

1960 presidential election to Kennedy. After a failed bid for the governorship of California in 1962, many believed Nixon's political career was over. But he emerged as the Republican candidate for president in 1968, and won a narrow victory over the Democratic candidate, Hubert H. Humphrey, becoming the 37th president of the U.S. In 1972, Nixon won a landslide victory over George McGovern. However, his second term was marred by the Watergate scandal, and Nixon resigned the presidency on August 9, 1974—the only president to resign the office. Over the next twenty years he wrote several books and somewhat rehabilitated his image. He died in New York City on April 22, 1994.

John F. Kennedy was born in Brookline, Massachusetts on May 29, 1917. He came from a prominent Massachusetts family; his father, Joseph P. Kennedy, was a wealthy businessman who had been the U.S. Ambassador to Great Britain prior to World War II. Kennedy attended Harvard University, and worked briefly as a journalist before World War II. He served as an officer in the U.S. Navy in the Pacific in World War II, and received medals for heroism for his actions in command of a PT boat that was sunk in a collision with a Japanese war ship. In 1946, he was elected to the U.S. House from a district in Boston. He was elected to the U.S. Senate in 1952, and re-elected in 1956. He made an unsuccessful attempt to secure the Democratic vice-presidential nomination in 1956, and then set his sights on becoming the president nominee in 1960. He was elected the 35th president of the U.S. in November 1960, defeating Richard M. Nixon. He was the first Roman Catholic elected to the U.S. presidency. He was assassinated in Dallas, Texas, on November 22, 1963.

HISTORICAL DOCUMENT

[The debate began with an introduction by Howard K. Smith of CBS, followed by opening statements of approximately 8 minutes by the two candidates. Senator Kennedy was the first speaker.]

MR. KENNEDY.

Mr. Smith, Mr. Nixon. In the election of 1860, Abraham Lincoln said the question was whether this Nation could exist half slave or half free. In the election of 1960, and with the world around us, the question is whether the world will exist half slave or half free, whether it will move in the direction of freedom, in the direction of the road that we are taking, or whether it will move in the direction of slavery. I think it will depend in great measure upon what we do here in the United States, on the kind of society that we build, on the kind of strength that we maintain...

This is a great country, but I think it could be a greater country; and this is a powerful country but I think it could be a more powerful country. I'm not satisfied to have 50 percent of our steel-mill capacity unused. I'm not satisfied when the United States had last year the lowest rate of economic growth of any major industrialized society in the world—because economic growth means strength and vitality. It means we're able to sustain our defenses; it means we're able to meet our commitments abroad. I'm not satisfied, when we have over $9 billion worth of food, some of it rotting even though there is a hungry world and even though 4 million Americans wait every month for a food package from the Government, which averages 5 cents a day per individual. I saw cases in West Virginia, here in the United States, where children took home part of their school lunch in order to feed their families because I don't think we're meeting our obligations toward these Americans. I'm not satisfied when the Soviet Union is turning out twice as many scientists and engineers as we are. I'm not satisfied when many of our teachers are inadequately paid, or when our children go to school part-time shifts. I think we should have an educational system second to none...

I'm not satisfied when we are failing to develop the natural resources of the United States to the fullest. Here in the United States, which developed the Tennessee Valley and which built the Grand Coulee and the other dams in the Northwest United States, at the present rate of hydropower production—and that is the hallmark of an industrialized society—the Soviet Union by 1975 will be producing more power than we are. These are all the things I think in this country that can make our society strong, or can mean that it stands still.

I'm not satisfied until every American enjoys his full constitutional rights. If a Negro baby is born, and this is true also of Puerto Ricans and Mexicans in some of our cities, he has about one-half as much chance to get through high school as a white baby. He has one-third as much chance to get through college as a white student. He has about a third as much chance to be a professional man, and about half as much chance to own a house. He has about four times as much chance that he'll be out of work in his life as the white baby. I think we can do better. I don't want the talents of any American to go to waste. I know that there are those who want to turn everything over to the Government. I don't at all. I want the individuals to meet their responsibilities and I want the States to meet their responsibilities. But I think there is also a national responsibility... I don't believe in big government, but I believe in effective governmental action, and I think that's the only way that the United States is going to maintain its freedom; it's the only way that we're going to move ahead. I think we can do a better job. I think we're going to have to do a better job if we are going to meet the responsibilities which time and events have placed upon us...

MR. SMITH.

And now the opening statement by Vice President Richard M. Nixon.

MR. NIXON.

Mr. Smith, Senator Kennedy. The things that Senator Kennedy has said many of us can agree with. There is no question but that we cannot discuss our internal affairs in the United States without recognizing that they have a tremendous bearing on our international position. There is no question but that this nation cannot stand still, because we are in a deadly competition, a competition not only with the men in the Kremlin, but the men in Peking. We're ahead in this competition, as Senator Kennedy, I think, has implied. But when you're in a race, the only way to stay ahead is to move ahead, and I subscribe completely to the spirit that Senator Kennedy has expressed tonight, the spirit that the United States should move ahead.

Where then do we disagree? I think we disagree on the implication of his remarks tonight and on the state-ments that he has made on many occasions during his campaign to the effect that the United States has been standing still... Is it true that this administration, as Senator Kennedy has charged, has been an administration of retreat, of defeat, of stagnation? Is it true that, as far as this country is concerned, in the field of electric power, and all of the fields that he has mentioned, we have not been moving ahead? Well, we have a comparison that we can make. We have the record of the Truman administration of 7 years, and the 7 years of the Eisenhower administration. When we compare these two records in the areas that Senator Kennedy has discussed tonight, I think we find that America has been moving ahead. Let's take schools. We have built more schools in these 7 years than we built in the previous 7, for that matter in the previous 20 years. Let's take hydroelectric power. We have developed more hydroelectric power in these 7 years than was developed in any previous administration in history. Let us take hospitals. We find that more have been built in this administration than in the previous administration. The same is true of highways.

Let's put it in terms that all of us can understand. We often hear gross national product discussed, and in that respect may I say that when we compare the growth in this administration with that of the previous administration, that then there was a total growth of 11 percent over 7 years; in this administration there has been a total growth of 19 percent over 7 years. That shows that there's been more growth in this administration than in its predecessor... What kind of programs are we for? We are for programs that will expand educational opportunities, that will give to all Americans their equal chance for education, for all of the things which are necessary and dear to the hearts of our people. We are for programs, in addition, which will see that our medical care for the aged is much better handled than it is at the present time. Here again, may I indicate that Senator Kennedy and I are not in disagreement as to the aim. We both want to help the old people. We want to see that they do have adequate medical care. The question is the means. I think that the means that I advocate will reach that goal better than the means that he advocates. I could give better examples but for whatever it is, whether it's in the field of housing or health or medical care or schools, or the development of electric power, we have programs which we believe will move America, move her forward and build on the wonderful record that we have made over these past 7 years.

Now, when we look at these programs might I suggest that in evaluating them we often have a tendency to say that the test of a program is how much you're spending. I will concede that in all the areas to which I have referred, Senator Kennedy would have the Federal Government spend more than I would have it spend. I costed out the cost of the Democratic platform. It runs a minimum of $13.2 billion a year more than we are presently spending to a maximum of $18 billion a year more than we're presently spending. Now the Republican platform will cost more too. It will cost a minimum of $4 billion a year more, a maximum of $4.9 billion a year more than we're presently spending. Now, does this mean that his program is better than ours? Not at all, because it isn't a question of how much the Federal Government spends. It isn't a question of which government does the most. It's a question of which administration does the right things, and in our case, I do believe that our programs will stimulate the creative energies of 180 million free Americans. I believe the programs that Senator Kennedy advocates will have a tendency to stifle those creative energies. I believe, in other words, that his programs would lead to the stagnation of the motive power that we need in this country to get progress... I know Senator Kennedy feels as deeply about these problems as I do, but our disagreement is not about the goals for America but only about the means to reach those goals.

MR. SMITH.
Thank you, Mr. Nixon...

MR. FLEMING (ABC News).
Senator, the Vice President in his campaign has said that you are naive and at times immature. He has raised the question of leadership. On this issue, why do you think people should vote for you rather than the Vice President?

MR. KENNEDY.
Well, the Vice President and I came to the Congress together in 1946. We both served in the Labor Committee. I've been there now for fourteen years, the same period of time that he has, so that our experience in government is comparable. Secondly, I think the question is "What are the programs that we advocate?" What is the party record that we lead? I come out of the Democratic party, which in this century has produced Woodrow Wilson and Franklin Roosevelt and Harry Truman, and which supported and sustained these programs which I've discussed tonight. Mr. Nixon comes out of the Republican Party. He was nominated by it. And it is a fact that through most of these last 25 years the Republican leadership has opposed Federal aid for education, medical care for the aged, development of the Tennessee Valley, development of our natural resources. I think Mr. Nixon is an effective leader of his party. I hope he would grant me the same. The question before us is: Which point of view and which party do we want to lead the United States?

MR. SMITH.
Mr. Nixon, would you like to comment on that statement?

MR. NIXON.
I have no comment.

...

MR. VANOCUR (NBC News).
Mr. Vice President, since the question of executive leadership is a very important campaign issue, I would like to follow Mr. Novins' question. Now, Republican campaign slogans—you'll see them on signs around the country as we did last week—say it's experience that counts (that's over a picture of yourself; sir), implying that you've had more governmental, executive decision-making experience than your opponent. Now, in his news conference on August 24, President Eisenhower was asked to give one example of a major idea of yours that he adopted. His reply was, and I'm quoting: "If you give me a week, I might think of one. I don't remember." Now that was a month ago, sir, and the President hasn't brought it up since, and I am wondering, sir, if you can clarify which version is correct, the one put out by Republican campaign leaders or the one put out by President Eisenhower?

MR. NIXON.

Well, I would suggest, Mr. Vanocur, that if you know the President, that that was probably a facetious remark. I would also suggest that insofar as his statement is concerned, that I think it would be improper for the President of the United States to disclose the instances in which members of his official family had made recommendations, as I have made them through the years to him, which he has accepted or rejected...

The President has asked for my advice, I have given it; sometimes my advice has been taken, sometimes it has not. I do not say that I have made the decisions, and I would say that no President should ever allow anybody else to make the major decisions. The President only makes the decisions. All that his advisers do is to give counsel when he asks for it. As far as what experience counts and whether that is experience that counts, that isn't for me to say. I can only say that my experience is there for the people to consider, Senator Kennedy's is there for the people to consider. As he pointed out, we came to the Congress in the same year; his experience has been different from mine, mine has been in the executive branch, his has been in the legislative branch. I would say that the people now have the opportunity to evaluate his as against mine, and I think both he and I are going to abide by whatever the people decide.

MR. SMITH.

Senator Kennedy?

MR. KENNEDY.

Well, I'll just say that the question is of experience and the question also is what our judgment is of the future and what our goals are for the United States and what ability we have to implement those goals. Abraham Lincoln came to the Presidency in 1860 after a rather little known session in the House of Representatives and after being defeated for the Senate in '58, and was a distinguished President. There is no certain road to the Presidency. There are no guarantees that if you take one road or another that you will be a successful President.... The question really is: which candidate and which party can meet the problems that the United States is going to face in the '60's?

MR. SMITH.

The next question to Vice President Nixon from Mr. Fleming.

MR. FLEMING.

(ABC News) Mr. Vice President, do I take it, then, you believe that you could work better with Democratic majorities in the House and Senate than Senator Kennedy could work with Democratic majorities in the House and Senate?

MR. NIXON.

I would say this: That we, of course, expect to pick up some seats in both in the House and the Senate. We would hope to control the House, to get a majority in the House in this election. We cannot, of course, control the Senate. I would say that a President will be able to lead; a President will be able to get his program through to the effect that he has the support of the country, the support of the people.

Sometimes we—we get the opinion that in getting programs through the House or the Senate it's purely a question of legislative finagling and all that sort of thing. It isn't really that. Whenever a majority of the people are for a program, the House and the Senate responds to it; and whether this House and Senate, in the next session is Democratic or Republican, if the country will have voted for the candidate for the Presidency and for the proposals that he has made, I believe that you will find that the President, if it were a Republican, as it would be in my case, would be able to get his program through that Congress.

Now I also say that as far as Senator Kennedy's proposals are concerned, that again the question is not simply one of a Presidential veto stopping programs. You must always remember that a President can't stop anything unless he has the people behind him, and the reason President Eisenhower's vetoes have been sustained, the reason the Congress does not send up bills to him which they think will be vetoed is because the people and the Congress, the majority of them, know the country is behind the President.

MR. SMITH.

Senator Kennedy.

MR. KENNEDY.

Well, now let's look at these bills that the Vice President suggests were too extreme. One was a bill for a dollar twenty-five cents an hour for anyone who works in a store or company that has a million dollars a year business. I don't think that's extreme at all, and yet nearly two-thirds to three-fourths of the Republicans in the House of Representatives voted against that proposal.

Secondly was the Federal aid to education bill. It - it was a very—because of the defeat of teacher salaries, it was not a bill that met, in my opinion, the needs. The fact of the matter is it was a bill that was less than you recommended, Mr. Nixon, this morning in your proposal. It was not an extreme bill, and yet we could not get one Republican to join; at least, I think, four of the eight

Democrats voted to send it to the floor of the House, not one Republican, and they joined with those Democrats who were opposed to it. I don't say the Democrats are united in their support of the program, but I do say a majority are and I say a majority of the Republicans are opposed to it... One party is ready to move in these programs; the other party gives them lip service.

MR. SMITH.

Can I have the summation time please?

We've completed our questions and our comments. In just a moment we'll have the summation time.

[The debate ended with 3-minute closing statements.]

Document Analysis

In their opening statements, both candidates addressed what they believed were the principal problems and challenges facing the nation. Both agreed that forceful U.S. leadership was needed because of the international struggle against the communist powers in the Soviet Union and China. Senator Kennedy implied that the U.S. had stagnated under President Eisenhower, and that new leadership was needed to move forward. Vice President Nixon, while agreeing with the need to continue moving forward, attempted to refute the idea that the nation was standing still.

Both Kennedy and Nixon expressed the belief that the U.S. was strong domestically and as an international leader, but Kennedy argued that more needed to be done. He believed that if the U.S. failed to move forward in economic development and in addressing the civil rights and economic opportunities of its minority citizens, then it would fall behind in the struggle to lead the rest of the world to embrace freedom rather than communist dictatorship. Making the first opening statement, Kennedy seemed to anticipate that Nixon would attack his proposals on the grounds of cost and the expansion of federal power, so he preemptively asserted, "I don't believe in big government, but I believe in effective governmental action, and I think that's the only way that the United States is going to maintain its freedom, it's the only way that we're going to move ahead."

Nixon responded to Kennedy's opening statement with a standard debate tactic from his days as a successful

high school and college debater—noting that there was much to agree with in what Kennedy had said, and then proceeding to explore the differences between their positions. He agreed that the nation could not stand still, but he cited statistics on various areas of growth which he believed refuted the argument that the nation was stagnating. He suggested that he and Kennedy did not disagree on the aims for a better life for the American people, but only in the means used to achieve these aims. He pointed out that Kennedy wanted the federal government to spend more on the domestic programs he had outlined; he believed that the Democratic platform would call for over $13 billion in additional federal spending. Nixon argued, "I do believe that our programs [the Republican policies] will stimulate the creative energies of 180 million free Americans. I believe the programs that Senator Kennedy advocates will have a tendency to stifle those creative energies."

After both candidates had made their opening statements, the questions posed by the journalists present focused on leadership and the readiness to govern. Kennedy was asked about remarks that Nixon had previously made suggesting that he was "naïve and at times immature." Kennedy responded that he and Nixon had both come to Congress in 1946, and that their experience at the national level was comparable. He turned the question back to what kind of programs do the two parties advocate? Nixon was asked about a damaging remark that President Eisenhower had made when asked if he could recall any decisions on which Nixon had made major contributions. Eisenhower had said, "If you give me a week, I might think of one. I don't remember." Nixon responded that knowing Eisenhower, this was no doubt a facetious remark, but he went on to say that he had made suggestions on policies and decisions, but the president should never reveal who contributed to such decisions, because the final responsibility rests with the president alone.

Neither candidate said anything new in this debate. But the impact of this debate was not so much in what was said, but in the image of the two men portrayed by television. Nixon, who had recently been sick, did not come across well on television, and later admitted he had made a mistake in not taking more pains to address this problem. Kennedy was more photogenic, and came across as more eloquent, despite Nixon's year of experience in political speaking. Many took away from this debate a lasting favorable impression of Kennedy's youth and energy. The later debates did little to change these perceptions. There is no way to measure how much impact the first debate had on the election of 1960, but given the narrowness of Kennedy's victory, any gains he made from it may have been significant.

Essential Themes

In this first televised debate between U.S. presidential candidates, it quickly became clear that was said or not said was not as important as tone, approach, and image. Anyone who had heard or read the stump speeches that both candidates had been making for weeks could have predicted what was going to be said. Nixon had a reputation as a great debater; Kennedy's aides and supporters went into this debate somewhat fearful of Nixon's skill. But Kennedy emerged as the more forceful presence on the stage. Nixon sometimes stressed his agreement with much of what Kennedy said, and at times simply replied with "No comment." Many of Nixon's supporters were surprised and shocked by his somewhat subdued manner. Nixon's running mate, Henry Cabot Lodge, Jr., believed that Nixon lost the election with his performance in this first debate. Ironically, Lodge was one of the people who had encouraged Nixon to abandon his "attack" image in this debate.

The theme of moving ahead was emphasized by both candidates. Without directly criticizing President Eisen-

hower, who, as Kennedy knew, was admired by many Americans, Kennedy implied that the United States was stagnating under the present administration. He said, "This is a great country, but I think it could be a better country; this is a powerful country, but I believe it could be a more powerful country." Because Nixon, as vice-president, was a part of that administration, he was inevitably put on the defensive, and cited evidence to counter the perception that the nation was standing still. He questioned the direction and the potential costs of the kinds of programs Kennedy endorsed.

Both candidates also emphasized the theme of their preparedness to lead. Since Nixon's experience in the executive branch might be perceived as giving him an advantage in claiming leadership potential, Kennedy pointed out that Abraham Lincoln had come to the presidency with no executive experience and only one undistinguished term in the U.S. House. Nixon stressed his experience as vice president, including his foreign travels during which he had met with the leaders of many nations. Nixon also had to deal with the damaging quip by Eisenhower about not remembering any contribution made by Nixon to a major decision.

More than anything that was said in the debate, the significance of this encounter was the forceful demonstration of the impact television was going to have on politics going forward, and the concomitant importance of a candidate's image.

—*Mark S. Joy, PhD*

Bibliography and Additional Reading

Ambrose, Stephen E. *Nixon: The Education of a Politician 1913-1962.* New York: Simon and Schuster, 1987. Print.

Farrell, John A. *Richard Nixon: The Life.* New York: Doubleday, 2017.

Matthews, Christopher. *Kennedy and Nixon: The Rivalry That Shaped Postwar America.* New York: Simon and Schuster, 1996. Print.

Nixon, Richard M. *RN: The Memoirs of Richard Nixon.* New York: Grosset and Dunlap, 1978. Print.

Oliphant, Thomas, and Wilkie, Curtis. *The Road to Camelot: Inside JFK's Five-Year Campaign.* New York: Simon and Schuster, 2017. Print.

Eisenhower's Farewell Address

Date: January 17, 1961
Author: Dwight D. Eisenhower
Genre: Speech

Summary Overview

Dwight D. Eisenhower gave this speech at the end of his second term as president of the United States. He had held the nation's highest office since 1953. Though he had overseen the development of military technology and capability beyond the imagining of previous generations, Eisenhower grew increasingly concerned about the power of the "military-industrial complex" he had helped to create. The nation's wealth was being funneled into military contracts. He warned the people of the nation that they were in danger of losing free scientific thought, as universities were increasingly driven by government contracts and public policy was in danger of being controlled by a "scientific-technological elite." Though the Cold War and the Soviet threat necessitated a powerful standing military and defensive infrastructure, Eisenhower warned that this powerful element could lead the nation away from the peaceful principles that it was supposed to protect. A fiscal conservative, Eisenhower warned that the nation must resist the deficit-spending, "live for today" mentality that the prosperity and youth of the age encouraged and be responsible also to future generations.

Defining Moment

World War II essentially ended the belief by U.S. officials that the best policy in international affairs was to remain isolated and neutral, positions that had been popular at the beginnings of both world wars. American public opinion and policy turned to a greatly expanded role in international affairs, and the president's influence and power over foreign policy steadily grew, particularly under Eisenhower, who was a military hero in his own right. The driver for this was, in large part, the rise of aggressive Communism at the end of the war and the inability of a devastated European economy to recover on its own. Relations with the Soviet Union, an ally during the war, were deteriorating, and another ally, Winston Churchill, had warned that there was an "Iron Curtain"

coming down between Eastern and Western Europe. The ideological conflict between the Soviet Union and the United States defined the next four decades in world history, as both sides endeavored to block the expansion and influence of the other.

The Truman Doctrine of 1947, which pledged military support to contain the spread of Communism, led to an increase in the military budget the following year. In 1949, the Soviet Union successfully detonated its first atomic bomb, and Communist rebels took control of China. The following year, the Korean War broke out, pitting the United States against the Communist North Koreans and their Chinese and Soviet allies. The events of 1949 and 1950 further entrenched the rivalry between the United States and the Soviet Union, ensuring that the struggle for military and technological supremacy would continue. The military budget, and the role of the United States as the defender of the world against Communism, continued to grow until the end of the Korean War in 1953, the year that Eisenhower took office. Despite Eisenhower's "New Look" policy, which emphasized nuclear deterrents over maintaining a large traditional army, the military budget took up between 9 and 14 percent of the gross national product during his administration, averaging three times higher than in 1947. Though Eisenhower was not able to successfully curb military spending, and acknowledged that the Cold War necessitated a strong and swift defensive capability, he was never comfortable with the dedication of so much of the nation's wealth and talent to weapons development and production. His "Chance for Peace" speech, in which he compared the cost of a bomber to the cost of schools and hospitals, and his farewell speech, in which he warned against the increasing power of the military-industrial complex, bookended a presidency in which military buildup seemed the only deterrent to the threat from the Soviet Union.

Author Biography

Dwight David Eisenhower was born in Denison, Texas, on October 14, 1890. He was the third son of seven born, and when he was two years old, his parents moved to Abilene, Kansas. Eisenhower graduated from Abilene High School in 1909, and was accepted to West Point in 1911. He was an officer in the Army during World War I. He continued his military career after the war and became a brigadier general in 1941. Eisenhower commanded the Allied landing in North Africa in November 1942. In 1943, President Franklin D. Roosevelt made Eisenhower supreme Allied commander in Europe, and he was in charge of the Allied forces that invaded occupied France on June 6, 1944, D-Day. After a postwar position as the military commander of occupied Germany, Eisenhower was named chief of staff of the Army, until becoming president of Columbia University in 1948. He was named supreme commander of the North Atlantic Treaty Organization (NATO) in 1950, but retained the presidency of Columbia until 1953, when he became president of the United States. After serving a second term as president, Eisenhower retired to Pennsylvania. He died of congestive heart failure on March 28, 1969, and is buried on the grounds of the Eisenhower Presidential Library in Abilene.

HISTORICAL DOCUMENT

Good evening, my fellow Americans.

First, I should like to express my gratitude to the radio and television networks for the opportunities they have given me over the years to bring reports and messages to our nation. My special thanks go to them for the opportunity of addressing you this evening.

Three days from now, after half century in the service of our country, I shall lay down the responsibilities of office as, in traditional and solemn ceremony, the authority of the Presidency is vested in my successor. This evening, I come to you with a message of leave-taking and farewell, and to share a few final thoughts with you, my countrymen.

Like every other—Like every other citizen, I wish the new President, and all who will labor with him, Godspeed. I pray that the coming years will be blessed with peace and prosperity for all.

Our people expect their President and the Congress to find essential agreement on issues of great moment, the wise resolution of which will better shape the future of the nation. My own relations with the Congress, which began on a remote and tenuous basis when, long ago, a member of the Senate appointed me to West Point, have since ranged to the intimate during the war and immediate post-war period, and finally to the mutually interdependent during these past eight years. In this final relationship, the Congress and the Administration have, on most vital issues, cooperated well, to serve the nation good, rather than mere partisanship, and so have assured that the business of the nation should go forward. So, my official relationship with the Congress ends in a feeling—on my part—of gratitude that we have been able to do so much together.

We now stand ten years past the midpoint of a century that has witnessed four major wars among great nations. Three of these involved our own country. Despite these holocausts, America is today the strongest, the most influential, and most productive nation in the world. Understandably proud of this pre-eminence, we yet realize that America's leadership and prestige depend, not merely upon our unmatched material progress, riches, and military strength, but on how we use our power in the interests of world peace and human betterment.

Throughout America's adventure in free government, our basic purposes have been to keep the peace, to foster progress in human achievement, and to enhance liberty, dignity, and integrity among peoples and among nations. To strive for less would be unworthy of a free and religious people. Any failure traceable to arrogance, or our lack of comprehension, or readiness to sacrifice would inflict upon us grievous hurt, both at home and abroad.

Progress toward these noble goals is persistently threatened by the conflict now engulfing the world. It commands our whole attention, absorbs our very beings. We face a hostile ideology global in scope, atheistic in character, ruthless in purpose, and insiduous [insidious] in method. Unhappily, the danger it poses promises to be of indefinite duration. To meet it successfully, there is called for, not so much the emotional and transitory sacrifices of crisis, but rather those which enable us to carry forward steadily, surely, and without complaint the burdens of a prolonged and complex struggle with liberty the stake. Only thus shall we remain, despite every provocation, on our charted course toward permanent peace and human betterment.

Crises there will continue to be. In meeting them, whether foreign or domestic, great or small, there is a recurring temptation to feel that some spectacular and costly action could become the miraculous solution to all current difficulties. A huge increase in newer elements of our defenses; development of unrealistic programs to cure every ill in agriculture; a dramatic expansion in basic and applied research—these and many other possibilities, each possibly promising in itself, may be suggested as the only way to the road we wish to travel.

But each proposal must be weighed in the light of a broader consideration: the need to maintain balance in and among national programs, balance between the private and the public economy, balance between the cost and hoped for advantages, balance between the clearly necessary and the comfortably desirable, balance between our essential requirements as a nation and the duties imposed by the nation upon the individual, balance between actions of the moment and the national welfare of the future. Good judgment seeks balance and progress. Lack of it eventually finds imbalance and frustration. The record of many decades stands as proof that our people and their Government have, in the main, understood these truths and have responded to them well, in the face of threat and stress.

But threats, new in kind or degree, constantly arise. Of these, I mention two only.

A vital element in keeping the peace is our military establishment. Our arms must be mighty, ready for instant action, so that no potential aggressor may be tempted to risk his own destruction. Our military organization today bears little relation to that known of any of my predecessors in peacetime, or, indeed, by the fighting men of World War II or Korea.

Until the latest of our world conflicts, the United States had no armaments industry. American makers of plowshares could, with time and as required, make swords as well. But we can no longer risk emergency improvisation of national defense. We have been compelled to create a permanent armaments industry of vast proportions. Added to this, three and a half million men and women are directly engaged in the defense establishment. We annually spend on military security alone more than the net income of all United States cooperations—corporations.

Now this conjunction of an immense military establishment and a large arms industry is new in the American experience. The total influence—economic, political, even spiritual—is felt in every city, every Statehouse, every office of the Federal government. We recognize the imperative need for this development. Yet, we must not fail to comprehend its grave implications. Our toil, resources, and livelihood are all involved. So is the very structure of our society.

In the councils of government, we must guard against the acquisition of unwarranted influence, whether sought or unsought, by the military-industrial complex. The potential for the disastrous rise of misplaced power exists and will persist. We must never let the weight of this combination endanger our liberties or democratic processes. We should take nothing for granted. Only an alert and knowledgeable citizenry can compel the proper meshing of the huge industrial and military machinery of defense with our peaceful methods and goals, so that security and liberty may prosper together.

Akin to, and largely responsible for the sweeping changes in our industrial-military posture, has been the technological revolution during recent decades. In this revolution, research has become central; it also becomes more formalized, complex, and costly. A steadily increasing share is conducted for, by, or at the direction of, the Federal government.

Today, the solitary inventor, tinkering in his shop, has been overshadowed by task forces of scientists in laboratories and testing fields. In the same fashion, the free university, historically the fountainhead of free ideas and scientific discovery, has experienced a revolution in the conduct of research. Partly because of the huge costs involved, a government contract becomes virtually a substitute for intellectual curiosity. For every old blackboard there are now hundreds of new electronic computers. The prospect of domination of the nation's scholars by Federal employment, project allocations, and the power of money is ever present—and is gravely to be regarded.

Yet, in holding scientific research and discovery in respect, as we should, we must also be alert to the equal and opposite danger that public policy could itself become the captive of a scientific-technological elite.

It is the task of statesmanship to mold, to balance, and to integrate these and other forces, new and old, within the principles of our democratic system—ever aiming toward the supreme goals of our free society.

Another factor in maintaining balance involves the element of time. As we peer into society's future, we—you and I, and our government—must avoid the impulse to live only for today, plundering for our own ease and convenience the precious resources of tomorrow. We cannot mortgage the material assets of our grandchildren without risking the loss also of their political and spiritual heritage. We want democracy to survive for all generations to come, not to become the insolvent phantom of tomorrow.

During the long lane of the history yet to be written, America knows that this world of ours, ever growing smaller, must avoid becoming a community of dreadful fear and hate, and be, instead, a proud confederation of mutual trust and respect. Such a confederation must be one of equals. The weakest must come to the conference table with the same confidence as do we, protected as we are by our moral, economic, and military strength. That table, though scarred by many past frustrations—past frustrations, cannot be abandoned for the certain agony of disarmament—of the battlefield.

Disarmament, with mutual honor and confidence, is a continuing imperative. Together we must learn how to compose differences, not with arms, but with intellect and decent purpose. Because this need is so sharp and apparent, I confess that I lay down my official responsibilities in this field with a definite sense of disappointment. As one who has witnessed the horror and the lin-gering sadness of war, as one who knows that another war could utterly destroy this civilization which has been so slowly and painfully built over thousands of years, I wish I could say tonight that a lasting peace is in sight.

Happily, I can say that war has been avoided. Steady progress toward our ultimate goal has been made. But so much remains to be done. As a private citizen, I shall never cease to do what little I can to help the world advance along that road.

So, in this, my last good night to you as your President, I thank you for the many opportunities you have given me for public service in war and in peace. I trust in that—in that—in that service you find some things worthy. As for the rest of it, I know you will find ways to improve performance in the future.

You and I, my fellow citizens, need to be strong in our faith that all nations, under God, will reach the goal of peace with justice. May we be ever unswerving in devotion to principle, confident but humble with power, diligent in pursuit of the Nation's great goals.

To all the peoples of the world, I once more give expression to America's prayerful and continuing aspiration: We pray that peoples of all faiths, all races, all nations, may have their great human needs satisfied; that those now denied opportunity shall come to enjoy it to the full; that all who yearn for freedom may experience its few spiritual blessings. Those who have freedom will understand, also, its heavy responsibility; that all who are insensitive to the needs of others will learn charity; and that the sources—scourges of poverty, disease, and ignorance will be made [to] disappear from the earth; and that in the goodness of time, all peoples will come to live together in a peace guaranteed by the binding force of mutual respect and love.

Now, on Friday noon, I am to become a private citizen. I am proud to do so. I look forward to it.

Thank you, and good night.

Document Analysis

Eisenhower begins his farewell address by wishing the new president, John F. Kennedy, well, and reminding him that the American people expect him to work productively with Congress. He also looks back at his own long relationship with Congress, from his appointment to West Point as a young man to "intimate" years during and after the war, to "mutual interdependence" during his presidency. He is grateful for the work they have accomplished together.

The people of the United States are justifiably proud of their "pre-eminence" in the world, despite all of the upheaval and wars of the twentieth century, but Eisenhower changes the tone of the speech at this point. The United States must not measure success by material gain alone, but by its contributions to "world peace and human betterment." Eisenhower identifies a primary purpose of the United States as the keeping of peace "between nations," and the support of freedom among its people. To turn away from this purpose because of the current state of the world would be a grievous error. The goals of freedom and peace are threatened by Communism, the "hostile ideology" that poses a danger of "indefinite duration." It is tempting to think that in an era of amazing scientific and technological advances, the world's problems can be solved through "spectacular and costly action," but this is a trap.

Eisenhower reminds Americans that what they are most in need of is not spectacular technological power, but balance. The continuous growth of the military and weapons technology has dangerously tilted the scales away from the private, individual economy toward public spending, and toward immediate action versus sustained long-term growth. There is no question that the military is needed to keep the peace, Eisenhower says, and that the military must be well armed and able to respond immediately. However, the military has evolved out of necessity into something never before seen in American history, he adds. Whereas in the past, weapons were made as needed, and then those industries converted to peacetime use, Eisenhower notes that there is now a standing armament industry with no peacetime purpose outside of defense. Indeed, the defense industry is a larger sector of the economy than "the net income of all United States corporations." Where there is money, there is power, he reminds his listeners. The influence of the defense industries, the "military-industrial complex," is "economic, political, even spiritual."

In addition, the role of science and technology in the defense industry has necessitated that research universities work closely with the government. The free-thinking scholars of the past are replaced with government employees working on military contracts. Eisenhower does not offer an alternative to this, just a warning. The citizens of the United States must be on guard, to ensure that "security and liberty may prosper together," and they must focus on the future, providing fiscal stability for future generations.

Essential Themes

In 2011, fifty years after this speech was given, President Eisenhower's granddaughter Susan published an article in the *Washington Post* arguing that the world had failed to heed the warning in her grandfather's final speech. The nation was spending beyond its means, she argued, and the post-9/11 military budget had grown to a staggering $700 billion, an amount that was equivalent to spending during World War II.

Eisenhower's speech has been quoted and discussed at length since it was given, particularly its caution against allowing the power of the military-industrial complex to grow unchecked and its concern that defense spending would place future economic stability at risk. Eisenhower intended his speech to inform primarily the administration that followed his, but during the Kennedy administration, military spending did not drop appreciably. The Kennedy and Johnson administrations dealt with the same difficult decisions that Eisenhower did, and the U.S. involvement between North and South Vietnam prompted another jump in the budget, pushing spending to nearly 10 percent of GDP in 1968. By 1970, defense spending began to decline as a percentage of the U.S. economy, but it remained the largest single expenditure of the federal government until surpassed by Social Security in 1976. Defense industries remain a powerful lobby, and the debate over how to cut defense spending without compromising the security of the United States continues.

—*Bethany Groff Dorau, MA*

Bibliography and Additional Reading

Ambrose, Stephen E. *Eisenhower, Vol. II: The President.* New York: Simon, 1984. Print.

Eisenhower, Susan. "Fifty Years Later, We're Still Ignoring Ike's Warning." *Washington Post.* Washington Post, 16 Jan. 2011. Web.

Thomas, Evans. *Ike's Bluff: President Eisenhower's Secret Battle to Save the World.* New York: Little, 2012. Print.

Walker, Martin. *The Cold War: A History.* New York: Holt, 1993. Print.

■ *Baker v. Carr*

Date: March 26, 1962
Author: Justice William J. Brennan, Jr.
Area of Law: Court decision

Summary Overview

Among the landmark rulings of the Supreme Court, some have mandated specific changes within the American system of government, while others have delineated philosophical principles of governance, which have been the foundation for later court rulings or actions. Justice Brennan's majority opinion in *Baker v. Carr* fell into the latter category. For Justice Brennan, this was the first major case in which he had been assigned the task of writing the majority opinion.

The case, in which the plaintiff sought changes to the voting districts in Tennessee, was appealed to the Supreme Court because the District Court would not hear the case. Brennan's ruling did not directly address the complaint filed by Charles Baker; thus, it did not mandate any changes in the voting districts. However, the ruling clearly stated that the federal courts did have the power to review state legislative districts. The results of this assertion not only included the District Court being ordered to hear the suit, but similar suits were filed in more than thirty states. These suits resulted in later Supreme Court rulings, such as *Gray v. Sanders* and *Reynolds v. Sims*, which did force states to create electoral districts essentially equal in population. Thus, during the 1960s, state legislatures were transformed, generally increasing representation from urban areas so that, on a per capita basis, it was proportional with that from rural regions of a state.

Defining Moment

From the foundation of the United States until the 1920s, the rural population was greater than the urban. Thus, in the early years of most states, creating legislative districts based upon land area, or the population distribution at that time, did not result in many major instances of disproportionate representation of people from one region of the state. However over the years, there was strong inertia, and desire by those in power, to keep at least part of the political system tilted in favor of rural regions of the state. This was partially because these regions would have had to give up political power, which they did not want to do, and partially because many viewed cities as suspect, being contaminated by non-American ideas and people. As the decades passed, the per capita disparity changed dramatically with increased urbanization. The rural sections of the various states would not willingly give up the political power they had as a result of having a greater land area, or from previous censuses. Many, in the growing urban areas, felt disenfranchised by having relatively fewer representatives in state legislatures. In one earlier Supreme Court non-ruling, as the result of a tie vote and a swing vote not clearly addressing the situation, federal judicial review of state electoral processes did not seem to be allowed. However, this did not deter Baker from filing a suit seeking changes in the legislative district which had been created for the Tennessee legislature.

Baker v. Carr came to the Supreme Court during the 1960-61 term, but no consensus was reached by the justices at that time. It was re-argued during the next Court term, on October 9, 1961, with Brennan taking the lead in trying to create a consensus in favor of federal court jurisdiction over state elections and electoral districts. Eventually, this resulted in a 6-2 decision supporting his position. Although *Baker v. Carr* did not establish the principle of "one person, one vote," (which would come the following year with William O. Douglas's opinion in *Gray v. Sanders*), Brennan's opinion for the Court certainly set the stage for what came to be known as the "reapportionment revolution." Prior to Baker, state-mandated legislative districts normally continued to favor rural voters, even after populations had shifted to urban areas. In Baker, for example, residents of Memphis, Nashville, and Knoxville, Tennessee, sued Joe C. Carr, the Tennessee secretary of state, to force him to redraw the state's existing legislative districts. The boundaries of these districts had remained unchanged since 1901. As a result, the votes of those inhabiting rural districts in Tennessee carried more weight, individually and collectively, than did those of their more numerous urban counterparts, including those in Shelby County where Baker resided.

Author Biography

William J. Brennan, Jr. was the son of William and Agnes Brennan, both of whom had emigrated from Ireland. Born on April 25, 1906, in Newark, New Jersey, William Brennan, Jr. was raised a Catholic, which was an issue when he was nominated for the Supreme Court. He attended public schools and then the University of Pennsylvania, during which time he married Marjorie Leonard, whom he had known in high school. Brennan attended and, in 1931, graduated from Harvard Law School.

Prior to becoming a judge, Brennan was in private practice, except during World War II when he served in the Army as a judge advocate general. In 1949, Albert Driscoll, the Republican governor of New Jersey, appointed Brennan (a Democrat) to the Superior Court, a trial court. Then, in 1951, the same governor appointed Brennan to the New Jersey Supreme Court. At that time there was no indication that Brennan would become a liberal judicial leader, although he was not as conservative as he seemed to those advising President Eisenhower when a U.S. Supreme Court vacancy occurred in 1956.

To demonstrate his bipartisanship, Eisenhower appointed Brennan to the court during a 1956 Congressional recess, so he began serving immediately. His name was submitted for Senate approval during the next Congressional session and he was approved with only ultra-conservative Sen. Joseph McCarthy voting against him. For many of the other senators, Brennan's confirmation was only possible because he had made it clear that his decisions would be based on U.S. law, not on Catholic doctrines.

In his first term, it would seem that McCarthy's view of him was confirmed because in twelve cases Brennan was the swing vote supporting the individual rights of Communists against government intrusion. Within a few years, Brennan was seen as the leading liberal intellectual force on the Supreme Court. During his term, which lasted until 1990, Brennan put forward strong arguments generally on the liberal side of court cases. Currently, Brennan holds second place in the number of opinions written (1,360). After retirement for health reasons, he was moderately active in legal and academic circles, until his death on July 24, 1997.

HISTORICAL DOCUMENT

The District Court was uncertain whether our cases withholding federal judicial relief rested upon a lack of federal jurisdiction or upon the inappropriateness of the subject matter for judicial consideration—what we have designated "nonjusticiability." The distinction between the two grounds is significant. In the instance of nonjusticiability, consideration of the cause is not wholly and immediately foreclosed; rather, the Court's inquiry necessarily proceeds to the point of deciding whether the duty asserted can be judicially identified and its breach judicially determined, and whether protection for the right asserted can be judicially molded. In the instance of lack of jurisdiction the cause either does not "arise under" the Federal Constitution, laws or treaties (or fall within one of the other enumerated categories of Art. III, 2), or is not a "case or controversy" within the meaning of that section; or the cause is not one described by any jurisdictional statute. Our conclusion ... that this cause presents no nonjusticiable "political question" settles the only possible doubt that it is a case or controversy....

It is clear that the cause of action is one which "arises under" the Federal Constitution. The complaint alleges that the 1901 statute effects an apportionment that deprives the appellants of the equal protection of the laws in violation of the Fourteenth Amendment. Dismissal of the complaint upon the ground of lack of jurisdiction of the subject matter would, therefore, be justified only if that claim were "so attenuated and unsubstantial as to be absolutely devoid of merit."... Since the complaint plainly sets forth a case arising under the Constitution, the subject matter is within the federal judicial power defined in Art. III, 2, and so within the power of Congress to assign to the jurisdiction of the District Courts....

The appellees refer to *Colegrove v. Green* ... as

authority that the District Court lacked jurisdiction of the subject matter. Appellees misconceive the holding of that case. The holding was precisely contrary to their reading of it. Seven members of the Court participated in the decision. Unlike many other cases in this field which have assumed without discussion that there was jurisdiction, all three opinions filed in *Colegrove* discussed the question....

We hold that the District Court has jurisdiction of the subject matter of the federal constitutional claim asserted in the complaint....

Have the appellants alleged such a personal stake in the outcome of the controversy as to assure that concrete adverseness which sharpens the presentation of issues upon which the court so largely depends for illumination of difficult constitutional questions? This is the gist of the question of standing. It is, of course, a question of federal law....

We hold that the appellants do have standing to maintain this suit.... These appellants seek relief in order to protect or vindicate an interest of their own, and of those similarly situated. Their constitutional claim is, in substance, that the 1901 statute constitutes arbitrary and capricious state action, offensive to the Fourteenth Amendment in its irrational disregard of the standard of apportionment prescribed by the State's Constitution or of any standard, effecting a gross disproportion of representation to voting population. The injury which appellants assert is that this classification disfavors the voters in the counties in which they reside, placing them in a position of constitutionally unjustifiable inequality vis-a-vis voters ... in irrationally favored counties. A citizen's right to a vote free of arbitrary impairment by state action has been judicially recognized as a right secured by the Constitution....

It would not be necessary to decide whether appellants' allegations of impairment of their votes by the 1901 apportionment will, ultimately, entitle them to any relief, in order to hold that they have standing to seek it. If such impairment does produce a legally cognizable injury, they are among those who have sustained it.... They are entitled to a hearing and to the District Court's decision on their claims....

In holding that the subject matter of this suit was not justiciable, the District Court relied on *Colegrove v. Green* .... We understand the District Court to have read the cited cases as compelling the conclusion that since the appellants sought to have a legislative apportionment held unconstitutional, their suit presented a "political question" and was therefore nonjusticiable. We hold that this challenge to an apportionment presents no nonjusticiable "political question."...

We come, finally, to the ultimate inquiry whether our precedents as to what constitutes a nonjusticiable "political question" bring the case before us under the umbrella of that doctrine.... The question here is the consistency of state action with the Federal Constitution. We have no question decided, or to be decided, by a political branch of government coequal with this Court. Nor do we risk embarrassment of our government abroad, or grave disturbance at home if we take issue with Tennessee as to the constitutionality of her action here challenged. Nor need the appellants, in order to succeed in this action, ask the Court to enter upon policy determinations for which judicially manageable standards are lacking. Judicial standards under the Equal Protection Clause are well developed and familiar, and it has been open to courts since the enactment of the Fourteenth Amendment to determine, if on the particular facts they must, that a discrimination reflects no policy, but simply arbitrary and capricious action.

We conclude that the complaint's allegations of a denial of equal protection present a justiciable constitutional cause of action upon which appellants are entitled to a trial and a decision. The right asserted is within the reach of judicial protection under the Fourteenth Amendment.

The judgment of the District Court is reversed and the cause is remanded for further proceedings consistent with this opinion.

GLOSSARY

appellants: persons bringing a case on appeal to the Supreme Court.

appellees: persons against whom a case is appealed to the Supreme Court.

holding: the Supreme Court's ruling.

judicial relief: the means by which a court applies a judicial remedy—that is, a solution to the problem presented to it by a given case.

nonjusticiability: issues which do not fall within the purview of the court's power.

offensive to: in violation of.

relief: judicial relief.

remanded: sent back to a lower court.

standing: legal right to bring a lawsuit, which in the United States requires, among other things, clear proof that the party bringing the suit is directly and materially affected by the issue at hand.

Document Analysis

Possible judicial review by federal courts of all laws passed by Congress and all actions taken by the executive branch of the federal government had been clearly stated in an 1803 Supreme Court decision (*Marbury v. Madison*). However, even though one of the issues related to the Civil War was the supremacy of the federal government in certain areas, it was unclear whether or not the federal courts had the power to mandate actions in what were seen as state "political activities." This included drawing the borders for state legislative districts. As the District Court had ruled that it did not have jurisdiction in this type of case, the Supreme Court initially dealt with this matter. If it ruled that federal courts had jurisdiction (which it ultimately did), only then would it deal with other questions, such as to whether the plaintiff had standing to file the suit and whether the issue was significant enough to warrant a trial by the District Court. Once the case was brought to the Supreme Court, Brennan became the leader in supporting the plaintiff's assertion that federal courts did have jurisdiction, while Justice Felix Frankfurter argued strongly against this position. After a second hearing of the case, Brennan was able to obtain support from a majority of the justices, that Section 1 of the 14th Amendment did apply to laws regulating state elections, thereby giving federal courts the right of judicial review, which resulted in the case

being remanded to the District Court, restarting the process of determining the merits of the case.

The plaintiffs, believing that only a federal forum could bring redress, brought their suit in federal district court, asking that the Tennessee apportionment act, which required reapportionment of the state's ninety-five counties only every ten years (a directive that had plainly been disregarded since 1901) be declared unconstitutional and that state officials be enjoined from conducting further elections under the existing act. The district court, citing the principle requiring that so-called legal questions were for legislatures, rather than courts to decide, dismissed the case. The plaintiffs then appealed directly to the U.S. Supreme Court, claiming, as they had in the lower court, that their right to equal protection under the laws, granted by the Fourteenth Amendment, had been violated.

The ostensible issue before the high bench was whether federal courts could mandate equality among legislative districts, however, this was not the specific issue coming to the Supreme Court. At its core, Baker concerned the scope and power of the Supreme Court itself. Seventeen years earlier, in *Colegrove v. Green* (1946), Frankfurter had written a plurality opinion for a seven-member Court (one justice was absent, and a recent vacancy had not been filled) declaring that the high court had no authority to entertain cases concerning apportionment of state legislatures. Now, in the last opinion he would write before retiring from the Court, Frankfurter—always the advocate for judicial restraint—dissented from the majority, once again warning against the Court's entry into a "political thicket." Colegrove had been decided by a vote of three to three to one, with Justice Wiley B. Rutledge concurring in the result but not with Frankfurter's reasoning. Because of the unusual circumstances surrounding that decision, the status of Colegrove as precedent had always been shaky. Brennan's opinion for the Court in Baker destroyed that status entirely.

The appellants in Baker had appealed to the Supreme Court for a writ of certiorari, meaning that Court review was discretionary and requiring the justices to vote first on the issue of hearing the case. When this vote was taken, a bare majority of the justices (five) supported Frankfurter's contention that Baker was a political case outside Court jurisdiction. Only four justices are required to grant certiorari, however, and thus the Court agreed to hear the case. After two days of oral argument, on April 19 and 20, 1961, the Court was still split four to four on the merits of the appeal, with Justice Potter Stewart undecided. Chief Justice Earl Warren, cognizant of Baker's significance and potential for overturning Colegrove, held the case over for re-argument in the next Court term. When Baker was reargued on October 9, 1961, neither side introduced anything new. Afterward Frankfurter attacked the plaintiffs' case with a sixty-page memorandum written to his colleagues. Only Brennan responded in kind, and his lengthy memo, addressing the injustice of malapportionment but asking only that Tennessee be obliged to defend its apportionment system (and intending to convince the still recalcitrant Stewart), carried the day. For his part, Warren, too, was convinced by Brennan's argument, and he assigned Brennan to write an opinion for what would eventually be a six-member majority (two justices dissented, and one did not participate) to overturn Colegrove and grant the Tennessee plaintiffs their day in court.

Brennan's opinion, though ultimately supporting the appellants' contention that Tennessee had acted unconstitutionally, comes at the matter tangentially. After rehearsing the facts of the case, Brennan addresses more technical matters. The lower court had dismissed the case on grounds that federal courts lacked jurisdiction and that Baker presented a question that could not be resolved by judicial means. Brennan carefully distinguishes between these two arguments: Whereas a case that is

nonjusticiable can still be considered by a court up to the point of decision, the court is barred from entertaining a case over which it lacks jurisdiction. In Baker the court ruled that the complaint clearly sets forth a case that arises under the Constitution; therefore, the district court unquestionably has jurisdiction. What is more, the appellants have sufficient interest in the value of their votes to be granted standing to sue. Justiciability presents a knottier problem for Brennan, who nonetheless succeeds in distinguishing this case, which concerns a question of federalism, from one raising a political question about the relationship among the three branches of government. The appellants, Brennan concludes, have a cause of action, and he sends their case back to the lower court "for further proceedings consistent with this opinion."

Baker was decided on very narrow grounds, but it was nonetheless hard fought. Justice Charles Whittaker found the pressure put on him by some of his colleagues during the Court's consideration of the case too much to bear. He was hospitalized for exhaustion before Baker was decided, and he took no part in its decision. A week after Baker was handed down on March 26, 1962, Whittaker resigned from the Court. Frankfurter, embittered by his defeat, suffered a debilitating stroke a few weeks later. On August 28, 1962, he, too, resigned from the Court.

For urban residents of Tennessee—and other states—Baker had a happier aftermath. Within a year of its decision, thirty-six other states were involved in reapportionment suits. A string of Supreme Court cases that followed effectively declared the apportionment of every state legislature unconstitutional. Soon population equality was required of virtually all electoral districts, and even state senate seats were apportioned on the basis of population.

Earl Warren often referred to Baker v. Carr as the most interesting and important case decided during his tenure. Because the case succeeded in transferring political power from the largely landowning, largely conservative rural population to the more heterogeneous populace of the cities, Baker can be said to have opened the door to the major social restructuring America underwent during the Warren era as well as, perhaps, the conservative backlash that ensued decades later. This ruling also partially laid the legal foundation for various federal voter rights laws as they applied to state elections.

Essential Themes

Although the formal result of *Baker v. Carr* was the case being remanded to the District Court to hear the merits of the complaint by Baker, the case's impact went far beyond voting districts in Tennessee. The six justices who supported Brennan's majority opinion, in effect supported the extension of federal judicial review into an area of state politics not specifically mentioned in Article III of the Constitution or the 14th Amendment. They did this on the grounds that the "equal protection" section of the 14th Amendment applied to legislative districts beyond those of the House of Representatives. The creation of these districts, according to this opinion, was not just a political decision by state leaders, but rather it was an action through which a state could demonstrate the equality of all of its citizens. However, in remanding the case to the District Court for a hearing upon its merits, the Supreme Court was also saying that it was possible that states might, contrary to Constitutional principles, illegally create different classes of citizenship based upon the location of a person's residence. For this reason, the case should be heard by the District Court.

After the adoption of several amendments soon after the Civil War, federal judicial review was extended into some areas of state government which had previously been ignored. The decision of *Baker v. Carr* made a clear statement that the federal courts had the right to intervene into the political systems of states, when those systems did not uphold the principle of equality for all citizens of the state. This is what made *Baker v. Carr* such an important case, not the fact that Tennessee ultimately had to deal with legislative redistricting, which it had put off for sixty years. The statement that states could "not deny . . . the equal protection of the laws" was found to apply to all areas of governmental (and thereby political) activity. This clearly included establishing the composition of state legislatures.

In finding that the "appellants are entitled to a trial and a decision" the Court indicated that citizens of a state had standing to bring suit regarding the legislative districts. While Brennan's opinion did not specifically say whether or not a thing could be solely a "political question," he clearly stated that the creation of state legislative districts was not a "political question," but rather a question of the equal treatment of a state's citizens.

Thus, as outlined in the parts of Brennan's opinion contained in this essay: the federal courts have broader powers of judicial review than previously thought; the plaintiffs (appellants) had standing to file a suit; there was the possibility that the plaintiffs were being treated unequally (although no ruling was made on this issue); and, therefore, the full case should be heard by the district court. In line with the philosophy contained in this ruling, not only did the district judge rule that Tennessee needed to update its legislative districts, but people in the majority of states filed similar suits to bring greater equity within their legislative elections.

—*Donald A. Watt, Ph.D.*

Bibliography and Additional Reading

Digital History. "*Baker v. Carr.*" *Digital History.* Houston: Digital History, 2016. Web. 3 August 2017.

Hansen, Richard. *The Supreme Court and Election Law: Judging from* Baker v. Carr *to* Bush v. Gore. New edition. New York: New York University Press, 2006. Print.

Legal Information Institute. "*Baker v. Carr.*" Cornell: Cornell Law School, 2017. Web. 3 August 2017.

C-SPAN with Theodore Olson and J. Douglas Smith. "Baker v. Carr, 1962." *Landmark Cases.* Washington: National Cable Satellite Corporation, 2017. Web. 3 August 2017.

Stern, Seth and Stephen Wermiel. *Justice Brenan.* New York: Houghton Mifflin Harcourt Publishing Company, 2010. Print.

Washington Secretary of State. "*Baker v. Carr et al.,* March 2, 1962." *Shifting Boundaries: Redistricting in Washington State.* Olympia: Office of the Secretary of State, 2017. Web. 7 August 2017.

President Lyndon B. Johnson signs the Voting Rights Act of 1965 while Martin Luther King and others look on. (Yoichi Okamoto, LBJ Library)

■ LBJ's "The Great Society" Speech

Date: May 22, 1964
Author: Lyndon B. Johnson
Genre: Speech

Summary Overview

Lyndon B. Johnson became president of the United States in the wake of the assassination of President John F. Kennedy on November 22, 1963. Johnson found immediate support for his proposals for civil rights and tax reform, and he continued to build on progressive initiatives launched by Kennedy, proposing sweeping domestic reforms in his vision of a "Great Society." Elected by a landslide in his own right in 1964, Johnson, with Democratic majorities in both houses of Congress, was able to achieve many of the Great Society initiatives he proposed, including Medicare and Medicaid, antipoverty initiatives, and passage of the Civil Rights Act of 1964, along with education, immigration, and infrastructure reforms. In this speech, delivered at the University of Michigan at Ann Arbor in May 1964, Johnson proposed some of the initiatives of the Great Society, notably education reform, urban renewal, and environmental reforms.

Defining Moment

Kennedy, president of the United States since January 1961, was assassinated on November 22, 1963, in Dallas, Texas. Vice President Johnson, a former senator from Texas who had served as Senate majority leader, was three cars behind the president. About an hour and a half after Kennedy's death, Johnson was sworn in as president.

During Kennedy's less than three years in office, he had embraced the vision of a "New Frontier" for the United States. The nation's young, dynamic president had asked the country to respond to a progressive vision in international and domestic affairs, and they had responded with great enthusiasm. Thousands joined the newly formed Peace Corps, and many more worked for social justice and civil rights. Kennedy had enacted wage reforms for women, increased some government benefits to combat poverty, and raised the minimum wage. Some New Frontier initiatives, however, including the protec-

tion of wilderness land, education reform, and Medicare, failed to gain the support of Congress and consequently stalled.

When Johnson took office, the nation was in shock and eager to honor the legacy of its slain president. Johnson continued many New Frontier initiatives in the first months of his presidency, including a civil rights bill, which was signed into law in July 1964. This legislation outlawed discrimination based on race, gender, and other factors in employment and public facilities. Johnson also initiated the War on Poverty and established the Office of Economic Opportunity, designed to provide vocational training and reduce barriers to employment. Head Start, a preschool program designed to help struggling students in disadvantaged communities, was also proposed as part of the effort to combat poverty. Johnson referenced his own experience of poverty, and his early career as an educator, and enacted sweeping education reforms. He used the idea of the Great Society, without poverty or injustice, to express his vision of the future in the United States, first employing the term in a speech at Ohio University on May 7, 1964.

Task forces of experts were convened to study how to best achieve the Great Society, and Johnson used these groups to formulate and defend his policies. During his presidency, he formed over one hundred groups to study and report on issues as varied as education and land conservation. His vision of the Great Society, which was focused on education reform, land conservation, and urban renewal, broadened to include the most far-reaching social reform agenda in history, and greatly expanded the role of the federal government in the everyday lives of its citizens.

Author Biography

Lyndon Baines Johnson was born near Stonewall, Texas, on August 27, 1908. His parents were farmers, and he was raised in relative poverty. Three years after graduating from Johnson City High School in 1924, he enrolled in Southwest Texas State Teachers College. Working his way through school, he taught at the segregated Welhausen School for children of Mexican descent. Following graduation, he entered political circles while continuing to teach, and in 1937, he was elected to the House of Representatives. During World War II, he served in the Navy. After the war ended, he was elected to the U.S. Senate. In 1953, he became the youngest Senate minority leader in its history, and when the Democrats won the Senate a year later, he became the majority leader. As John F. Kennedy's running mate in 1960, he was elected vice president. When Kennedy was assassinated on November 22, 1963, Johnson was sworn in as president. In 1964, he was elected president with a huge popular margin, and he used his time in office to build on Kennedy's vision for civil rights and combating poverty. His tenure was also marred by the unpopular war in Vietnam and by urban racial unrest. After leaving office in January 1969, Johnson returned home to Texas. He died suddenly on January 22, 1973, and is buried in his family cemetery in Stonewall, Texas.

HISTORICAL DOCUMENT

President Hatcher, Governor Romney, Senators McNamara and Hart, Congressmen Meader and Staebler, and other members of the fine Michigan delegation, members of the graduating class, my fellow Americans:

It is a great pleasure to be here today. This university has been coeducational since 1870, but I do not believe it was on the basis of your accomplishments that a Detroit high school girl said, "In choosing a college, you first have to decide whether you want a coeducational school or an educational school."

Well, we can find both here at Michigan, although perhaps at different hours.

I came out here today very anxious to meet the Michigan student whose father told a friend of mine that his son's education had been a real value. It stopped his mother from bragging about him.

I have come today from the turmoil of your Capital to the tranquility of your campus to speak about the future of your country.

The purpose of protecting the life of our Nation and preserving the liberty of our citizens is to pursue the happiness of our people. Our success in that pursuit is the test of our success as a Nation.

For a century we labored to settle and to subdue a continent. For half a century we called upon unbounded invention and untiring industry to create an order of plenty for all of our people.

The challenge of the next half century is whether we have the wisdom to use that wealth to enrich and elevate our national life, and to advance the quality of our American civilization.

Your imagination, your initiative, and your indignation will determine whether we build a society where progress is the servant of our needs, or a society where old values and new visions are buried under unbridled growth. For in your time we have the opportunity to move not only toward the rich society and the powerful society, but upward to the Great Society.

The Great Society rests on abundance and liberty for all. It demands an end to poverty and racial injustice, to which we are totally committed in our time. But that is just the beginning.

The Great Society is a place where every child can find knowledge to enrich his mind and to enlarge his talents. It is a place where leisure is a welcome chance to build and reflect, not a feared cause of boredom and restlessness. It is a place where the city of man serves not only the needs of the body and the demands of commerce but the desire for beauty and the hunger for community.

It is a place where man can renew contact with nature. It is a place which honors creation for its own sake and for what it adds to the understanding of the race. It is a place where men are more concerned with the quality of their goals than the quantity of their goods. But most of all, the Great Society is not a safe harbor, a resting place, a final objective, a finished work. It is a challenge constantly renewed, beckoning us toward a destiny where the meaning of our lives matches the marvelous products of our labor.

So I want to talk to you today about three places where we begin to build the Great Society—in our cities, in our countryside, and in our classrooms.

Many of you will live to see the day, perhaps 50 years from now, when there will be 400 million Americans—four-fifths of them in urban areas. In the remainder of this century urban population will double, city land will double, and we will have to build homes, highways, and facilities equal to all those built since this country was first settled. So in the next 40 years we must rebuild the entire urban United States.

Aristotle said: "Men come together in cities in order to live, but they remain together in order to live the good life." It is harder and harder to live the good life in American cities today.

The catalog of ills is long: there is the decay of the centers and the despoiling of the suburbs. There is not enough housing for our people or transportation for our traffic. Open land is vanishing and old landmarks are violated.

Worst of all expansion is eroding the precious and time honored values of community with neighbors and communion with nature. The loss of these values breeds loneliness and boredom and indifference.

Our society will never be great until our cities are great. Today the frontier of imagination and innovation is inside those cities and not beyond their borders.

New experiments are already going on. It will be the task of your generation to make the American city a place where future generations will come, not only to live but to live the good life.

I understand that if I stayed here tonight I would see that Michigan students are really doing their best to live the good life.

This is the place where the Peace Corps was started. It is inspiring to see how all of you, while you are in this country, are trying so hard to live at the level of the people.

A second place where we begin to build the Great Society is in our countryside. We have always prided ourselves on being not only America the strong and America the free, but America the beautiful. Today that beauty is in danger. The water we drink, the food we eat, the very air that we breathe, are threatened with pollution. Our parks are overcrowded, our seashores overburdened. Green fields and dense forests are disappearing.

A few years ago we were greatly concerned about the "Ugly American." Today we must act to prevent an ugly America.

For once the battle is lost, once our natural splendor is destroyed, it can never be recaptured. And once man can no longer walk with beauty or wonder at nature his spirit will wither and his sustenance be wasted.

A third place to build the Great Society is in the classrooms of America. There your children's lives will be shaped. Our society will not be great until every young mind is set free to scan the farthest reaches of thought and imagination. We are still far from that goal.

Today, 8 million adult Americans, more than the entire population of Michigan, have not finished 5 years of school. Nearly 20 million have not finished 8 years of school. Nearly 54 million—more than one-quarter of all America—have not even finished high school.

Each year more than 100,000 high school graduates, with proved ability, do not enter college because they cannot afford it. And if we cannot educate today's youth, what will we do in 1970 when elementary school enrollment will be 5 million greater than 1960? And high school enrollment will rise by 5 million. College enrollment will increase by more than 3 million.

In many places, classrooms are overcrowded and curricula are outdated. Most of our qualified teachers are underpaid, and many of our paid teachers are unqualified. So we must give every child a place to sit and a teacher to learn from. Poverty must not be a bar to learning, and learning must offer an escape from poverty.

But more classrooms and more teachers are not enough. We must seek an educational system which grows in excellence as it grows in size. This means better training for our teachers. It means preparing youth to enjoy their hours of leisure as well as their hours of labor. It means exploring new techniques of teaching, to find new ways to stimulate the love of learning and the capacity for creation.

These are three of the central issues of the Great Society. While our Government has many programs directed at those issues, I do not pretend that we have the full answer to those problems.

But I do promise this: We are going to assemble the best thought and the broadest knowledge from all over the world to find those answers for America. I intend to establish working groups to prepare a series of White

House conferences and meetings—on the cities, on natural beauty, on the quality of education, and on other emerging challenges. And from these meetings and from this inspiration and from these studies we will begin to set our course toward the Great Society.

The solution to these problems does not rest on a massive program in Washington, nor can it rely solely on the strained resources of local authority. They require us to create new concepts of cooperation, a creative federalism, between the National Capital and the leaders of local communities.

Woodrow Wilson once wrote: "Every man sent out from his university should be a man of his Nation as well as a man of his time."

Within your lifetime powerful forces, already loosed, will take us toward a way of life beyond the realm of our experience, almost beyond the bounds of our imagination.

For better or for worse, your generation has been appointed by history to deal with those problems and to lead America toward a new age. You have the chance never before afforded to any people in any age. You can help build a society where the demands of morality, and the needs of the spirit, can be realized in the life of the Nation.

So, will you join in the battle to give every citizen the full equality which God enjoins and the law requires, whatever his belief, or race, or the color of his skin?

Will you join in the battle to give every citizen an escape from the crushing weight of poverty?

Will you join in the battle to make it possible for all nations to live in enduring peace—as neighbors and not as mortal enemies?

Will you join in the battle to build the Great Society, to prove that our material progress is only the foundation on which we will build a richer life of mind and spirit?

There are those timid souls who say this battle cannot be won; that we are condemned to a soulless wealth. I do not agree. We have the power to shape the civilization that we want. But we need your will, your labor, your hearts, if we are to build that kind of society.

Those who came to this land sought to build more than just a new country. They sought a new world. So I have come here today to your campus to say that you can make their vision our reality. So let us from this moment begin our work so that in the future men will look back and say: It was then, after a long and weary way, that man turned the exploits of his genius to the full enrichment of his life.

Thank you. Goodbye.

Document Analysis

President Johnson opens this speech with several jokes, designed to put the students at the University of Michigan at ease and keep their attention, but then he gets to the purpose of his speech: discussing America's future. The president first focuses on the theme of the pursuit of happiness. The mark of a successful government is whether it allows its people to pursue their happiness, and the time has come to see whether the extraordinary wealth and progress that has been made in the United States in the previous fifty years will be put to the service of the happiness of its people. It is up to young people such as the students of the University of Michigan to ensure that the United States is not only moving toward the "rich society and the powerful society, but upward to the Great Society." Johnson spends the next part of his speech laying out his vision for the Great Society as a place where there is justice and equality for all citizens, educational and recreational opportunities, and cities that serve the needs of people rather than just the demands of commerce. The Great Society is not static, however. It will be a "challenge constantly renewed," he stresses, pushing the nation toward a life that has meaning, where people are not just machines.

Three of the places where the Great Society will be built are "in our cities, in our countryside, and in our classrooms," according to Johnson, and he looks at these in depth in the remainder of his speech. Cities will be home to four-fifths of some four hundred million Americans in the next fifty years, he predicts. Cities face myriad problems, however; as suburbs expand, city centers decay. Landmarks and open space are being swept away as development expands. He closes his case for invigorating and renewing urban life with another joke: people want to live "the good life," and Michigan students have mastered it.

Another area where the Great Society will be built is in the countryside, and Johnson uses this term "countryside" to represent various elements of the environment. Pollution is rising, he says, and areas of natural beauty are being lost. The United States is in danger of becoming "ugly." Humankind depends on "natural splendor" to nurture the spirit, and if it is spoiled, the Great Society will be irrevocably lost.

The Great Society also depends on access to a quality education. Johnson bemoans the number of people who have limited education. Nearly one quarter of Americans do not finish high school, he emphasizes. Many qualified students who do finish high school have difficulty affording to pay for college. Teachers need supplies, modern classroom materials, and appropriate pay. They also need to find new ways of teaching in order to inspire students' creativity.

Johnson moves from discussion of these specific areas of need to a general call to action, and he promises that he will dedicate groups to study and report on each of the aspects crucial to the success of the Great Society. At the same time, he stresses that the generation of Americans represented on the University of Michigan campus will be responsible for implementing any necessary changes. The president asks them if they are willing to "join in the battle to build the Great Society." It will be the fulfillment of the desire of the founders of the nation to build "a new world."

Essential Themes

President Johnson dedicated his administration to an ambitious agenda of social reforms, and when he won the presidency in his own right in 1964 by a wide margin, he used this momentum, and the support of the Democratic-controlled Congress, to build his Great Society. In addition to passing the Civil Rights Act of 1964, he founded Head Start, and his Volunteers in Service to America (VISTA) program sent volunteers to work on various projects in needy and poverty-stricken communities throughout the country. Educational funding was increased, as was aid of all kinds to disadvantaged areas. Johnson had declared that he would wage a War on Poverty, and he set out to do just that. Funds were designated to construct low-income housing, and Medicare and Medicaid provided healthcare for retirees and those in need. He also worked to eliminate barriers to full civic participation for African Americans and eliminated immigration quotas.

Johnson also focused on consumer protection and the environment during the early years of his presidency, working to reduce pollution through clean air and water acts, and tighter controls of food safety and consumer products. He protected millions of acres of open land from future development.

War in Vietnam would spell the end of much of Johnson's progressive agenda by the conclusion of his presidency, however, as funds were increasingly diverted abroad, and he lost support from many of his antiwar colleagues in Congress and in the population at large. Still, the Johnson presidency is responsible for many of the social programs still in place in the United States today.

—*Bethany Groff Dorau, MA*

Bibliography and Additional Reading

Andrew, John A. *Lyndon Johnson and the Great Society*. Chicago: Dee, 1998. Print.

Califano, Joseph A., Jr. *The Triumph and Tragedy of Lyndon Johnson: The White House Years*. New York: Simon, 1991. Print.

Zelizer, Julian E. *The Fierce Urgency of Now: Lyndon Johnson*, Congress, and the Battle for the Great Society. New York: Penguin, 2015. Print.

■ *Reynolds v. Sims*

Date: Decided June 15, 1964
Author: Justice Earl Warren
Genre: Court case

Summary Overview

Earl Warren led the U.S. Supreme Court during the turbulent years of the 1950s and 1960s. Driven by his own moral compass rather than politics, Warren shocked those on the left and right as he made the transition from crime-fighting district attorney to liberal chief justice. He became known as a protector of the rights of minorities and the oppressed, a stance reflected in many of his rulings. The case of *Reynolds v. Sims* addressed disenfranchisement of blacks in the South, which was ongoing despite the protections offered by the Fourteenth Amendment. A group of voters challenged legislative reapportionment in Alabama, which left urban counties drastically underrepresented. In its decision the Court ruled that state legislative districts had to be roughly equal in population, based on the principle of "one person, one vote."

Defining Moment

Starting as early as the 1950's, there was a movement within the United States encouraging political leaders to do something to ensure the fair apportionment of state legislative districts. Because cities and suburbs were experiencing periods of extreme growth in terms of population counts, many did not believe it was fair to continue allowing the government to be controlled primarily by those coming from rural districts. More specifically, there was growing concern that the system of apportionment being used was a major cause for the disenfranchisement of black voters. In particular, within the state of Alabama there were huge discrepancies between the number of voters in various districts, which lead to the underrepresentation of large portions of the Alabama population. In one shocking example, the number of eligible voters casting their votes for one senator was 41 times the number of voters in another district. Upon examination, it was evident the districts in Alabama still reflected the population counts from the 1900 census report. To challenge the existing ap-

portionment practices of their state legislatures, many reapportionment cases came before the Supreme Court of the United States, with the case of *Reynolds v. Sims* stemming from the Alabama legislature, taking the spotlight as the lead case.

In an 8-1 decision, the Supreme Court decided state legislatures must undergo a system of reapportionment that would align with the population of the state. Noting the right to vote as being a fundamental right, the inequalities promoted in the faulty apportionment of legislative districts was struck down by the Court, causing a nationwide change in the political scene. Redrawing district maps was mandated, a call for districts to be drawn as equally as possible according to population, and the reign of rural lawmakers in states with increasingly urban populations was effectively ended.

Author Biography

As governor of California and chief justice of the United States, Earl Warren defied political categorization, confounding his supporters and critics alike. Although he proved to be a notoriously "liberal" judge, he had been head of the Republican Party in California and had won the vice presidential nomination on the Republican ticket in 1948. Prominent in California politics during the reformist Progressive Era, Warren pursued an agenda as district attorney and later as governor that included elimination of corruption within law enforcement, cracking down on gambling rings, and prison reform. Under his leadership as chief justice, the Supreme Court issued several landmark rulings, among them, decisions on religious freedom, criminal law procedure, civil rights and equal protection under the law, and freedom of speech and obscenity. With a long career spanning the years of the Progressive Era, the Great Depression, World War II, the cold war, and the civil rights movement, Warren epitomizes the American struggle to answer many of the moral questions of the twentieth century.

Warren was born on March 19, 1891, and grew up in the booming oil town of Bakersfield, California, where his father worked as a handyman. He graduated from Kern County High School in 1908 and enrolled at the University of California, Berkeley, where he earned both a bachelor's and a law degree. Following President Woodrow Wilson's call for a congressional declaration of war against Germany on April 2, 1917, Warren joined the army and completed officer training. In 1919 a college friend helped him secure a position as clerk of the California State Assembly Judiciary Committee. Warren soon became deputy city attorney of Oakland, working his way up to the position of district attorney of Alameda County in 1925.

His professional reputation growing, Warren was elected state chairman of the Republican Party in 1934, despite his belief in nonpartisanship; he repeatedly campaigned as a political independent. In 1938 he was elected attorney general and, in 1942, governor of California. As governor, Warren irked the Republican right when he called for compulsory medical insurance, but his record of fiscal responsibility pleased most conservatives. Under Warren's watch, the University of California system expanded, the teachers' retirement fund regained solvency, and the state began developing its massive highway system. Perhaps the most notorious act of Warren's gubernatorial stint was his support for the evacuation and internment of Japanese residents, including U.S. citizens, following the attack on Pearl Harbor, Hawaii.

After his decisive reelection victory in 1946, Warren was considered a candidate for president. He was nominated for vice president on the Republican ticket in the 1948 election, in which the Republican Thomas Dewey lost to the Democrat Harry Truman. He then lost the presidential nomination to Dwight Eisenhower in 1952. When Chief Justice Fred Vinson died of a heart attack in 1953, Eisenhower named Warren as Vinson's replacement. Under Warren's leadership, the Supreme Court handed down several historic decisions. One of the first and most important of these cases was *Brown v. Board of Education of Topeka* (1954), which paved the way for school desegregation. The chief justice wrote dissenting opinions in four separate obscenity cases, arguing that pornographers did not deserve First Amendment protection. Nevertheless, decisions such as *Engel v. Vitale* (1962), which ruled school prayer unconstitutional, fueled public outcry against the liberal nature of the Warren Court. The Court addressed the issue of voting rights in *Baker v. Carr* (1962) and the subsequent case, *Reynolds v. Sims* (1964), handing down the famous "one man, one vote" edict, which essentially extended the Court's power to the legislative branch of government. The obligation of law enforcement officials to advise criminal suspects of their rights was confirmed by the Court's 1966 ruling in *Miranda v. Arizona*. Perhaps Warren's most well-known activity, however, was his investigation into the 1963 assassination of President John F. Kennedy. The President's Commission on the Assassination of President Kennedy, popularly known as the Warren Commission, produced a report that received enormous public scrutiny and has been the subject of ongoing debate into the twenty-first century. Warren retired from the Court in 1969. He died on July 9, 1974, in Washington, D.C.

HISTORICAL DOCUMENT

Undeniably, the Constitution of the United States protects the right of all qualified citizens to vote, in state as well as in federal, elections. A consistent line of decisions by this Court in cases involving attempts to deny or restrict the right of suffrage has made this indelibly clear. It has been repeatedly recognized that all qualified voters have a constitutionally protected right to vote, *Ex parte Yarbrough*, and to have their votes counted, *United States v. Mosley*. In *Mosley*, the Court stated that it is "as equally unquestionable that the right to have one's vote counted is as open to protection… as the right to put a ballot in a box." The right to vote can neither be denied outright, *Guinn v. United States, Lane v. Wilson*, nor destroyed by alteration of ballots, *see United States v. Classic*, nor diluted by ballot box stuffing, *Ex parte Siebold, United States v. Saylor*. As the Court stated in *Classic*, "Obviously included within the right to choose, secured by the Constitution, is the right of qualified voters within a state to cast their ballots and have them counted."

Racially based gerrymandering… and the conducting

of white primaries,... both of which result in denying to some citizens their right to vote, have been held to be constitutionally impermissible. And history has seen a continuing expansion of the scope of the right of suffrage in this country. The right to vote freely for the candidate of one's choice is of the essence of a democratic society, and any restrictions on that right strike at the heart of representative government. And the right of suffrage can be denied by a debasement or dilution of the weight of a citizen's vote just as effectively as by wholly prohibiting the free exercise of the franchise.

In *Baker v. Carr*, we held that a claim asserted under the Equal Protection Clause challenging the constitutionality of a State's apportionment of seats in its legislature, on the ground that the right to vote of certain citizens was effectively impaired, since debased and diluted, in effect presented a justiciable controversy subject to adjudication by federal courts. The spate of similar cases filed and decided by lower courts since our decision in *Baker* amply shows that the problem of state legislative malapportionment is one that is perceived to exist in a large number of the States. In *Baker*, a suit involving an attack on the apportionment of seats in the Tennessee Legislature, we remanded to the District Court, which had dismissed the action, for consideration on the merits. We intimated no view as to the proper constitutional standards for evaluating the validity of a state legislative apportionment scheme. Nor did we give any consideration to the question of appropriate remedies. Rather, we simply stated: "Beyond noting that we have no cause at this stage to doubt the District Court will be able to fashion relief if violations of constitutional rights are found, it is improper now to consider what remedy would be most appropriate if appellants prevail at the trial."

We indicated in *Baker*, however, that the Equal Protection Clause provides discoverable and manageable standards for use by lower courts in determining the constitutionality of a state legislative apportionment scheme, and we stated:

"Nor need the appellants, in order to succeed in this action, ask the Court to enter upon policy determinations for which judicially manageable standards are lacking. Judicial standards under the Equal Protection Clause are well developed and familiar, and it has been open to courts since the enactment of the Fourteenth Amend-ment to determine if, on the particular facts they must, that a discrimination reflects no policy, but simply arbitrary and capricious action."

Subsequent to *Baker*, we remanded several cases to the courts below for reconsideration in light of that decision....

Legislators represent people, not trees or acres. Legislators are elected by voters, not farms or cities or economic interests. As long as ours is a representative form of government, and our legislatures are those instruments of government elected directly by and directly representative of the people, the right to elect legislators in a free and unimpaired fashion is a bedrock of our political system. It could hardly be gainsaid that a constitutional claim had been asserted by an allegation that certain otherwise qualified voters had been entirely prohibited from voting for members of their state legislature. And, if a State should provide that the votes of citizens in one part of the State should be given two times, or five times, or 10 times the weight of votes of citizens in another part of the State, it could hardly be contended that the right to vote of those residing in the disfavored areas had not been effectively diluted. It would appear extraordinary to suggest that a State could be constitutionally permitted to enact a law providing that certain of the State's voters could vote two, five, or 10 times for their legislative representatives, while voters living elsewhere could vote only once. And it is inconceivable that a state law to the effect that, in counting votes for legislators, the votes of citizens in one part of the State would be multiplied by two, five, or 10, while the votes of persons in another area would be counted only at face value, could be constitutionally sustainable. Of course, the effect of state legislative districting schemes which give the same number of representatives to unequal numbers of constituents is identical. Overweighting and overvaluation of the votes of those living here has the certain effect of dilution and undervaluation of the votes of those living there. The resulting discrimination against those individual voters living in disfavored areas is easily demonstrable mathematically. Their right to vote is simply not the same right to vote as that of those living in a favored part of the State. Two, five, or 10 of them must vote before the effect of their voting is equivalent to that of their favored neighbor. Weighting the votes of citizens differently, by any method or means, merely because of where they happen to reside, hardly seems justifiable. One must be ever aware that the Constitution forbids "sophisticated, as well as simpleminded, modes of discrimination."...

State legislatures are, historically, the fountainhead of representative government in this country. A number of them have their roots in colonial times, and substantially antedate the creation of our Nation and our Federal Government. In fact, the first formal stirrings of American political independence are to be found, in large part, in the views and actions of several of the colonial legislative bodies. With the birth of our National Government, and the adoption and ratification of the Federal Constitution, state legislatures retained a most important place in our Nation's governmental structure. But representative government is, in essence, self-government through the medium of elected representatives of the people, and each and every citizen has an inalienable right to full and effective participation in the political processes of his State's legislative bodies. Most citizens can achieve this participation only as qualified voters through the election of legislators to represent them. Full and effective participation by all citizens in state government requires, therefore, that each citizen have an equally effective voice in the election of members of his state legislature. Modern and viable state government needs, and the Constitution demands, no less.

Logically, in a society ostensibly grounded on representative government, it would seem reasonable that a majority of the people of a State could elect a majority of that State's legislators. To conclude differently, and to sanction minority control of state legislative bodies, would appear to deny majority rights in a way that far surpasses any possible denial of minority rights that might otherwise be thought to result. Since legislatures are responsible for enacting laws by which all citizens are to be governed, they should be bodies which are collectively responsive to the popular will. And the concept of equal protection has been traditionally viewed as requiring the uniform treatment of persons standing in the same relation to the governmental action questioned or challenged. With respect to the allocation of legislative representation, all voters, as citizens of a State, stand in the same relation regardless of where they live. Any suggested criteria for the differentiation of citizens are insuf-

ficient to justify any discrimination, as to the weight of their votes, unless relevant to the permissible purposes of legislative apportionment. Since the achieving of fair and effective representation for all citizens is concededly the basic aim of legislative apportionment, we conclude that the Equal Protection Clause guarantees the opportunity for equal participation by all voters in the election of state legislators. Diluting the weight of votes because of place of residence impairs basic constitutional rights under the Fourteenth Amendment just as much as invidious discriminations based upon factors such as race, *Brown v. Board of Education*, or economic status, *Griffin v. Illinois, Douglas v. California*. Our constitutional system amply provides for the protection of minorities by means other than giving them majority control of state legislatures. And the democratic ideals of equality and majority rule, which have served this Nation so well in the past, are hardly of any less significance for the present and the future.

We are told that the matter of apportioning representation in a state legislature is a complex and many-faceted one. We are advised that States can rationally consider factors other than population in apportioning legislative representation. We are admonished not to restrict the power of the States to impose differing views as to political philosophy on their citizens. We are cautioned about the dangers of entering into political thickets and mathematical quagmires. Our answer is this: a denial of constitutionally protected rights demands judicial protection; our oath and our office require no less of us....

We hold that, as a basic constitutional standard, the Equal Protection Clause requires that the seats in both houses of a bicameral state legislature must be apportioned on a population basis. Simply stated, an individual's right to vote for state legislators is unconstitutionally impaired when its weight is in a substantial fashion diluted when compared with votes of citizens living in other parts of the State....

By holding that, as a federal constitutional requisite, both houses of a state legislature must be apportioned on a population basis, we mean that the Equal Protection Clause requires that a State make an honest and good faith effort to construct districts, in both houses of its legislature, as nearly of equal population as is practicable....

History indicates, however, that many States have

deviated, to a greater or lesser degree, from the equal population principle in the apportionment of seats in at least one house of their legislatures. So long as the divergences from a strict population standard are based on legitimate considerations incident to the effectuation of a rational state policy, some deviations from the equal population principle are constitutionally permissible with respect to the apportionment of seats in either or both of the two houses of a bicameral state legislature. But neither history alone, nor economic or other sorts of group interests, are permissible factors in attempting to justify disparities from population-based representation. Citizens, not history or economic interests, cast votes.

GLOSSARY

bicameral consisting of two legislative bodies, generally one made up of statewide representatives and the other of local representatives

concededly: admittedly

gainsaid: denied

gerrymandering: the act of drawing congressional boundary lines for the purpose of giving an advantage to a party, group of constituents, or candidate in an election

justiciable: able to be evaluated and ruled on in the courts

remanded: returned to a lower court for further consideration

Document Analysis

Despite the protections of the Fourteenth Amendment, black voters continued to be disenfranchised in the South through the 1950s. Disenfranchisement took many forms, including literacy tests and poll taxes. The process of apportionment, which determined the boundaries of congressional districts, also effectively disenfranchised voters, particularly those who lived in urban areas. Even though many states' populations were shifting from the country to the city, most states continued to allocate representatives by county, which effectively robbed urban voters of proportional representation in their legislatures. Rural interests thus governed increasingly urban populations.

In 1959 Charles Baker and nine other urban residents sued the Tennessee secretary of state, Joe C. Carr, noting that the state had not reapportioned its districts since 1901 and had thus effectively denied its urban voters their Fourteenth Amendment rights. *Baker v. Carr* represented a challenge to the Warren Court. First of all, the courts had traditionally shied away from matters involving political districting, concerned that judicial rulings in this area could be construed as a violation of separation of powers; legislative questions were considered political matters not appropriate for Court involvement. Furthermore, the right to vote is not clearly established by the Constitution. The Founders had a restrictive view of who should be able to vote: Slaves, women, and unpropertied males were not considered eligible. In considering *Baker v. Carr*, the Court was entering new territory. Written by William J. Brennan, the 1962 *Baker* decision was carefully worded, stating only that reapportionment could be taken up in the courts. The ruling thus let individual federal district courts decide how they would solve problems of malapportionment. Soon after the decision was announced, attorneys filed cases challenging apportionments in several states. By the end of 1962, the Supreme Court had twelve cases pending that related to redistricting. These state cases were decided collectively under *Reynolds v. Sims* on June 15, 1964.

In *Reynolds v. Sims*, several voters in Alabama sued state election officials, charging that their Fourteenth Amendment rights, as well as their rights under the Alabama Constitution, had been violated by the state's existing legislative apportionment. The case also involved a dispute over proposed reapportionment plans, which the plaintiffs argued were unconstitutional. Having established in *Baker v. Carr* that the courts did, in fact, have jurisdiction over such matters, the Warren Court now needed to address specific cases handed up by the federal district courts.

In the first paragraph of the excerpt of Warren's decision, he makes clear his opinion that the Court has jurisdiction over questions of redistricting. One of the roles of the Supreme Court is to evaluate the constitutionality of state and federal laws; by stating that the Constitution protects the right of qualified voters, Warren establishes the Court's role in striking down laws that violate those rights.

As was the case in *Brown v. Board*, Warren's decision in this case was strongly influenced by his attitude toward racial discrimination. He mentions the practice of "gerrymandering," which is the manipulation of election district boundaries in order to influence election results. The term derives from Elbridge Gerry, governor of Massachusetts from 1810 to 1812, who redistricted the state to benefit his political party. Warren refers to racial gerrymandering, which was practiced in both southern and northern states; by redrawing legislative district lines, politicians could create segregated, all-black districts or, in some cases, eliminate black voters from an area when it was expedient. Warren points out that malapportionment disenfranchises voters just as effectively as prohibiting them from voting at all.

Warren's decisions are noteworthy for their clear, straightforward language. This particular document contains an especially unusual and oft-quoted passage: "Legislators represent people, not trees or acres. Legislators are elected by voters, not farms or cities or economic interests." This verbiage was actually crafted by the law clerk Francis X. Beytagh, who worked on the case with Warren. Warren read this in the draft statement and thought that the language captured the essence of his "one man, one vote" argument. The passage stands out for the very reason that its tone differs from that of the rest of the document.

A key component of Warren's decision is his statement that "seats in both houses of a bicameral state legislature must be apportioned on a population basis." Important here is the assertion that both houses had to use population as a means of determining representation. Following *Baker v. Carr*, many states refused to reapportion their districts, instead using what was known as the "federal plan," in which one house of the legislature was apportioned geographically and the other by population. *Reynolds v. Sims* made clear that the federal plan was no longer an option. Warren allowed for some flexibility in redistricting in order to prevent gerrymandering or to provide for fair representation in more rural states with many counties. However, he reiterates in his decision that population is the overriding factor that should determine the number of representatives.

Reynolds v. Sims was a much broader decision than *Baker v. Carr* in the sense that it had a dramatic and lasting impact on the political landscape. By specifically defining constitutional districting plans in terms of population rather than geography, Warren summarily eliminated the jobs of many powerful rural senators and assemblymen; rural districts disappeared as states redrew boundaries to conform to the new requirements. Today, Congress and state legislatures are overwhelmingly filled with lawmakers from cities and suburbs. In addition to reshaping the makeup of legislatures and the state level, *Reynolds v. Sims* is cited as helping end one method of black voter disenfranchisement in America.

Essential Themes

According to the majority opinion of the Court on the *Reynolds* case, the principle of democracy was clearly based on the Equal Protection Clause of the Fourteenth Amendment. The concept of democracy in America, in large part, hinges on the right to vote in democratic elections. By ruling to create more equal legislative districts throughout the nation, the Court established the standard of "one person, one vote". In other words, each person voting in an election should have equal weight in determining the result of the election they voted in.

The Court's decision to end the unfair apportionment of legislative districts was a move to uphold the new "one person, one vote" standard, and simultaneously caused a major shakeup in the political landscape of America. Because the Court insisted upon reapportionment on the basis of population by calling for districts to be made as equal as possible, state legislative districts were overhauled across the country. The redrawing of state legislative districts meant there would be an end to the legislative stronghold held by rural lawmakers, and instead legislatures would be dominated by elected officials from cities and suburbs. The roughly 2% of Americans still living on farms would experience a loss of power in terms of their legislative representation. This was a seriously controversial ruling at the time, with many claiming the Supreme Court had no right to interfere in state politics. A constitutional amendment was proposed to combat the Court's ruling, but this attempt to reverse the decision was unsuccessful. Regardless of the pushback, the Court, and Justice Warren in particular, were confident this was the only fair ruling according to the Constitution. While the Court certainly has respect for states' rights, they must also fiercely defend individuals' rights and they ruling of *Reynolds* emphasizes that stance.

—*Karen Linkletter, PhD*
—*Amber R. Dickinson, PhD*

Bibliography and Additional Reading

Douglas, Joshua, and Eugene Mazeo. *Election Law Stories*. Foundation Press, 2016. Print.

Irons, Peter. *A People's History of the Supreme Court*. New York, NY: Penguin, 1999. Print.

McBride, Alex. "Landmark Cases: *Reynolds V. Sims*." *PBS*, Public Broadcasting Services, www.pbs.org/wnet/supremecourt/rights/landmark_reynolds.html. Accessed 24 Aug. 2017.

McClosky, Robert G. *The American Supreme Court: Fourth Edition*. University of Chicago Press, 2005. Print.

■ Barry Goldwater's "Extremism in the Defense of Liberty Is No Vice" Speech

Date: July 16, 1964
Author: Barry Goldwater
Genre: Speech

Summary Overview

In 1964, Senator Barry Goldwater ran for president against incumbent Lyndon B. Johnson and lost by a wide margin. Though his bid failed, he is widely seen as ushering in a new era in the conservative movement in the United States. The presidential campaign of 1964 gave conservative philosophy a national and international stage, crafting the message of the Republican Party for decades to come. The popular support of Goldwater's positions, considered extreme by many in his own party, was a surprise to leaders from both sides of the aisle. Goldwater embraced the term "conservative" in an era when most leaders distanced themselves from the term. Republicans struggled to persuade Goldwater to accept the nomination, and his acceptance speech—given at the Cow Palace in Daly City, California (bordering San Francisco) in July 1964—was not the anticipated conciliatory call for party unity but a clear articulation of a kind of small-government, hawkish conservatism that had not been part of mainstream American politics in the twentieth century.

Defining Moment

The Republican Party in the 1950s still suffered from the effects of the stock-market crash of 1929 and the Great Depression. These events exposed the weakness in unregulated top-down economic policy, and the social programs in place were woefully inadequate to cope with the human impact of the crash. First elected in 1932, President Franklin D. Roosevelt embarked on a sweeping social-welfare campaign that many credited for saving the nation, and the Democratic administration lasted through World War II. Republicans recaptured control of Congress in 1946, and took the nation's highest office again in 1952 with Dwight D. Eisenhower. During Eisenhower's presidency, the Republican Party leaders tended to be moderate, privileged, well-educated, East

Coast elites; conservative elements of the party were marginalized.

By the late 1950s, however, the conservative element of the Republican Party was starting to gain ground, thanks in large part to so-called Sunbelt conservatives, political leaders from the Southwest who espoused a brand of frontier conservatism that valued small-government individualism. The postwar oil boom across the country increased the wealth and influence of these leaders, who were joined by midwesterners and others who felt that the Republican Party had become virtually indistinguishable from New Deal Democrats, supporting social programs and expanding U.S. foreign aid.

By 1960, the Republican Party was gaining ground in several key areas, while moderates were losing their hold on the party. Some states in the South, Democratic since the Civil War, were unhappy with the advance of civil rights legislation under Democrats John F. Kennedy and Johnson and resented the involvement of the federal government in what they considered state issues; this new brand of conservatism appealed to them. It was also virulently anti-Communist, and conservative leaders accused both the Democrats and moderate Republicans of pandering to the enemy. These conservatives championed state's rights (which would have drastically undercut the civil rights movement) and argued that individual initiative, not social welfare, was the basis of American freedom. In 1960, Senator Goldwater, one of the few Republican senators who had voted against the Civil Rights Act of 1964, published *The Conscience of a Conservative*, a book that articulated the new conservatism in a succinct and appealing way. The book blasted social welfare as the end of individual freedom and identified the government's involvement in the lives of its citizens as a step on the road to totalitarianism. Goldwater drew a bold line between freedom and New Deal liberalism, arguing that the government had trampled on the rights of its citizens, while offering only weak resistance to the Communist threat inside the United States and abroad. By identifying conservatism with individual rights and American tradition, Goldwater gave conservatives an organizing principal and a moral imperative.

After the congressional elections of 1962, conservative Republicans met to find and fund a viable conservative candidate for the 1964 presidential election. Goldwater was a natural choice, despite his protests that he did not wish to run. In 1963, the "Draft Goldwater Committee" was formed in order to persuade him to run. Despite heavy opposition from moderate Republicans, led by New York governor Nelson Rockefeller, a groundswell of support developed for Goldwater. On Friday, January 20, 1964, Goldwater announced his candidacy from his home in Phoenix, Arizona, and six months later, he was the Republican nominee for president.

Author Biography

Barry Morris Goldwater was born in Phoenix, Arizona, on January 1, 1909. His family owned Goldwater's Department Store in Phoenix and were considered moderately wealthy. Goldwater attended local schools until high school, when he attended the Staunton Military Academy in Virginia and graduated at the top of his class. Goldwater enrolled in the University of Arizona in 1928, but he left after one year to help manage the family store. During World War II, he served in Ferry Command, a unit that delivered wartime supplies across the world. After the war, he became interested in city government, serving on the Phoenix city council in 1949. In 1952, he won a tight election to the Senate, a seat he kept with little opposition in 1958. In the Presidential election of 1964, he ran as a conservative Republican against President Johnson's progressive Democratic ticket. He was defeated decisively and returned to the Senate, where he served until his retirement in 1987. Goldwater died on May 29, 1998, in Paradise Valley, Arizona.

HISTORICAL DOCUMENT

To my good friend and great Republican, Dick Nixon, and your charming wife, Pat; my running mate and that wonderful Republican who has served us well for so long, Bill Miller and his wife, Stephanie; to Thurston Morton who has done such a commendable job in chairmaning this Convention; to Mr. Herbert Hoover, who I hope is watching; and to that great American and his wife, General and Mrs. Eisenhower; to my own wife, my family, and to all of my fellow Republicans here assembled, and Americans across this great Nation.

From this moment, united and determined, we will go forward together, dedicated to the ultimate and undeniable greatness of the whole man. Together we will win.

I accept your nomination with a deep sense of humility. I accept, too, the responsibility that goes with it, and I seek your continued help and your continued guidance. My fellow Republicans, our cause is too great for any man to feel worthy of it. Our task would be too great for any man, did he not have with him the heart and the hands of this great Republican Party, and I promise you tonight that every fiber of my being is consecrated to our cause; that nothing shall be lacking from the struggle that can be brought to it by enthusiasm, by devotion, and plain hard work. In this world no person, no party can guarantee anything, but what we can do and what we shall do is to deserve victory, and victory will be ours.

The good Lord raised this mighty Republic to be a home for the brave and to flourish as the land of the free—not to stagnate in the swampland of collectivism, not to cringe before the bully of communism.

Now, my fellow Americans, the tide has been running against freedom. Our people have followed false prophets. We must, and we shall, return to proven ways—not because they are old, but because they are true. We must, and we shall, set the tide running again in the cause of freedom. And this party, with its every action, every word, every breath, and every heartbeat, has but a single resolve, and that is freedom—freedom made orderly for this nation by our constitutional government; freedom under a government limited by laws of nature and of nature's God; freedom—balanced so that liberty lacking order will not become the slavery of the prison cell; balanced so that liberty lacking order will not become the license of the mob and of the jungle.

Poster of Senator Barry Goldwater of Arizona, in his 1964 presidential campaign

Now, we Americans understand freedom. We have earned it, we have lived for it, and we have died for it. This Nation and its people are freedom's model in a searching world. We can be freedom's missionaries in a doubting world. But, ladies and gentlemen, first we must renew freedom's mission in our own hearts and in our own homes.

During four futile years, the administration which we shall replace has distorted and lost that faith. It has talked and talked and talked and talked the words of freedom. Now, failures cement the wall of shame in Berlin. Failures blot the sands of shame at the Bay of Pigs. Failures mark the slow death of freedom in Laos. Failures infest the jungles of Vietnam. And failures haunt the houses of our once great alliances and undermine the greatest bulwark ever erected by free nations—the NATO community. Failures proclaim lost leadership, obscure purpose, weakening wills, and the risk of inciting our sworn enemies to new aggressions and to new excesses. Because of this administration we are tonight a world divided—we are a Nation becalmed. We have lost the brisk pace of diversity and the genius of individual creativity. We are plodding at a pace set by centralized planning, red tape, rules without responsibility, and regimentation without recourse.

Rather than useful jobs in our country, people have been offered bureaucratic "make work," rather than moral leadership, they have been given bread and circuses, spectacles, and, yes, they have even been given scandals. Tonight there is violence in our streets, corruption in our highest offices, aimlessness among our youth, anxiety among our elders and there is a virtual despair among the many who look beyond material success for the inner meaning of their lives. Where examples of morality should be set, the opposite is seen. Small men, seeking great wealth or power, have too often and too long turned even the highest levels of public service into mere personal opportunity.

Now, certainly, simple honesty is not too much to demand of men in government. We find it in most. Republicans demand it from everyone. They demand it from everyone no matter how exalted or protected his position might be. The growing menace in our country tonight, to personal safety, to life, to limb and property, in homes, in churches, on the playgrounds, and places of business, particularly in our great cities, is the mounting concern, or should be, of every thoughtful citizen in the United States.

Security from domestic violence, no less than from foreign aggression, is the most elementary and fundamental purpose of any government, and a government that cannot fulfill that purpose is one that cannot long command the loyalty of its citizens. History shows us— demonstrates that nothing—nothing prepares the way for tyranny more than the failure of public officials to keep the streets from bullies and marauders.

Now, we Republicans see all this as more, much more, than the rest: of mere political differences or mere political mistakes. We see this as the result of a fundamentally and absolutely wrong view of man, his nature and his destiny. Those who seek to live your lives for you, to take your liberties in return for relieving you of yours, those who elevate the state and downgrade the citizen must see ultimately a world in which earthly power can be substituted for divine will, and this Nation was founded upon the rejection of that notion and upon the acceptance of God as the author of freedom.

Those who seek absolute power, even though they seek it to do what they regard as good, are simply demanding the right to enforce their own version of heaven on earth. And let me remind you, they are the very ones who always create the most hellish tyrannies. Absolute power does corrupt, and those who seek it must be suspect and must be opposed. Their mistaken course stems from false notions of equality, ladies and gentlemen. Equality, rightly understood, as our founding fathers understood it, leads to liberty and to the emancipation of creative differences. Wrongly understood, as it has been so tragically in our time, it leads first to conformity and then to despotism.

Fellow Republicans, it is the cause of Republicanism to resist concentrations of power, private or public, which enforce such conformity and inflict such despotism. It is the cause of Republicanism to ensure that power remains in the hands of the people. And, so help us God, that is exactly what a Republican president will do with the help of a Republican Congress. It is further the cause of Republicanism to restore a clear understanding of the tyranny of man over man in the world at large. It is our cause to dispel the foggy thinking which avoids hard decisions in the illusion that a world of conflict will somehow mysteriously resolve itself into a world of harmony, if we just don't rock the boat or irritate the forces of aggression—and this is hogwash.

It is further the cause of Republicanism to remind ourselves, and the world, that only the strong can remain free, that only the strong can keep the peace.

Now, I needn't remind you, or my fellow Americans regardless of party, that Republicans have shouldered this hard responsibility and marched in this cause before. It was Republican leadership under Dwight Eisenhower that kept the peace, and passed along to this administration the mightiest arsenal for defense the world has ever known. And I needn't remind you that it was the strength and the unbelievable will of the Eisenhower years that kept the peace by using our strength, by using it in the Formosa Straits and in Lebanon and by showing it courageously at all times.

It was during those Republican years that the thrust of Communist imperialism was blunted. It was during those years of Republican leadership that this world moved closer, not to war, but closer to peace, than at any other time in the three decades just passed.

And I needn't remind you—but I will—that it's been during Democratic years that our strength to deter war has stood still, and even gone into a planned decline. It has been during Democratic years that we have weakly stumbled into conflict, timidly refusing to draw our own lines against aggression, deceitfully refusing to tell even our people of our full participation, and tragically, letting our finest men die on battlefields (unmarked by purpose, unmarked by pride or the prospect of victory).

Yesterday it was Korea. Tonight it is Vietnam. Make no bones of this. Don't try to sweep this under the rug. We are at war in Vietnam. And yet the President, who is Commander-in-Chief of our forces, refuses to say—refuses to say, mind you, whether or not the objective over there is victory. And his Secretary of Defense continues to mislead and misinform the American people, and enough of it has gone by.

And I needn't remind you, but I will; it has been during Democratic years that a billion persons were cast into Communist captivity and their fate cynically sealed.

Today in our beloved country we have an administration which seems eager to deal with communism in every coin known—from gold to wheat, from consulates to confidence, and even human freedom itself.

The Republican cause demands that we brand communism as a principal disturber of peace in the world today. Indeed, we should brand it as the only significant disturber of the peace, and we must make clear that until its goals of conquest are absolutely renounced and its rejections with all nations tempered, communism and the governments it now controls are enemies of every man on earth who is or wants to be free.

We here in America can keep the peace only if we remain vigilant and only if we remain strong. Only if we keep our eyes open and keep our guard up can we prevent war. And I want to make this abundantly clear—I don't intend to let peace or freedom be torn from our grasp because of lack of strength or lack of will—and that I promise you Americans.

I believe that we must look beyond the defense of freedom today to its extension tomorrow. I believe that the communism which boasts it will bury us will, instead, give way to the forces of freedom. And I can see in the distant and yet recognizable future the outlines of a world worthy our dedication, our every risk, our every effort, our every sacrifice along the way. Yes, a world that will redeem the suffering of those who will be liberated from tyranny. I can see and I suggest that all thoughtful men must contemplate the flowering of an Atlantic civilization, the whole world of Europe unified and free, trading openly across its borders, communicating openly across the world. This is a goal far, far more meaningful than a moon shot.

It's a truly inspiring goal for all free men to set for themselves during the latter half of the twentieth century. I can also see—and all free men must thrill to—the events of this Atlantic civilization joined by its great ocean highway to the United States. What a destiny, what a destiny can be ours to stand as a great central pillar linking Europe, the Americans and the venerable and vital peoples and cultures of the Pacific. I can see a day when all the Americas, North and South, will be linked in a mighty system, a system in which the errors and misunderstandings of the past will be submerged one by one in a rising tide of prosperity and interdependence. We know that the misunderstandings of centuries are not to be wiped away in a day or wiped away in an hour. But we pledge—we pledge that human sympathy—what our neighbors to the South call that attitude of "simpatico"—no less than enlightened self-interest will be our guide.

I can see this Atlantic civilization galvanizing and guiding emergent nations everywhere.

I know this freedom is not the fruit of every soil. I know that our own freedom was achieved through centuries, by unremitting efforts by brave and wise men. I know that the road to freedom is a long and a challenging road. I know also that some men may walk away from it, that some men resist challenge, accepting the false security of governmental paternalism.

And I pledge that the America I envision in the years ahead will extend its hand in health, in teaching and in cultivation, so that all new nations will be at least encouraged to go our way, so that they will not wander down the dark alleys of tyranny or to the dead-end streets of collectivism. My fellow Republicans, we do no man a service by hiding freedom's light under a bushel of mistaken humility.

I seek an American proud of its past, proud of its ways, proud of its dreams, and determined actively to proclaim them. But our example to the world must, like charity, begin at home.

In our vision of a good and decent future, free and peaceful, there must be room for deliberation of the energy and talent of the individual—otherwise our vision is blind at the outset.

We must assure a society here which, while never abandoning the needy or forsaking the helpless, nurtures incentives and opportunity for the creative and the productive. We must know the whole good is the product of many single contributions.

I cherish a day when our children once again will restore as heroes the sort of men and women who—unafraid and undaunted—pursue the truth, strive to cure disease, subdue and make fruitful our natural environment and produce the inventive engines of production, science, and technology.

This Nation, whose creative people have enhanced this entire span of history, should again thrive upon the greatness of all those things which we, as individual citizens, can and should do. During Republican years, this again will be a nation of men and women, of families proud of their role, jealous of their responsibilities,

unlimited in their aspirations—a Nation where all who can will be self-reliant.

We Republicans see in our constitutional form of government the great framework which assures the orderly but dynamic fulfillment of the whole man, and we see the whole man as the great reason for instituting orderly government in the first place.

We see, in private property and in economy based upon and fostering private property, the one way to make government a durable ally of the whole man, rather than his determined enemy. We see in the sanctity of private property the only durable foundation for constitutional government in a free society. And beyond that, we see, in cherished diversity of ways, diversity of thoughts, of motives and accomplishments. We do not seek to lead anyone's life for him—we seek only to secure his rights and to guarantee him opportunity to strive, with government performing only those needed and constitutionally sanctioned tasks which cannot otherwise be performed.

We Republicans seek a government that attends to its inherent responsibilities of maintaining a stable monetary and fiscal climate, encouraging a free and a competitive economy and enforcing law and order. Thus do we seek inventiveness, diversity, and creativity within a stable order, for we Republicans define government's role where needed at many, many levels, preferably through the one closest to the people involved.

Our towns and our cities, then our counties, then our states, then our regional contacts—and only then, the national government. That, let me remind you, is the ladder of liberty, built by decentralized power. On it also we must have balance between the branches of government at every level.

Balance, diversity, creativity—these are the elements of Republican equation. Republicans agree, Republicans agree heartily to disagree on many, many of their applications, but we have never disagreed on the basic fundamental issues of why you and I are Republicans. This is a party, this Republican Party, a Party for free men, not for blind followers, and not for conformists.

Back in 1858 Abraham Lincoln said this of the Republican party—and I quote him, because he probably could have said it during the last week or so: "It was composed of strained, discordant, and even hostile elements" in 1858. Yet all of these elements agreed on one paramount objective: To arrest the progress of slavery, and place it in the course of ultimate extinction.

Today, as then, but more urgently and more broadly than then, the task of preserving and enlarging freedom at home and safeguarding it from the forces of tyranny abroad is great enough to challenge all our resources and to require all our strength. Anyone who joins us in all sincerity, we welcome. Those who do not care for our cause, we don't expect to enter our ranks in any case. And let our Republicanism, so focused and so dedicated, not be made fuzzy and futile by unthinking and stupid labels.

I would remind you that extremism in the defense of liberty is no vice. And let me remind you also that moderation in the pursuit of justice is no virtue.

The beauty of the very system we Republicans are pledged to restore and revitalize, the beauty of this Federal system of ours is in its reconciliation of diversity with unity. We must not see malice in honest differences of opinion, and no matter how great, so long as they are not inconsistent with the pledges we have given to each other in and through our Constitution. Our Republican cause is not to level out the world or make its people conform in computer regimented sameness. Our Republican cause is to free our people and light the way for liberty throughout the world.

Ours is a very human cause for very humane goals.

This Party, its good people, and its unquestionable devotion to freedom, will not fulfill the purposes of this campaign which we launch here now until our cause has won the day, inspired the world, and shown the way to a tomorrow worthy of all our yesteryears.

I repeat, I accept your nomination with humbleness, with pride, and you and I are going to fight for the goodness of our land. Thank you.

Document Analysis

Senator Goldwater begins his acceptance speech at the Republican National Convention by thanking the leaders of the Republican Party who are present and have given him their support. He also makes a brief call for unity, important since his nomination was divisive for the Republican Party, which should be, from that point, "united and determined." He wastes no time laying out the two principal points that shape his candidacy: The nation has deviated from its sacred purpose; it was not destined to "stagnate in the swampland of collectivism, not to cringe before the bully of communism." These two themes, the exchange of individual freedom for a big-government welfare state and the weakness of the Democratic administration in the face of aggressive Communism, thread through this speech.

Goldwater defines freedom as a uniquely American tradition that its citizens must pursue "in our own hearts and in our own homes." He slams the Kennedy and Johnson administrations for their failures, accusing them of "lost leadership, obscure purpose, weakening wills." The Berlin Wall and the disintegrating situation in Southeast Asia are both evidence of the weakness of the administration, he says. The passivity of the United States encourages the Communists to be ever more aggressive, and under the Democratic administration, "our strength to deter war has stood still, and even gone into a planned decline."

Rather than seeing progressive social reforms as a service to the people, Goldwater warns that they are the opposite. Government programs "elevate the state and downgrade the citizen," robbing them of the freedom to act and their will to succeed. The nation has lost its momentum and will, and is bogged down in "centralized planning (and) red tape." Goldwater believes the government must be decentralized. He articulates his vision of the proper order as "towns and our cities, then our counties, then our states, then our regional contacts—and only then, the national government." He answers the charge that his positions are extreme with the famous line, "Extremism in the defense of liberty is no vice."

Essential Themes

Despite being a clear and sweeping victory for President Johnson, the election of 1964 is considered a watershed moment in American political history. Goldwater garnered 38 percent of the popular vote to Johnson's 61, with Goldwater carrying only the southern states of Alabama, Georgia, Louisiana, Mississippi, and South Carolina, as well as his home state of Arizona. This shift in the southern states is one legacy of the election, as these states had been solidly Democratic since the Civil War. Largely because of the role the federal government played in the civil rights movement, they switched to a Republican candidate. In addition, Goldwater's conservatism pushed the Republican Party further to the right and marginalized its moderate leaders. Furthermore, the election of 1964 proved that conservatives could muster a committed, grassroots base. The campaign itself utilized slick negative television spots and candidates who were unapologetically at opposite ends of the political spectrum and willing to accuse each other of destroying the American way of life. Johnson accused Goldwater of being willing to start a nuclear war, and Goldwater accusing Johnson of moving the United States toward totalitarianism.

Actor Ronald Reagan gave a nationally televised speech in support of Goldwater before the 1964 election, and Reagan, the future governor of California and president of the United States, continued Goldwater's conservative legacy in his own political career. Many Republican leaders since then have identified Goldwater's conservatism as expressed in *The Conscience of a Conservative* as formative to their own development.

—*Bethany Groff Dorau, MA*

Bibliography and Additional Reading

Brennan, Mary. *Turning Right in the Sixties: The Conservative Capture of the GOP*. Chapel Hill: U of North Carolina P, 1995. Print.

Goldberg, Robert Alan. *Barry Goldwater*. New Haven: Yale UP, 1995. Print.

Middendorf, John William. *A Glorious Disaster: Barry Goldwater's Presidential Campaign and the Origins of the Conservative Movement*. New York: Basic, 2006. Print.

Skipper, John C. *The 1964 Republican Convention: Barry Goldwater and the Beginning of the Conservative Movement*. Jefferson: McFarland, 2016. Print.

■ Ronald Reagan's "A Time for Choosing" Speech

Date: October 27, 1964
Author: Ronald Reagan
Genre: Speech

Summary Overview

In the month before the 1964 U.S. presidential election between Democratic incumbent Lyndon B. Johnson and Republican challenger Barry Goldwater, Ronald Reagan, a popular actor, delivered a speech supporting Goldwater that encapsulated the vision of a libertarian Republican government. Reagan gave the speech several times, but a televised presentation at the bequest of Republican donors brought widespread attention and proved highly influential. Though the speech did not ultimately help Goldwater win the election, it propelled Reagan's own political career and gave him the national stature that would lead him to the California governorship and eventually the presidency. Many scholars trace the beginnings of anti-big government Republican ideology to the Goldwater campaign and Reagan's speech.

Defining Moment

Ronald Reagan's speech in support of Arizona senator Barry Goldwater's 1964 presidential campaign came at a difficult time for the Republican Party. The 1963 assassination of popular Democratic president John F. Kennedy was still fresh in the nation's consciousness, and Kennedy's vice president and successor, Lyndon B. Johnson, built on that popularity by promising to continue to push for progress in areas ranging from space exploration to civil rights. While Democrats were unified behind Johnson, Republicans faced an ideological split between more moderate politicians, such as New York governor Nelson Rockefeller and conservative ideologues led by Goldwater.

As the election season progressed, the Johnson administration worked to start the implementation of a large-scale expansion of the role of the federal government in American life, known as the Great Society. Johnson, even more so than Kennedy, saw the federal government as the main solution to the social ills present in American society. His experience as Senate majority leader had given him the skills and personal connections to get legislation passed through Congress rapidly. By identifying himself as a politically effective moderate and harnessing the generally popularity of his party, Johnson generated widespread support. Even the growing unrest regarding U.S. military involvement in Vietnam did not weaken his campaign.

While Johnson portrayed himself as the one to continue the Kennedy legacy, Goldwater's propensity for iconoclastic statements and lack of support from the Republican establishment allowed Democrats to paint him as an extremist and a warmonger. This strategy was seen in a famous television commercial by the Johnson campaign in which a child picking petals off a daisy morphs into a countdown to a nuclear detonation, critiquing Goldwater's support for using nuclear weapons. Coming at the height of the Cold War, when the United States and Soviet Union had narrowly avoided a nuclear war over the Soviets' deployment of missiles in Cuba only two years before, this argument proved particularly effective. It also demonstrated the importance of the media, especially television, to the political landscape.

But while the country largely supported Johnson's continuation of Kennedy's policies, well-known actor Ronald Reagan—a longtime Democrat—was becoming more conservative. He had spent most of the 1950s as a spokesman for the General Electric, giving pro-business speeches and honing anti-big government ideas that fit well with Goldwater's political rhetoric.

Author Biography

Ronald Wilson Reagan was born on February 6, 1911, in Illinois. A successful athlete in school, he found a career as an actor and appeared in many films during the 1930s and 1940s. During this time he was an active supporter of Democratic president Franklin D. Roosevelt's New Deal policies. Like many others during the 1940s Reagan was an outspoken opponent of Communism. As a secret FBI informant he passed on information about

Hollywood figures suspected of being Communist sympathizers. In 1947, Reagan's own political life began to take shape when he became president of the Screen Actors Guild and testified before the House Committee on Un-American Activities about the presence of Communists throughout the motion picture industry.

Reagan's political views moved to the right during the 1950s, and by 1962, he had become a Republican. His speech in support of Barry Goldwater's 1964 presidential campaign launched him into the political spotlight, and he was elected governor of California in 1966. In 1980,

he won the Republican nomination for president after two earlier failed bids and defeated Democrat Jimmy Carter in the general election. His two terms as president were marked by a strong national shift toward conservative policies that would become Republican mainstays for years to come, including tax cuts and deregulation. His foreign policy focused on military spending and opposing the Soviet Union, which he dubbed the "evil empire." After leaving the White House, Reagan revealed in 1994 that he had Alzheimer's disease. He died in 2004.

HISTORICAL DOCUMENT

Thank you. Thank you very much. Thank you and good evening. The sponsor has been identified, but unlike most television programs, the performer hasn't been provided with a script. As a matter of fact, I have been permitted to choose my own words and discuss my own ideas regarding the choice that we face in the next few weeks.

I have spent most of my life as a Democrat. I recently have seen fit to follow another course. I believe that the issues confronting us cross party lines. Now, one side in this campaign has been telling us that the issues of this election are the maintenance of peace and prosperity. The line has been used, "We've never had it so good."

But I have an uncomfortable feeling that this prosperity isn't something on which we can base our hopes for the future. No nation in history has ever survived a tax burden that reached a third of its national income. Today, 37 cents out of every dollar earned in this country is the tax collector's share, and yet our government continues to spend 17 million dollars a day more than the government takes in. We haven't balanced our budget 28 out of the last 34 years. We've raised our debt limit three times in the last twelve months, and now our national debt is one and a half times bigger than all the combined debts of all the nations of the world. We have 15 billion dollars in gold in our treasury; we don't own an ounce. Foreign dollar claims are 27.3 billion dollars. And we've just had announced that the dollar of 1939 will now purchase 45 cents in its total value.

As for the peace that we would preserve, I wonder who among us would like to approach the wife or mother

whose husband or son has died in South Vietnam and ask them if they think this is a peace that should be maintained indefinitely. Do they mean peace, or do they mean we just want to be left in peace? There can be no real peace while one American is dying some place in the world for the rest of us. We're at war with the most dangerous enemy that has ever faced mankind in his long climb from the swamp to the stars, and it's been said if we lose that war, and in so doing lose this way of freedom of ours, history will record with the greatest astonishment that those who had the most to lose did the least to prevent its happening. Well I think it's time we ask ourselves if we still know the freedoms that were intended for us by the Founding Fathers.

Not too long ago, two friends of mine were talking to a Cuban refugee, a businessman who had escaped from Castro, and in the midst of his story one of my friends turned to the other and said, "We don't know how lucky we are." And the Cuban stopped and said, "How lucky you are? I had someplace to escape to." And in that sentence he told us the entire story. If we lose freedom here, there's no place to escape to. This is the last stand on earth.

And this idea that government is beholden to the people, that it has no other source of power except the sovereign people, is still the newest and the most unique idea in all the long history of man's relation to man. This is the issue of this election: Whether we believe in our capacity for self-government or whether we abandon the American revolution and confess that a little intellectual elite in a far-distant capitol can plan our lives for us better than we can plan them ourselves.

You and I are told increasingly we have to choose between a left or right. Well I'd like to suggest there is no such thing as a left or right. There's only an up or down. Up to man's age-old dream, the ultimate in individual freedom consistent with law and order, or down to the ant heap of totalitarianism. And regardless of their sincerity, their humanitarian motives, those who would trade our freedom for security have embarked on this downward course.

In this vote-harvesting time, they use terms like the "Great Society," or as we were told a few days ago by the President, we must accept a greater government activity in the affairs of the people. But they've been a little more explicit in the past and among themselves; and all of the things I now will quote have appeared in print. These are not Republican accusations. For example, they have voices that say, "The cold war will end through our acceptance of a not undemocratic socialism." Another voice says, "The profit motive has become outmoded. It must be replaced by the incentives of the welfare state." Or, "Our traditional system of individual freedom is incapable of solving the complex problems of the twentieth century." Senator Fullbright has said at Stanford University that the Constitution is outmoded. He referred to the President as "our moral teacher and our leader," and he says he is "hobbled in his task by the restrictions of power imposed on him by this antiquated document." He must "be freed," so that he "can do for us" what he knows "is best." And Senator Clark of Pennsylvania, another articulate spokesman, defines liberalism as "meeting the material needs of the masses through the full power of centralized government."

Well, I, for one, resent it when a representative of the people refers to you and me, the free men and women of this country, as "the masses." This is a term we haven't applied to ourselves in America. But beyond that, "the full power of centralized government"—this was the very thing the Founding Fathers sought to minimize. They knew that governments don't control things. A government can't control the economy without controlling people. And they know when a government sets out to do that, it must use force and coercion to achieve its purpose. They also knew, those Founding Fathers, that outside of its legitimate functions, government does noth-

ing as well or as economically as the private sector of the economy.

Now, we have no better example of this than government's involvement in the farm economy over the last 30 years. Since 1955, the cost of this program has nearly doubled. One-fourth of farming in America is responsible for 85 percent of the farm surplus. Three-fourths of farming is out on the free market and has known a 21 percent increase in the per capita consumption of all its produce. You see, that one-fourth of farming that's regulated and controlled by the federal government. In the last three years we've spent 43 dollars in the feed grain program for every dollar bushel of corn we don't grow.

Senator Humphrey last week charged that Barry Goldwater, as President, would seek to eliminate farmers. He should do his homework a little better, because he'll find out that we've had a decline of 5 million in the farm population under these government programs. He'll also find that the Democratic administration has sought to get from Congress [an] extension of the farm program to include that three-fourths that is now free. He'll find that they've also asked for the right to imprison farmers who wouldn't keep books as prescribed by the federal government. The Secretary of Agriculture asked for the right to seize farms through condemnation and resell them to other individuals. And contained in that same program was a provision that would have allowed the federal government to remove 2 million farmers from the soil.

At the same time, there's been an increase in the Department of Agriculture employees. There's now one for every 30 farms in the United States, and still they can't tell us how 66 shiploads of grain headed for Austria disappeared without a trace and Billie Sol Estes never left shore.

Every responsible farmer and farm organization has repeatedly asked the government to free the farm economy, but how who are farmers to know what's best for them? The wheat farmers voted against a wheat program. The government passed it anyway. Now the price of bread goes up; the price of wheat to the farmer goes down.

Meanwhile, back in the city, under urban renewal the assault on freedom carries on. Private property rights [are] so diluted that public interest is almost anything a few government planners decide it should be. In a program that takes from the needy and gives to the greedy, we see such spectacles as in Cleveland, Ohio, a million-and-a-half-dollar building completed only three years ago must be destroyed to make way for what government officials call a "more compatible use of the land." The President tells us he's now going to start building public housing units in the thousands, where heretofore we've only built them in the hundreds. But FHA [Federal Housing Authority] and the Veterans Administration tell us they have 120,000 housing units they've taken back through mortgage foreclosure. For three decades, we've sought to solve the problems of unemployment through government planning, and the more the plans fail, the more the planners plan. The latest is the Area Redevelopment Agency.

They've just declared Rice County, Kansas, a depressed area. Rice County, Kansas, has two hundred oil wells, and the 14,000 people there have over 30 million dollars on deposit in personal savings in their banks. And when the government tells you you're depressed, lie down and be depressed.

We have so many people who can't see a fat man standing beside a thin one without coming to the conclusion the fat man got that way by taking advantage of the thin one. So they're going to solve all the problems of human misery through government and government planning. Well, now, if government planning and welfare had the answer—and they've had almost 30 years of it—shouldn't we expect government to read the score to us once in a while? Shouldn't they be telling us about the decline each year in the number of people needing help? The reduction in the need for public housing?

But the reverse is true. Each year the need grows greater; the program grows greater. We were told four years ago that 17 million people went to bed hungry each night. Well that was probably true. They were all on a diet. But now we're told that 9.3 million families in this country are poverty-stricken on the basis of earning less than 3,000 dollars a year. Welfare spending [is] 10 times greater than in the dark depths of the Depression. We're spending 45 billion dollars on welfare. Now do a little arithmetic, and you'll find that if we divided the 45 billion dollars up equally among those 9 million poor families, we'd be able to give each family 4,600 dollars a year. And this added to their present income should eliminate poverty. Direct aid to the poor, however, is only running only about 600 dollars per family. It would seem that someplace there must be some overhead.

So now we declare "war on poverty," or "You, too, can be a Bobby Baker." Now do they honestly expect us to believe that if we add 1 billion dollars to the 45 billion we're spending, one more program to the 30-odd we have—and remember, this new program doesn't replace any, it just duplicates existing programs—do they believe that poverty is suddenly going to disappear by magic? Well, in all fairness I should explain there is one part of the new program that isn't duplicated. This is the youth feature. We're now going to solve the dropout problem, juvenile delinquency, by reinstituting something like the old CCC camps [Civilian Conservation Corps], and we're going to put our young people in these camps. But again we do some arithmetic, and we find that we're going to spend each year just on room and board for each young person we help 4,700 dollars a year. We can send them to Harvard for 2,700! Course, don't get me wrong. I'm not suggesting Harvard is the answer to juvenile delinquency.

But seriously, what are we doing to those we seek to help? Not too long ago, a judge called me here in Los Angeles. He told me of a young woman who'd come before him for a divorce. She had six children, was pregnant with her seventh. Under his questioning, she revealed her husband was a laborer earning 250 dollars a month. She wanted a divorce to get an 80 dollar raise. She's eligible for 330 dollars a month in the Aid to Dependent Children Program. She got the idea from two women in her neighborhood who'd already done that very thing.

Yet anytime you and I question the schemes of the do-gooders, we're denounced as being against their humanitarian goals. They say we're always "against" things—we're never "for" anything. Well, the trouble with our liberal friends is not that they're ignorant; it's just that they know so much that isn't so.

Now we're for a provision that destitution should not follow unemployment by reason of old age, and to that end we've accepted Social Security as a step toward meeting the problem.

But we're against those entrusted with this program when they practice deception regarding its fiscal shortcomings, when they charge that any criticism of the program means that we want to end payments to those people who depend on them for a livelihood. They've called it "insurance" to us in a hundred million pieces of literature. But then they appeared before the Supreme Court and they testified it was a welfare program. They only use the term "insurance" to sell it to the people. And they said Social Security dues are a tax for the general use of the government, and the government has used that tax. There is no fund, because Robert Byers, the actuarial head, appeared before a congressional committee and admitted that Social Security as of this moment is 298 billion dollars in the hole. But he said there should be no cause for worry because as long as they have the power to tax, they could always take away from the people whatever they needed to bail them out of trouble. And they're doing just that.

A young man, 21 years of age, working at an average salary—his Social Security contribution would, in the open market, buy him an insurance policy that would guarantee 220 dollars a month at age 65. The government promises 127. He could live it up until he's 31 and then take out a policy that would pay more than Social Security. Now are we so lacking in business sense that we can't put this program on a sound basis, so that people who do require those payments will find they can get them when they're due that the cupboard isn't bare?

Barry Goldwater thinks we can.

At the same time, can't we introduce voluntary features that would permit a citizen who can do better on his own to be excused upon presentation of evidence that he had made provision for the non-earning years? Should we not allow a widow with children to work, and not lose the benefits supposedly paid for by her deceased husband? Shouldn't you and I be allowed to declare who our beneficiaries will be under this program, which we cannot do? I think we're for telling our senior citizens that no one in this country should be denied medical care because of a lack of funds. But I think we're against forcing all citizens, regardless of need, into a compulsory government program, especially when we have such examples, as was announced last week, when France admitted that their Medicare program is now bankrupt. They've come to the end of the road.

In addition, was Barry Goldwater so irresponsible when he suggested that our government give up its program of deliberate, planned inflation, so that when you do get your Social Security pension, a dollar will buy a dollar's worth, and not 45 cents worth?

I think we're for an international organization, where the nations of the world can seek peace. But I think we're against subordinating American interests to an organization that has become so structurally unsound that today you can muster a two-thirds vote on the floor of the General Assembly among nations that represent less than 10 percent of the world's population. I think we're against the hypocrisy of assailing our allies because here and there they cling to a colony, while we engage in a conspiracy of silence and never open our mouths about the millions of people enslaved in the Soviet colonies in the satellite nations.

I think we're for aiding our allies by sharing of our material blessings with those nations which share in our fundamental beliefs, but we're against doling out money government to government, creating bureaucracy, if not socialism, all over the world. We set out to help 19 countries. We're helping 107. We've spent 146 billion dollars. With that money, we bought a 2 million dollar yacht for Haile Selassie. We bought dress suits for Greek undertakers, extra wives for Kenya[n] government officials. We bought a thousand TV sets for a place where they have no electricity. In the last six years, 52 nations have bought 7 billion dollars worth of our gold, and all 52 are receiving foreign aid from this country.

No government ever voluntarily reduces itself in size. So governments' programs, once launched, never disappear.

Actually, a government bureau is the nearest thing to eternal life we'll ever see on this earth.

Federal employees—federal employees number two and a half million; and federal, state, and local, one out of six of the nation's work force employed by government. These proliferating bureaus with their thousands of regulations have cost us many of our constitutional safeguards. How many of us realize that today federal agents can invade a man's property without a warrant? They can impose a fine without a formal hearing, let alone a trial by jury? And they can seize and sell his property at auction to enforce the payment of that fine. In Chico County, Arkansas, James Wier over-planted his rice allotment.

The government obtained a 17,000 dollar judgment. And a U.S. marshal sold his 960-acre farm at auction. The government said it was necessary as a warning to others to make the system work.

Last February 19th at the University of Minnesota, Norman Thomas, six-times candidate for President on the Socialist Party ticket, said, "If Barry Goldwater became President, he would stop the advance of socialism in the United States." I think that's exactly what he will do.

But as a former Democrat, I can tell you Norman Thomas isn't the only man who has drawn this parallel to socialism with the present administration, because back in 1936, Mr. Democrat himself, Al Smith, the great American, came before the American people and charged that the leadership of his Party was taking the Party of Jefferson, Jackson, and Cleveland down the road under the banners of Marx, Lenin, and Stalin. And he walked away from his Party, and he never returned 'til the day he died—because to this day, the leadership of that Party has been taking that Party, that honorable Party, down the road in the image of the labor Socialist Party of England.

Now it doesn't require expropriation or confiscation of private property or business to impose socialism on a people. What does it mean whether you hold the deed to or the title to your business or property if the government holds the power of life and death over that business or property? And such machinery already exists. The government can find some charge to bring against any concern it chooses to prosecute. Every businessman has his own tale of harassment. Somewhere a perversion has taken place. Our natural, unalienable rights are now considered to be a dispensation of government, and freedom has never been so fragile, so close to slipping from our grasp as it is at this moment.

Our Democratic opponents seem unwilling to debate these issues. They want to make you and I believe that this is a contest between two men—that we're to choose just between two personalities.

Well what of this man that they would destroy—and in destroying, they would destroy that which he represents, the ideas that you and I hold dear? Is he the brash and shallow and trigger-happy man they say he is? Well I've been privileged to know him "when." I knew him

long before he ever dreamed of trying for high office, and I can tell you personally I've never known a man in my life I believed so incapable of doing a dishonest or dishonorable thing.

This is a man who, in his own business before he entered politics, instituted a profit-sharing plan before unions had ever thought of it. He put in health and medical insurance for all his employees. He took 50 percent of the profits before taxes and set up a retirement program, a pension plan for all his employees. He sent monthly checks for life to an employee who was ill and couldn't work. He provides nursing care for the children of mothers who work in the stores. When Mexico was ravaged by the floods in the Rio Grande, he climbed in his airplane and flew medicine and supplies down there.

An ex-GI told me how he met him. It was the week before Christmas during the Korean War, and he was at the Los Angeles airport trying to get a ride home to Arizona for Christmas. And he said that [there were] a lot of servicemen there and no seats available on the planes. And then a voice came over the loudspeaker and said, "Any men in uniform wanting a ride to Arizona, go to runway such-and-such," and they went down there, and there was a fellow named Barry Goldwater sitting in his plane. Every day in those weeks before Christmas, all day long, he'd load up the plane, fly it to Arizona, fly them to their homes, fly back over to get another load.

During the hectic split-second timing of a campaign, this is a man who took time out to sit beside an old friend who was dying of cancer. His campaign managers were understandably impatient, but he said, "There aren't many left who care what happens to her. I'd like her to know I care." This is a man who said to his 19-year-old son, "There is no foundation like the rock of honesty and fairness, and when you begin to build your life on that rock, with the cement of the faith in God that you have, then you have a real start." This is not a man who could carelessly send other people's sons to war. And that is the issue of this campaign that makes all the other problems I've discussed academic, unless we realize we're in a war that must be won.

Those who would trade our freedom for the soup kitchen of the welfare state have told us they have a utopian solution of peace without victory. They call their policy "accommodation." And they say if we'll only avoid any direct confrontation with the enemy, he'll forget his evil ways and learn to love us. All who oppose them are indicted as warmongers. They say we offer simple answers to complex problems. Well, perhaps there is a simple answer—not an easy answer, but simple—If you and I have the courage to tell our elected officials that we want our national policy based on what we know in our hearts is morally right.

We cannot buy our security, our freedom from the threat of the bomb by committing an immorality so great as saying to a billion human beings now enslaved behind the Iron Curtain, "Give up your dreams of freedom because to save our own skins, we're willing to make a deal with your slave masters." Alexander Hamilton said, "A nation which can prefer disgrace to danger is prepared for a master, and deserves one." Now let's set the record straight. There's no argument over the choice between peace and war, but there's only one guaranteed way you can have peace—and you can have it in the next—second surrender.

Admittedly, there's a risk in any course we follow other than this, but every lesson of history tells us that the greater risk lies in appeasement, and this is the specter our well-meaning liberal friends refuse to face that their policy of accommodation is appeasement, and it gives no choice between peace and war, only between fight or surrender. If we continue to accommodate, continue to back and retreat, eventually we have to face the final demand the ultimatum. And what then—when Nikita Khrushchev has told his people he knows what our answer will be? He has told them that we're retreating under the pressure of the Cold War, and someday when the time comes to deliver the final ultimatum, our surrender will be voluntary, because by that time we will have been weakened from within spiritually, morally, and economically. He believes this because from our side he's

heard voices pleading for "peace at any price" or "better Red than dead," or as one commentator put it, he'd rather "live on his knees than die on his feet." And therein lies the road to war, because those voices don't speak for the rest of us.

You and I know and do not believe that life is so dear and peace so sweet as to be purchased at the price of chains and slavery. If nothing in life is worth dying for, when did this begin just in the face of this enemy? Or should Moses have told the children of Israel to live in slavery under the pharaohs? Should Christ have refused the cross? Should the patriots at Concord Bridge have thrown down their guns and refused to fire the shot heard 'round the world? The martyrs of history were not fools, and our honored dead who gave their lives to stop the advance of the Nazis didn't die in vain. Where, then, is the road to peace? Well it's a simple answer after all.

You and I have the courage to say to our enemies, "There is a price we will not pay." "There is a point beyond which they must not advance." And this, this is the meaning in the phrase of Barry Goldwater's "peace through strength." Winston Churchill said, "The destiny of man is not measured by material computations. When great forces are on the move in the world, we learn we're spirits, not animals." And he said, "There's something going on in time and space, and beyond time and space, which, whether we like it or not, spells duty."

You and I have a rendezvous with destiny.

We'll preserve for our children this, the last best hope of man on earth, or we'll sentence them to take the last step into a thousand years of darkness.

We will keep in mind and remember that Barry Goldwater has faith in us. He has faith that you and I have the ability and the dignity and the right to make our own decisions and determine our own destiny.

Thank you very much.

Document Analysis

"A Time for Choosing" was crafted for a television audience, and Reagan, a seasoned actor and public speaker, was at home in front of the camera. From the outset, Reagan delivers the libertarian-leaning ideas that were staples of Goldwater's political philosophy, arguing that the expansion of the federal government into the lives of the American people is oppressive and must be stopped. However, his speech, while impassioned, avoids the divisive, extreme language and theoretical slant of Goldwater's own rhetoric in favor of an appeal to American ideals and an emphasis on vivid, easily understandable storytelling. For example, he provides anecdotes portraying Goldwater as a caring, thoughtful person.

The 1964 election, to Reagan, is a referendum on the most basic American concept: individual freedom. Like Goldwater he uses the political establishment, both Republican and Democratic, as his foil, stating that the central issue is "Whether we believe in our capacity for self-government or whether we abandon the American Revolution and confess that a little intellectual elite in a far-distant capitol can plan our lives for us better than we can plan them ourselves." Equating libertarianism with the freedom espoused by the Founding Fathers and big government programs such as Johnson's Great Society with totalitarianism, Reagan again and again drives home the idea that government spending is not the answer to the domestic and foreign challenges facing the country.

Reagan goes on to address individual programs. He expresses limited acceptance of things like foreign aid and Social Security as a safety net for the aged on a moral basis, but argues for greater fiscal constraint and the elimination of waste and bureaucracy. He suggests that whenever possible the free market should hold sway rather than government intervention. He advocates lower taxes and provides statistics regarding economic issues such as the tax burden and federal debt. Again his strong imagery comes into play when describing examples of the welfare state system gone wrong, as in the story of a pregnant woman with six children seeking a divorce in order to qualify for government assistance.

Reagan concludes his speech by further equating big government programs with socialism and warning that the election is America's "rendezvous with destiny," implying that appeasement of Communism will lead to the collapse of the free world. He asserts that he and the majority of the American people believe freedom is worth fighting for and that appeals to peace at all costs are misguided. He uses richly symbolic language alluding to biblical and heroic imagery such as Moses leading resistance against the pharaohs, Christ on the cross, patriots of the American Revolution, and the Allies battle against the Nazis. He takes a dramatic position by claiming that the election will either provide "the last best hope on earth" or be "the last step into a thousand years of darkness."

Essential Themes

Reagan's "A Time for Choosing" speech was effective, but not necessarily in the way that the Republican Party might have hoped. Although his speech succeeded in raising $1 million for the Goldwater's presidential campaign, it did little to help the Republican candidate avoid one of the most lopsided defeats in the history of American presidential elections. Goldwater carried only his home state of Arizona and five states in the Deep South, where Johnson's signing of the Civil Rights Act of 1964 had made him politically toxic to the mostly white vot-

ing base. Goldwater's views were not yet dominant in his own political party and seemed even more extreme to the American electorate, over 60 percent of which voted for Johnson.

However, the speech represented a milestone in the history of American politics for two main reasons. First, it propelled Ronald Reagan to prominence as a national political figure. Two years later, Reagan would run for political office for the first time, winning the California gubernatorial election in a landslide. Then in 1980, Reagan easily won the Republican presidential nomination and, in the context of a faltering economy and international troubles such as the Iranian hostage crisis, defeated incumbent Democrat Jimmy Carter by a wide margin. His two terms would prove one of the most consequential presidencies of the late twentieth century.

Second, while Goldwater's libertarianism was deemed radical in 1964, Reagan's speech was a harbinger of things to come in Republican politics. Republicans increasingly pointed to big, expensive government programs as the reason for economic problems in the late 1970s and beyond. Although Reagan did little as president to curb federal spending, the rhetoric of the Republican Party and its tax policies shifted toward those outlined in "A Time for Choosing." In many ways, what became known as the Reagan Revolution of the 1980s had its roots in the 1964 speech.

—*Steven L. Danver, PhD*

Bibliography and Additional Reading

Brands, H. W. *Reagan: The Life*. New York: Doubleday, 2015. Print.

Johnson, Robert David. *All the Way with LBJ: The 1964 Presidential Election*. New York: Cambridge UP, 2009. Print.

Ritter, Kurt W. "Ronald Reagan and 'The Speech': The Rhetoric of Public Relations Politics." *Western Speech* 32.1 (1968): 50–58. Print.

Reagan, Ronald. *An American Life: The Autobiography*. New York: Simon, 2011. Print.

■ LBJ's Speech Before Congress on Voting Rights

Date: March 15, 1965
Author: Lyndon B. Johnson
Genre: Speech

Summary Overview

By early 1965, substantial gains had been made in the push for equality for all Americans. However, there were many regions of the country where significant roadblocks prevented full equality from being realized. In most Southern states, these roadblocks included efforts to keep African Americans from becoming eligible to vote and, when eligible, from registering to vote or participating in the electoral process. For months, civil rights leaders had been trying to register voters in Alabama. On March 7, 1965, a small group of marchers who supported voting rights left Selma with the aim of walking the 54 miles to the capital, Montgomery. The actions that Alabama law enforcement officials took to turn back the demonstrators were televised nationally, exposing police violence and producing sympathy for the marchers and their cause. The time seemed ripe for the introduction of legislation that would give federal officials the authority to intervene in situations where voting rights were being denied on the basis of race. President Lyndon Johnson appeared before Congress and delivered the speech included here two days before sending the bill to Congress. The speech identifies the president's set of priorities regarding the right to vote.

Defining Moment

African Americans were given their freedom in 1865 (following the Civil War), granted equal rights in 1868 (Fourteenth Amendment), and the right to vote in 1870 (Fifteenth Amendment). However, for many African American citizens these rights and freedoms were only words on paper. After the end of Reconstruction, Southern states slowly made African Americans second-class citizens and instituted a system of racial segregation. The latter was ratified at the national level by the U.S. Supreme Court in its 1896 ruling *Plessy v. Ferguson,* which allowed that the doctrine of "separate but equal" was acceptable. Not all Americans, and particularly not African-Americans, found the practice acceptable. Throughout the first half of the twentieth century, efforts were made to change such laws, especially through legal proceedings. The landmark case *Brown v. Board of Education* (1954) not only invalidated segregated schools but also ruled that the "separate but equal" doctrine was flawed. Emerging from that case were a series of additional civil rights cases as well as the beginnings of efforts to change the system through public demonstrations. The Birmingham Bus Boycott of 1955-56, for example, proved that non-violent demonstrations and pressure tactics could work to draw attention and turn matters around.

From that time forward, demonstrations and community-wide efforts were used to try to obtain equal rights for all people throughout the land. In 1964, the Civil Rights Act became the first major piece of Congressional legislation to advance the cause of broad equality regardless of race. Because voting rights were already covered under the Fifteenth Amendment, consideration of voting rights was dropped from the 1964 law. But as 1965 opened, the strong effort to register African American voters in Selma proved that state laws and local attitudes still hindered the process. A march to the state capital was planned by civil rights leaders to focus on these laws. Yet, the marchers were attacked by state and local police and by mobs wielding rocks. The brutal response pushed many moderates, citizens and lawmakers alike, toward supporting a federal voting rights bill. Senate leaders of the Democratic and Republican Parties joined as co-sponsors in an attempt to overcome a possible filibuster by Southern senators. President Johnson gave a televised address to a joint session of Congress, thus indicating the strength of his commitment to the bill. Johnson's speech, in fact, is regarded by many as one of his best as president. He understood that this was a pivotal moment, and that without the right to vote the broader cause of equal rights generally might not be attained.

Author Biography

Lyndon Baines Johnson (1908-1973) was raised in central Texas, a member of a poor but influential family. He graduated from high school at fifteen but alternated work and college until earning his degree at twenty-two. An influential Congressional aide, he was then elected to and entered the House of Representatives in 1937, the Senate in 1949, and the vice presidency in 1961. He became president when John F. Kennedy was assassinated, serving from 1963 to 1969. Johnson sponsored what is called "The Great Society" legislation, which included anti-poverty measures in addition to civil rights laws. Outside of civil rights, his most influential pieces of legislation included Medicare, Head Start, work-study for students, and the Gulf of Tonkin Resolution, which legitimized America's expanded participation in the Vietnam War. Although willing to use virtually any means to prevail in politics, Johnson also held a basic belief in the equality of all people.

HISTORICAL DOCUMENT

[Note: this transcript contains the published text of the speech, not the actual words spoken. Thus, there may be some differences between the transcript and the audio content.]

Mr. Speaker, Mr. President, Members of the Congress:

I speak tonight for the dignity of man and the destiny of democracy.

I urge every member of both parties, Americans of all religions and of all colors, from every section of this country, to join me in that cause.

At times history and fate meet at a single time in a single place to shape a turning point in man's unending search for freedom. So it was at Lexington and Concord. So it was a century ago at Appomattox. So it was last week in Selma, Alabama.

There, long-suffering men and women peacefully protested the denial of their rights as Americans. Many were brutally assaulted. One good man, a man of God, was killed.

There is no cause for pride in what has happened in Selma. There is no cause for self-satisfaction in the long denial of equal rights of millions of Americans. But there is cause for hope and for faith in our democracy in what is happening here tonight.

For the cries of pain and the hymns and protests of oppressed people have summoned into convocation all the majesty of this great Government—the Government of the greatest Nation on earth.

Our mission is at once the oldest and the most basic of this country: to right wrong, to do justice, to serve man.

In our time we have come to live with moments of great crisis. Our lives have been marked with debate about great issues; issues of war and peace, issues of prosperity and depression. But rarely in any time does an issue lay bare the secret heart of America itself. Rarely are we met with a challenge, not to our growth or abundance, our welfare or our security, but rather to the values and the purposes and the meaning of our beloved Nation.

The issue of equal rights for American Negroes is such an issue. And should we defeat every enemy, should we double our wealth and conquer the stars, and still be unequal to this issue, then we will have failed as a people and as a nation.

For with a country as with a person, "What is a man profited, if he shall gain the whole world, and lose his own soul ?"

There is no Negro problem. There is no Southern problem. There is no Northern problem. There is only an American problem. And we are met here tonight as Americans—not as Democrats or Republicans—we are met here as Americans to solve that problem.

This was the first nation in the history of the world to be founded with a purpose. The great phrases of that purpose still sound in every American heart, North and South: "All men are created equal"—"government by consent of the governed"—"give me liberty or give me death." Well, those are not just clever words, or those are not just empty theories. In their name Americans have fought and died for two centuries, and tonight around the world they stand there as guardians of our liberty, risking their lives.

Those words are a promise to every citizen that he shall share in the dignity of man. This dignity cannot be found in a man's possessions; it cannot be found in his power, or in his position. It really rests on his right to be treated as a man equal in opportunity to all others. It says that he shall share in freedom, he shall choose his leaders, educate his children, and provide for his family according to his ability and his merits as a human being.

To apply any other test—to deny a man his hopes because of his color or race, his religion or the place of his birth—is not only to do injustice, it is to deny America and to dishonor the dead who gave their lives for American freedom.

Our fathers believed that if this noble view of the rights of man was to flourish, it must be rooted in democracy. The most basic right of all was the right to choose your own leaders. The history of this country, in large measure, is the history of the expansion of that right to all of our people.

Many of the issues of civil rights are very complex and most difficult. But about this there can and should be no argument. Every American citizen must have an equal right to vote. There is no reason which can excuse the denial of that right. There is no duty which weighs more heavily on us than the duty we have to ensure that right.

Yet the harsh fact is that in many places in this country men and women are kept from voting simply because they are Negroes.

Every device of which human ingenuity is capable has been used to deny this right. The Negro citizen may go to register only to be told that the day is wrong, or the hour is late, or the official in charge is absent. And if he persists, and if he manages to present himself to the registrar, he may be disqualified because he did not spell out his middle name or because he abbreviated a word on the application.

And if he manages to fill out an application he is given a test. The registrar is the sole judge of whether he passes this test. He may be asked to recite the entire Constitution, or explain the most complex provisions of State law. And even a college degree cannot be used to prove that he can read and write.

For the fact is that the only way to pass these barriers is to show a white skin.

Experience has clearly shown that the existing process of law cannot overcome systematic and ingenious discrimination. No law that we now have on the books—and I have helped to put three of them there—can ensure the right to vote when local officials are determined to deny it.

In such a case our duty must be clear to all of us. The Constitution says that no person shall be kept from voting because of his race or his color. We have all sworn an oath before God to support and to defend that Constitution. We must now act in obedience to that oath.

Wednesday I will send to Congress a law designed to eliminate illegal barriers to the right to vote.

The broad principles of that bill will be in the hands of the Democratic and Republican leaders tomorrow. After they have reviewed it, it will come here formally as a bill. I am grateful for this opportunity to come here tonight at the invitation of the leadership to reason with my friends, to give them my views, and to visit with my former colleagues.

I have had prepared a more comprehensive analysis of the legislation which I had intended to transmit to the clerk tomorrow but which I will submit to the clerks tonight. But I want to really discuss with you now briefly the main proposals of this legislation.

This bill will strike down restrictions to voting in all elections—federal, state, and local—which have been used to deny Negroes the right to vote.

This bill will establish a simple, uniform standard which cannot be used, however ingenious the effort, to flout our Constitution.

It will provide for citizens to be registered by officials of the United States Government if the State officials refuse to register them.

It will eliminate tedious, unnecessary lawsuits which delay the right to vote.

Finally, this legislation will ensure that properly registered individuals are not prohibited from voting.

I will welcome the suggestions from all of the Members of Congress—I have no doubt that I will get some—on ways and means to strengthen this law and to make it effective. But experience has plainly shown that this is the only path to carry out the command of the Constitution.

To those who seek to avoid action by their National Government in their own communities; who want to and who seek to maintain purely local control over elections, the answer is simple:

Open your polling places to all your people.

Allow men and women to register and vote whatever the color of their skin.

Extend the rights of citizenship to every citizen of this land.

There is no constitutional issue here. The command of the Constitution is plain.

There is no moral issue. It is wrong—deadly wrong—to deny any of your fellow Americans the right to vote in this country.

There is no issue of States rights or national rights. There is only the struggle for human rights.

I have not the slightest doubt what will be your answer.

The last time a President sent a civil rights bill to the Congress it contained a provision to protect voting rights in federal elections. That civil rights bill was passed after eight long months of debate. And when that bill came to my desk from the Congress for my signature, the heart of the voting provision had been eliminated.

This time, on this issue, there must be no delay, no hesitation and no compromise with our purpose.

We cannot, we must not, refuse to protect the right of every American to vote in every election that he may desire to participate in. And we ought not and we cannot and we must not wait another 8 months before we get a bill. We have already waited a hundred years and more, and the time for waiting is gone.

So I ask you to join me in working long hours—nights and weekends, if necessary—to pass this bill. And I don't make that request lightly. For from the window where I sit with the problems of our country I recognize that outside this chamber is the outraged conscience of a nation, the grave concern of many nations, and the harsh judgment of history on our acts.

But even if we pass this bill, the battle will not be over. What happened in Selma is part of a far larger movement which reaches into every section and State of America. It is the effort of American Negroes to secure for themselves the full blessings of American life.

Their cause must be our cause too. Because it is not just Negroes, but really it is all of us, who must overcome the crippling legacy of bigotry and injustice. And we shall overcome.

As a man whose roots go deeply into Southern soil, I know how agonizing racial feelings are. I know how difficult it is to reshape the attitudes and the structure of our society.

But a century has passed, more than a hundred years, since the Negro was freed. And he is not fully free tonight.

It was more than a hundred years ago that Abraham Lincoln, a great President of another party, signed the Emancipation Proclamation, but emancipation is a proclamation and not a fact.

A century has passed, more than a hundred years, since equality was promised. And yet the Negro is not equal.

A century has passed since the day of promise. And the promise is unkept.

The time of justice has now come. I tell you that I believe sincerely that no force can hold it back. It is right in the eyes of man and God that it should come. And when it does, I think that day will brighten the lives of every American.

For Negroes are not the only victims. How many white children have gone uneducated, how many white families have lived in stark poverty, how many white lives have been scarred by fear, because we have wasted our energy and our substance to maintain the barriers of hatred and terror?

So I say to all of you here, and to all in the Nation tonight, that those who appeal to you to hold on to the past do so at the cost of denying you your future.

This great, rich, restless country can offer opportunity and education and hope to all: black and white, North and South, sharecropper and city dweller. These are the enemies: poverty, ignorance, disease. They are the enemies and not our fellow man, not our neighbor. And these enemies too, poverty, disease and ignorance, we shall overcome.

Now let none of us in any sections look with prideful righteousness on the troubles in another section, or on the problems of our neighbors. There is really no part of America where the promise of equality has been fully kept. In Buffalo as well as in Birmingham, in Philadelphia as well as in Selma, Americans are struggling for the fruits of freedom.

This is one Nation. What happens in Selma or in Cincinnati is a matter of legitimate concern to every American. But let each of us look within our own hearts and our own communities, and let each of us put our shoulder to the wheel to root out injustice wherever it exists.

As we meet here in this peaceful, historic chamber tonight, men from the South, some of whom were at Iwo Jima, men from the North who have carried Old Glory to far corners of the world and brought it back without a stain on it, men from the East and from the West, are all fighting together without regard to religion, or color, or region, in Viet-Nam. Men from every region fought for us across the world 20 years ago.

And in these common dangers and these common sacrifices the South made its contribution of honor and gallantry no less than any other region of the great Republic—and in some instances, a great many of them, more.

And I have not the slightest doubt that good men from everywhere in this country, from the Great Lakes to the Gulf of Mexico, from the Golden Gate to the harbors along the Atlantic, will rally together now in this cause to vindicate the freedom of all Americans. For all of us owe this duty; and I believe that all of us will respond to it.

Your President makes that request of every American.

The real hero of this struggle is the American Negro. His actions and protests, his courage to risk safety and even to risk his life, have awakened the conscience of this Nation. His demonstrations have been designed to call attention to injustice, designed to provoke change, designed to stir reform.

He has called upon us to make good the promise of America. And who among us can say that we would have made the same progress were it not for his persistent bravery, and his faith in American democracy.

For at the real heart of battle for equality is a deep-seated belief in the democratic process. Equality depends not on the force of arms or tear gas but upon the force of moral right; not on recourse to violence but on respect for law and order.

There have been many pressures upon your President and there will be others as the days come and go. But I pledge you tonight that we intend to fight this battle where it should be fought: in the courts, and in the Congress, and in the hearts of men.

We must preserve the right of free speech and the right of free assembly. But the right of free speech does not carry with it, as has been said, the right to holler fire in a crowded theater. We must preserve the right to free assembly, but free assembly does not carry with it the right to block public thoroughfares to traffic.

We do have a right to protest, and a right to march under conditions that do not infringe the constitutional rights of our neighbors. And I intend to protect all those rights as long as I am permitted to serve in this office.

We will guard against violence, knowing it strikes from our hands the very weapons which we seek—progress, obedience to law, and belief in American values.

In Selma as elsewhere we seek and pray for peace. We seek order. We seek unity. But we will not accept the peace of stifled rights, or the order imposed by fear, or the unity that stifles protest. For peace cannot be purchased at the cost of liberty.

In Selma tonight, as in every—and we had a good day there—as in every city, we are working for just and peaceful settlement. We must all remember that after this speech I am making tonight, after the police and the FBI and the Marshals have all gone, and after you have promptly passed this bill, the people of Selma and the other cities of the Nation must still live and work together. And when the attention of the Nation has gone elsewhere they must try to heal the wounds and to build a new community.

This cannot be easily done on a battleground of violence, as the history of the South itself shows. It is in recognition of this that men of both races have shown such an outstandingly impressive responsibility in recent days—last Tuesday, again today.

The bill that I am presenting to you will be known as a civil rights bill. But, in a larger sense, most of the program I am recommending is a civil rights program. Its object is to open the city of hope to all people of all races.

Because all Americans just must have the right to vote. And we are going to give them that right.

All Americans must have the privileges of citizenship regardless of race. And they are going to have those privileges of citizenship regardless of race.

But I would like to caution you and remind you that to exercise these privileges takes much more than just legal right. It requires a trained mind and a healthy body. It requires a decent home, and the chance to find a job, and the opportunity to escape from the clutches of poverty.

Of course, people cannot contribute to the Nation if they are never taught to read or write, if their bodies are stunted from hunger, if their sickness goes untended, if their life is spent in hopeless poverty just drawing a welfare check.

So we want to open the gates to opportunity. But we are also going to give all our people, black and white, the help that they need to walk through those gates.

My first job after college was as a teacher in Cotulla, Texas, in a small Mexican-American school. Few of them could speak English, and I couldn't speak much Spanish. My students were poor and they often came to class without breakfast, hungry. They knew even in their youth the pain of prejudice. They never seemed to know why people disliked them. But they knew it was so, because I saw it in their eyes. I often walked home late in the afternoon, after the classes were finished, wishing there was more that I could do. But all I knew was to teach them the little that I knew, hoping that it might help them against the hardships that lay ahead.

Somehow you never forget what poverty and hatred can do when you see its scars on the hopeful face of a young child.

I never thought then, in 1928, that I would be standing here in 1965. It never even occurred to me in my fondest dreams that I might have the chance to help the sons and daughters of those students and to help people like them all over this country.

But now I do have that chance—and I'll let you in on a secret—I mean to use it. And I hope that you will use it with me.

This is the richest and most powerful country which ever occupied the globe. The might of past empires is little compared to ours. But I do not want to be the President who built empires, or sought grandeur, or extended dominion.

I want to be the President who educated young children to the wonders of their world. I want to be the President who helped to feed the hungry and to prepare them to be taxpayers instead of tax-eaters.

I want to be the President who helped the poor to find their own way and who protected the right of every citizen to vote in every election.

I want to be the President who helped to end hatred among his fellow men and who promoted love among the people of all races and all regions and all parties.

I want to be the President who helped to end war among the brothers of this earth.

And so at the request of your beloved Speaker and the Senator from Montana; the majority leader, the Senator from Illinois; the minority leader, Mr. McCulloch, and other Members of both parties, I came here tonight—not as President Roosevelt came down one time in person to veto a bonus bill, not as President Truman came down one time to urge the passage of a railroad bill—but I came down here to ask you to share this task with me and to share it with the people that we both work for. I want this to be the Congress, Republicans and Democrats alike, which did all these things for all these people.

Beyond this great chamber, out yonder in 50 States, are the people that we serve. Who can tell what deep and unspoken hopes are in their hearts tonight as they sit there and listen. We all can guess, from our own lives, how difficult they often find their own pursuit of happiness, how many problems each little family has. They look most of all to themselves for their futures. But I think that they also look to each of us.

Above the pyramid on the great seal of the United States it says—in Latin—"God has favored our undertaking."

God will not favor everything that we do. It is rather our duty to divine His will. But I cannot help believing that He truly understands and that He really favors the undertaking that we begin here tonight.

PUBLIC LAW 89-110

S. 1564

Eighty-ninth Congress of the United States of America

AT THE FIRST SESSION

Begun and held at the City of Washington on Monday, the fourth day of January,
one thousand nine hundred and sixty-five

An Act

To enforce the fifteenth amendment to the Constitution of the United States,
and for other purposes.

Be it enacted by the Senate and House of Representatives of the
United States of America in Congress assembled, That this Act shall
be known as the "Voting Rights Act of 1965".

SEC. 2. No voting qualification or prerequisite to voting, or standard,
practice, or procedure shall be imposed or applied by any State or
political subdivision to deny or abridge the right of any citizen of
the United States to vote on account of race or color.

SEC. 3. (a) Whenever the Attorney General institutes a proceeding
under any statute to enforce the guarantees of the fifteenth amendment in any State or political subdivision the court shall authorize
the appointment of Federal examiners by the United States Civil
Service Commission in accordance with section 6 to serve for such
period of time and for such political subdivisions as the court shall
determine is appropriate to enforce the guarantees of the fifteenth
amendment (1) as part of any interlocutory order if the court deter-
mines that the appointment of such examiners is necessary to enforce
such guarantees or (2) as part of any final judgment if the court finds
that violations of the fifteenth amendment justifying equitable relief
have occurred in such State or subdivision: *Provided,* That the court
need not authorize the appointment of examiners if any incidents of
denial or abridgement of the right to vote on account of race or color
(1) have been few in number and have been promptly and effectively
corrected by State or local action, (2) the continuing effect of such
incidents has been eliminated, and (3) there is no reasonable proba-
bility of their recurrence in the future.

(b) If in a proceeding instituted by the Attorney General under
any statute to enforce the guarantees of the fifteenth amendment in
any State or political subdivision the court finds that a test or device
has been used for the purpose or with the effect of denying or abridging the right of any citizen of the United States to vote on account
of race or color, it shall suspend the use of tests and devices in such
State or political subdivisions as the court shall determine is appropriate and for such period as it deems necessary.

(c) If in any proceeding instituted by the Attorney General under
any statute to enforce the guarantees of the fifteenth amendment in
any State or political subdivision the court finds that violations of the
fifteenth amendment justifying equitable relief have occurred within
the territory of such State or political subdivision, the court, in
addition to such relief as it may grant, shall retain jurisdiction for
such period as it may deem appropriate and during such period no
voting qualification or prerequisite to voting, or standard, practice,
or procedure with respect to voting different from that in force or
effect at the time the proceeding was commenced shall be enforced
unless and until the court finds that such qualification, prerequisite,
standard, practice, or procedure does not have the purpose and will
not have the effect of denying or abridging the right to vote on
account of race or color: *Provided,* That such qualification, prerequisite, standard, practice, or procedure may be enforced if the
qualification, prerequisite, standard, practice, or procedure has been
submitted by the chief legal officer or other appropriate official of
such State or subdivision to the Attorney General and the Attorney
General has not interposed an objection within sixty days after such

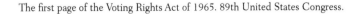

The first page of the Voting Rights Act of 1965. 89th United States Congress.

Document Analysis

As President Johnson points out, this is not the first civil rights bill to be submitted with a provision guaranteeing voting rights. However, in his mind, the time is right for finally enacting such legislation. Johnson believes that events in Alabama have made it clear that voting rights are not going to be granted unless the federal government steps in. The lack of equal rights for any one group in the United States makes the matter "an American problem." Johnson contrasts the eloquent statements of the Founding Fathers with the situation in which non-white citizens find themselves in many Southern states. He states that the time has come for full equality, in all aspects of life, for all American citizens. The shocking images of police assaulting peaceful demonstrators is something that Johnson knows will eventually fade from awareness. Thus, he is adamant that the new legislation must be passed quickly, or else it could languish forever in Congressional committees.

Although, from a 21st-century perspective, the language of the speech might seem a bit archaic (e.g., the use of the word Negro and referring to groups using only male terms), Johnson takes a somewhat extreme position to reflect his strong support of the right of non-white citizens to vote. Johnson understands that what is at stake here are the "values and the purposes" of America. Quoting the Declaration of Independence, the president sees that there has been a failure in living up to the phrase "All men are created equal." He suggests that this expression will be validated when all people have access to the vote.

The fact that the Civil Rights Act of 1964 had been stripped, during the legislative process, of any provisions regarding voting rights, is an indication to Johnson that quick action is needed. Outlining the history from 1865 to the present, he is able to demonstrate that even the most patient person would be worn thin by events. He continually refers to what took place during the first two Selma marches, as well as to the murder of a New England minister, to remind listeners of the urgency of redressing these wrongs. Although most of the laws restricting voting by non-whites had been passed in the South, Johnson presents his case that given the unity of the country, the march in Selma and the larger struggle for which it stands "reaches into every section" of the United States.

Using Biblical and American images and references, Johnson strengthens his case for action. He believes that failure in obtaining equal rights for all citizens is more important than any physical or monetary gains the nation might make. He states that if the only way a person can gain equality, including the right to vote, is to "show a white skin," then the nation is a failure. It is that simple for Johnson. He sees substantial resources being wasted on segregation, resources that could help whites as well as members of minority groups to move out of poverty. In Johnson's mind, this is part of the unity of the nation and of all its citizens.

Essential Themes

In this speech, President Johnson presents a vision of justice and equality for all Americans without qualification. Participation in the political process is a basic part of what it means to be an American. Thus, he speaks about the need to treat a person on the "merits" of his (or her) status as a human being, regardless of what color or ethnicity the person might be. To denigrate anyone because of his or her race or color, in Johnson's perspective, is to deny all that Americans have struggled for in the preceding centuries. Although he was confronting some in the South who seemed to deny such a view, he insists that the matter is part of the great American tradition. Speaking to Congress and to the nation, Johnson seeks to bring that tradition into focus. All must share equally in opportunity, or all will be harmed.

Once signed into law, the Voting Rights Act was quickly implemented. By the end of 1966, nine of the thirteen Southern states had more than half their African American citizens registered to vote, two-thirds of them by local officials. However, this did not mean that opponents of the law stopped their efforts completely. The matter, rather, moved to the courts. Initially, the Supreme Court upheld the basic provisions of the law. Over the years, however, seven Supreme Court decisions have come to limited various provisions of the law. The strongest such rulings have limited the federal government's power to approve/disapprove electoral districts prior to their implementation, based on the government's understanding of how and why the electoral lines were established. With this provision being declared unconstitutional in 2013, only challenges by individuals who believe their constitutional rights have been violated can be file a complaint, with the burden of proof falling to the individual filing the case.

President Johnson sought to move the nation toward political equality for all people by adding this legislation to his Great Society quiver. Fifty years later, the issue is still a subject of political and legal debate, some of it quite heated. Advocates for voting rights and similar laws believe that historic injustices have not yet been fully redressed, while opponents believe that institutionalized injustices from the past are dead history as far as current concerns go. President Johnson intentionally drew on words from the Civil Rights Movement when he stated that "we shall overcome" the problems that he describes. Yet, whether the nation has indeed overcome these problems or whether they linger as continuing concerns, remains, it seems, unsettled.

—Donald A. Watt, PhD

Bibliography and Additional Reading

Ellis, Sylvia. *Freedom's Pragmatist: Lyndon Johnson and Civil Rights*. Gainesville: University of Florida Press, 2013. Print.

Kearns, Doris. *Lyndon Johnson and the American Dream*. New York: St. Martins Griffin, 1991. Print.

LBJ Presidential Library. "LBJ and Civil Rights." Austin: Lyndon Baines Johnson Library and Museum, 2015. Web 10 September 2015.

National Voting Rights Museum and Institute. "Selma Movement." Selma, Alabama: National Voting Rights Museum and Institute, 2015. Web.

Our Documents.Gov. "100 Milestone Documents: Voting Rights Act (1965)." Washington, D.C.: *National Archives and Records Administration*, 2015. Web.

Senator Eugene McCarthy's Announcement of Presidential Run

Date: November 30, 1967
Author: Eugene McCarthy
Genre: Speech

Summary Overview

The fall of 1967 was a critical moment in the history of domestic opposition to the Vietnam War. U.S. involvement in the war in South Vietnam had been escalating since 1965 and protest against the war had grown in size and militancy. Three major protests in October signaled the intensifying opposition to the war: the Oakland Anti-Draft Riot, the "Dow Day" protest at the University of Wisconsin and the March on the Pentagon in Washington, D.C. Mainstream opposition to the war had been expressed mostly through the Senate Foreign Affairs Committee, of which Senator Eugene McCarthy was a member. Antiwar liberals, seeking a political alternative to radical street protest, were searching for a peace candidate to oppose Lyndon Johnson in the Democratic primaries the following year. Initially hoping to enlist a wavering Senator Robert Kennedy, it was instead Eugene McCarthy who stepped forward to challenge the incumbent president of his own party. The intellectual and calm McCarthy soon attracted passionate, young volunteers to his campaign. In February and March of 1968 McCarthy's "Children's Crusade," as some dubbed it, descended on New Hampshire, going "Clean for Gene" (being well groomed and conventionally dressed) and went door to door for the McCarthy campaign. On March 12, McCarthy outstripped expectations, winning 42 percent of the vote to Johnson's 49 percent. This revealed Johnson's vulnerability and on March 16 Robert Kennedy entered the Democratic primary to challenge Johnson as well. Faced with this growing opposition to the war in his own party, on March 31, 1968 Johnson shocked the American public by announcing he would not seek a second term as president. The McCarthy and Kennedy peace campaigns competed in several primaries through June. After Kennedy's victory in California and his devastating assassination later that day, McCarthy's volunteers largely disbanded and the once vibrant Mc-Carthy campaign lost steam. That August the Democrats ended up nominating Vice President Hubert Humphrey on a prowar platform in Chicago, amidst deep divisions within the Convention Hall and battles between police and protesters outside. Nevertheless, McCarthy's historic campaign had made opposition to the war respectable and a major campaign issue in 1968.

Defining Moment

After years of U.S. military advisors supporting South Vietnam's pro-American government against a communist insurgency, in 1965 President Lyndon Johnson began sending U.S. ground troops to defend the tottering South Vietnamese government and launched a bombing campaign against North Vietnam. Due to the Cold War consensus of containing communism, America's direct entry into the Vietnam War was initially met with widespread public and Congressional support. A small and peaceful antiwar movement emerged in 1965, which many dismissed as outside of the American political mainstream. As the war escalated each year with the introduction of more U.S. troops and a wider bombing campaign, the antiwar movement grew in size and intensity.

By late 1967, America's commitment to South Vietnam had grown to approximately 500,000 troops and a segment of the antiwar movement announced a transition from "protest to resistance." Protests in Oakland, Madison, Wisconsin, and Washington, D.C. led to violent confrontations with police and numerous protesters arrested or hospitalized.

Meanwhile, mild Congressional opposition to the war grew in the Senate Foreign Relations Committee led by Arkansas Senator J. William Fulbright. Unlike the rest of Congress, where support for the war was strong, the Foreign Affairs Committee included members who were critical of the war like Eugene McCarthy, Frank Church, and Al Gore, Sr. During televised hearings, the committee and many of its witnesses revealed skepticism of the rationales for the war as well as the Johnson administration's claims of progress.

In the fall of 1967, antiwar liberal activist Allard Lowenstein began a "Dump Johnson" campaign to recruit someone to challenge Lyndon Johnson for the presidency on a peace platform. Lowenstein believed it was critical to move opposition to the war from the streets into mainstream political channels. Lowenstein hoped to recruit Senator Robert Kennedy, brother of the assassinated president John F. Kennedy, but Kennedy was deeply torn about challenging an incumbent president with whom he had a long and ugly rivalry, and declined.

It was Minnesota Senator Eugene McCarthy who agreed to take up the mantle of opposing Johnson and the war. On November 30, 1967, McCarthy entered the Senate Caucus Room and announced to the press his intention to challenge Johnson in select Democratic primaries in 1968 to raise the issue of ending the war in Vietnam. He declared he only sought to raise the issue ending the war. Since only 15 states even held primaries in 1968, with most states sending delegates to the Democratic Convention chosen by state conventions dominated by established party officials, McCarthy's campaign was dismissed by many political insiders. McCarthy's announcement, however, energized many idealistic college students who rallied to the Senator's campaign. Often, McCarthy's dry, cerebral and sometimes meandering speeches contrasted dramatically with the raucous energy of the youth attending his rallies. Many of McCarthy's supporters, however, viewed the Senator's calm demeanor as reassuring and validating.

The McCarthy campaign received a huge boost after the Tet Offensive in South Vietnam, launched by the Viet Cong and North Vietnamese Army on January 31, 1968, in which the communist forces left their rural strongholds to launch a surprise attack on all of South Vietnam's cities and provincial capitals. Although the U.S. and South Vietnamese militaries eventually repelled the communist offensive, the mere fact the communist could launch such a large-scale offensive belied the Administration's claims of progress and highlighted the fact that America was mired in a stalemate.

The Tet Offensive made McCarthy seem prescient and his strong showing in New Hampshire upended the 1968 presidential campaign, which practically everyone had assumed would see Johnson easily winning re-nomination. The now unpredictable election would be held in a year of racial unrest, assassinations, militant campus protest, a growing hippie counterculture and deepening divisions throughout American society.

Author Biography

Eugene Joseph McCarthy was born on March 29, 1916 in Watkins, Minnesota. He attended St. John's Preparatory School and St. John's University. McCarthy's intellectual outlook was shaped by Catholic social thought, and he became a Benedictine novitiate at St. John's Abbey in 1942. He was expelled from the monastery for "intellectual pride," and after serving in the Army Signal Corps code breaking in Washington, D.C. during World War II, he returned to Minnesota as a professor of sociology at the College of St. Thomas. In 1948, McCarthy won a seat in Congress as a candidate of the Minnesota Democratic Farmer-Labor Party. He was an ally of liberal Minnesota Senator and future Vice President Hubert Humphrey. In 1958 McCarthy was elected to the Senate, and was considered, along with Humphrey, as a potential vice-presidential running mate of Lyndon Johnson's in the 1964 presidential election. After his historic run for president in 1968, McCarthy retired from the Senate in 1970 for a career writing poetry, teaching and periodic runs for president, campaigns which garnered little support. He married Abigail Quigley in 1945 with whom he had four children: Ellen, Mary, Michael and Margaret. The couple separated in 1970 but never divorced. McCarthy died on December 10, 2005.

HISTORICAL DOCUMENT

I intend to enter the Democratic primaries in four states: Wisconsin, Oregon, California and Nebraska. The decision with reference to Massachusetts, and also New Hampshire, will be made within the next two or three weeks. Insofar as Massachusetts is concerned, it will depend principally upon the outcome of a meeting which is being held there if they finish their work this weekend—a meeting of the Democratic State Committee.

Since I first said that I thought the issue of Vietnam and the issues related to it should be raised in the primaries of the country, I have talked with Democratic leaders from about 25 or 26 states; I have talked particularly to candidates for, re-election to the Senate (Democratic candidates), to some House members and also to students on campus and to other people throughout the country.

My decision to challenge the President's position and the Administration's position has been strengthened by recent announcements out of the Administration—the evident intention to escalate and to intensify the war in Vietnam and, on the other hand, the absence of any positive indications or suggestions for a compromise or for a negotiated political settlement. I am concerned that the Administration seems to have set no limit to the price which it is willing to pay for a military victory.

Let me summarize the cost of the war up to this point:

—the physical destruction of much of a small and weak nation by military operations of the most powerful nation in the world;

—100,000 to 150,000 civilian casualties in south Vietnam alone, to say nothing of the destruction of life and property in north Vietnam;

—the uprooting and the fracturing of the structure of the society of South Vietnam, where one-fourth to one-third of the population are now reported to be refugees;

—for the United States—as of yesterday—over 15,000 combat dead and nearly 95,000 wounded through November.

—a monthly expenditure in pursuit of the war running somewhere between $2 and $3 billion.

I am also concerned about the bearing of the war on other areas of United States responsibility, both at home and abroad:

—the failure to appropriate adequate funds for the poverty program here, for housing, for education and to meet other national needs, and the prospect of additional cuts as a condition to a possible passage of the surtax tax bill;

—the drastic reduction of our foreign aid program in other parts of the world;

—a dangerous rise in inflation; and one of the indirect and serious consequences of our involvement in Vietnam—the devaluation of the British pound, which in many respects is more important east of Suez today that the British Navy.

In addition, there's a growing evidence of the deepening moral crisis in America: discontent and frustration, and a disposition to take extra-legal—if not illegal—actions to manifest protest.

I am hopeful that this challenge which I am making—which I hope will be supported by other members of the Senate and other politicians—may alleviate at least in some degree of this sense of political helplessness and restore to many people a belief in the processes of American politics and of American government; that on the college campuses especially and also among adult, thoughtful Americans, it may come to the growing sense of alienation from politics which I think is currently reflected in a tendency to withdraw from political action, to talk of non-participation, to become cynical and to make threats of support for third parties or fourth parties or other irregular political movements.

I do not see in my move any great threat to the unity and strength of the Democratic Party—whatever that unity may be today and whenever that strength may be.

The issue of the war in Vietnam is not really a separate issue, but one which must be dealt with in the configuration of other problems to which it is related. And it is within this broader context that I intend to make the case to the people of the United States.

Let me say that—as I am sure I shall be charge—I am not for peace at any price, but for an honorable, rational and political solution to this war; a solution which I believe will enhance our world position, encourage the respect of our Allies and our potential adversaries, which will permit us to get the necessary attention to other commitments—both at home and abroad, militarily and did not militarily—and leave us with resources and moral energy to deal effectively with a pressing domestic problems of the United States itself. In this total effort, I believe we can restore to this nation a clear sense of purpose and of dedication to the achievement of our traditional purposes as a great nation in the twentieth century.

Document Analysis

The prosaic announcement of McCarthy's candidacy for president stands in stark contrast to the emotional reaction his announcement would stir in supporters. McCarthy does not indicate he is even running to win the nomination, merely to enter four, possibly more, primaries to raise the issue of the war and make the case for a negotiated end to the conflict. McCarthy doesn't mention Lyndon Johnson's name, but rather refers simply to "the President" and "the Administration. He declares he was prompted to run by the Administration's intention to continue escalating the war without any indication of a willingness to negotiate with the enemy

McCarthy cites the impact of the war on domestic programs to alleviate poverty and fund education, and the devastation visited upon the impoverished people of Vietnam by the greatest power on earth. He further asserts his belief that the war is undermining America's reputation abroad.

McCarthy's announcement seems as much concerned with restoring faith in American democracy and institutions as ending the war. He describes a "deepening moral crisis" in America, and a "sense of political helplessness… [and] alienation…" manifesting itself in "extra-legal—if not illegal—protests." McCarthy hopes his campaign will re-engage young Americans, especially college students, in the political process. Some radicals accused McCarthy of running merely to sap the antiwar movement of its revolutionary fervor and divert young Americans from confronting the power structure head on and diverting them into harmless, established political channels. But by bringing opposition to the war into the mainstream, McCarthy's campaign helped break the political consensus that dismissed the peace movement as marginal and perpetuated the war.

Essential Themes

McCarthy was known in the Senate for being intellectual, dispassionate, and having a dry wit. He was seen by some colleagues as disengaged, more interested in poetry and philosophy than the day-to-day details of legislating. Still, McCarthy had a strong liberal voting record

and had grown increasingly concerned by the "Imperial Presidency" during the war; namely, Johnson's ability to expand the war with minimal input from Congress. McCarthy called for greater Congressional oversight of the C.I.A. and F.B.I. as well greater Congressional input on the war. McCarthy's institutional reform positions as well as his professorial demeanor appealed to his college student and educated middle-class base.

After McCarthy's surprise showing in New Hampshire on March 12, Senator Robert Kennedy announced his campaign for the Democratic presidential nomination on March 16. Many of McCarthy's supporters viewed Kennedy as an opportunist trying to steal the fruits of their hard-fought victory. Robert Kennedy's entrance, however, was the realization of a deep fear Johnson had harbored since President John Kennedy's assassination of a Kennedy restoration. The worsening situation in Vietnam and Kennedy's entrance into the race led Johnson to announce his withdrawal from the race for re-election on March 31.

Standing as a peace candidate and aspiring national unifier, Kennedy ran both a more charismatic and more professional campaign than McCarthy. Whereas McCarthy had deep support among white college students and educated white middle-class reformers, Kennedy ran strong with minorities. The 1960s was a decade of racial progress with Lyndon Johnson's milestone civil rights legislation, as well as growing racial divisions and urban rebellions/riots, especially after the April 4, 1968 assassination of Rev. Martin Luther King, Jr. McCarthy had compiled a strong civil rights voting record, yet was unable to connect with African American, Puerto Rican and Mexican American voters during his 1968 campaign, unlike the more empathetic and inspirational Robert Kennedy.

Kennedy entered too late to contest the Wisconsin primary, which McCarthy won. Thereafter, McCarthy and Kennedy slugged it out in the primaries with Kennedy winning in Indiana, Florida (which McCarthy didn't contest) and Nebraska, and McCarthy winning in Oregon. The final showdown came in California where Kennedy's strong minority support propelled him to a 46% to 42%

victory over McCarthy on June 4. After an energetic speech at his victory rally at the Ambassador Hotel in Los Angeles, Kennedy was shot while passing through a kitchen by a mentally unstable assassin, Sirhan Sirhan.

After the final primary in California, McCarthy's student volunteers disbanded and the energy disappeared from the McCarthy campaign. Although McCarthy still made appearances on TV and at small rallies, close friends believed McCarthy entered a period of emotional depression leading up to the Democratic Convention in late August.

McCarthy's old ally from Minnesota, Vice President Hubert Humphrey entered the race for the Democratic nomination in April, eschewing the primaries and seeking to build up a lead in delegates among party regulars. Humphrey's support with labor unions and big city mayors allowed him to defeat McCarthy and the other peace candidate Senator George McGovern, who ran in Kennedy's place.

During the Convention, McCarthy and his delegates were shocked by the violence wielded by Chicago Mayor Richard Daley's police against antiwar protestor (a mix of nonviolent and militant activists). After losing to Humphrey and the defeat of the peace plank at the Convention, many supporters of McCarthy and Kennedy were unwilling to support the prowar Humphrey.

Behind in the polls to Republican nominee, former Vice President Richard M. Nixon, Humphrey announced support for a bombing halt against North Vietnam a week before the November election and saw his poll numbers begin to climb overnight. McCarthy, in response, gave a grudging endorsement of Humphrey on October 29, mere days before the election. Nixon defeated Humphrey and third party "Law and Order" candidate Governor George Wallace of Alabama in one of the closest elections in American history.

McCarthy's campaign signaled a growing rift in the Democratic Party between college-educated, middle-class white progressives, who questioned the premises of U.S. cold war foreign policy and embraced the cultural changes of the 1960s, and the party's blue collar union members and urban ethnic white base. The former would henceforth, alongside African Americans and other minorities, form the base of the Democratic Party as many white, blue-collar workers began drifting to the Republican Party. After the loss of Democratic white voters in the South in 1964 due to Lyndon Johnson's support for civil rights, the further split in the party over Vietnam in 1968 marked the death knell of the New Deal coalition forged in the Depression era which had kept the Democratic Party in the White House for all but eight years between 1933 and 1969. Many historians regard the 1968 election as the beginning of the Republican ascendancy that kept the Republicans in the White House for all but eight years between 1969 and 1993.

—*Robert Surbrug, PhD*

Bibliography and Additional Reading

Cohen, Michael A. *American Maelstrom: The 1968 Election and the Politics of Division.* New York: Oxford University Press, 2016.

O'Donnell, Lawrence. *Playing with Fire: 1968 and the Transformation of American Politics.* New York: Penguin House, 2017.

Sandbrook, Dominic. *Eugene McCarthy: The Rise and Fall of Postwar American Liberalism.* New York: Alfred A. Knopf, 2004.

White, Theodore H. White. *The Making of the President: 1968.* New York: Atheneum House, 1969.

■ RFK's "An Unwinnable War" Speech

Date: February 8, 1968
Author: Robert F. Kennedy
Genre: Speech; address

Summary Overview

On February 8, 1968 Senator Robert F. Kennedy of New York announced his opposition to the Vietnam War during a speech in Chicago. His speech occurred as American soldiers and soldiers of the Republic of Vietnam (RVN, or South Vietnam) were fighting to dislodge communist forces that had seized military bases and cities in the RVN during the Tet Offensive. He provided a critical assessment of the American military intervention in Vietnam, arguing that the war was having a devastating effect on both the Vietnamese and Americans. He argued that the Tet Offensive proved once and for all that the war was unwinnable. The only sensible course was to withdraw all American forces from Vietnam. An influential member of the Democratic Party, Kennedy's denunciation put him in direct opposition to the war policies of Democratic president Lyndon Johnson and provided him with a platform with which to seek the Democratic presidential nomination in 1968.

Defining the Moment

In many respects, Kennedy's "Unwinnable War" speech represented a dramatic shift in his views. As a close advisor to his brother, John F. Kennedy, Robert Kennedy had supported American aid to South Vietnam in the early 1960s. His support for the war continued during the first years of Lyndon Johnson's presidency, even as Johnson sent hundreds of thousands of American combat troops to fight in the south against anti-government communist forces.

Kennedy's relationship with Johnson was complex. Although Johnson appreciated Kennedy's earlier support for escalation, he was also paranoid about his potential influence. Johnson thought that Kennedy's views on Vietnam were far more hawkish than his own. He feared that if he did not aggressively fight the war, Kennedy would use it as an opportunity to criticize him, undercut his support, and improve his own popularity among democrats.

Over time, Kennedy became more critical of American involvement in the war, but he largely kept his criticisms to himself as he did not want to appear disloyal or create divisions within the Democratic Party. Kennedy's "Unwinnable War" speech was the first time he publicly called for an end to the war. His comments were largely a reaction to the Tet Offensive. For months, the Johnson administration had told the American people that the United States was winning the war and that it would be over soon. On January 30, 1968, the Vietnamese New Year, the National Liberation Front (NLF) and North Vietnamese Army (NVA) conducted a series of coordinated attacks against important and symbolic military and civilian targets throughout South Vietnam. As scenes of insurgents attacking the U.S. embassy flashed across millions of American TV screens, any hope that the war would soon be over was permanently broken. Kennedy's speech was meant to address this new and troubling reality. His criticisms of the war were likely shared by many Americans listening who had similarly concluded that the events of the past days had proven once and for all that the Vietnam War was in fact an unwinnable war.

Author Biography

Born in Brookline, Massachusetts on November 20, 1925, Robert Francis Kennedy was not only the brother of President John F. Kennedy, but also an influential political actor in his own right. After military service in World War II, Kennedy earned a law degree from the University of Virginia and served as council for several congressional committees during the 1950s. When his older brother was elected president in 1960, Kennedy was appointed attorney general of the United States. He was one of his brother's closest advisors and, as attorney general, played an instrumental role in determining the Kennedy administration's response to the civil rights movement. In 1964, Kennedy was elected to the U.S. Senate. He had long had reservations about Johnson's policy in Vietnam, but after the Tet Offensive began in late January 1968, he publicly expressed his opposition to the war. On March 31, 1968, he announced his candidacy for the Democratic presidential nomination. After winning several state Democratic primaries, he was assassinated by Sirhan Sirhan in Los Angeles on June 5, 1968.

HISTORICAL DOCUMENTS

Our enemy, savagely striking at will across all of South Vietnam, has finally shattered the mask of official illusion with which we have concealed our true circumstances, even from ourselves. But a short time ago we were serene in our reports and predictions of progress.

The Vietcong will probably withdraw from the cities, as they were forced to withdraw from the American Embassy. Thousands of them will be dead.

But they will, nevertheless, have demonstrated that no part or person of South Vietnam is secure from their attacks: neither district capitals nor American bases, neither the peasant in his rice paddy nor the commanding general of our own great forces.

No one can predict the exact shape or outcome of the battles now in progress, in Saigon or at Khesanh. Let us pray that we will succeed at the lowest possible cost to our young men.

But whatever their outcome, the events of the last two weeks have taught us something. For the sake of those young Americans who are fighting today, if for no other reason, the time has come to take a new look at the war in Vietnam, not by cursing the past but by using it to illuminate the future.

And the first and necessary step is to face the facts. It is to seek out the austere and painful reality of Vietnam, freed from wishful thinking, false hopes and sentimental dreams. It is to rid ourselves of the "good company," of those illusions which have lured us into the deepening swamp of Vietnam.

We must, first of all, rid ourselves of the illusion that the events of the past two weeks represent some sort of victory. That is not so.

It is said the Vietcong will not be able to hold the cities. This is probably true. But they have demonstrated despite all our reports of progress, of government strength and enemy weakness, that half a million American soldiers with 700,000 Vietnamese allies, with total command of the air, total command of the sea, backed by huge resources and the most modern weapons, are unable to secure even a single city from the attacks of an enemy whose total strength is about 250,000. . . .

For years we have been told that the measure of our success and progress in Vietnam was increasing security and control for the population. Now we have seen that none of the population is secure and no area is under sure control.

Four years ago when we only had about 30,000 troops in Vietnam, the Vietcong were unable to mount the assaults on cities they have now conducted against our enormous forces. At one time a suggestion that we protect enclaves was derided. Now there are no protected enclaves.

This has not happened because our men are not brave or effective, because they are. It is because we have misconceived the nature of the war: It is because we have sought to resolve by military might a conflict whose issue depends upon the will and conviction of the South Vietnamese people. It is like sending a lion to halt an epidemic of jungle rot.

This misconception rests on a second illusion—the illusion that we can win a war which the South Vietnamese cannot win for themselves.

You cannot expect people to risk their lives and endure hardship unless they have a stake in their own society. They must have a clear sense of identification with their own government, a belief they are participating in a cause worth fighting for.

People will not fight to line the pockets of generals or swell the bank accounts of the wealthy. They are far more likely to close their eyes and shut their doors in the face of their government—even as they did last week.

More than any election, more than any proud boast, that single fact reveals the truth. We have an ally in name only. We support a government without supporters. Without the efforts of American arms that government would not last a day.

The third illusion is that the unswerving pursuit of military victory, whatever its cost, is in the interest of either ourselves or the people of Vietnam.

For the people of Vietnam, the last three years have meant little but horror. Their tiny land has been devastated by a weight of bombs and shells greater than Nazi Germany knew in the Second World War.

We have dropped 12 tons of bombs for every square mile in North and South Vietnam. Whole provinces have been substantially destroyed. More than two million South Vietnamese are now homeless refugees.

Imagine the impact in our own country if an equivalent number—over 25 million Americans—were wandering homeless or interned in refugee camps, and millions more refugees were being created as New York and Chicago, Washington and Boston, were being destroyed by a war raging in their streets.

Whatever the outcome of these battles, it is the people we seek to defend who are the greatest losers.

Nor does it serve the interests of America to fight this war as if moral standards could be subordinated to immediate necessities. Last week, a Vietcong suspect was turned over to the chief of the Vietnamese Security Services, who executed him on the spot—a flat violation of the Geneva Convention on the Rules of War.

The photograph of the execution was on front pages all around the world—leading our best and oldest friends to ask, more in sorrow than in anger, what has happened to America?

The fourth illusion is that the American national interest is identical with—or should be subordinated to—the selfish interest of an incompetent military regime.

We are told, of course, that the battle for South Vietnam is in reality a struggle for 250 million Asians—the beginning of a Great Society for all of Asia. But this is pretension.

We can and should offer reasonable assistance to Asia; but we cannot build a Great Society there if we cannot build one in our own country. We cannot speak extravagantly of a struggle for 250 million Asians, when a struggle for 15 million in one Asian country so strains our forces, that another Asian country, a fourth-rate power which we have already once defeated in battle, dares to seize an American ship and hold and humiliate her crew.

The fifth illusion is that this war can be settled in our own way and in our own time on our own terms. Such a settlement is the privilege of the triumphant: of those who crush their enemies in battle or wear away their will to fight.

We have not done this, nor is there any prospect we will achieve such a victory.

Unable to defeat our enemy or break his will—at least without a huge, long and ever more costly effort—we must actively seek a peaceful settlement. We can no longer harden our terms every time Hanoi indicates it may be prepared to negotiate; and we must be willing to foresee a settlement which will give the Vietcong a chance to participate in the political life of the country.

These are some of the illusions which may be discarded if the events of last week are to prove not simply a tragedy, but a lesson: a lesson which carries with it some basic truths.

First, that a total military victory is not within sight or around the corner; that, in fact, it is probably beyond our grasp; and that the effort to win such a victory will only result in the further slaughter of thousands of innocent and helpless people—a slaughter which will forever rest on our national conscience.

Second, that the pursuit of such a victory is not necessary to our national interest, and is even damaging that interest.

Third, that the progress we have claimed toward increasing our control over the country and the security of the population is largely illusory.

Fourth, that the central battle in this war cannot be measured by body counts or bomb damage, but by the extent to which the people of South Vietnam act on a sense of common purpose and hope with those that govern them.

Fifth, that the current regime in Saigon is unwilling or incapable of being an effective ally in the war against the Communists.

Sixth, that a political compromise is not just the best path to peace, but the only path, and we must show as much willingness to risk some of our prestige for peace as to risk the lives of young men in war.

Seventh, that the escalation policy in Vietnam, far from strengthening and consolidating international resistance to aggression, is injuring our country through the world, reducing the faith of other peoples in our wisdom and purpose and weakening the world's resolve to stand together for freedom and peace.

Eighth, that the best way to save our most precious stake in Vietnam—the lives of our soldiers—is to stop the enlargement of the war, and that the best way to end casualties is to end the war.

Ninth, that our nation must be told the truth about this war, in all its terrible reality, both because it is right—and because only in this way can any Administration rally the public confidence and unity for the shadowed days which lie ahead.

No war has ever demanded more bravery from our people and our Government—not just bravery under fire or the bravery to make sacrifices—but the bravery to dis-card the comfort of illusion—to do away with false hopes and alluring promises.

Reality is grim and painful. But it is only a remote echo of the anguish toward which a policy founded on illusion is surely taking us.

This is a great nation and a strong people. Any who seek to comfort rather than speak plainly, reassure rather than instruct, promise satisfaction rather than reveal frustration—they deny that greatness and drain that strength. For today as it was in the beginning, it is the truth that makes us free.

Robert Kennedy campaigns in Los Angeles (photo by Evan Freed)

Document Analysis

As American and Army of the Republic of Vietnam (ARVN) forces continued to battle communist forces throughout South Vietnam, Kennedy declared his opposition to the Vietnam War in a speech in Chicago on February 8, 1968. Kennedy justified his opposition, arguing that the war did not serve the interests of either the Vietnamese or the American people and was unwinnable. He also noted that the Johnson administration had purposely misled the American people about the true nature and status of the war.

Clearly, the Tet Offensive loomed large in his thinking. He maintained that the attacks had "shattered the mask of official illusion" that American forces were winning the war and that it would soon be over. He noted that while the NLF's immediate goal of overthrowing the South Vietnamese government would fail, thousands of American soldiers would ultimately be killed in the process. The Tet Offensive also proved that the Johnson administration's claim that communist forces were near defeat was nothing more than an illusion. The simple fact that the NLF was able to conduct coordinated attacks throughout the South was proof that "no part or person of South Vietnam is secure from their attacks: neither district capitals nor American bases, neither the peasant in his rice paddy nor the commanding general of our own great forces."

In Kennedy's estimation, the only way forward was to accept the reality of the war. First and foremost, the offensive proved once and for all that despite having more than half a million American soldiers in Vietnam, supported by 700,000 allied ARVN soldiers with the most modern weaponry and total control of the air and sea, communist forces could not be prevented from attacking nearly every city and important military installation in South Vietnam simultaneously. In the past, Johnson's administration had justified the need for more American forces in Vietnam with the argument that they were needed to control enemy forces and maintain security. Kennedy claimed that the recent offensive proved that no quantity of soldiers and resources would be enough to secure these goals.

Kennedy maintained that victory depended "upon the will and conviction of the South Vietnamese people." Yet they were largely led by corrupt military officials, whose dedication to popular rule was tenuous at best and whose primary concern was making money. Many Vietnamese had little confidence in their officials and, therefore, little interest in defending the country they represented.

Additionally, American bombing campaigns had done little to gain support from Vietnamese civilians especially as thousands were killed or injured. The South had more than 2 million refugees as a result of the bombing.

Equally important, the war not only placed American soldiers in the difficult position of fighting, and even dying, for a corrupt regime, it also diverted American resources from more pressing domestic needs. Kennedy noted that "we cannot build a Great Society there if we cannot build one in our own country." Even at the international level, Kennedy maintained that continued escalation of the war damaged American standing abroad, "reducing the faith of other peoples in our wisdom and purpose and weakening the world's resolve to stand together for freedom and peace."

Kennedy concluded that the only sensible reaction to the realities of the Vietnam War was to seek a peaceful settlement with the Democratic Republic of Vietnam (DRV, or North Vietnam) and the NLF. He believed that a peace settlement was the only way to avoid continued suffering and the only way for the Johnson administration to regain the trust and confidence of the American people.

Essential Themes

Robert F. Kennedy served as an influential advisor during his brother's presidency. During this time he expressed support for American intervention in Vietnam, a position which he maintained during the first years of Johnson's presidency. By late 1967, Kennedy had become increasingly skeptical about American involvement in Vietnam, but he hesitated to express these views publicly for fear of appearing disloyal to the president. However, the Tet Offensive permanently destroyed Kennedy's confidence that the war could be won in a timely matter. In his mind, the fact that the Vietnamese communist forces could conduct such a significant military attack meant that the war was unwinnable. Thus, Kennedy's "Unwinnable War" speech represented a significant shift in how he viewed American military intervention. It also led a significant break in his relationship with Johnson's administration.

Kennedy's speech established his reputation as an antiwar politician. Overnight, he became the most prominent antiwar politician. In the months before the Tet Offensive antiwar Democrats had tried unsuccessfully to convince Kennedy to run against Johnson in the 1968 Democratic nomination race. When he turned them down, they turned to Senator Eugene McCarthy of Minnesota. Quite unexpectedly, McCarthy came close to defeating Johnson in the New Hampshire primary on March 12, 1968. This close election motivated Kennedy to announce his entry into the race. Influenced at least in part by the entry of such a formidable candidate, Johnson announced on March 31 that he would not be seeking the Democratic nomination. After winning the California primary in early June, Kennedy established himself as a major contender for the nomination. However, his journey to the presidency was cut short when he was assassinated on June 5, 1968.

—Gerald F. Goodwin, PhD

Bibliography and Additional Reading

Clarke, Thurston. *The Last Campaign: Robert F. Kennedy and 82 Days That Inspired America*. New York: Henry Holt and Company, 2008. Print.

Moss, George Donelson. *Vietnam: An American Ordeal*. Upper Saddle River, New Jersey: Pearson Prentice Hall, 2006. Print.

Oberdorfer, Don. *Tet!: The Turning Point in the Vietnam War*. Baltimore, MD: Johns Hopkins UP, 2001. Print.

Small, Melvin. Antiwarriors: *The Vietnam War and the Battle for America's Hearts and Minds*. Lanham, MD: Rowman & Littlefield Publishers, 2002. Vietnam: America in the War Years Ser. Print.

■ LBJ's Address to the Nation Announcing Steps to Limit the War in Vietnam

Date: March 31, 1968
Author: Lyndon B. Johnson
Genre: Speech

Summary Overview

President Lyndon B. Johnson's nationally televised speech of March 31, 1968, included two major announcements: his decision to curtail the bombing campaign over North Vietnam as a way to induce the North Vietnamese into engaging in peace talks and his decision not to seek reelection as president. Both decisions are practically buried in the lengthy presentation, especially the latter announcement, which came in the penultimate paragraph, with little preparation. It marked a precipitous fall for a politician who, just four years earlier, had been elected in a landslide of historic proportions.

Defining Moment

Multiple contexts came together in President Johnson's March 31 speech, encompassing both the war in Vietnam and politics at home. Johnson had always wanted to be remembered as a great president based on his domestic policies, a program that he had termed the Great Society. He became closely identified with the Vietnam War, which he viewed as a threat to that domestic legacy. He feared that defeat in Vietnam would undermine political support for the Great Society. His decisions to escalate had been motivated by that fear as much as by events on the battlefield.

Until 1968, the escalation of the war, not the prospect of defeat, roiled U.S. politics and fueled the antiwar movement. Then came the Viet Cong's Tet Offensive of January–February 1968, which undermined public faith in the official narrative of how well the war was going. (This was compounded by the Pentagon's confusing analysis that the offensive had backfired, resulting in the decimation of the Viet Cong, but also that U.S. military leaders would now need 205,000 more troops.) On March 26, the "Wise Men," a team of elder statesmen that Johnson consulted, changed their previously optimistic view of the war's prospects, determining that it was time to move toward disengagement. Turmoil extended into the president's party. Senator Eugene McCarthy (D-MN), whom Johnson had considered as a possible running mate in 1964, challenged him for the Democratic nomination on an antiwar platform. Although Johnson defeated McCarthy in the New Hampshire primary, the outcome was close enough (49.4 percent to 42.4 percent) to be a humiliation for an incumbent president. Moreover, Johnson was trailing in the polls for the next primary, Wisconsin's, scheduled for April 2. Senator Robert Kennedy (D-NY), encouraged by these results, joined the race within days. At the same time that the war was dividing the Democratic Party, segregationist Southern Democrats were reacting to Johnson's civil rights agenda by rallying around Governor George Wallace (D-GA), who was running for president as an independent.

Also, unknown to the public at the time, Johnson's health was deteriorating. It was not certain that he would live through another term, and he had struggled with the idea of announcing his retirement during his State of the Union address in January. He had already fulfilled his domestic agenda, and he may have concluded that he had become controversial enough that stepping down was the surest way to secure his domestic legacy. The war in Vietnam clearly was not going well, but if nothing else, he could structure his exit in such a way that he left the scene as a peacemaker. This he sought to do in his March 31 speech. Still, the announcement that he would not seek reelection took the public by surprise. Johnson eventually endorsed Vice President Hubert Humphrey, who had not challenged him before his decision to retire from office, but only after Humphrey agreed to continue Johnson's policies. Humphrey was nominated at the Democratic National Convention in August, but then distanced himself from the war starting in late September. Johnson continued to voice support for him, but only as a Democrat and the candidate most likely to sustain the Great Society, without reference to Vietnam.

Author Biography

Lyndon Baines Johnson was born on Aug. 27, 1908, in Stonewall, Texas. He was elected to the U.S. House of Representatives (1937–49) and to the U.S. Senate (1949–61), where he served as Senate majority leader for six years. After unsuccessfully seeking the Democratic nomination for president in 1960 (the first Southerner to make such as attempt since the Civil War), he served as John F. Kennedy's running mate and vice president (1961–63). He succeeded to the presidency upon Kennedy's assassination on November 22, 1963 and was reelected in 1964 in a landslide. Johnson had been a New Deal Democrat in the House, developed a more conservative reputation in the Senate (which he viewed as necessary to win state-wide elections in Texas) and was a noted liberal in the White House. As president, he prioritized civil rights legislation, federal aid to education, and a "War on Poverty," but he also drew the country into the Vietnam War. He acquired a legendary reputation for passing legislation, but this owed as much to the dramatic way in which he came to office, the existing support in Congress for his legislative agenda, and the 2–1 Democratic majorities in both houses (in 1965–66) as it did to Johnson's personal political skills. Johnson was known as LBJ, following the tradition of Democratic presidents Franklin Delano Roosevelt (FDR) and Kennedy (JFK). He died on Jan. 22, 1973, just four years and two days after leaving office.

HISTORICAL DOCUMENT

Good evening, my fellow Americans:

Tonight I want to speak to you of peace in Vietnam and Southeast Asia.

No other question so preoccupies our people. No other dream so absorbs the 250 million human beings who live in that part of the world. No other goal motivates American policy in Southeast Asia.

For years, representatives of our Government and others have traveled the world, seeking to find a basis for peace talks.

Since last September, they have carried the offer that I made public at San Antonio. That offer was this:

That the United States would stop its bombardment of North Vietnam when that would lead promptly to productive discussions—and that we would assume that North Vietnam would not take military advantage of our restraint.

Hanoi denounced this offer, both privately and publicly. Even while the search for peace was going on, North Vietnam rushed their preparations for a savage assault on the people, the government, and the allies of South Vietnam.

Their attack—during the Tet holidays—failed to achieve its principal objectives.

It did not collapse the elected government of South Vietnam or shatter its army—as the Communists had hoped.

It did not produce a "general uprising" among the people of the cities as they had predicted.

The Communists were unable to maintain control of any of the more than 30 cities that they attacked. And they took very heavy casualties.

But they did compel the South Vietnamese and their allies to move certain forces from the countryside into the cities.

They caused widespread disruption and suffering. Their attacks, and the battles that followed, made refugees of half a million human beings.

The Communists may renew their attack any day.

They are, it appears, trying to make 1968 the year of decision in South Vietnam—the year that brings, if not final victory or defeat, at least a turning point in the struggle. This much is clear:

If they do mount another round of heavy attacks, they will not succeed in destroying the fighting power of South Vietnam and its allies.

But tragically, this is also clear: Many men—on both sides of the struggle—will be lost. A nation that has already suffered 20 years of warfare will suffer once again. Armies on both sides will take new casualties. And the war will go on.

There is no need for this to be so.

There is no need to delay the talks that could bring an end to this long and this bloody war.

Tonight, I renew the offer I made last August—to stop the bombardment of North Vietnam. We ask that talks begin promptly, that they be serious talks on the substance of peace. We assume that during those talks Hanoi will not take advantage of our restraint.

We are prepared to move immediately toward peace through negotiations.

So, tonight, in the hope that this action will lead to early talks, I am taking the first step to deescalate the conflict. We are reducing—substantially reducing—the present level of hostilities.

And we are doing so unilaterally, and at once.

Tonight, I have ordered our aircraft and our naval vessels to make no attacks on North Vietnam, except in the area north of the demilitarized zone where the continuing enemy buildup directly threatens allied forward positions and where the movements of their troops and supplies are clearly related to that threat.

The area in which we are stopping our attacks includes almost 90 percent of North Vietnam's population, and most of its territory. Thus there will be no attacks around the principal populated areas, or in the food-producing areas of North Vietnam.

Even this very limited bombing of the North could come to an early end—if our restraint is matched by restraint in Hanoi. But I cannot in good conscience stop all bombing so long as to do so would immediately and directly endanger the lives of our men and our allies. Whether a complete bombing halt becomes possible in the future will be determined by events.

Our purpose in this action is to bring about a reduction in the level of violence that now exists.

It is to save the lives of brave men—and to save the lives of innocent women and children. It is to permit the contending forces to move closer to a political settlement.

And tonight, I call upon the United Kingdom and I call upon the Soviet Union—as cochairmen of the Geneva Conferences, and as permanent members of the United Nations Security Council—to do all they can to move from the unilateral act of deescalation that I have just announced toward genuine peace in Southeast Asia.

Now, as in the past, the United States is ready to send its representatives to any forum, at any time, to discuss the means of bringing this ugly war to an end.

I am designating one of our most distinguished Americans, Ambassador Averell Harriman, as my personal representative for such talks. In addition, I have asked Ambassador Llewellyn Thompson, who returned from Moscow for consultation, to be available to join Ambassador Harriman at Geneva or any other suitable place—just as soon as Hanoi agrees to a conference.

I call upon President Ho Chi Minh to respond positively, and favorably, to this new step toward peace.

But if peace does not come now through negotiations, it will come when Hanoi understands that our common resolve is unshakable, and our common strength is invincible.

Tonight, we and the other allied nations are contributing 600,000 fighting men to assist 700,000 South Vietnamese troops in defending their little country.

Our presence there has always rested on this basic belief: The main burden of preserving their freedom must be carried out by them—by the South Vietnamese themselves.

We and our allies can only help to provide a shield behind which the people of South Vietnam can survive and can grow and develop. On their efforts—on their determination and resourcefulness—the outcome will ultimately depend.

That small, beleaguered nation has suffered terrible punishment for more than 20 years.

I pay tribute once again tonight to the great courage and endurance of its people. South Vietnam supports armed forces tonight of almost 700,000 men—and I call your attention to the fact that this is the equivalent of more than 10 million in our own population. Its people maintain their firm determination to be free of domination by the North.

There has been substantial progress, I think, in building a durable government during these last 3 years. The South Vietnam of 1965 could not have survived the enemy's Tet offensive of 1968. The elected government of South Vietnam survived that attack—and is rapidly repairing the devastation that it wrought.

The South Vietnamese know that further efforts are going to be required:

to expand their own armed forces,

to move back into the countryside as quickly as possible,

to increase their taxes,

to select the very best men that they have for civil and military responsibility,

to achieve a new unity within their constitutional government, and

to include in the national effort all those groups who wish to preserve South Vietnam's control over its own destiny.

Last week President Thiêu ordered the mobilization of 135,000 additional South Vietnamese. He plans to reach—as soon as possible—a total military strength of more than 800,000 men.

To achieve this, the Government of South Vietnam started the drafting of 19-year-olds on March 1st. On May 1st, the Government will begin the drafting of 18-year-olds.

Last month, 10,000 men volunteered for military service—that was two and a half times the number of volunteers during the same month last year. Since the middle of January, more than 48,000 South Vietnamese have joined the armed forces—and nearly half of them volunteered to do so.

All men in the South Vietnamese armed forces have had their tours of duty extended for the duration of the war, and reserves are now being called up for immediate active duty.

President Thiêu told his people last week: "We must make greater efforts and accept more sacrifices because, as I have said many times, this is our country. The existence of our nation is at stake, and this is mainly a Vietnamese responsibility."

He warned his people that a major national effort is required to root out corruption and incompetence at all levels of government.

We applaud this evidence of determination on the part of South Vietnam. Our first priority will be to support their effort.

We shall accelerate the reequipment of South Vietnam's armed forces—in order to meet the enemy's increased firepower. This will enable them progressively to undertake a larger share of combat operations against the Communist invaders.

On many occasions I have told the American people that we would send to Vietnam those forces that are required to accomplish our mission there. So, with that as our guide, we have previously authorized a force level of approximately 525,000.

Some weeks ago—to help meet the enemy's new offensive—we sent to Vietnam about 11,000 additional Marine and airborne troops. They were deployed by air in 48 hours, on an emergency basis. But the artillery, tank, aircraft, medical, and other units that were needed to work with and to support these infantry troops in combat could not then accompany them by air on that short notice.

In order that these forces may reach maximum combat effectiveness, the Joint Chiefs of Staff have recommended to me that we should prepare to send—during the next 5 months—support troops totaling approximately 13,500 men.

A portion of these men will be made available from our active forces. The balance will come from reserve component units which will be called up for service.

The actions that we have taken since the beginning of the year

--to reequip the South Vietnamese forces,

--to meet our responsibilities in Korea, as well as our responsibilities in Vietnam,

--to meet price increases and the cost of activating and deploying reserve forces,

--to replace helicopters and provide the other military supplies we need, all of these actions are going to require additional expenditures.

The tentative estimate of those additional expenditures is $2.5 billion in this fiscal year, and $2.6 billion in the next fiscal year.

These projected increases in expenditures for our national security will bring into sharper focus the Nation's need for immediate action: action to protect the prosperity of the American people and to protect the strength and the stability of our American dollar.

On many occasions I have pointed out that, without a tax bill or decreased expenditures, next year's deficit would again be around $20 billion. I have emphasized the need to set strict priorities in our spending. I have stressed that failure to act and to act promptly and decisively would raise very strong doubts throughout the world about America's willingness to keep its financial house in order.

Yet Congress has not acted. And tonight we face the sharpest financial threat in the postwar era—a threat to the dollar's role as the keystone of international trade and finance in the world.

Last week, at the monetary conference in Stockholm, the major industrial countries decided to take a big step toward creating a new international monetary asset that will strengthen the international monetary system. I am very proud of the very able work done by Secretary Fowler and Chairman Martin of the Federal Reserve Board.

But to make this system work the United States just must bring its balance of payments to—or very close to—equilibrium. We must have a responsible fiscal policy in this country. The passage of a tax bill now, together with expenditure control that the Congress may desire and dictate, is absolutely necessary to protect this Nation's security, to continue our prosperity, and to meet the needs of our people.

What is at stake is 7 years of unparalleled prosperity. In those 7 years, the real income of the average American, after taxes, rose by almost 30 percent—a gain as large as that of the entire preceding 19 years.

So the steps that we must take to convince the world are exactly the steps we must take to sustain our own economic strength here at home. In the past 8 months, prices and interest rates have risen because of our inaction.

We must, therefore, now do everything we can to move from debate to action—from talking to voting. There is, I believe—I hope there is—in both Houses of the Congress—a growing sense of urgency that this situation just must be acted upon and must be corrected.

My budget in January was, we thought, a tight one. It fully reflected our evaluation of most of the demanding needs of this Nation.

But in these budgetary matters, the President does not decide alone. The Congress has the power and the duty to determine appropriations and taxes.

The Congress is now considering our proposals and they are considering reductions in the budget that we submitted.

As part of a program of fiscal restraint that includes the tax surcharge, I shall approve appropriate reductions in the January budget when and if Congress so decides

that that should be done.

One thing is unmistakably clear, however: Our deficit just must be reduced. Failure to act could bring on conditions that would strike hardest at those people that all of us are trying so hard to help.

These times call for prudence in this land of plenty. I believe that we have the character to provide it, and tonight I plead with the Congress and with the people to act promptly to serve the national interest, and thereby serve all of our people.

Now let me give you my estimate of the chances for peace:

the peace that will one day stop the bloodshed in South Vietnam,

that will permit all the Vietnamese people to rebuild and develop their land,

that will permit us to turn more fully to our own tasks here at home.

I cannot promise that the initiative that I have announced tonight will be completely successful in achieving peace any more than the 30 others that we have undertaken and agreed to in recent years.

But it is our fervent hope that North Vietnam, after years of fighting that have left the issue unresolved, will now cease its efforts to achieve a military victory and will join with us in moving toward the peace table.

And there may come a time when South Vietnamese—on both sides—are able to work out a way to settle their own differences by free political choice rather than by war.

As Hanoi considers its course, it should be in no doubt of our intentions. It must not miscalculate the pressures within our democracy in this election year.

We have no intention of widening this war.

But the United States will never accept a fake solution to this long and arduous struggle and call it peace.

No one can foretell the precise terms of an eventual settlement.

Our objective in South Vietnam has never been the annihilation of the enemy. It has been to bring about a recognition in Hanoi that its objective—taking over the South by force—could not be achieved.

We think that peace can be based on the Geneva Accords of 1954—under political conditions that permit the South Vietnamese—all the South Vietnamese— to chart their course free of any outside domination or interference, from us or from anyone else.

So tonight I reaffirm the pledge that we made at Manila—that we are prepared to withdraw our forces from South Vietnam as the other side withdraws its forces to the north, stops the infiltration, and the level of violence thus subsides.

Our goal of peace and self-determination in Vietnam is directly related to the future of all of Southeast Asia—where much has happened to inspire confidence during the past 10 years. We have done all that we knew how to do to contribute and to help build that confidence.

A number of its nations have shown what can be accomplished under conditions of security. Since 1966, Indonesia, the fifth largest nation in all the world, with a population of more than 100 million people, has had a government that is dedicated to peace with its neighbors and improved conditions for its own people. Political and economic cooperation between nations has grown rapidly.

I think every American can take a great deal of pride in the role that we have played in bringing this about in Southeast Asia. We can rightly judge—as responsible Southeast Asians themselves do—that the progress of the past 3 years would have been far less likely—if not completely impossible—if America's sons and others had not made their stand in Vietnam.

At Johns Hopkins University, about 3 years ago, I announced that the United States would take part in the great work of developing Southeast Asia, including the Mekong Valley, for all the people of that region. Our determination to help build a better land-a better land for men on both sides of the present conflict—has not diminished in the least. Indeed, the ravages of war, I think, have made it more urgent than ever.

So, I repeat on behalf of the United States again tonight what I said at Johns Hopkins—that North Vietnam could take its place in this common effort just as soon as peace comes.

Over time, a wider framework of peace and security in Southeast Asia may become possible. The new cooperation of the nations of the area could be a foundation-stone. Certainly friendship with the nations of such a Southeast Asia is what the United States seeks—and that is all that the United States seeks.

One day, my fellow citizens, there will be peace in Southeast Asia.

It will come because the people of Southeast Asia want it—those whose armies are at war tonight, and those who, though threatened, have thus far been spared.

Peace will come because Asians were willing to work for it—and to sacrifice for it—and to die by the thousands for it.

But let it never be forgotten: Peace will come also because America sent her sons to help secure it.

It has not been easy—far from it. During the past 4-1/2 years, it has been my fate and my responsibility to be Commander in Chief. I have lived—daily and nightly—with the cost of this war. I know the pain that it has inflicted. I know, perhaps better than anyone, the misgivings that it has aroused.

Throughout this entire, long period, I have been sustained by a single principle: that what we are doing now, in Vietnam, is vital not only to the security of Southeast Asia, but it is vital to the security of every American.

Surely we have treaties which we must respect. Surely we have commitments that we are going to keep. Resolutions of the Congress testify to the need to resist aggression in the world and in Southeast Asia.

But the heart of our involvement in South Vietnam—under three different presidents, three separate administrations—has always been America's own security.

And the larger purpose of our involvement has always been to help the nations of Southeast Asia become independent and stand alone, self-sustaining, as members of a great world community—at peace with themselves, and at peace with all others.

With such an Asia, our country—and the world—will be far more secure than it is tonight.

I believe that a peaceful Asia is far nearer to reality because of what America has done in Vietnam. I believe that the men who endure the dangers of battle—fighting there for us tonight—are helping the entire world avoid far greater conflicts, far wider wars, far more destruction, than this one.

The peace that will bring them home someday will come. Tonight I have offered the first in what I hope will be a series of mutual moves toward peace.

I pray that it will not be rejected by the leaders of North Vietnam. I pray that they will accept it as a means by which the sacrifices of their own people may be ended. And I ask your help and your support, my fellow citizens, for this effort to reach across the battlefield toward an early peace.

Finally, my fellow Americans, let me say this:

Of those to whom much is given, much is asked. I cannot say and no man could say that no more will be asked of us.

Yet, I believe that now, no less than when the decade began, this generation of Americans is willing to "pay any price, bear any burden, meet any hardship, support any friend, oppose any foe to assure the survival and the success of liberty."

Since those words were spoken by John F. Kennedy, the people of America have kept that compact with mankind's noblest cause.

And we shall continue to keep it.

Yet, I believe that we must always be mindful of this one thing, whatever the trials and the tests ahead. The ultimate strength of our country and our cause will lie not in powerful weapons or infinite resources or boundless wealth, but will lie in the unity of our people.

This I believe very deeply.

Throughout my entire public career I have followed the personal philosophy that I am a free man, an American, a public servant, and a member of my party, in that order always and only.

For 37 years in the service of our Nation, first as a Congressman, as a Senator, and as Vice President, and now as your President, I have put the unity of the people first. I have put it ahead of any divisive partisanship.

And in these times as in times before, it is true that a house divided against itself by the spirit of faction, of party, of region, of religion, of race, is a house that cannot stand.

There is division in the American house now. There is divisiveness among us all tonight. And holding the trust that is mine, as President of all the people, I cannot disregard the peril to the progress of the American people and the hope and the prospect of peace for all peoples.

So, I would ask all Americans, whatever their personal interests or concern, to guard against divisiveness and all its ugly consequences.

Fifty-two months and 10 days ago, in a moment of tragedy and trauma, the duties of this office fell upon me. I asked then for your help and God's, that we might continue America on its course, binding up our wounds, healing our history, moving forward in new unity, to clear the American agenda and to keep the American commitment for all of our people.

United we have kept that commitment. United we have enlarged that commitment.

Through all time to come, I think America will be a stronger nation, a more just society, and a land of greater opportunity and fulfillment because of what we have all done together in these years of unparalleled achievement.

Our reward will come in the life of freedom, peace, and hope that our children will enjoy through ages ahead.

What we won when all of our people united just must not now be lost in suspicion, distrust, selfishness, and politics among any of our people.

Believing this as I do, I have concluded that I should not permit the Presidency to become involved in the partisan divisions that are developing in this political year.

With America's sons in the fields far away, with America's future under challenge right here at home, with our hopes and the world's hopes for peace in the balance every day, I do not believe that I should devote an hour or a day of my time to any personal partisan causes or to any duties other than the awesome duties of this office—the Presidency of your country.

Accordingly, I shall not seek, and I will not accept, the nomination of my party for another term as your President.

But let men everywhere know, however, that a strong, a confident, and a vigilant America stands ready tonight to seek an honorable peace—and stands ready tonight to defend an honored cause—whatever the price, whatever the burden, whatever the sacrifice that duty may require.

Thank you for listening. Good night and God bless all of you.

Document Analysis

The administration was divided over whether outcome of the Tet Offensive represented a breakthrough to be exploited militarily, through yet another troop escalation, or an opportunity to pursue peace talks and a negotiated settlement. Secretary of Defense Robert McNamara, who had gradually turned against the war, resigned at the end of February and was replaced by Clark Clifford. Clifford, who came into office supporting the war, turned against it in a matter of weeks, having concluded that the military was unable to justify its latest troop request. In Clifford's view, escalation would result only in renewed stalemate at a higher level of violence. On the other hand, Secretary of State Dean Rusk and National Security Adviser Walt W. Rostow were convinced that conditions increasingly favored the United States. Johnson typically refused to accept either argument fully. He generally responded to their appeals with compromises and halfway measures. The March 31 speech represents one such compromise. At the same time, in announcing his resignation, he stresses that he would be able to negotiate and pursue the war without having to yield to electoral considerations.

Essential Themes

The top theme in the speech is peace, or rather the prospect of peace, in Vietnam, but it was to be a peace in which the United States still expected to achieve all its objectives. Johnson had made various quiet offers to halt the bombing of North Vietnam and one public offer in a speech in San Antonio in September 1967, but he had conditioned these offers on the other side's engaging in productive peace talks and not taking advantage of U.S. restraint on the battlefield. Hanoi had refused, and the half of Johnson's advisers were skeptical of the idea anyway. At the same time, Johnson stressed that the war was going well and that the nation could afford to pursue both the war in Vietnam and his Great Society program at home. His initial response to the Tet Offensive had been to strengthen his commitment to the ongoing course in Vietnam with allusions to the lessons of Munich and the Domino Theory. In the March 31 speech, however, he did not allude to Munich or the Domino Theory, and his call for higher taxes was the first suggestion that scarce resources would force him to make difficult choices.

The new strategy would be to fight and negotiate simultaneously. In his March 31 speech, Johnson again spoke of halting the bombing in return for meaningful negotiations and for not taking advantage of U.S. restraint, but

this time, he did not make them preconditions. He curtailed the bombing immediately and unilaterally. (Bombing was halted north of the twentieth parallel, with the theory that the area south of that line was actively being used to supply communist forces in South Vietnam.) He also offered to send representatives "to any forum, at any time" for talks. He noted that the U.S. objectives in Vietnam were not to annihilate North Vietnam, but to create conditions in which South Vietnam could live in peace without outside domination or interference, adding that the United States would be willing to provide economic assistance to the whole of Southeast Asia after the war ended. (This, however, ignored Hanoi's contention that there was only one Vietnam and that its artificial division into two was itself an artefact of outside domination and interference.) At the same time, Johnson announced that he was sending more troops to South Vietnam, although not nearly as many as the Pentagon had requested. The United States intensified air and ground operations against communist forces within South Vietnam to maintain pressure on Hanoi to make concessions.

By stressing the pro-peace element of his position— in effect, the position of McCarthy and Kennedy— Johnson may have hoped to undermine their chances for the nomination and make it harder for them to attack his policies or to attack Humphrey for defending his legacy. He also implied that the two were divisive partisans indifferent to America's best interests, while he stated explicitly that he was putting the "unity of the people" above partisan interests.

Hanoi agreed to negotiations, which began in May. In October 1968, after Hanoi had agreed to allow Saigon (hitherto dismissed as a U.S. puppet) to participate in the talks—and at a time when the U.S. military position on the ground was improving—Johnson agreed to a complete halt of the bombing of North Vietnam (although the bombing of supply routes through Laos was intensified). The Saigon government, however, delayed and obstructed. President Nguyen Van Thiêu feared that the Johnson administration intended to abandon him and hoped to get more solid support from a Republican administration. (It later emerged that Republican presidential candidate Richard M. Nixon secretly encouraged him to stall the talks.) Indeed, even as the talks proceeded, the Johnson administration remained divided on goals, whether to seek the survival of a viable, independent South Vietnam or simply to extract the United States from its quagmire. In any event, the talks made little progress. Both Hanoi and Washington resisted

Washington, D.C. in October 1967—support for the Vietnam War was dropping and the anti-Vietnam War movement strengthened. (By Frank Wolfe - Lyndon B. Johnson Library)

making concessions, each in the apparent belief that the other was on the verge of capitulation.

—*Scott C. Monje, PhD*

Bibliography and Additional Reading

Berman, Larry. *Lyndon Johnson's War: The Road to Stalemate in Vietnam.* New York: W. W. Norton, 1989. Print.

Busby, Horace. *The Thirty-First of March: Lyndon Johnson's Final Days in Office.* New York: Farrar, Straus, and Giroux, 2005. Print.

Herring, George C. *LBJ and Vietnam: A Different Kind of War.* Austin, TX: University of Texas Press, 1994. Print.

Jamieson, Patrick E. "Seeing the Lyndon B. Johnson Presidency through the March 31, 1968, Withdrawal Speech." *Presidential Studies Quarterly* 29.1 (March 1999): 134–49. Print.

Warner, Geoffrey. "Lyndon Johnson's War? Part 2: From Escalation to Negotiation." *International Affairs* 81.1 (January 2005): 187–215. Print.

■ Richard Nixon's Acceptance Speech at the 1968 Republican National Convention

Date: August 8, 1968
Author: Richard M. Nixon
Genre: Speech; address

Summary Overview

Richard Nixon officially announced his candidacy on February 1, 1968, just after the beginning of the Tet Offensive in South Vietnam, where communist forces struck U.S. strongholds across the country, convincing many Americans that the United States was mired in a military stalemate. The coming months witnessed Lyndon Johnson announce he would not seek re-election, the assassination of Martin Luther King, Jr. followed by an explosion of rage in America's cities, intensifying campus protest against the Vietnam War and the assassination of presidential candidate Robert Kennedy.

Amidst this chaos, Nixon ran a strong campaign in Republican primaries. The Republicans held their convention in Miami from August 5 to 8 in a controlled environment that projected an orderly contrast to the unrest seen nightly by Americans on their TVs. Off camera, Nixon and his campaign team worked diligently to line up the requisite delegates to win the nomination. These included many whose hearts were with the more ideologically conservative and personally congenial California governor Ronald Reagan. Nixon further had to win the support of moderate Republicans who supported New York governor Nelson Rockefeller. Nixon engineered the support of southern delegates with the help of South Carolina Senator Strom Thurmond and plotted a "Southern strategy" to head off the more extreme independent "Law and Order" campaign of segregationist Alabama governor George Wallace, who was polling at 20 percent nationally. Nixon unified the factions in the Republican Party and was nominated for president amidst enthusiastic applause. His acceptance speech outlined a vision of law and order at home, regained respect for America abroad and an unspecified plan for peace with honor in Vietnam. Nixon wove together themes in his speech that were designed to appeal to many audiences, including the Reagan right wing, populist supporters of Wallace

and moderate Americans looking for steady leadership. Nixon melded the statesman-like "New Nixon" with divisive appeals to those he depicted as the majority of good Americans against the "demonstrators" and "shouters" spreading "lawlessness," prefiguring his "Moral Majority" speech of a year later.

Defining Moment

The election of 1968 represented not one, but two, remarkable political comebacks. The first was that of Nixon himself, whose political obituary had been written in 1962, when, after losing the race for California governor, Nixon peevishly announced his retirement at a press conference and declared "you don't have Nixon to kick around anymore." Having lost two elections in two years, pundits declared Americans had seen the last of Richard Nixon.

The second comeback was that of the Republican Party, which had lost the 1964 election to Democrat Lyndon B. Johnson in a historic landslide. Right-wing Arizona Senator Barry Goldwater had run on a platform of hard-line anti-communism, states' rights, unrestrained free enterprise and dismantling the social welfare state. At the 1964 Republican Convention, Goldwater had defended his sometimes extremist supporters by proclaiming that "extremism in the defense of liberty is no vice." As the Democrats won a historic landslide for president and Congress, liberalism was riding high and commentators wondered if conservatism, and perhaps even the Republican Party itself, were dead.

Nineteen-sixty-five, however, began to unleash political forces that had been germinating beneath the surface. In the summer a major riot/rebellion broke out in Watts, Los Angeles, marking the beginning of consecutive years of racial unrest in America's urban centers and the emergence of a more militant phase of the African American freedom struggle. Waves of urban revolt struck

U.S. cities each summer in 1966 and 1967 ("the Long Hot Summer") and exploded nation-wide in 1968 in the wake of the assassination of Martin Luther King, Jr. The growing unrest in black America on the heels of Johnson's historic civil rights bills fueled white racial resentment in the North and West as well as the South, which manifested in huge Republican gains in Congress in the 1966 mid-term elections.

Nineteen-sixty-five also marked the year President Johnson introduced ground troops to fight in South Vietnam, where an unpopular U.S.-backed government was fighting against the Viet Cong insurgency supported by communist North Vietnam. Johnson's transition from a military advisory effort to the Americanization of the war led to increasing draft calls and an escalation of U.S. troop strength to 550,000 by 1968. As the war expanded with no end in sight, a small peace movement grew until by 1968 the movement was a major force in U.S. society. The fall of 1967 witnessed violent confrontations between protesters and police.

These changes were paralleled by a growing hippie counterculture which rejected consumerism, materialism and social conformity for sex, drugs, rock music and communal living. As the baby boom swelled a generation gap widened. By 1968 these changes were accompanied by a rising crime rate and inflation, and the optimism and idealism of the early 1960s gave way to division, violence and a breakdown in what conservatives now called "law and order."

During these years, as the forces of revolution and reaction intensified, Nixon quietly rehabilitated his image. Although he considered Barry Goldwater an extremist in 1964, Nixon campaigned for him, winning the respect of the hardline conservative activists who were the party's future. In 1966, Nixon campaigned for Republican congressional candidates across America. When the Republicans scored huge pick-ups in 1966, scores of new members of Congress were indebted to Nixon.

In 1966-1967 Nixon toured the world and visited South Vietnam to bolster his image as a foreign policy veteran. But Nixon also had a darker reputation as "Tricky Dick," which he had developed during his days on the House Un-American Activities Committee (HUAC) and in his election campaigns for Congress when he smeared his opponents as communist sympathizers.

As Nixon prepared for his 1968 run, he employed media-savvy consultants to remake his image. He adopted a self-deprecating sense of humor and appeared more comfortable on TV. During the campaign he employed a young Roger Ailes (future founder of *Fox News*), who organized highly controlled events designed to look like Nixon was comfortably interacting with ordinary Americans.

Amidst the upheavals of 1968 Nixon evoked memories of the placid Eisenhower years and associated himself with hard-working, law-abiding Americans. He charged two terms of Democratic governance with the breakdown in law and order and stalemate in Vietnam and skillfully exploited the divisions in American society.

Author Biography

Richard Milhouse Nixon was born in Yorba Linda, California on January 9, 1913. He attended Whittier College and Duke University Law School. During World War II Nixon served in the Navy in a non-combat role in the Pacific Theater. He was elected as a Republican to the United States House of Representatives from a California district in 1946 and to the U.S. Senate in 1950. Nixon served as Vice President under President Dwight D. Eisenhower from 1953-1961. He lost his bid for president to John F. Kennedy in 1960. In 1962 he lost a run for California governor. Nixon was elected president of the United States in 1968 and re-elected by a landslide in 1972. On August 9, 1974, amidst the Watergate scandal, Nixon became the first president in U.S. history to resign from the presidency. Nixon died on April 22, 1994.

HISTORICAL DOCUMENT

Mr. Chairman, delegates to this convention, my fellow Americans.

Sixteen years ago I stood before this Convention to accept your nomination as the running mate of one of the greatest Americans of our time—or of any time—Dwight D. Eisenhower.

Eight years ago, I had the highest honor of accepting your nomination for President of the United States.

Tonight, I again proudly accept that nomination for President of the United States.

But I have news for you. This time there is a difference.

This time we are going to win.

We're going to win for a number of reasons: first a personal one. General Eisenhower, as you know, lies critically ill in the Walter Reed Hospital tonight... there is nothing that he lives more for and there is nothing that would lift him more than for us to win in November and I say let's win this one for Ike! ...

We are going to win because at a time that America cries out for the unity that this Administration has destroyed, the Republican Party—after a spirited contest for its nomination for President and for Vice President—stands united before the nation tonight.

I congratulate Governor Reagan. I congratulate Governor Rockefeller [on their runs] ...

[A] party that can unite itself will unite America...

And the question that we answer tonight: can America meet this great challenge?

For a few moments, let us look at America, let us listen to America to find the answer to that question. As we look at America, we see cities enveloped in smoke and flame. We hear sirens in the night. We see Americans dying on distant battlefields abroad. We see Americans hating each other; fighting each other; killing each other at home. And as we see and hear these things, millions of Americans cry out in anguish. Did we come all this way for this? Did American boys die in Normandy, and Korea, and in Valley Forge for this?

Listen to the answer to those questions.

It is another voice. It is the quiet voice in the tumult and the shouting. It is the voice of the great majority of Americans, the forgotten Americans—the non-shouters; the non-demonstrators. They are not racists or sick; they are not guilty of the crime that plagues the land. They are black and they are white—they're native born and foreign born —they're young and they're old. They work in America's factories. They run America's businesses. They serve in government. They provide most of the soldiers who died to keep us free. They give drive to the spirit of America. They give lift to the American Dream. They give steel to the backbone of America.

They are good people, they are decent people; they work, and they save, and they pay their taxes, and they care...

Let's never forget that despite her faults, America is a great nation. And America is great because her people are great... America is in trouble today not because her people have failed but because her leaders have failed. And what America needs are leaders to match the greatness of her people. And this great group of Americans, the forgotten Americans, and others know that the great; question Americans must answer by their votes in November is this: Whether we shall continue for four more years the policies of the last five years.

And this is their answer and this is my answer to that question.

When the strongest nation in the world can be tied down for four years in a war in Vietnam with no end in sight; When the richest nation in the world can't manage its own economy; When the nation with the greatest tradition of the rule of law is plagued by unprecedented lawlessness; When a nation that has been known for a century for equality of opportunity is torn by unprecedented racial violence; And when the President of the United States cannot travel abroad or to any major city at home without fear of a hostile demonstration—then it's time for new leadership for the United States of America.

My fellow Americans, tonight I accept the challenge and the commitment to provide that new leadership for America...

Look at our problems abroad. Do you realize that we face the stark truth that we are worse off in every area of the world tonight than we were when President Eisenhower left office eight years ago. That's the record. And there is only one answer to such a record of failure and that is a complete housecleaning of those responsible for the failures of that record. The answer is a complete re-appraisal of America's policies in every section of the world.

We shall begin with Vietnam.

We all hope in this room that there is a chance that current negotiations may bring an honorable end to that war. And we will say nothing during this campaign that might destroy that chance. But if the war is not ended when the people choose in November, the choice will be clear. Here it is. For four years this Administration has had at its disposal the greatest military and economic advantage that one nation has ever had over another in any war in history. For four years, America's fighting men have set a record for courage and sacrifice unsurpassed in our history. For four years, this Administration has had the support of the Loyal Opposition for the objective of seeking an honorable end to the struggle. Never has so much military and economic and diplomatic power been used so ineffectively. And if after all of this time and all of this sacrifice and all of this support there is still no end in sight, then I say the time has come for the American people to turn to new leadership—not tied to the mistakes and the policies of the past. That is what we offer to America.

And I pledge to you tonight that the first priority foreign policy objective of our next Administration will be to bring an honorable end to the war in Vietnam. We shall not stop there—we need a policy to prevent more Vietnams…

And now to the leaders of the Communist world, we say: After an era of confrontation, the time has come for an era of negotiation. Where the world's super powers are concerned, there is no acceptable alternative to peaceful negotiation. Because this will be a period of negotiation, we shall restore the strength of America so that we shall always negotiate from strength and never from weakness…

And as we commit to new policies for America tonight, let us make one further pledge:

My friends, America is a great nation…[but today] America is an example to be avoided and not followed. A nation that can't keep the peace at home won't be trusted to keep the peace abroad. A President who isn't treated with respect at home will not be treated with respect abroad. A nation which can't manage its own economy can't tell others how to manage theirs.

If we are to restore prestige and respect for America abroad, the place to begin is at home in the United States of America…

And tonight, it is time for some honest talk about the problem of order in the United States…

[T]he first civil right of every American is to be free from domestic violence, and that right must be guaranteed in this country… The wave of crime is not going to be the wave of the future in the United States of America. We shall re-establish freedom from fear in America

so that America can take the lead in re-establishing freedom from fear in the world.

And to those who say that law and order is the code word for racism, there and here is a reply: Our goal is justice for every American.

If we are to have respect for law in America, we must have laws that deserve respect…

We are a great nation. And we must never forget how we became great. America is a great nation today not because of what government did for people—but because of what people did for themselves over a hundred- ninety years in this country… And let us build bridges, my friends, build bridges to human dignity across that gulf that separates black America from white America.

Black Americans, no more than white Americans, they do not want more government programs which perpetuate dependency. They don't want to be a colony in a nation. They want the pride, and the self-respect, and the dignity that can only come if they have an equal chance to own their own homes, to own their own businesses, to be managers and executives as well as workers…

My fellow Americans, I believe that historians will recall that 1968 marked the beginning of the American generation in world history… I see a day when Americans are once again proud of their flag. When once again at home and abroad, it is honored as the world's greatest symbol of liberty and justice…

And tonight, therefore, as we make this commitment, let us look into our hearts and let us look down into the faces of our children. Is there anything in the world that should stand in their way? None of the old hatreds mean anything when we look down into the faces of our children. In their faces is our hope, our love, and our courage.

Tonight, I see the face of a child.

He lives in a great city. He is black. Or he is white. He is Mexican, Italian, Polish. None of that matters. What matters, he's an American child. That child in that great city is more important than any politician's promise. He is America. He is a poet. He is a scientist, he is a great teacher, he is a proud craftsman. He is everything we ever hoped to be and everything we dare to dream to be. He sleeps the sleep of childhood and he dreams the dreams of a child. And yet when he awakens, he awakens to a living nightmare of poverty, neglect and despair. He fails in school. He ends up on welfare. For him the American system is one that feeds his stomach and starves his soul. It breaks his heart. And in the end it may take his life on some distant battlefield. To millions of children in this rich land, this is their prospect of the future.

But this is only part of what I see in America.

I see another child tonight. He hears the train go by at night and he dreams of faraway places where he'd like to go. It seems like an impossible dream. But he is helped on his journey through life. A father who had to go to work before he finished the sixth grade, sacrificed everything he had so that his sons could go to college. A gentle, Quaker mother, with a passionate concern for peace, quietly wept when he went to war but she understood why he had to go. A great teacher, a remarkable football coach, an inspirational minister encouraged him on his way. A courageous wife and loyal children stood by him in victory and also defeat. And in his chosen profession of politics, first there were scores, then hundreds, then thousands, and finally millions worked for his success.

And tonight he stands before you—nominated for President of the United States of America. You can see why I believe so deeply in the American Dream...

The next President of the United States will face challenges which in some ways will be greater than those of Washington or Lincoln. Because for the first time in our nation's history, an American President will face not only the problem of restoring peace abroad but of restoring peace at home.

Without God's help and your help, we will surely fail; but with God's help and your help, we shall surely succeed.

My fellow Americans, the long dark night for America is about to end.

The time has come for us to leave the valley of despair and climb the mountain so that we may see the glory of the dawn—a new day for America, and a new dawn for peace and freedom in the world.

Document Analysis

Nixon's televised acceptance speech, excerpted here, weaves together several interlocking themes: nostalgia for the 1950s, divisions between patriotic "forgotten Americans" and the "shouters" and "demonstrators" responsible for "unprecedented lawlessness," promises of peace under restored American global leadership and the rebirth of the American Dream.

Nixon begins by invoking the ailing Dwight D. Eisenhower, Supreme Allied Commander in World War II and popular president from 1953-61. After congratulating his Republican opponents he hails the unity in the Republican Party which he proclaims will go on to unify the country.

Nixon then moves from standard campaign themes to the divisions of 1968, asking his audience to "listen to America." He uses the device of two competing sounds to represent two Americas, one the "shouting" of "protest," "lawlessness" and "tumult," the other "the voice of the great majority of Americans, the forgotten Americans—the non-shouters; the non-demonstrators," who "cry out in anguish" at the loss of the America they once knew. Nixon evokes visual images and sounds of an America descending into anarchy: "cities enveloped in smoke and flame," "sirens in the night," "Americans hating each other" and "Americans dying on distant battlefields..."

Nixon then asks, "Did we come all this way for this?" and invokes the sacrifices of American soldiers from Valley Forge through Normandy to Korea. He pays tribute to the majority of Americans "who work in the factories... run the businesses... died to keep us free... drive the American Spirit...give lift to the American Dream... [and] pay their taxes..." Only by rejecting the Democratic leadership of the last five years (Nixon astutely does not include the three years under the beloved John F. Kennedy) can the America of "decent Americans" be reclaimed from the forces chaos.

Even as Nixon weaves this dark vision of America, he is careful to include the diversity of the American people among the good Americans. Thus, while his evocation of law and order appealed to "white backlash" voters, his inclusiveness avoided sounding explicitly racist.

Nixon then moves on to America's place in the world, which he argues is linked to a strong America at home. He again evokes what many Americans remembered as the peace and prosperity of the Eisenhower years. He turns to Vietnam and appeals to a war-weary nation with vague promises of peace and reaching out to communist super powers to de-escalate the tensions of the Cold War. Here Nixon plays to his image as a statesman with vast foreign policy experience.

Republican nominee Richard Nixon gives his trademark 'V' sign as he stands atop a motorcade vehicle during a Tickertape parade in the Chicago Loop, shortly after the Democratic Convention in the same city. (U.S. National Archives and Records Administration)

Richard Nixon's Acceptance Speech at the 1968 Republican National Convention • **379**

Nixon concludes by juxtaposing the images of two children, one a contemporary child who becomes dependent on welfare and sees his dreams wither away, and another child from an older America when the American Dream was still alive – Nixon himself – who grows up to become at that moment the Republican nominee for president.

Essential Themes

Nineteen-sixty-eight was one of the most tumultuous years in American history and the election that year was a turning point in American politics, marking the end of an era of Democratic dominance in national politics and the beginning of an era of Republican ascendancy. After the Republicans' unified convention, the Democrats gathered in Chicago from August 26 to 29. The Democrats were deeply divided over the war in Vietnam. The Democratic Convention erupted in chaos on the floor as supporters of Eugene McCarthy and the late Robert Kennedy (the peace candidates) got into shouting matches and sometimes fisticuffs with delegates loyal to prowar candidate Hubert Humphrey. As the party delegates nominated Humphrey and defeated the peace plank in the party platform, battles between police and antiwar protesters raged throughout Chicago. The images on TV showed a party in disarray and under siege. Seizing on the divisions among his opponents Nixon declared that if the Democrats could not unite their party they could not unite the country.

Members of the radical New Left had already given up on electoral politics and believed only a revolution could end war, racism, poverty and a culture of repression in America. As the election approached, many peace Democrats refused to support the prowar Humphrey. Nixon had opened a comfortable lead over Humphrey and the independent Wallace campaign, but when Humphrey broke with Johnson and announced support for a bombing halt of North Vietnam, he began closing the gap. After losing one of the closest elections in U.S. history in 1960, Nixon won one of the closest in 1968. Nixon received 43.4 percent of the popular vote to Humphrey's 42.7 percent and Wallace's 13.5 percent.

The first years of Nixon's presidency were marked by continuing polarization in American society. His policy of Vietnamization slowly withdrew U.S. troops while building up the South Vietnamese Army. Nixon expanded the war into Cambodia and Laos and intensified the bombing, but by the end of his first term U.S. troops had shrunk from 550,000 to 25,000 in South Vietnam.

Meanwhile, Nixon enacted liberal domestic legislation like the Environmental Protection Act while nominating conservative judges to the judiciary. His biggest achievement was détente with the Soviet Union and the People's Republic of China in which he sought to ease Cold War tensions between the superpowers.

Exhausted from the tumultuous 1960s, and with U.S. troops almost out of Vietnam, American voters gave Nixon one of the largest election victories in U.S. history in 1972. Nixon defeated progressive, antiwar candidate Senator George McGovern in a landslide, winning 49 of 50 states. Many interpreted Nixon's victory as the triumph of traditional, predominantly white Americans against a coalition of peace activists, feminists, minorities and those embracing the cultural liberalization of the 1960s.

Nixon's triumph was soon overshadowed by the Watergate scandal. Members of Nixon's team had carried out phone taps and covert "dirty tricks" against Nixon's opponents, including the wire-tapping of Democratic campaign headquarters at the Watergate Hotel in Washington, D.C. in 1972.

The final two years of Nixon's presidency were marked by independent investigations and Congressional hearings into the Watergate break-in and subsequent cover-up, resulting in Nixon's unprecedented resignation on August 9, 1974.

Despite the Watergate scandal, Nixon's landslide re-election in 1972 signaled a rejection of 1960s liberalism and radicalism and a move to the right by the electorate. That right-ward shift culminated in the 1980 election of Ronald Reagan — Nixon's right-wing challenger in 1968 – to the presidency of the United States.

Nixon's 1968 victory was the dividing line marking the slow decline of liberalism and the gradual rise of conservatism. Although the conservative trajectory was interrupted by the Watergate scandal and the centrist presidency of Democrat Jimmy Carter in the late 1970s, the political realignments revealed in the 1968 election would define American politics into the twenty-first century.

—*Robert Surbrug, PhD*

Bibliography and Additional Readings

Cohen, Michael A. *American Maelstrom: The 1968 Election and the Politics of Division*. New York: Oxford University Press, 2016.

O'Donnell, Lawrence. *Playing with Fire: 1968 and the Transformation of American Politics*. New York: Penguin House, 2017.

White, Theodore H. White. *The Making of the President: 1968*. New York: Atheneum House, 1969.

Wills, Gary. *Nixon Agonistes: The Crisis of the Self-Made Man*. New York: First Mariner Books, 2002.

■ Richard Nixon's Second Inaugural Address

Date: January 20, 1973
Author: Richard M. Nixon
Genre: Speech

Summary Overview

Richard Nixon's inaugural address, delivered at the beginning of his second term as U.S. president in January 1973, set forth a policy of limiting America's commitments abroad and aiming for a less confrontational relationship with other great powers, in addition to a program of domestic reform based on locating the initiative for change outside of the federal government. Nixon celebrated the impending end of the American involvement in the Vietnam War and expressed hope for domestic tranquility after the turmoil of the 1960s and early 1970s. While this optimistic speech was meant to mark the beginning of an ambitious second term following a landslide victory that had signified his popularity with the American public, Nixon would experience a significant downfall within months that would bring his time in office to a bitter and premature end and forever taint his presidential legacy.

Defining Moment

In 1972, Nixon, the Republican president running for reelection, won one of the most crushing electoral victories in American history, winning forty-nine states. His Democratic opponent, Senator George McGovern, won only Massachusetts and the District of Columbia. Nixon's victory was somewhat marred by the capture of several individuals tied to his campaign during an attempted break-in at the Watergate building, the temporary headquarters of the Democratic National Committee, on June 17; however, in January, that scandal was still relatively minor and not directly connected to Nixon, and it goes unmentioned in this speech. Instead of viewing the presidency as weakened, observers were wondering what Nixon would do with his overwhelming mandate.

Nixon's victory in 1972 came after an extraordinarily divisive period in American life. There were massive riots fueled by racial conflict in American cities. The Vietnam War and other issues had led to huge demonstrations on college campuses and elsewhere. In 1970, four

students at Kent State University in Ohio protesting the invasion of Cambodia that the Nixon administration had launched were shot and killed by the National Guard. Many Americans considered U.S. involvement in Vietnam to have been ill-advised, and Nixon himself championed "Vietnamizing" the conflict, transferring the burden of protecting the South from the North to the people of South Vietnam themselves.

Nixon's great foreign policy triumph in his first term had been, after decades of estrangement, the effort to normalize relations between the United States and Communist-ruled China. His visit to China in 1972 had been expected to help his campaign for reelection. However, Nixon had also received a great deal of criticism for expanding the Vietnam War to Laos and Cambodia, as well as the ruthless bombing of North Vietnam itself. At the same time, following lengthy negotiations, a peace agreement that included American withdrawal from Vietnam and a cease-fire between North and South Vietnam had recently been reached in Paris and would be formally signed by all parties seven days after this speech. As Nixon spoke, America was in the process of winding down its direct military involvement in the Vietnam War.

Author Biography

Richard Milhous Nixon was the thirty-seventh president of the United States. A veteran of World War II, he was a Republican who served as a congressman, a senator, and a vice president under President Dwight D. Eisenhower. He ran unsuccessfully for president against John F. Kennedy in 1960. Eight years later, he campaigned for the presidency again, defeating Democrat Hubert H. Humphrey in a close election dominated by the issue of Vietnam. Nixon's achievements in his first term included the opening to China and détente with the Soviet Union. On the domestic front, his first term saw the last great expansion of the federal government, with the establishment of new agencies such as the Occupational Safety and Health Administration and the Environmental Protection Agency.

Though Nixon's presidency was marked by controversy, he was reelected with an overwhelming majority in 1972. During that campaign, a group of Nixon's supporters broke into the Democratic National Committee's headquarters at the Watergate building in Washington, DC. Although Nixon most likely did not know about the initial break-in, he became deeply involved in the ensuing cover-up, and the growing scandal forced him to resign on August 9, 1974. After suffering a stroke, he died on April 22, 1994. He remains the only president to have resigned the office.

HISTORICAL DOCUMENT

I, RICHARD NIXON, do solemnly swear that I will faithfully execute the Office of President of the United States, and will to the best of my ability, preserve, protect and defend the Constitution of the United States, so help me God.

Mr. Vice President, Mr. Speaker, Mr. Chief Justice, Senator Cook, Mrs. Eisenhower, and my fellow citizens of this great and good country we share together:

When we met here 4 years ago, America was bleak in spirit, depressed by the prospect of seemingly endless war abroad and of destructive conflict at home.

As we meet here today, we stand on the threshold of a new era of peace in the world.

The central question before us is: How shall we use that peace?

Let us resolve that this era we are about to enter will not be what other postwar periods have so often been: a time of retreat and isolation that leads to stagnation at home and invites new danger abroad.

Let us resolve that this will be what it can become: a time of great responsibilities greatly borne, in which we renew the spirit and the promise of America as we enter our third century as a nation.

This past year saw far-reaching results from our new policies for peace. By continuing to revitalize our traditional friendships, and by our missions to Peking and to Moscow, we were able to establish the base for a new and more durable pattern of relationships among the nations of the world. Because of America's bold initiatives, 1972 will be long remembered as the year of the greatest progress since the end of World War II toward a lasting peace in the world.

The peace we seek in the world is not the flimsy peace which is merely an interlude between wars, but a peace which can endure for generations to come.

It is important that we understand both the necessity and the limitations of America's role in maintaining that peace.

Unless we in America work to preserve the peace, there will be no peace.

Unless we in America work to preserve freedom, there will be no freedom.

But let us clearly understand the new nature of America's role, as a result of the new policies we have adopted over these past 4 years.

We shall respect our treaty commitments.

We shall support vigorously the principle that no country has the right to impose its will or rule on another by force.

We shall continue, in this era of negotiation, to work for the limitation of nuclear arms and to reduce the danger of confrontation between the great powers.

We shall do our share in defending peace and freedom in the world. But we shall expect others to do their share.

The time has passed when America will make every other nation's conflict our own, or make every other nation's future our responsibility, or presume to tell the people of other nations how to manage their own affairs.

Just as we respect the right of each nation to determine its own future, we also recognize the responsibility of each nation to secure its own future.

Just as America's role is indispensable in preserving the world's peace, so is each nation's role indispensable in preserving its own peace.

Together with the rest of the world, let us resolve to move forward from the beginnings we have made. Let us continue to bring down the walls of hostility which have divided the world for too long, and to build in their place bridges of understanding—so that despite profound differences between systems of government, the people of the world can be friends.

Let us build a structure of peace in the world in which the weak are as safe as the strong, in which each respects the right of the other to live by a different system, in which those who would influence others will do so by the strength of their ideas and not by the force of their arms.

Let us accept that high responsibility not as a burden, but gladly—gladly because the chance to build such a peace is the noblest endeavor in which a nation can engage; gladly also because only if we act greatly in meeting our responsibilities abroad will we remain a great nation, and only if we remain a great nation will we act greatly in meeting our challenges at home.

We have the chance today to do more than ever before in our history to make life better in America—to ensure better education, better health, better housing, better transportation, a cleaner environment-to restore respect for law, to make our communities more livable—and to ensure the God-given right of every American to full and equal opportunity.

Because the range of our needs is so great, because the reach of our opportunities is so great, let us be bold in our determination to meet those needs in new ways.

Just as building a structure of peace abroad has required turning away from old policies that have failed, so building a new era of progress at home requires turning away from old policies that have failed.

Abroad, the shift from old policies to new has not been a retreat from our responsibilities, but a better way to peace.

And at home, the shift from old policies to new will not be a retreat from our responsibilities, but a better way to progress.

Abroad and at home, the key to those new responsibilities lies in the placing and the division of responsibility. We have lived too long with the consequences of attempting to gather all power and responsibility in Washington.

Abroad and at home, the time has come to turn away from the condescending policies of paternalism—-of "Washington knows best."

A person can be expected to act responsibly only if he has responsibility. This is human nature. So let us encourage individuals at home and nations abroad to do more for themselves, to decide more for themselves. Let us locate responsibility in more places. And let us measure what we will do for others by what they will do for themselves.

That is why today I offer no promise of a purely governmental solution for every problem. We have lived too long with that false promise. In trusting too much in government, we have asked of it more than it can deliver. This leads only to inflated expectations, to reduced individual effort, and to a disappointment and frustration that erode confidence both in what government can do and in what people can do.

Government must learn to take less from people so that people can do more for themselves.

Let us remember that America was built not by government, but by people; not by welfare, but by work; not by shirking responsibility, but by seeking responsibility.

In our own lives, let each of us ask-not just what will government do for me, but what can I do for myself?

In the challenges we face together, let each of us ask—not just how can government help, but how can I help?

Your National Government has a great and vital role to play. And I pledge to you that where this Government should act, we will act boldly and we will lead boldly. But just as important is the role that each and every one of us must play, as an individual and as a member of his own community.

From this day forward, let each of us make a solemn commitment in his own heart: to bear his responsibility, to do his part, to live his ideals—so that together we can see the dawn of a new age of progress for America, and together, as we celebrate our 200th anniversary as a nation, we can do so proud in the fulfillment of our promise to ourselves and to the world.

As America's longest and most difficult war comes to an end, let us again learn to debate our differences with civility and decency. And let each of us reach out for that one precious quality government cannot provide—a new level of respect for the rights and feelings of one another, a new level of respect for the individual human dignity which is the cherished birthright of every American.

Above all else, the time has come for us to renew our faith in ourselves and in America.

In recent years, that faith has been challenged.

Our children have been taught to be ashamed of their country, ashamed of their parents, ashamed of America's record at home and its role in the world.

At every turn we have been beset by those who find everything wrong with America and little that is right. But I am confident that this will not be the judgment of history on these remarkable times in which we are privileged to live.

America's record in this century has been unparalleled in the world's history for its responsibility, for its generosity, for its creativity, and for its progress.

Let us be proud that our system has produced and provided more freedom and more abundance, more widely shared, than any system in the history of the world.

Let us be proud that in each of the four wars in which we have been engaged in this century, including the one we are now bringing to an end, we have fought not for our selfish advantage, but to help others resist aggression.

And let us be proud that by our bold, new initiatives, by our steadfastness for peace with honor, we have made a breakthrough toward creating in the world what the world has not known before—a structure of peace that can last, not merely for our time, but for generations to come. We are embarking here today on an era that presents challenges as great as those any nation, or any generation, has ever faced.

We shall answer to God, to history, and to our conscience for the way in which we use these years.

As I stand in this place, so hallowed by history, I think of others who have stood here before me. I think of the dreams they had for America and I think of how each recognized that he needed help far beyond himself in order to make those dreams come true.

Today I ask your prayers that in the years ahead I may have God's help in making decisions that are right for America, and I pray for your help so that together we may be worthy of our challenge.

Let us pledge together to make these next 4 years the best 4 years in America's history, so that on its 200th birthday America will be as young and as vital as when it began, and as bright a beacon of hope for all the world.

Let us go forward from here confident in hope, strong in our faith in one another, sustained by our faith in God who created us, and striving always to serve His purpose.

President Richard Nixon is sworn in for a second term as First Lady Pat Nixon holds the Bibles at the East Front of the Capitol in Washington, D.C. Chief Justice Warren Burger administers the oath. (Ollie Atkins, Official White House photographer.)

Document Analysis

Like most inaugural speeches, the emphasis is on broad themes rather than the details of policy. Nixon discusses his second-term agenda in terms of the principles he plans to apply, but says little or nothing about how these principles will apply to specific cases.

Foreign policy issues, the areas Nixon considered central to the work of a president and to his own presidency specifically, come first. The atmosphere of Nixon's discussion of foreign policy is positive, with a primary emphasis on peace and peacemaking. He presents his first term as a success in terms of making peace, not mentioning the fact that American troops were still in Vietnam and that the conflict between North and South Vietnam was far from over. Nixon primarily thought of foreign policy in terms of great power relations; therefore, the hard-won good relations with the Soviet Union and China dominate the picture of the world he gives. He explicitly describes the present as a "postwar" period. While he states that the period will not see a retreat into isolation (by this point in American history "isolationism" was more a rhetorical strawman than a serious policy option), he is also establishing that in the post-Vietnam era American interventions in the affairs of other nations would need to be more limited. The speech's emphasis on the limitations of American power and commitment contrasts with Kennedy's claim in his inaugural address twelve years earlier that America "shall pay any price, bear any burden, meet any hardship, support any friend, oppose any foe to assure the survival and the success of liberty." For Nixon, it was time to lay some of that burden down and allow other nations to work to support themselves to ensure that they could thrive and maintain peace independently.

In the domestic sphere, Nixon explains that the expansion of the federal government characteristic of his first term is now over, and that the initiative for reform will now rest on the state and local level. He advises everyone to think about "not just what will government do for me, but what can I do for myself?" This question harkens back once again to another famous statement in Kennedy's inaugural address: "Ask not what your country can do for you—ask what you can do for your country." Nixon's vision is more individualist and more concerned with self-reliance than with sacrifice for a "national" cause; this policy is consistent with the greater emphasis on individualism in Republican rhetoric.

Nixon expresses the hope that the divisions in the country caused by Vietnam will begin to be healed and that his second term will see peace at home as well as abroad. His conclusion invokes the forthcoming bicentennial of the American Declaration of Independence in 1976, looked forward to as a major occasion for the festive demonstration of American patriotism and the last year of Nixon's second term. Although religion seems to have played little role in Nixon's life, he also employs the religious rhetoric characteristic of public orations on significant occasions in America.

Essential Themes

President Nixon's hopes and plans for his second term came to naught, as his role in the cover-up of the Watergate break-in became apparent over the ensuing months. Investigations also revealed numerous other illegal activities directed at political opponents from the Nixon campaign and the Nixon administration, many undertaken with Nixon's personal approval. Even before his resignation, his administration was increasingly distracted by defending the president from various Watergate investigations, including a court case that challenged his attempt to protect audio tapes recorded in the Oval Office under the presidential prerogative of executive privilege, which left him little time or political capital to carry out policy changes.

Even the president's triumph in Vietnam was tainted. Despite the withdrawal of American troops from Vietnam on March 29, 1973, there was no peace between South and North Vietnam. Both sides began violating the cease-fire that had been part of the peace agreement almost immediately. The South would surrender in 1975, leading to the formation of the Communist-ruled Socialist Republic of Vietnam and what many Americans viewed as a profound national humiliation. In addition, Nixon's vice president, Spiro T. Agnew, was implicated in taking bribes from his days as a county executive in Maryland and had to resign the office. It would be the person appointed as Agnew's successor in the vice presidency, Gerald Ford, who would succeed to the presidency upon Nixon's resignation in 1974 and preside over the national bicentennial festivities in 1976.

Nixon's policy of détente was ended beginning in the late 1970s, partly in reaction to the Communist triumph in Vietnam as well as other changes on the international scene, such as the Soviet invasion of Afghanistan in December 1979. This process began under Ford's successor as president, the Democrat Jimmy Carter. However, the Republican Party in particular turned toward a more confrontational relationship with the Soviets after Nixon and Ford, especially with the rise of Ronald Reagan as the party's leading figure in the post-Nixon era. On the domestic front, Nixon's vision of removing the initiative from the federal government was carried further by Reagan's vision of small government and of government at all levels, but particularly the federal, as inherently suspect.

—*William E. Burns, PhD*

Bibliography and Additional Reading

Drew, Elizabeth. *Richard M. Nixon*. New York: Times, 2007. Print.

Hoff, Joan. *Nixon Reconsidered*. New York: Basic, 1994. Print.

Perlstein, Rick. *Nixonland: The Rise of a President and the Fracturing of America*. New York: Scribner, 2008. Print.

Weiner, Tim. *One Man against the World: The Tragedy of Richard Nixon*. New York: Holt, 2015. Print.

THE SIXTH PARTY SYSTEM, PART II, 1974-2016

Despite the constitutional crisis that was Watergate, the nation moved on and the Republican Party survived. Indeed, with Nixon having successfully captured the South in his two successful election campaigns, the Republicans continued to find strength there in later years. They were supported as well by rural and suburban voters in other parts of the nation and by conservatives generally. The Democratic Party, on the other hand, drew most of its support from urban centers, liberals/progressives, and African American and Latino voters. The election of Jimmy Carter in 1976 threw off some aspects of those party alignments, as some white southerners returned, temporarily, to the Democratic Party and some mainline and progressive Democratic constituents chaffed at Carter's "born-again" religiosity and traditional outlook.

A true cementing of political lines, for the remainder of the century and beyond, however, came about with the election of Carter's successor, Ronald Reagan, in 1980. The Reagan Era saw the South go once again to the Republicans—and stay there for decades. Reagan's conservative policies called for small government, large tax cuts, aggressive anticommunism measures, a major military buildup, law and order at home, and a traditionalist morality drawn from fundamentalist Christian doctrine. Indeed, the recently formed Moral Majority, a Christian right political organization, had contributed significantly to Reagan's victory, and it or its successor organizations would continue to hold sway in Republican politics throughout the remainder of the sixth party system. Another increasingly important Republican constituency, aligned with rural voters, was gun owners and gun-rights advocates.

During this period, too, the Soviet Union collapsed—largely of its own accord, but Reagan is given credit for forcing the issue (partly through his military buildup, which the USSR could no longer match). The actual collapse occurred on the watch of Reagan's successor, his former vice president George H.W. Bush. But Reagan indelibly marked the Republican Party and it continued to hold true, more or less, to his principles through successive presidential campaigns, whether Republicans were on the winning side (George W. Bush, 2001-09) or lost to Democratic candidates (Bill Clinton, 1993-2001; Barack Obama, 2009-17). Under George W. Bush, the United States responded to the 9/11 attacks against the nation, launching military campaigns in Afghanistan and Iraq. Both, particularly the latter, proved highly controversial.

Meanwhile, the Democrats under Bill Clinton became a more centrist party, willing to entertain alliances with business groups and Wall Street financiers. The Democrats ushered in the election of the first African American president, Barack Obama, in 2008. Although he managed to achieve some legislative successes, he was blocked at every turn by an entrenched Republican opposition.

Throughout this period, hostility between the two major parties became such that battles were continuously being fought over redistricting efforts, or the redrawing of voter districts by state legislatures to advantage themselves. (Republicans controlled most state legislatures from the 1990s onward, so most of the redistricting benefited them.) The U.S. Supreme Court is expected to rule on the issue in summer 2018. Other voting issues being fought tooth and nail by the parties were voter I.D. laws and the shaping of the 2020 Census, whose results will contribute to the defining of future voter districts.

To the Congress of the United States:

Pursuant to the provisions of Section 2 of the Twenty-fifth Amendment to the Constitution of the United States, I hereby nominate Nelson A. Rockefeller, of New York, to be the Vice President of the United States.

Gerald R. Ford

The White House,
August 20, 1974.

Message to Congress nominating Nelson A. Rockefeller to be Vice President (August 20, 1974)

Ford's Remarks on Assuming the Presidency

Date: August 9, 1974
Author: Gerald Ford
Genre: Speech

Summary Overview

Gerald Ford's ascent to the U.S. presidency was unique in the annals of American political history. Appointed by President Richard M. Nixon to fill the vacancy created by the resignation of Spiro T. Agnew, Ford became vice president in December 1973. Just nine months later he assumed the presidency when Nixon resigned in order to avoid the possibility of impeachment over the Watergate crisis. Ford's first speech after taking the oath of office was designed to reassure the American people that the constitutional system of government had worked effectively. He promised transparency in his conduct as president and pledged to work closely with Congress in moving ahead. Ford wanted to heal the nation after the damage done by Watergate, and he attempted to do so by both acknowledging the loss of the American people's trust in government and committing to regaining it.

Defining Moment

When Ford took the presidential oath of office following the resignation of President Nixon, he knew it was a unique transition in the history of the U.S. presidency. In 1967, the Twenty-Fifth Amendment was ratified, codifying the official succession processes for both the presidency and vice presidency. In the latter case the amendment required that the president make a nomination to be confirmed by a majority of both houses of Congress. Six years later the process was put into action for the first time. After Vice President Agnew resigned amid scandal in October 1973, Nixon nominated Ford, the minority leader in the House of Representatives, to replace him. Ford, a genial, well-respected veteran of the House, was confirmed easily despite being a Republican while Congress was controlled by Democrats, and he became vice president on December 6, 1973.

Meanwhile, President Nixon was facing increasing pressure over the growing Watergate scandal, which began when burglars entered the office of the Democratic National Committee in 1972. An investigation proved the thieves were connected to Nixon's reelection campaign, sparking a deeper examination of conspiracy and corruption in the government. It was subsequently revealed that the scandal ran deep in the Nixon administration, with the president himself involved in the attempted cover-up—despite his claims otherwise—even if he may not have personally authorized the break-in. The episode shook the faith of the American public in the presidency and stirred calls for Nixon's impeachment. These calls grew louder as more evidence of Nixon's abuse of power came to light and he refused to release potentially incriminating audio tapes.

By the summer of 1974 the House of Representatives moved to impeach Nixon and he was forced to release the tapes by the Supreme Court. Before the Senate could confirm the impeachment, Nixon decided to resign. His aides had alerted Ford to the possibility of such an action, but Nixon did not tell Ford of his final decision until the day before he made his public announcement. Nixon announced his resignation in a televised address on the evening of August 8, 1974, effective at noon the following day. Shortly after noon on August 9, Ford took the presidential oath of office. He became the first person to hold the office of president who had not been elected to either the vice presidency or the presidency.

Author Biography

Gerald R. Ford was born in Omaha, Nebraska, on July 14, 1913. His birth name was Leslie Lynch King Jr., but his parents divorced two years after his birth and he was renamed after his stepfather. Ford attended public schools in Grand Rapids, Michigan. He then attended the University of Michigan, where he was a football star, and Yale University Law School. He began a legal practice in Grand Rapids but left to enter the U.S. Navy in 1942, serving in World War II.

In 1948, Ford was elected to the U.S. House of Representatives for Michigan's Fifth Congressional District.

He would be reelected twelve times and served in the House for nearly twenty-five years, becoming the minority leader for the Republican Party in 1965, until he was appointed by President Nixon to fill the vacancy created by Vice President Agnew's resignation. After being confirmed by Congress, Ford became vice president on December 6, 1973. Nine months later, Nixon resigned as a result of the Watergate crisis and Ford became president. He subsequently ran for the presidency in 1976 but lost to Democratic candidate Jimmy Carter. After leaving the presidency Ford retired to California. He died at his home in Rancho Mirage, California, on December 26, 2006.

HISTORICAL DOCUMENT

Mr. Chief Justice, my dear friends, my fellow Americans:

The oath that I have taken is the same oath that was taken by George Washington and by every President under the Constitution. But I assume the Presidency under extraordinary circumstances never before experienced by Americans. This is an hour of history that troubles our minds and hurts our hearts.

Therefore, I feel it is my first duty to make an unprecedented compact with my countrymen. Not an inaugural address, not a fireside chat, not a campaign speech—just a little straight talk among friends. And I intend it to be the first of many.

I am acutely aware that you have not elected me as your President by your ballots, and so I ask you to confirm me as your President with your prayers. And I hope that such prayers will also be the first of many.

If you have not chosen me by secret ballot, neither have I gained office by any secret promises. I have not campaigned either for the Presidency or the Vice Presidency. I have not subscribed to any partisan platform. I am indebted to no man, and only to one woman—my dear wife—as I begin this very difficult job.

I have not sought this enormous responsibility, but I will not shirk it. Those who nominated and confirmed me as Vice President were my friends and are my friends. They were of both parties, elected by all the people and acting under the Constitution in their name. It is only fitting then that I should pledge to them and to you that I will be the President of all the people.

Thomas Jefferson said the people are the only sure reliance for the preservation of our liberty. And down the years, Abraham Lincoln renewed this American article of faith asking, "Is there any better way or equal hope in the world?"

I intend, on Monday next, to request of the Speaker of the House of Representatives and the President pro tempore of the Senate the privilege of appearing before the Congress to share with my former colleagues and with you, the American people, my views on the priority business of the Nation and to solicit your views and their views. And may I say to the Speaker and the others, if I could meet with you right after these remarks, I would appreciate it.

Even though this is late in an election year, there is no way we can go forward except together and no way anybody can win except by serving the people's urgent needs. We cannot stand still or slip backwards. We must go forward now together.

To the peoples and the governments of all friendly nations, and I hope that could encompass the whole world, I pledge an uninterrupted and sincere search for peace. America will remain strong and united, but its strength will remain dedicated to the safety and sanity of the entire family of man, as well as to our own precious freedom.

I believe that truth is the glue that holds government together, not only our Government but civilization itself. That bond, though strained, is unbroken at home and abroad.

In all my public and private acts as your President, I expect to follow my instincts of openness and candor with full confidence that honesty is always the best policy in the end. My fellow Americans, our long national nightmare is over.

Our Constitution works; our great Republic is a government of laws and not of men. Here the people rule. But there is a higher Power, by whatever name we honor Him, who ordains not only righteousness but love, not only justice but mercy.

As we bind up the internal wounds of Watergate,

more painful and more poisonous than those of foreign wars, let us restore the golden rule to our political process, and let brotherly love purge our hearts of suspicion and of hate.

In the beginning, I asked you to pray for me. Before closing, I ask again your prayers, for Richard Nixon and for his family. May our former President, who brought peace to millions, find it for himself. May God bless and comfort his wonderful wife and daughters, whose love and loyalty will forever be a shining legacy to all who bear the lonely burdens of the White House.

I can only guess at those burdens, although I have witnessed at close hand the tragedies that befell three Presidents and the lesser trials of others.

With all the strength and all the good sense I have gained from life, with all the confidence my family, my friends, and my dedicated staff impart to me, and with the good will of countless Americans I have encountered in recent visits to 40 States, I now solemnly reaffirm my promise I made to you last December 6: to uphold the Constitution, to do what is right as God gives me to see the right, and to do the very best I can for America.

God helping me, I will not let you down.

Thank you.

Document Analysis

President Ford describes his remarks as "a little straight talk among friends," noting that this is different from a traditional inaugural address, a campaign speech, or other normal channels of presidential communication to the people. He acknowledges that he has become president under unique circumstances, implicitly referencing President Nixon's resignation. Due to the unprecedented scandal Ford felt a special need to reassure the American people that the constitutional process was working, and he uses these remarks to do just that.

Ford notes that he was not elected to the presidency or the vice presidency but asks that the people accept him in good faith, promising to carry out the "enormous responsibility" of the presidency according to their wishes. He suggests he is a legitimate leader because the bipartisan members of Congress who confirmed his selection as vice president had been elected by the people. He avows that he has not become president through "any secret promise," reassuring a public devastated by the conspiracies of the Nixon administration. Ford even poses his unique status as a buffer against corruption, noting that he never had to campaign, take partisan stances, or owe a debt to anyone—except his wife—to gain his office.

Ford urges that he and Congress should begin working together immediately, directly asking the Speaker of the House and other leaders to meet with him right after the speech. He announces plans to appear before each house of Congress to share his ideas about the most important issues facing the nation. He pleads for bipartisan cooperation, claiming that "there is no way we can go forward except together and no way anybody can win ex-cept by serving the people's urgent needs." He asserts his continued faith in the government and the democratic process despite the "long national nightmare" the United States has just faced and vows to work for peace and safety both domestically and abroad.

Importantly, Ford promises to "follow my instincts of openness and candor with full confidence that honesty is always the best policy," making a blatant appeal to the American people that he is the opposite of Nixon. Finally, he references the Watergate scandal by name, asserting that its damage will be repaired and that the public should "purge our hearts of suspicion and hate" in order to move forward. Ford ends his remarks by asking the people to pray for him as well as for Nixon and his family, suggesting that the former president did good things as well as bad. He pledges to "do the very best I can for America" on a platform of honesty and forgiveness.

Essential Themes

A key theme that is apparent throughout this document is Ford's sense of humility. He was keenly aware of the extraordinary chain of events that had led to his ascension to the presidency and presents himself as someone in tune with the people rather than a power-hungry politician. His religious references and calls for bipartisanship foreshadow the conservative and morally principled platform he would follow throughout his presidency The stability of government is also a prominent theme, as Ford sought to reassure the nation that constitutional procedures were functioning properly, America's political institutions were still viable, and the rule of law had proven superior to the power of an individual—even the power of an incumbent president.

Ford also stressed compassion and the need to move forward as a country, both on a general level and regarding his predecessor. He was a longtime friend and supporter of President Nixon, so his appeal to the American people to pray for Nixon and his family while keeping in mind his positive accomplishments as president can be seen as coming both personally and professionally. Ford further carried out this compassionate viewpoint when he pardoned Nixon a month into his presidency. The American people, however, did not seem to agree with forgiving such unprecedented crimes, as Ford's popularity dropped sharply after the pardon. The act even caused many to question Ford's otherwise unblemished reputation of integrity.

Ford's attempts to move the country forward met with considerable obstacles, including a declining economy complicated by an energy crisis and the unacknowledged defeat of the United States in Vietnam. His foreign policies were largely unsuccessful and he faced two attempted assassinations. In addition, he gained a reputation as a well-meaning but clumsy dolt and became a subject of parody. He managed to win the Republican nomination for the 1976 presidential election but lost the general election to Democrat Jimmy Carter.

—*Mark S. Joy, PhD*

Bibliography and Additional Reading

Ambrose, Stephen E. *Nixon: Ruin and Recovery, 1973–1990*. New York: Simon, 1991. Print.

DeFrank, Thomas. *Write It When I'm Gone: Remarkable Off-the-Record Conversations with Gerald R. Ford*. New York: Putnam's, 2007. Print.

Ford, Gerald R. *A Time to Heal: The Autobiography of Gerald R. Ford*. New York: Harper, 1979. Print.

Greene, John Robert. *The Presidency of Gerald R. Ford*. Lawrence: UP of Kansas, 1995. Print.

Barbara Jordan's Keynote Address at the 1976 Democratic National Convention

Date: July 12, 1976
Author: Barbara Jordan
Genre: Speech

Summary Overview

During the summer of 1976, Congresswoman Barbara Jordan of Texas—the first African American woman from a southern state elected to the House of Representatives—took to the stage of the Democratic National Convention in New York City. Jordan cited the Democratic Party's image—one of inclusiveness and innovation—as the reason Americans were looking to the party to move the United States forward after two terms of Republican leadership in the White House. Acknowledging that both the Democratic and Republican parties had made many mistakes in previous years, Jordan said that all elected officials should lead by moral and ethical example. Leaders, she added, should join together with all Americans to create a national community committed to moving the United States forward once again.

Defining Moment

One of the most politically tumultuous periods in modern U.S. history was the decade between the mid-1960s and the mid-1970s. During this time, U.S. military involvement in Vietnam reached its peak, along with antiwar protests at home and an insurgent counterculture that seemed to strain the nation's social fabric. The civil rights movement saw great victories, but the decade also witnessed the assassinations of major national leaders such as Martin Luther King Jr. and Robert F. Kennedy. When President Richard M. Nixon took office in 1969, he pledged to bring "peace with honor" to the Vietnam conflict, working to turn responsibility for the fighting increasingly over to the South Vietnamese. By the time a cease-fire was negotiated during the Paris talks in 1973, however, 58,000 Americans had been killed in action and over 150,000 had been wounded in the conflict, which ultimately ended in a Communist victory.

In June of 1972, five men were arrested breaking into and attempting to bug the Democratic National Committee's offices at Washington DC's Watergate Hotel. During the months that followed, more and more of Nixon's staff were found to be connected to the break-in as a major political conspiracy unfolded, pointing increasingly toward the involvement of the president himself. Over the course of several months into Nixon's second term, more and more of his aides and appointees resigned over the scandal while nationally televised Senate hearings on Watergate again dominated American viewers' attention. In 1973, Vice President Spiro T. Agnew resigned under suspicion of tax evasion and bribery, and Nixon named Congressman Gerald Ford to be his new vice president. In 1974, Nixon, threatened with impeachment proceedings on suspicion of attempting to cover up the Watergate scandal, resigned from office, leaving Ford as his successor. Ford put forth a valiant effort as president—particularly in the fight against inflation—but his pardon of Nixon and his inability to unify a toxic political environment in Washington led to calls for new blood in the White House. In 1976, Ford faced a daunting reelection campaign, as Democrats put forth as their candidate a relative political outsider: Georgia governor Jimmy Carter. During the summer of 1976, the Democratic Party held its nominating convention at Madison Square Garden in New York City.

Author Biography

Barbara Charline Jordan was born on February 21, 1936, in Houston, Texas. Educated in Houston public schools, Jordan graduated from Texas Southern University in 1956 and from Boston University School of Law in 1959. Inspired by her work on John F. Kennedy's 1960 presidential campaign, Jordan unsuccessfully ran twice for the Texas House of Representatives, in 1962 and 1964.

In 1966, however, she was successful in running for the Texas Senate. The first African American in the United States since 1883 to win a state senate seat, Jordan rose to the rank of president pro tempore. In 1972, Jordan was victorious in her campaign for U.S. House of Representatives, garnering 80 percent of the vote. In 1974, she was among the members of the House Judiciary Committee to support articles of impeachment against President Nixon. She remained in office until 1979, stepping down after three terms to teach at the University of Texas at Austin. Jordan died from complications of leukemia on January 17, 1996.

HISTORICAL DOCUMENT

Thank you ladies and gentlemen for a very warm reception.

It was one hundred and forty-four years ago that members of the Democratic Party first met in convention to select a Presidential candidate. Since that time, Democrats have continued to convene once every four years and draft a party platform and nominate a Presidential candidate. And our meeting this week is a continuation of that tradition. But there is something different about tonight. There is something special about tonight. What is different? What is special?

I, Barbara Jordan, am a keynote speaker.

When—A lot of years passed since 1832, and during that time it would have been most unusual for any national political party to ask a Barbara Jordan to deliver a keynote address. But tonight, here I am. And I feel—I feel that notwithstanding the past that my presence here is one additional bit of evidence that the American Dream need not forever be deferred.

Now—Now that I have this grand distinction, what in the world am I supposed to say? I could easily spend this time praising the accomplishments of this party and attacking the Republicans—but I don't choose to do that. I could list the many problems which Americans have. I could list the problems which cause people to feel cynical, angry, frustrated: problems which include lack of integrity in government; the feeling that the individual no longer counts; the reality of material and spiritual poverty; the feeling that the grand American experiment is failing or has failed. I could recite these problems, and then I could sit down and offer no solutions. But I don't choose to do that either. The citizens of America expect more. They deserve and they want more than a recital of problems.

We are a people in a quandary about the present. We are a people in search of our future. We are a people in search of a national community. We are a people trying not only to solve the problems of the present, unemployment, inflation, but we are attempting on a larger scale to fulfill the promise of America. We are attempting to fulfill our national purpose, to create and sustain a society in which all of us are equal.

Throughout—Throughout our history, when people have looked for new ways to solve their problems and to uphold the principles of this nation, many times they have turned to political parties. They have often turned to the Democratic Party. What is it? What is it about the Democratic Party that makes it the instrument the people use when they search for ways to shape their future? Well I believe the answer to that question lies in our concept of governing. Our concept of governing is derived from our view of people. It is a concept deeply rooted in a set of beliefs firmly etched in the national conscience of all of us.

Now what are these beliefs? First, we believe in equality for all and privileges for none. This is a belief—This is a belief that each American, regardless of background, has equal standing in the public forum—all of us. Because—Because we believe this idea so firmly, we are an inclusive rather than an exclusive party. Let everybody come.

I think it no accident that most of those immigrating to America in the nineteenth century identified with the Democratic Party. We are a heterogeneous party made up of Americans of diverse backgrounds. We believe that the people are the source of all governmental power; that the authority of the people is to be extended, not restricted.

This—This can be accomplished only by providing each citizen with every opportunity to participate in the management of the government. They must have that, we believe. We believe that the government which represents the authority of all the people, not just one interest group, but all the people, has an obligation to actively—underscore actively—seek to remove those obstacles which would block individual achievement—obstacles emanating from race, sex, economic condition. The government must remove them, seek to remove them. We.

We are a party—We are a party of innovation. We do not reject our traditions, but we are willing to adapt to changing circumstances, when change we must. We are willing to suffer the discomfort of change in order to achieve a better future. We have a positive vision of the future founded on the belief that the gap between the promise and reality of America can one day be finally closed. We believe that.

This, my friends is the bedrock of our concept of governing. This is a part of the reason why Americans have turned to the Democratic Party. These are the foundations upon which a national community can be built. Let all understand that these guiding principles cannot be discarded for short-term political gains. They represent what this country is all about. They are indigenous to the American idea. And these are principles which are not negotiable.

In other times—In other times, I could stand here and give this kind of exposition on the beliefs of the Democratic Party and that would be enough. But today that is not enough. People want more. That is not sufficient reason for the majority of the people of this country to decide to vote Democratic. We have made mistakes. We realize that. We admit our mistakes. In our haste to do all things for all people, we did not foresee the full consequences of our actions. And when the people raised their voices, we didn't hear. But our deafness was only a temporary condition, and not an irreversible condition.

Even as I stand here and admit that we have made mistakes, I still believe that as the people of America sit in judgment on each party, they will recognize that our mistakes were mistakes of the heart. They'll recognize that.

And now—now we must look to the future. Let us heed the voice of the people and recognize their common sense. If we do not, we not only blaspheme our political heritage, we ignore the common ties that bind all Americans. Many fear the future. Many are distrustful of their leaders, and believe that their voices are never heard. Many seek only to satisfy their private work—wants; to

satisfy their private interests. But this is the great danger America faces—that we will cease to be one nation and become instead a collection of interest groups: city against suburb, region against region, individual against individual; each seeking to satisfy private wants. If that happens, who then will speak for America? Who then will speak for the common good?

This is the question which must be answered in 1976: Are we to be one people bound together by common spirit, sharing in a common endeavor; or will we become a divided nation? For all of its uncertainty, we cannot flee the future. We must not become the "New Puritans" and reject our society. We must address and master the future together. It can be done if we restore the belief that we share a sense of national community, that we share a common national endeavor. It can be done.

There is no executive order; there is no law that can require the American people to form a national community. This we must do as individuals, and if we do it as individuals, there is no President of the United States who can veto that decision.

As a first step—As a first step, we must restore our belief in ourselves. We are a generous people, so why can't we be generous with each other? We need to take to heart the words spoken by Thomas Jefferson:

Let us restore the social intercourse—"Let us restore to social intercourse that harmony and that affection without which liberty and even life are but dreary things."

A nation is formed by the willingness of each of us to share in the responsibility for upholding the common good. A government is invigorated when each one of us is willing to participate in shaping the future of this nation. In this election year, we must define the "common good" and begin again to shape a common future. Let each person do his or her part. If one citizen is unwilling to participate, all of us are going to suffer. For the American idea, though it is shared by all of us, is realized in each one of us.

And now, what are those of us who are elected public officials supposed to do? We call ourselves "public servants" but I'll tell you this: We as public servants must set an example for the rest of the nation. It is hypocritical for the public official to admonish and exhort the people to uphold the common good if we are derelict in upholding the common good. More is required—More is required of public officials than slogans and handshakes and press releases. More is required. We must hold ourselves strictly accountable. We must provide the people with a vision of the future.

If we promise as public officials, we must deliver. If—If we as public officials propose, we must produce. If we say to the American people, "It is time for you to be sacrificial"—sacrifice. If the public official says that, we [public officials] must be the first to give. We must be. And again, if we make mistakes, we must be willing to admit them. We have to do that. What we have to do is strike a balance between the idea that government should do everything and the idea, the belief, that government ought to do nothing. Strike a balance.

Let there be no illusions about the difficulty of forming this kind of a national community. It's tough, difficult, not easy. But a spirit of harmony will survive in America only if each of us remembers that we share a common destiny; if each of us remembers, when self-interest and bitterness seem to prevail, that we share a common destiny.

I have confidence that we can form this kind of national community.

I have confidence that the Democratic Party can lead the way.

I have that confidence.

We cannot improve on the system of government handed down to us by the founders of the Republic. There is no way to improve upon that. But what we can do is to find new ways to implement that system and realize our destiny.

Now I began this speech by commenting to you on the uniqueness of a Barbara Jordan making a keynote address. Well I am going to close my speech by quoting a Republican President and I ask you that as you listen to these words of Abraham Lincoln, relate them to the concept of a national community in which every last one of us participates:

"As I would not be a slave, so I would not be a master." This—This—"This expresses my idea of Democracy. Whatever differs from this, to the extent of the difference, is no Democracy."

Thank you.

Barbara Jordan delivering the keynote address on the first day of the convention. By Warren K. Leffler, *U.S. News & World Report* Magazine (Library of Congress)

Document Analysis

Barbara Jordan understood the momentum her party enjoyed at this juncture of the presidential campaign. The American public perceived the incumbent, President Ford, as someone who had made a number of missteps. However, those stumbles were by far overshadowed by both the missteps of Ford's predecessor and the upheavals of the previous decade. Thus, her speech to the delegates is one that called for new leadership but, more importantly, calls for the nation to turn the page, reunite, and get back on track toward a positive future.

Jordan begins her speech by noting the significance of her own presence as the DNC keynote speaker. While not mentioning her race or gender—or, indeed, mentioning any specific political or social issues facing the nation, in a speech meant more to set a tone than lay out an agenda—she observes that "my presence here is one additional bit of evidence that the American Dream need not forever be deferred." She then notes the political opportunity her party had before it. The Democrats could use this convention for "attacking the Republicans" for the scandals and inequities that plague the American political landscape. However, Jordan says that Americans "want more than a recital of problems."

She notes instead that Americans, as a result of the current environment, are in a "quandary" about the American way of life. The United States was built on a solid foundation, she says, but the people are concerned about the direction in which the nation is moving. It is not just a question of the specific issues of unemployment or inflation; it is a larger question of how American society can move toward the promise of being a nation of equality.

On this point, Jordan says, the Democratic Party is well-equipped to restore the people's faith in governing. Democrats, she argues, long held a "concept of governing" driven by the principle of "equality for all and privileges for none." Democrats espouse an inclusive, rather than exclusive, philosophy built on a respect for diversity. In other words, Jordan says, government should be driven by the will of all Americans, regardless of their race, gender, or socioeconomic status.

Furthermore, Jordan argues, the Democratic Party aims to use this heterogeneity to create innovative policies that will better serve the country over the long term. Democrats are "willing to suffer the discomfort of change in order to achieve a better future." In order to move out of the morass of the previous decade, the United States needs the innovation and vision of the Democratic Party, she says.

Several times in the speech, Jordan invokes the theme of building a "national community," one that could not be legislated but will have to be created by individuals coming together. She speaks to a need to reunite an American society that had been for years deeply divided. As a result of these divisions, Americans are at risk of diverging into smaller adversarial interest groups. It is, therefore, imperative that Americans reconnect as one society, accepting responsibility for one another and pursuing a common good. A high ethical standard needs to be established, particularly among the nation's public servants and elected officials, she says. She closes by quoting Abraham Lincoln—the first Republican president—on the spirit of democracy: "As I would not be a slave, so I would not be a master," urging Americans to relate this idea to the task of building an inclusive national community.

Essential Themes

After nearly a decade of enormous challenges, including the Vietnam War and the Watergate scandal, the Democratic National Convention looked to retake the White House from the Republicans. Barbara Jordan did not rail against the specific missteps of the previous administration. Rather, she called upon the nation's leaders to be a shining example for others to follow. She also extolled what she saw as the characteristics that made her party appealing to the voters: inclusiveness, diversity, and innovation. Such characteristics, she argued, made the Democratic Party the ideal vehicle to move the nation through the challenges of the day.

Jordan also called for national healing. Striking an optimistic tone, Jordan argued for the forging of a new national community that would underpin a restored faith in American government. Everyone had a part to play, she argued, to build upon what she saw as a near-perfect system of government. Doing so, Jordan exclaimed, would help move the United States closer to its destiny.

—*Michael P. Auerbach, MA*

Bibliography and Additional Reading

Brass, Chelsea. "The Life and Work of Barbara Jordan: Remembering a Legacy." Lyndon B. Johnson School of Public Affairs. U of Texas, 2011. Web. 15 Apr. 2016.

Clines, Francis X. "Barbara Jordan Dies at 59; Her Voice Stirred the Nation." *New York Times*. New York Times, 18 Jan. 1996. Web. 15 Apr. 2016

"Jordan, Barbara Charline." U.S. House of Representatives: History, Art & Archives. Office of the Historian, n.d. Web. 15 Apr. 2016.

■ Ronald Reagan's Speech at the 1976 Republican National Convention

Date: August 19, 1976
Author: Ronald Reagan
Genre: Speech

Summary Overview

Ronald Reagan believed that President Gerald Ford's 1974 pardon of former president Richard M. Nixon had damaged Ford politically to the point that he could not win the general election in 1976. Therefore, Reagan campaigned to gain the Republican nomination himself. After Ford's narrow victory at the Republican National Convention in Kansas City in August 1976, Ford gave his acceptance speech; afterward, he invited Reagan and his wife to come to the convention stage. Reagan then delivered this speech, both expressing gratitude for how the convention members and President Ford had treated him and his wife and pledging his support for Ford and the convention's platform. He challenged the convention members to take the Republican message to the American people and to work with unity and determination to win the general election that fall.

Defining Moment

On November 20, 1975, Ronald Reagan announced his candidacy for the Republican Party's presidential nomination. The incumbent president, Gerald R. Ford, was already seeking the Republican nomination. While it is rare for a candidate to challenge a sitting president for the nomination of his or her own party, Reagan's challenge arose from the unique circumstances surrounding Ford's presidency. Ford had become vice president in October 1973 when Spiro T. Agnew resigned the office because of charges of corruption. Ford's appointment to become vice president was the first employment of the Twenty-Fifth Amendment, ratified in 1967, which outlines the procedure for filling such a vacancy. The amendment requires the president to nominate a candidate, who then must be confirmed by both houses of Congress. Because of Ford's solid reputation and long years of service in the House of Representatives, President Nixon believed, correctly, Ford would be confirmed easily. Ford became

vice president on December 6, 1973.

On August 9, 1974, Ford became president when Nixon resigned to avoid impeachment because of the Watergate scandal. Ford initially received an outpouring of support and goodwill, as the American public seemed anxious to move beyond Watergate. However, Ford believed the country could not move ahead as long as Nixon's ultimate judicial fate remained undetermined. So on September 8, 1974, he pardoned Nixon for any crimes he "committed or may have committed." Immediately, the public's goodwill toward Ford evaporated, as reaction to the pardon was overwhelmingly negative. Reagan believed the pardon had damaged Ford so badly that he could not be elected in 1976, so he decided to challenge Ford for the Republican nomination.

As the 1976 campaign began, Reagan lost several early primaries to Ford, before winning a string of southern primaries and carrying his adopted home state of California. By the time the Republican convention began in Kansas City, Missouri, in August, neither candidate seemed to have a lock on the nomination. Ford won the nomination on the first convention ballot, by a margin of 117 votes. After Ford delivered his acceptance speech as the Republican Party's candidate, Reagan made this impromptu speech to the convention after Ford had invited him and his wife, Nancy, to the convention stage as a gesture of unity.

Author Biography

Ronald Wilson Reagan was born on February 6, 1911, in Tampico, Illinois. In 1932, he graduated from Eureka College in Illinois and gained some regional notoriety as a radio sportscaster in Iowa. In 1937, he began a Hollywood film career that lasted more than twenty years and included more than fifty films. Reagan embraced New Deal liberalism in his youth, but he became more conservative in the 1950s, as he worked as a spokesman for the

General Electric Company. In 1966, he was elected governor of California; he was reelected in 1970. In 1968, he was a candidate for the Republican presidential nomination but did not campaign aggressively and lost the nomination to Richard M. Nixon. In 1976, Reagan believed that President Gerald Ford could not be reelected because of the backlash over his pardon of Nixon. There-fore, Reagan campaigned extensively for the Republican nomination. Ford won the nomination but lost the general election to Jimmy Carter. In 1980, Reagan secured the Republican nomination and defeated Carter. He was elected to a second term in 1984. After his second term ended, Reagan returned to private life at his California ranch. He died there on June 5, 2004.

HISTORICAL DOCUMENT

Mr. President, Mrs. Ford, Mr. Vice President, Mr. Vice President-to-be, the distinguished guests here, you ladies and gentlemen. I was going to say fellow Republicans here but those who are watching from a distance (including) all those millions of Democrats and independents who I know are looking for a cause around which to rally and which I believe we can give them. Mr. President, before you arrive tonight, these wonderful people, here, when we came in, gave Nancy and myself a welcome. That, plus this, plus your kindness and generosity in honoring us by bringing us down here will give us a memory that will live in our hearts forever.

Watching on television these last few nights I've seen also the warmth with which you greeted Nancy and you also filled my heart with joy when you did that. May I say some words. There are cynics who say that a party platform is something that no one bothers to read and is doesn't very often amount to much. Whether it is different this time than is has ever been before, I believe the Republican party has a platform that is a banner of bold, unmistakable colors with no pale pastel shades. We have just heard a call to arms, based on that platform.

And a call to us to really be successful in communicating and reveal to the American people the difference between this platform and the platform of the opposing party which is nothing but a revamp and a reissue and a rerunning of a late, late show of the thing that we have been hearing from them for the last 40 years.

If I could just take a moment, I had an assignment the other day. Someone asked me to write a letter for a time capsule that is going to opened in Los Angeles a hundred years from now, on our Tricentennial.

It sounded like an easy assignment. They suggested I write about the problems and issues of the day. And I set out to do so, riding down the coast in an automo-bile, looking at the blue Pacific out on one side and the Santa Ynez Mountains on the other, and I couldn't help but wonder if it was going to be that beautiful a hundred years from now as it was on that summer day.

And then as I tried to write-let your own minds turn to that task. You're going to write for people a hundred years from now who know all about us, we know nothing about them. We don't know what kind of world they'll be living in. And suddenly I thought to myself, "If I write of the problems, they'll be the domestic problems of which the President spoke here tonight; the challenges confronting us, the erosion of freedom taken place under Democratic rule in this country, the invasion of private rights, the controls and restrictions on the vitality of the great free economy that we enjoy." These are the challenges that we must meet and then again there is that challenge of which he spoke that we live in a world in which the great powers have aimed and poised at each other horrible missiles of destruction, nuclear weapons that can in a matter of minutes arrive at each other's country and destroy virtually the civilized world we live in.

And suddenly it dawned on me; those who would read this letter a hundred years from now will know whether those missiles were fired. They will know whether we met our challenge.

Whether they will have the freedom that we have known up until now will depend on what we do here. Will they look back with appreciation and say, "Thank God for those people in 1976 who headed off that loss of freedom? Who kept us now a hundred years later free? Who kept our world from nuclear destruction?"

And if we fail they probably won't get to read the letter at all because it spoke of individual freedom and they won't be allowed to talk of that or read of it.

This is our challenge and this is why we're here in this

hall tonight. Better than we've ever done before, we've got to quit talking to each other and about each other and go out and communicate to the world that we may be fewer in numbers than we've ever been but we carry the message they're waiting for. We must go forth from here united, determined and what a great general said a few years ago is true: "There is no substitute for victory." Mr. President.

Document Analysis

In his introductory greetings to the Republican National Convention, Reagan refers to the president, the vice president, and the "Vice President to be," referencing Ford, Nelson Rockefeller (who decided not to be a candidate in 1976), and Kansas senator Bob Dole, Ford's running mate. Reagan expresses gratitude to both the convention delegates for welcoming him and his wife and to Ford for his warmth toward him during the convention. Reagan alludes to Ford's acceptance speech as "a call to arms" to press for the agenda contained in the party platform, and contrasted it with the Democratic Party platform, which he says simply repeated the same ideas the Democrats had pursued for the past forty years.

Reagan then discusses a letter he was recently asked to write, to be included in a time capsule that would be opened one hundred years later, on the tercentennial of the founding of the city of Los Angeles. He naturally felt he should write about the problems and challenges facing the people of his own time, but then he realized: the people of the future will know all about him and his contemporaries, while the people of the 1970s know nothing about the people of the future. The people of 2076 will know whether the American people and their leaders successfully met the challenges of the 1970s. Reagan says the challenges facing the nation are the things Ford stressed in his acceptance speech—the erosion of personal freedom, the invasion of private rights, and excessive controls on the nation's economy. He also refers to the awesome challenge of maintaining peace in a world full of nuclear weapons. Reagan wonders if that later generation will look back with thanksgiving for what was done by "those people in 1976."

Reagan concludes by calling on the Republican Party to leave the convention "united" and "determined" to take its message to the American people. He reminds them, with a quote from General Douglas MacArthur, that "there is no substitute for victory." Reagan's speech is a call for party unity, a generous response to Ford's gracious treatment of him, and a challenge for the party to move toward victory in the general election.

Essential Themes

With this speech, Reagan positioned himself as a gracious loser but also as a faithful worker for the Republican Party. The 1976 campaign for the Republican nomination was not especially acrimonious, in part because of Reagan's adherence to what he often called the "eleventh commandment": "Thou shalt not speak ill of a fellow Republican." During the campaign, Reagan criticized particular policies and the overall direction in which the nation seemed to be moving but rarely attacked Ford. Nevertheless, Ford and some of the Republican Party faithful believed that Reagan's campaign was inherently divisive. Therefore, Reagan was anxious to heal any breaches within the party and to express his support for Ford.

Like any speech at a political nominating convention, Reagan's remarks also looked to the future. Naturally, he looked to the 1976 general election and the hoped-for victory of his party's candidates. But Reagan also looked far ahead into the future, reflecting on his recent experience of writing a letter to be placed in a time capsule that would be opened one hundred years later. He wondered if the policies adopted in his own time would be proven wise and successful and whether or not that future generation would look back with thankfulness on what the people of his generation had accomplished.

Reagan believed that Ford's candidacy and the platform the party had adopted were "a cause around which to rally." He encouraged the party faithful to take their message to the voting public at large and to be "united" and "determined" in doing so. With his long background in Hollywood and television, Reagan was an excellent public speaker and had earned the nickname "The Great Communicator." This speech, made with no text and presumably without any formal preparation, aptly illustrated Reagan's masterful speechmaking skills.

—*Mark S. Joy, PhD*

Bibliography and Additional Reading

Diggins, John Patrick. *Ronald Reagan: Fate, Freedom, and the Making of History*. New York: Norton, 2007. Print.

Ford, Gerald R. *A Time to Heal: The Autobiography of Gerald R. Ford*. New York: Harper, 1979. Print.

Knott, Stephen F., and Jeffrey L. Chidester. *Presidential Profiles: The Reagan Years*. New York: Facts on File, 2005. Print.

Reagan, Ronald. *An American Life*. New York: Simon, 1990. Print.

■ Jimmy Carter's Inaugural Address

Date: January 20, 1977
Author: Jimmy Carter
Genre: Speech

Summary Overview

In a period of great political division, economic stagnation, and general uncertainty, newly elected president Jimmy Carter presented his inaugural address in a spirit of hope and reconciliation. Carter called for national unity and urged Americans to remain true to the fundamental principles on which the United States was founded. He asked the people to join him in promoting American ideals—such as religious and racial diversity as well as equal application of the law—both at home and abroad. If the United States kept these ideals in mind while offering bold solutions for the issues facing the country, he said, it would maintain its national and international strength.

Defining Moment

The decade between the mid-1960s and the mid-1970s was a particularly tumultuous period in modern U.S. history. The country became involved in the Vietnam conflict at the beginning of the 1960s, and by the end of the decade, the war was impacting the American way of life back home. The images of this increasingly unpopular war—including film of American soldiers returning home in caskets—were splashed across Americans' television sets nightly. Stories of America's South Vietnamese allies committing war atrocities against civilians were also widely circulated. Despite leaders' frequent assurances that the American effort would prevail, the war dragged on seemingly without an end in sight.

Back home, American dissatisfaction with the war sparked a nationwide peace movement, with large-scale demonstrations occurring on a number of university campuses (including the infamous incident at Kent State University, during which Ohio National Guardsmen fired upon protesting students, killing four). The Vietnam conflict increasingly appeared to be unwinnable, despite heavy bombing campaigns and a continued investment of American forces in the region. Amid growing public dissent over the war, the United States experienced a major political schism in the late 1960s.

When President Richard M. Nixon took office in 1969, he pledged to bring "peace with honor" to the Vietnam conflict, working to negotiate a peaceful settlement with the rival Viet Cong and North Vietnamese Army while maintaining a U.S. presence in the country. Despite negotiations, the war continued as the American presence slowly dwindled. By the time a cease-fire was negotiated during the Paris Peace Accords in 1973, 58,000 Americans had been killed in action and over 150,000 had been wounded in the conflict.

Elevating Americans' political skepticism was a bizarre incident in Washington, DC. In June of 1972, five men were arrested breaking into and attempting to bug the Democratic National Committee's offices at the Watergate Hotel. As Nixon sailed to a landslide reelection victory, the incident continued to unfold, involving more and more people, including those in Nixon's inner circle. Over the course of several months into Nixon's second term, several of his aides and appointees resigned over the scandal. Nationally televised Senate hearings on Watergate dominated American viewers' attention. Under a growing call for his impeachment, Nixon was pressured to supply his office tapes, which, according to several former aides, contained conversations about the Watergate break-in.

In 1973, in a scandal unrelated to Watergate but still relevant to growing American distrust of the government, Vice President Spiro Agnew resigned under suspicion of tax evasion and bribery. Nixon named U.S. representative Gerald Ford to be his new vice president. In 1974, Nixon resigned from office, leaving the unelected vice president Ford as his successor. Ford put forth a valiant effort as president—particularly in the effort to fight inflation—but his pardon of Nixon and his inability to pacify a toxic political environment in Washington led to calls for a change of president.

In 1976, Ford faced a daunting election campaign, as

Democrats chose a relative political outsider, Georgia governor Jimmy Carter. Carter ran on a platform of healing the political schism and restoring America's standing in the world. Narrowly defeating Ford in the general election, Carter set about moving forward to address the myriad issues facing the United States.

Author Biography

James Earl "Jimmy" Carter Jr. was born in Plains, Georgia, on October 1, 1924. He attended Georgia Southwestern College and the Georgia Institute of Technology until 1942, when he applied for and was accepted to the U.S. Naval Academy. He served as a naval officer aboard a submarine until 1953. After retiring from the Navy, he returned to run his family farm. Carter was also heavily involved in the Plains community, both as a civic leader and a church deacon. In 1955, he ran successfully for the Sumter County Board of Education and then, in 1962, he won election to the Georgia state senate. In 1966, Carter ran for governor, but, as a pro–civil rights candidate, was soundly defeated by his conservative Democratic opponents. He ran again in 1970, winning by a narrow margin after appealing to the conservative base of his party. In 1976, Carter was elected president. One of his most notable successes as president was his work facilitating the Camp David Accords in 1978, which led to peace between Israel and Egypt. Defeated by Ronald Reagan in 1980, Carter continued to advocate for international peace. In honor of his efforts in this area, Carter received the Nobel Peace Prize in 2002.

HISTORICAL DOCUMENT

For myself and for our Nation, I want to thank my predecessor for all he has done to heal our land.

In this outward and physical ceremony, we attest once again to the inner and spiritual strength of our Nation. As my high school teacher, Miss Julia Coleman, used to say, "We must adjust to changing times and still hold to unchanging principles."

Here before me is the Bible used in the inauguration of our first President, in 1789, and I have just taken the oath of office on the Bible my mother gave me just a few years ago, opened to a timeless admonition from the ancient prophet Micah: "He hath showed thee, O man, what is good; and what doth the Lord require of thee, but to do justly, and to love mercy, and to walk humbly with thy God."

This inauguration ceremony marks a new beginning, a new dedication within our Government, and a new spirit among us all. A President may sense and proclaim that new spirit, but only a people can provide it.

Two centuries ago, our Nation's birth was a milestone in the long quest for freedom. But the bold and brilliant dream which excited the founders of this Nation still awaits its consummation. I have no new dream to set forth today, but rather urge a fresh faith in the old dream.

Ours was the first society openly to define itself in terms of both spirituality and human liberty. It is that unique self-definition which has given us an exceptional appeal, but it also imposes on us a special obligation to take on those moral duties which, when assumed, seem invariably to be in our own best interests.

You have given me a great responsibility—to stay close to you, to be worthy of you, and to exemplify what you are. Let us create together a new national spirit of unity and trust. Your strength can compensate for my weakness, and your wisdom can help to minimize my mistakes.

Let us learn together and laugh together and work together and pray together, confident that in the end we will triumph together in the right.

The American dream endures. We must once again have full faith in our country—and in one another. I believe America can be better. We can be even stronger than before.

Let our recent mistakes bring a resurgent commitment to the basic principles of our Nation, for we know that if we despise our own government, we have no future. We recall in special times when we have stood briefly, but magnificently, united. In those times no prize was beyond our grasp.

But we cannot dwell upon remembered glory. We cannot afford to drift. We reject the prospect of failure or mediocrity or an inferior quality of life for any person. Our Government must at the same time be both competent and compassionate.

We have already found a high degree of personal lib-

Campaign flyer from Democratic Party presidential primary.

erty, and we are now struggling to enhance equality of opportunity. Our commitment to human rights must be absolute, our laws fair, our national beauty preserved; the powerful must not persecute the weak, and human dignity must be enhanced.

We have learned that more is not necessarily better, that even our great Nation has its recognized limits, and that we can neither answer all questions nor solve all problems. We cannot afford to do everything, nor can we afford to lack boldness as we meet the future. So, together, in a spirit of individual sacrifice for the common good, we must simply do our best.

Our Nation can be strong abroad only if it is strong at home. And we know that the best way to enhance freedom in other lands is to demonstrate here that our democratic system is worthy of emulation.

To be true to ourselves, we must be true to others. We will not behave in foreign places so as to violate our rules and standards here at home, for we know that the trust which our Nation earns is essential to our strength.

The world itself is now dominated by a new spirit. Peoples more numerous and more politically aware are craving, and now demanding, their place in the sun—not just for the benefit of their own physical condition, but for basic human rights.

The passion for freedom is on the rise. Tapping this new spirit, there can be no nobler nor more ambitious task for America to undertake on this day of a new beginning than to help shape a just and peaceful world that is truly humane.

We are a strong nation, and we will maintain strength so sufficient that it need not be proven in combat—a quiet strength based not merely on the size of an arsenal but on the nobility of ideas.

We will be ever vigilant and never vulnerable, and we will fight our wars against poverty, ignorance, and injustice, for those are the enemies against which our forces can be honorably marshaled.

We are a proudly idealistic nation, but let no one confuse our idealism with weakness.

Because we are free, we can never be indifferent to the fate of freedom elsewhere. Our moral sense dictates a clear-cut preference for those societies which share with us an abiding respect for individual human rights. We do not seek to intimidate, but it is clear that a world which others can dominate with impunity would be inhospitable to decency and a threat to the well-being of all people.

The world is still engaged in a massive armaments race designed to ensure continuing equivalent strength among potential adversaries. We pledge perseverance and wisdom in our efforts to limit the world's armaments to those necessary for each nation's own domestic safety. And we will move this year a step toward our ultimate goal—the elimination of all nuclear weapons from this Earth. We urge all other people to join us, for success can mean life instead of death.

Within us, the people of the United States, there is evident a serious and purposeful rekindling of confidence. And I join in the hope that when my time as your President has ended, people might say this about our Nation:

—that we had remembered the words of Micah and renewed our search for humility, mercy, and justice;

—that we had torn down the barriers that separated those of different race and region and religion, and where there had been mistrust, built unity, with a respect for diversity;

—that we had found productive work for those able to perform it;

—that we had strengthened the American family, which is the basis of our society;

—that we had ensured respect for the law and equal treatment under the law, for the weak and the powerful, for the rich and the poor; and

—that we had enabled our people to be proud of their own Government once again.

I would hope that the nations of the world might say that we had built a lasting peace, based not on weapons of war but on international policies which reflect our own most precious values.

These are not just my goals—and they will not be my accomplishments—but the affirmation of our Nation's continuing moral strength and our belief in an undiminished, ever-expanding American dream.

Thank you very much.

Document Analysis

President Carter uses the occasion of his inaugural address to remind Americans of their values and traditions while seeking innovative and bold approaches to restoring the county's domestic and international strength. Carter emphasizes that the notions on which the country was founded could be used to strengthen the nation and its international status. He calls for the equal application of the law and respect for the country's racial, religious, and social diversity. Carter points to his admittedly idealistic goals for the nation and, although acknowledging that not all of his goals would be met during his tenure, hopes that he can at least lay the groundwork for the nation to meet those goals in the future.

Carter begins his speech by recognizing the inaugural ceremony in which he just participated. His oath of office and the traditions associated with it are centuries old, he said, providing a reminder of the fundamental principles on which the nation was founded in 1776. He says that the United States represents a bold "milestone"—a nation founded on personal liberty and spiritual values. These values remain in the present, Carter says, adding that if Americans restore their faith in those concepts, the American Dream will remain strong.

Acknowledging the mistakes of previous administrations, Carter stresses that dwelling on those missteps will only continue to keep the nation in the doldrums. He also urges Americans not to harp on the successes of the past. Such an obsession with the past, he warns, only leads to the nation remaining adrift. Instead, he says, the people's faith in their nation and in one another must be restored so that the country can pursue future success.

The key to future national glory, Carter argues, is embracing the fundamental ideals on which the nation was founded. The country must continue its tradition of respecting the diversity of its population, he states. He also reminds the people that the United States is dedicated to the equal application of the law to all citizens. Americans must remain true to those values and to one another, he adds. This practice must occur not just at home—where doing so has made the nation strong—but also on the international stage, he says. Applying these concepts in both arenas strengthened American society and the country's status as a global leader, Carter says.

Carter admits that his goals for the country—healing racial divides, restoring full strength to the economy and promoting freedom and liberty abroad—are idealistic. However, he argues that idealism should not be confused with weakness. Carter's idealistic goals are reflective of a strong nation seeking to become stronger. Carter also acknowledges that the goals he set for his tenure were equally idealistic and perhaps not fully achievable during his presidency. Still, he says, when he leaves the White House, he hopes that he at least helped the country heal its racial wounds, start rebuilding its economy, and restore the people's faith in their government and their fellow citizens. After all, Carter said, these are the goals of all citizens who believe in the American Dream.

Essential Themes

Jimmy Carter used the occasion of his inauguration to remind Americans of the traditions, ideals, and principles on which the nation was founded. His idealism signified a sea change from the politics of the decade that preceded his election, a time in which the integrity of the political establishment was greatly undermined. Carter's idealism perhaps cost him reelection in 1980, but it remained one of the attributes that drove his post-presidential career in public service.

—*Michael P. Auerbach, MA*

Bibliography and Additional Reading

Carter, Jimmy. *White House Diary*. New York: Farrar, 2010. Print.

"Jimmy Carter: Life before the Presidency." Miller Center. University of Virginia, 2016. Web. 5 Apr. 2016.

"Jimmy Carter: Thirty-Ninth President of the United States and Founder of the Carter Center." Carter Center, 2016. Web. 5 Apr. 2016.

Morris, Kenneth E. *Jimmy Carter, American Moralist*. Athens: U of Georgia P, 1997. Print.

Thompson, Kenneth W. *The Carter Presidency: Fourteen Intimate Perspectives of Jimmy Carter*. Lanham: UP of America, 1990. Print.

The Reagans in the inaugural parade. (White House Photographic Office - National Archives and Records Administration)

■ Ronald Reagan's First Inaugural Address

Date: January 20, 1981
Author: Ronald Reagan
Genre: Address, speech

Summary Overview

After winning the presidency in a landslide victory, Ronald Reagan delivered an inaugural speech that would serve as a shining example of the type of leader the world would come to know him as. Known for his cheerful, optimistic disposition and his decisive leadership style, Reagan officially addressed the nation as president of the United States on January 20, 1981. In his historic address, Reagan laid out his intentions to reign in the welfare state, reinforcing what had been his promise to the people in the country during the presidential election. He sent out a call to the people for unity, described the United States in a way that painted a catastrophic economic picture, and encouraged American citizens to have hope despite the current economic difficulties moving forward. He promised a time of renewal, and even though as a candidate he received many criticisms, he projected a strong leadership style on Inauguration Day in 1981 which gave people hope for the future.

Defining Moment

After several failed attempts to secure the Republican nomination for president in 1968 and 1976, Reagan was ready to face the incumbent president, Jimmy Carter, when he secured the party's nomination in 1980. Even though Reagan had the support of the party, criticisms of the candidate were rampant. Many believed that Reagan was too old, held too conservative positions on issues, and possessed a resumé that seemed unconventional for a person seeking to win the highest office in the land. Even though Reagan had previously served two terms as the governor of California, the fact that he had a past as a Hollywood actor was off-putting for some who did not feel that was a suitable career for a president to have held. He was viewed as being unqualified regardless of his tenure as California's chief executive. On the positive side, Reagan's middle-class roots gave him an everyman quality people could relate to. He projected a sense of optimism and made people feel as if it was possible

to recapture some of America's former glory. This man, with an appealing face and comforting voice, would go on to launch a campaign successful enough to lock down 489 Electoral College votes while the sitting president secured less than 50. This victory marks the highest number of Electoral College votes ever won by a nonincumbent presidential candidate in the history of the United States.

Throughout the 1970s in America, the country was riddled with significant economic problems. Inflation was high, people were faced with very high unemployment rates, gas shortages were causing long lines and frustrated consumers at the gas pump. By the start of the 1980s, the world also faced a hostage crisis in Iran, where more than fifty Americans were being held hostage by Shiite revolutionaries. In short, America was in turmoil. Jimmy Carter was the sitting president, and he faced serious criticism over his failed hostage rescue attempt which resulted in the death of eight American servicemen and his decision to boycott the 1980 Summer Olympics. Carter was viewed as being weak and lacking authority, and America was desperate for a powerful leader to comfort them in those upsetting times. For many Americans, Ronald Reagan appeared to be the strong leader they needed. Reagan launched a campaign focused on increasing defense spending, enacting targeted economic policies, and operating under a balanced budget. For voters who had been hit hard in their pocketbook and who felt their current leader was crumbling under international and economic threats and pressure, Reagan as a candidate became increasingly appealing. Carter did attempt to highlight Reagan's faults by painting a picture of Reagan as a right-wing extremist whose conservativism would cause problems for many Americans. Specifically, Carter called attention to certain social programs like Social Security, and warned that people might lose their social benefits if they gave their trust to Reagan. Despite this strategem, Reagan proved that he was not too conservative for voters in the Northeast by winning the New Hampshire primary. He performed very well in the campaign's single debate, and went on to win the presidency with a record-setting 489 Electoral College votes.

Author Biography

Ronald Reagan was born in 1911 to poor parents in Illinois, and grew up modestly. In his youth Reagan was a Democrat, but switched to the Republican Party upon realizing he more closely identified with that party's goals and values. A once-successful film actor and a two-term governor of California, Reagan served as the 40th president of the United States from 1981 to 1989. Reagan believed in "peace through strength," a philosophy that ultimately contributed to improvements in Soviet relations. The key result of that repaired relationship was an important nuclear agreement, which had been thought by many to be an unattainable goal prior to Reagan's time in office. During Reagan's tenure, he focused his efforts on cutting taxes and increasing defense spending. The commitment to those goals contributed to the longest period recorded for the United States going without a recession or a depression. Known as the "Great Communicator," Reagan died at the age of 93 following a well-publicized battle with Alzheimer's disease.

HISTORICAL DOCUMENT

Senator Hatfield, Mr. Chief Justice, Mr. President, Vice President Bush, Vice President Mondale, Senator Baker, Speaker O'Neill, Reverend Moomaw, and my fellow citizens:

To a few of us here today this is a solemn and most momentous occasion, and yet in the history of our nation it is a commonplace occurrence. The orderly transfer of authority as called for in the Constitution routinely takes place, as it has for almost two centuries, and few of us stop to think how unique we really are. In the eyes of many in the world, this every 4-year ceremony we accept as normal is nothing less than a miracle.

Mr. President, I want our fellow citizens to know how much you did to carry on this tradition. By your gracious cooperation in the transition process, you have shown a watching world that we are a united people pledged to maintaining a political system which guarantees individual liberty to a greater degree than any other, and I thank you and your people for all your help in maintaining the continuity which is the bulwark of our Republic.

The business of our nation goes forward. These United States are confronted with an economic affliction of great proportions. We suffer from the longest and one of the worst sustained inflations in our national history. It distorts our economic decisions, penalizes thrift, and crushes the struggling young and the fixed-income elderly alike. It threatens to shatter the lives of millions of our people.

Idle industries have cast workers into unemployment, human misery, and personal indignity. Those who do work are denied a fair return for their labor by a tax system which penalizes successful achievement and keeps us from maintaining full productivity.

But great as our tax burden is, it has not kept pace with public spending. For decades we have piled deficit upon deficit, mortgaging our future and our children's future for the temporary convenience of the present. To continue this long trend is to guarantee tremendous social, cultural, political, and economic upheavals.

You and I, as individuals, can, by borrowing, live beyond our means, but for only a limited period of time. Why, then, should we think that collectively, as a nation, we're not bound by that same limitation? We must act today in order to preserve tomorrow. And let there be no misunderstanding: We are going to begin to act, beginning today.

The economic ills we suffer have come upon us over several decades. They will not go away in days, weeks, or months, but they will go away. They will go away because we as Americans have the capacity now, as we've had in the past, to do whatever needs to be done to preserve this last and greatest bastion of freedom.

In this present crisis, government is not the solution to our problem; government is the problem. From time to time we've been tempted to believe that society has become too complex to be managed by self-rule, that government by an elite group is superior to government for, by, and of the people. Well, if no one among us is capable of governing himself, then who among us has the capacity to govern someone else? All of us together, in and out of government, must bear the burden. The solutions we seek must be equitable, with no one group singled out to pay a higher price.

We hear much of special interest groups. Well, our concern must be for a special interest group that has been too long neglected. It knows no sectional boundaries or ethnic and racial divisions, and it crosses political party lines. It is made up of men and women who raise our food, patrol our streets, man our mines and factories, teach our children, keep our homes, and heal us when we're sick—professionals, industrialists, shopkeepers, clerks, cabbies, and truck drivers. They are, in short, "We the people," this breed called Americans.

Well, this administration's objective will be a healthy, vigorous, growing economy that provides equal opportunities for all Americans, with no barriers born of bigotry or discrimination. Putting America back to work means putting all Americans back to work. Ending inflation means freeing all Americans from the terror of runaway living costs. All must share in the productive work of this "new beginning," and all must share in the bounty of a revived economy. With the idealism and fair play which are the core of our system and our strength, we can have a strong and prosperous America, at peace with itself and the world.

So, as we begin, let us take inventory. We are a nation that has a government—not the other way around. And this makes us special among the nations of the Earth. Our government has no power except that granted it by the people. It is time to check and reverse the growth of government, which shows signs of having grown beyond the consent of the governed.

It is my intention to curb the size and influence of the Federal establishment and to demand recognition of the distinction between the powers granted to the Federal Government and those reserved to the States or to the people. All of us need to be reminded that the Federal Government did not create the States; the States created the Federal Government.

Now, so there will be no misunderstanding, it's not my intention to do away with government. It is rather to make it work—work with us, not over us; to stand by our side, not ride on our back. Government can and must provide opportunity, not smother it; foster productivity, not stifle it.

If we look to the answer as to why for so many years we achieved so much, prospered as no other people on Earth, it was because here in this land we unleashed the energy and individual genius of man to a greater extent than has ever been done before. Freedom and the dignity of the individual have been more available and assured here than in any other place on Earth. The price for this freedom at times has been high, but we have never been unwilling to pay that price.

It is no coincidence that our present troubles parallel and are proportionate to the intervention and intrusion in our lives that result from unnecessary and excessive growth of government. It is time for us to realize that we're too great a nation to limit ourselves to small dreams. We're not, as some would have us believe, doomed to an inevitable decline. I do not believe in a fate that will fall on us no matter what we do. I do believe in a fate that will fall on us if we do nothing. So, with all the creative energy at our command, let us begin an era of national renewal. Let us renew our determination, our courage, and our strength. And let us renew our faith and our hope.

We have every right to dream heroic dreams. Those who say that we're in a time when there are not heroes, they just don't know where to look. You can see heroes every day going in and out of factory gates. Others, a handful in number, produce enough food to feed all of us and then the world beyond. You meet heroes across a counter, and they're on both sides of that counter. There are entrepreneurs with faith in themselves and faith in an idea who create new jobs, new wealth and opportunity. They're individuals and families whose taxes support the government and whose voluntary gifts support church, charity, culture, art, and education. Their patriotism is quiet, but deep. Their values sustain our national life.

Now, I have used the words "they" and "their" in speaking of these heroes. I could say "you" and "your," because I'm addressing the heroes of whom I speak— you, the citizens of this blessed land. Your dreams, your hopes, your goals are going to be the dreams, the hopes, and the goals of this administration, so help me God.

We shall reflect the compassion that is so much a part of your makeup. How can we love our country and not love our countrymen; and loving them, reach out a hand when they fall, heal them when they're sick, and provide opportunity to make them self-sufficient so they will be equal in fact and not just in theory?

Can we solve the problems confronting us? Well, the answer is an unequivocal and emphatic "yes." To paraphrase Winston Churchill, I did not take the oath I've just taken with the intention of presiding over the dissolution of the world's strongest economy.

In the days ahead I will propose removing the roadblocks that have slowed our economy and reduced productivity. Steps will be taken aimed at restoring the balance between the various levels of government. Progress may be slow, measured in inches and feet, not miles, but we will progress. It is time to reawaken this industrial giant, to get government back within its means, and to lighten our punitive tax burden. And these will be our first priorities, and on these principles there will be no compromise.

On the eve of our struggle for independence a man who might have been one of the greatest among the Founding Fathers, Dr. Joseph Warren, president of the Massachusetts Congress, said to his fellow Americans, "Our country is in danger, but not to be despaired of . . . . On you depend the fortunes of America. You are to decide the important questions upon which rests the happiness and the liberty of millions yet unborn. Act worthy of yourselves."

Well, I believe we, the Americans of today, are ready to act worthy of ourselves, ready to do what must be done to ensure happiness and liberty for ourselves, our children, and our children's children. And as we renew ourselves here in our own land, we will be seen as having greater strength throughout the world. We will again be the exemplar of freedom and a beacon of hope for those who do not now have freedom.

To those neighbors and allies who share our freedom, we will strengthen our historic ties and assure them of our support and firm commitment. We will match loyalty with loyalty. We will strive for mutually beneficial relations. We will not use our friendship to impose on their sovereignty, for our own sovereignty is not for sale.

As for the enemies of freedom, those who are potential adversaries, they will be reminded that peace is the highest aspiration of the American people. We will nego-

tiate for it, sacrifice for it; we will not surrender for it, now or ever.

Our forbearance should never be misunderstood. Our reluctance for conflict should not be misjudged as a failure of will. When action is required to preserve our national security, we will act. We will maintain sufficient strength to prevail if need be, knowing that if we do so we have the best chance of never having to use that strength.

Above all, we must realize that no arsenal or no weapon in the arsenals of the world is so formidable as the will and moral courage of free men and women. It is a weapon our adversaries in today's world do not have. It is a weapon that we as Americans do have. Let that be understood by those who practice terrorism and prey upon their neighbors.

I'm told that tens of thousands of prayer meetings are being held on this day, and for that I'm deeply grateful. We are a nation under God, and I believe God intended for us to be free. It would be fitting and good, I think, if on each Inaugural Day in future years it should be declared a day of prayer.

This is the first time in our history that this ceremony has been held, as you've been told, on this West Front of the Capitol. Standing here, one faces a magnificent vista, opening up on this city's special beauty and history. At the end of this open mall are those shrines to the giants on whose shoulders we stand.

Directly in front of me, the monument to a monumental man, George Washington, father of our country. A man of humility who came to greatness reluctantly. He led America out of revolutionary victory into infant nationhood. Off to one side, the stately memorial to Thomas Jefferson. The Declaration of Independence flames with his eloquence. And then, beyond the Reflecting Pool, the dignified columns of the Lincoln Memorial. Whoever would understand in his heart the meaning of America will find it in the life of Abraham Lincoln.

Beyond those monuments to heroism is the Potomac River, and on the far shore the sloping hills of Arlington National Cemetery, with its row upon row of simple white markers bearing crosses or Stars of David. They add up to only a tiny fraction of the price that has been paid for our freedom.

Each one of those markers is a monument to the kind of hero I spoke of earlier. Their lives ended in places called Belleau Wood, The Argonne, Omaha Beach, Salerno, and halfway around the world on Guadalcanal, Tarawa, Pork Chop Hill, the Chosin Reservoir, and in a hundred rice paddies and jungles of a place called Vietnam.

Under one such marker lies a young man, Martin Treptow, who left his job in a small town barbershop in 1917 to go to France with the famed Rainbow Division. There, on the western front, he was killed trying to carry a message between battalions under heavy artillery fire.

We're told that on his body was found a diary. On the flyleaf under the heading, "My Pledge," he had written these words: "America must win this war. Therefore I will work, I will save, I will sacrifice, I will endure, I will fight

cheerfully and do my utmost, as if the issue of the whole struggle depended on me alone."

The crisis we are facing today does not require of us the kind of sacrifice that Martin Treptow and so many thousands of others were called upon to make. It does require, however, our best effort and our willingness to believe in ourselves and to believe in our capacity to perform great deeds, to believe that together with God's help we can and will resolve the problems which now confront us.

And after all, why shouldn't we believe that? We are Americans.

God bless you, and thank you.

GLOSSARY

vista: a pleasant view or prospect

Document Analysis

On the date of his inauguration, January 20, 1981, Ronald Reagan was the oldest elected president to date at the age of 69. While his age had been scrutinized during the campaign, Reagan's pleasant disposition and clear direction for the nation's future led voters to select him as the 40th president. He was a speaker whom people could identify with, and he was so natural at oration that he would go on to be known as "the Great Communicator." Reagan's speech on Inauguration Day only helped to reinforce his level of relatability with the general public, and gave people hope that the nation would soon recover from the dismal economic situation it was facing.

In his Inauguration Day speech, Reagan began by telling his audience that they were a "united people," thereby beginning his speech with the traditional call to unity present in most inaugural addresses. One of the main focuses of the speech was to cite the economic hardships the country was confronted with, and Reagan chose to speak about this in terms that were applicable to the experiences that the average American experienced at the time. By highlighting the "personal indignity" that many were facing, and calling out the "human misery" familiar to people at the time, Reagan emphasized the truly catastrophic economic climate the United States had been plagued with throughout the 1970s (and into the early

1980s). While focusing on the economic state of the union, Reagan called out deficit spending and signaled to listeners that, under his administration, the practice of deficit spending would be ended. In his speech, Reagan did not shy away from clearly identifying government as the cause of these financial problems, not the solution, and condemned elite control which he argues had got America into the monetary crisis it was in. Even though this was a strong and direct message focused on negative conditions, it was not without its hopeful elements. In fact, the heart of the speech was dedicated to lifting up the spirits of Americans, and promising them a brighter future.

Reagan assured Americans that if the power of the government was checked and reduced, then people could look forward to a "new beginning." This promise included equal economic opportunities for all Americans, and Reagan reassured people that a revived economy would benefit all. For a nation that had been significantly troubled by a dismal economic situation for at least ten years, these words were welcomed with open arms. The pledge to bring forth a renewal period for the country was refreshing, and Reagan was intentionally reassuring people that they were not "doomed to an inevitable decline." Reagan was positioning himself to be a savior for the country, and he did not shy away from highlighting his plans for the future of the nation using a personal point of view.

Reagan further personalized his speech by discussing God and the prayers he was told he had received. Reagan claimed that he was so moved by these prayers he stated he believed future Inauguration Days should be a day of prayer in the country. While for some this statement may have signaled the personal religious beliefs of the new president could pervade policy choices, others were comforted by the readiness of Reagan to disclose his personal feelings about religious faith. Reagan closed his speech by assuring people they would succeed with God's help, and once again directed the citizenry towards unity by stating, "We are all Americans."

That positive message was something that most Americans were ready to hear at that time, particularly given the economic state many people were facing. As a result, President Carter left office being perceived as weak and unable to help the mass of people, and as someone who had unsuccessfully navigated a disturbing hostage situation. Reagan's speech was punctuated by the fact that while the speech was being delivered, the hostages in Iran were being released. Promises of economic rebirth that Reagan spoke of throughout the speech, and the release of the hostages during the speech, gave people a tremendous amount of faith and hope in Ronald Reagan's presidential prospects.

Essential Themes

Under the leadership of Ronald Reagan, taxes were reduced and the size and scope of government was lessened, as promised. The country experienced an eventual economic boom, and it was evident that the promises Reagan had made to the country regarding a positive change in the economic stance of America came to fruition. For those who shared Reagan's personal conservative stance on issues, and who benefitted from his economic policies, he was a beloved president. While there were periods of public disapproval, particularly over issues such as the Iran-Contra scandal, history recalls Reagan as one of the more outstanding and treasured presidents. Yet, however popular history might remember Reagan, there are those who did then and continue to criticize some of the choices that he made as president.

While Reagan's inaugural speech made mention of equal opportunity for all in the country, his domestic policy stances and action/inaction on certain issues

seemed to run contradictory to that portion of the speech. In particular, Reagan's stance on domestic policies regarding issues such as civil rights, poverty, and AIDS are extremely problematic for some. Critics of the administration firmly believe that Reagan did little if nothing to help fight the AIDS epidemic in the country. While Reagan's later personal battle with Alzheimer's garnered some sympathy, his critics remain very vocal on his administration's choice to do nothing about the AIDS crisis or to consider anything other than the "trickle down" economics and Christian-fundamentalist moral positions that he espoused.

Generally speaking, low wage earners in the country felt ignored and abandoned by a president who seemed so eager to help them on Inauguration Day. Images of "welfare queens" and black criminals were stereotypes propagated by the Reagan administration, and those stereotypes negatively impacted the ability for all to be given an equal opportunity in the country. Thus, while history may remember Reagan as a great and powerful leader, there are those who seem to have suffered disproportionately during his time in office. With an approval rating that fluctuated throughout his time as president, just a few months before leaving office Reagan's approval rating was around 63 percent, demonstrating that he was well thought of as a president. Loved by conservatives and criticized by liberals, Reagan's legacy is remembered generally positively in the context of U.S. presidential history.

—*Amber R. Dickinson, PhD*

Bibliography and Additional Reading

D'Souza, Dinesh. *Ronald Reagan: How an Ordinary Man Became an Extraordinary Leader.* New York: Simon & Schuster, 1997.

Pear, Robin Toner and Robert. "THE 40TH PRESIDENT: THE OPPONENTS; Critics See a Reagan Legacy Tainted by AIDS, Civil Rights and Union Policies." *The New York Times*, The New York Times, 9 June 2004, www.nytimes.com/2004/06/09/us/40th-president-opponents-critics-see-reagan-legacy-tainted-aids-civil-rights.html.

Rothman, Lily, and Arpita Aneja. "President Ronald Reagan Elected: Remembering That Day." *Time*, Time, 4 Nov. 2015, time.com/4090907/time-remembers-ronald-reagan-1980/.

"Ronald Reagan: Inaugural Address - January 20, 1981." *The American Presidency Project*, www.presidency.ucsb.edu/ws/?pid=43130.

Walsh, Kenneth T. "The Most Consequential Elections in History: Ronald Reagan and the Election of 1980." *U.S. News & World Report*, U.S. News & World Report, www.usnews.com/news/articles/2008/09/25/the-most-consequential-elections-in-history-ronald-reagan-and-the-election-of-1980.

■ "Willie Horton" Ad—and a Bush-Dukakis Debate Question

Date: September 1988; October 13, 1988
Authors: George H. W. Bush; Michael Dukakis; with Bernard Shaw
Genre: Television ad; debate; speech

Summary Overview

As the 1988 presidential campaign unfolded, the Republican nominee, Vice President George H.W. Bush, assailed the Democratic nominee, Governor Michael Dukakis of Massachusetts, on the issues of Dukakis' being regarded as a left-leaning liberal, someone who was "weak on crime," and a person unqualified to lead in the area of national defense. In a notorious television ad from September 1988 known as the "Willie Horton" ad, Bush supporters sought to stereotype Dukakis as a leftist intellectual who coddled criminals, leaving citizens exposed to potential harm. In the presidential debates that followed in October, the debate host, Bernard Shaw, put a question to Dukakis relating to the Horton ad. Although the question itself was fairly shocking, Dukakis' mild-mannered, reasoned response, and the contents of his answer, reinforced in many voters' minds the notion that Dukakis was too soft on crime.

Some polls in the early summer had shown Dukakis in the lead, yet by the time both parties held their national conventions Bush was leading in all the major polls. The Horton ad seemed only to strengthen Bush's lead, and many Dukakis supporters were left to hope that their candidate would excel in the upcoming debates—it could be their only chance for victory. In the event, however, not only did Dukakis' answer about the death penalty go over poorly, but his lack of emotion revealed him to be a somewhat robotic, unfeeling human being. Ultimately, the combination of these two television events assisted Bush in winning a landslide victory.

Defining Moment

Going into the 1988 presidential campaign, there were conflicting indicators as to which major party might have the best chance to win. Overall, the economy was strong, and the Republicans had won four of the last five presidential elections. However, one had to look back to the 1920s to find an example of a Republican candidate being successful when the preceding eight years had had a Republican president (as was the case here), and it had been more than one hundred and fifty years since a sitting vice-president had been elected president. As it turned out, however, Dukakis' popularity reached its peak the week of the Democratic Convention in July, and proceeded to decline from there. At the same time, Bush's campaign had begun to press hard on areas in which they believed Dukakis was vulnerable. One such area was crime, including a furlough program for prisoners in Massachusetts. This is the topic that Bush used to depict Dukakis as weak on crime.

An independent organization, "Americans for Bush," a group within the National Security Political Action Committee (PAC), created the ad called "Weekend Passes" which came to be known as the "Willie Horton" ad for one of the furloughed prisoners featured in it. Horton's case had been identified by the Bush campaign as a potential weakness for Dukakis. (Although allegations of illicit coordination between the official Bush campaign and the independent PAC were made, no finding supported these charges.) The ad describes Horton, a convicted murderer, as having received weekend furloughs, the last of which he used to go on the lam and commit further serious crimes. When Americans for Bush stopped running the ad, the Bush campaign began running a similar ad, although without specifically naming Horton. Through both, a strong negative image of Dukakis was created, turning many middle-of-the-road voters away from the Democratic governor and toward the Republican vice president. The effect of the ads, beyond the election, was twofold. Furlough programs, which at that time were used in all fifty states, were dramatically cut back or ended. In addition, for the next several years, changes to criminal codes went in the direction of stricter, stronger laws.

The 1988 presidential debate, sponsored by the Commission on Presidential Debates, was, in the opinion of most, won by Bush. Dukakis had been ill just prior to the debate, which hurt his performance. His answers to the questions, especially the one printed below, reinforced the negative image of him as an unfeeling intellectual who lived by statistics rather than by commonplace thought and emotion. His quick pivot from the question regarding the rape and murder of a loved one to the statistics on crime and drug abuse, left many viewers feeling that Dukakis was not the type of person they wanted as their president. Bush's projection of himself as a "values" candidate, on the other hand, who would seek the death penalty against someone who committed serious crimes, resonated with more viewers. Although Bush was doing well before both the ad and the debate, in the period afterward he seemed to seal the election, forcing Dukakis to play catch-up.

Author Biographies

George Herbert Walker Bush (born 1924) grew up in New England and after high school, became a naval aviator in World War II, earning several medals. After the war, he married Barbara Pierce and then attended Yale University, graduating in 1948. He moved to Texas, entering the oil industry and eventually became a millionaire. On the Republican ticket, he was twice elected to the House of Representatives in the 1960s, and at President Nixon's urging ran unsuccessfully for the senate in 1970. He was then appointed Ambassador to the United Nations (1971-1973), Chairman of the Republican National Committee (1973-74), Envoy to China (1974-1975), and Director of the Central Intelligence Agency (1976-1977), before returning to private business. Bush was defeated in the 1980 Republican presidential primaries by Ronald Reagan, who selected him to be his vice president. He won the 1988 presidential election but lost his 1992 re-election effort. As his health has permitted, Bush has continued to be active in Republican politics and has raised funds for various humanitarian and social causes.

Michael Dukakis (born 1933) grew up in Massachusetts and attended Swarthmore College, served in the Army, and then attended and graduated from Harvard Law School. As a Democrat, he was in the Massachusetts House of Representatives from 1963 to 1971. He was governor of that state from 1975 to 1979, and then from 1983 to 1991. Having been defeated in the 1988 presidential race, Dukakis decided against running for office in the future. He has held teaching and research positions in several academic institutions, taking time to assist Democratic candidates in Massachusetts. He married Katherine "Kitty" Dickson in 1963.

Bernard Shaw (born 1940) became interested in journalism while serving as a message center specialist in the Army. After returning to Chicago to attend college, he moved into journalism full-time. From 1980 to his retirement in 2001, he was one of the leading news anchors on CNN (Cable News Network). High-points in his career were moderating the second 1988 presidential debates and his coverage of the Gulf War in 1991.

HISTORICAL DOCUMENTS

Political Ad: "Willie Horton" 1988 (c. Sept. 1988)

NARRATOR: Bush and Dukakis on crime. Bush supports the death penalty for first-degree murderers. Dukakis not only opposes the death penalty; he allowed first-degree murderers to have weekend passes from prison. One was Willie Horton who murdered a boy in a robbery, stabbing him 19 times. Despite a life sentence, Horton received 10 weekend passes from prison. Horton fled, kidnapped a young couple, stabbing the man and repeatedly raping his girlfriend. Weekend prison passes. Dukakis on crime.

= = =

The Second Bush-Dukakis Presidential Debate, October 13, 1988

BERNARD SHAW: On behalf of the Commission on Presidential Debates, I am pleased to welcome you to the second presidential debate. I am Bernard Shaw of CNN, Cable News Network. My colleagues on the panel are Ann Compton of ABC NEWS; Margaret Warner of Newsweek magazine; and Andrea Mitchell of NBC NEWS. The candidates are Vice President George Bush, the Republican nominee; and Governor Michael Dukakis, the Democratic nominee. (Applause)

SHAW: For the next 90 minutes we will be questioning the candidates following a format designed and agreed to by representatives of the two campaigns. However, there are no restrictions on the questions that my colleagues and I can ask this evening, and the candidates have no prior knowledge of our questions. By agreement between the candidates, the first question goes to Governor Dukakis. You have two minutes to respond. Governor, if Kitty Dukakis were raped and murdered, would you favor an irrevocable death penalty for the killer?

DUKAKIS: No, I don't, Bernard. And I think you know that I've opposed the death penalty during all of my life. I don't see any evidence that it's a deterrent, and I think there are better and more effective ways to deal with violent crime. We've done so in my own state. And it's one of the reasons why we have had the biggest drop in crime of any industrial state in America; why we have the lowest murder rate of any industrial state in America. But we have work to do in this nation. We have work to do to fight a real war, not a phony war, against drugs. And that's something I want to lead, something we haven't had over the course of the past many years, even though the Vice President has been at least allegedly in charge of that war. We have much to do to step up that war, to double the number of drug enforcement agents, to fight both here and abroad, to work with our neighbors in this hemisphere. And I want to call a hemispheric summit just as soon after the 20th of January as possible to fight that war. But we also have to deal with drug education prevention here at home. And that's one of the things that I hope I can lead personally as the President of the United States. We've had great success in my own state. And we've reached out to young people and their families and been able to help them by beginning drug education and prevention in the early elementary grades. So we can fight this war, and we can win this war. And we can do so in a way that marshals our forces, that provides real support for state and local law enforcement officers who have not been getting that support, and do it in a way which will bring down violence in this nation, will help our youngsters to stay away from drugs, will stop this avalanche of drugs that's pouring into the country, and will make it possible for our kids and our families to grow up in safe and secure and decent neighborhoods.

SHAW: Mr. Vice President, your one-minute rebuttal.

BUSH: Well, a lot of what this campaign is about, it seems to me Bernie, goes to the question of values. And here I do have, on this particular question, a big difference with my opponent. You see, I do believe that some crimes are so heinous, so brutal, so outrageous, and I'd say particularly those that result in the death of a police officer, for those real brutal crimes, I do believe in the death penalty, and I think it is a deterrent, and I believe we need it. And I'm glad that the Congress moved on this drug bill and have finally called for that related to these narcotics drug kingpins. And so we just have an honest difference of opinion: I support it and he doesn't....

GLOSSARY

Commission on Presidential Debates: organization established in 1987 to host debates in order to provide the "best possible information" to voters in presidential elections

Kitty Dukakis: wife of Michael Dukakis

Willie Horton: one of three men convicted of the murder mentioned in the ad; the second crime for which he was convicted occurred ten months after he escaped incarceration in Massachusetts

Document Analysis

The first document reproduced here is the text of the narration of a televised political ad aired by an independent committee which supported George H.W. Bush in the 1988 presidential campaign. Formally titled "Weekend Passes," the ad is designed to give a negative impression of Massachusetts Governor, and Democratic presidential nominee, Michael Dukakis, specifically his support for a furlough program seeking to rehabilitate prisoners. The weekend pass/furlough program in Massachusetts was created by a Republican governor and was extended to individuals convicted of first-degree murder by a court ruling. Dukakis vetoed legislation that would have changed this. The wording of the ad is slightly misleading, however, in that it implies that the second crime for which Horton was convicted happened as he was fleeing, rather than almost a year after he escaped. In addition, the image of Horton in the ad, was a picture taken under unusual circumstances. Horton had been seriously wounded trying to escape the police during his second arrest and was in the hospital for weeks. The picture was taken as he was released from the hospital, not having been given any opportunity for personal grooming. The impact of the ad, including its racist implications (Horton actually went by his given name of William, not "Willy"), met its creators' goal of scaring white suburban voters. The viability of the subject of the ad had been discovered by Bush's campaign manager, Lee Atwater, in his work among potential voters. The fact that Atwater had developed the idea of making this a central issue against Dukakis, which was then taken up by the theoretically independent National Security PAC, was the reason questions were raised regarding whether the official campaign and the PAC were illegally working together. Bush's official campaign's decision to later air weekend passes ads, without specifically including Horton, was successful in keeping the previous ad in the minds of voters.

The second document here is the transcript of the opening portion of the second Bush-Dukakis debate. The initial reaction of many viewers was that it was hard to believe that Shaw would ask such a question (about murder) and do so by couching it in such personal terms. Shaw knew that Dukakis was opposed to capital punishment, and many believed that no matter how Dukakis answered it he would come out the loser. If he had changed his policy views because the situation involved his wife, obviously he would be thought to

lack conviction. If, however, he stuck with his position and answered as he did, he stood to appear unfeeling or unrealistic. The precise answer he gave was, in the eyes of his campaign advisors, even worse than they had imagined. Knowing that a question about crime would be asked, especially in light of the Horton ad, they had advised the candidate to use events in his own life as part of his response. (Dukakis' father, at age 77, had been robbed in his medical office and left tied up, and Dukakis' brother had been killed by a hit-and-run driver.) In the response he gives, however, Dukakis fails to mention either of those incidents. Rather, he makes statements about the death penalty not being a deterrent, and notes the drop in Massachusetts's murder rate while he served as governor. While Dukakis manages to present his position on the death penalty, his total absence of personal reflection, or emotion, acted to hurt him in the polls. His debate performance, which was otherwise unremarkable (as was Bush's), caused him to lose the support of one seventh of those who had previously been inclined to support him: his support decreased in the polls from 49 percent to 42 percent after the debate.

In Bush's rebuttal to Dukakis' statements, the Republican candidate makes it clear that he supports the death penalty. Indeed, he seeks to go beyond this straightforward assertion by bringing up the topic of "values," hoping, no doubt, that voters might see him as an individual who cares. The adjectives he uses to describe crimes—"heinous," "brutal," "outrageous"—are evocative words that tend to create an emotional response. This response was key for Bush taking control of the debate, or at least gaining an upper hand. His final point in this rebuttal is to repeat the he supports the death penalty and Dukakis does not. The rebuttal overall was a solid move on Bush's part, resulting in the debate virtually being over at that point. Although Bush had less time for his response, he makes better use of the opportunity to present himself as someone who stands strongly against crime.

Essential Themes

In American politics, candidates and their staffs have always sought new methods for ensuring success. In the 1988 election cycle, the Bush campaign, and its supporters, went back to one proven method, a negative campaign. This approach creates images of the opponent as not being up to the standards of the office, or having some major flaw. The Willie Horton ad was a forceful presentation of a set of facts that painted Dukakis as politically deficient and an uncaring person. It suggested that he was somehow responsible for the crimes Horton had committed, or that he had personally released Horton on furlough. Dukakis was a part of the governing system that allowed these events to occur, yet the ad seeks to suggest that he was more than that, that he somehow was complicit in the crimes. The attempt to create fear, including fear based on Horton's race, in this negative ad went well beyond the attempts of most previous negative campaigning. It was a rather blatant example that set the tone for negative campaign ads to come in the future.

The lesson illustrated by the debate, too, was that American voters wanted someone with whom they could identify. This meant that candidates who might be technically proficient at governing, or had the basic skills needed to occupy the Oval Office, could nevertheless be unqualified because they fail to touch the hearts of voters. While both Bush and Dukakis had the experience and qualifications to serve in high office, Bush, who was not otherwise known for his attractive personality, nevertheless proved to be the more personable candidate. Such evident qualities, in addition to running a strong campaign and promising to hold the line on taxes, gave Bush the support of more than 53 percent of the voters, allowing him to win 426 of the 538 electoral votes.

—*Donald A Watt, PhD*

Bibliography and Additional Reading

Commission on Presidential Debates. "1988 Debates." *Commission on Presidential Debates.* Washington: The Commission on Presidential Debates, 2018. Web. 27 March 2018.

Gains, Richard and Michael Segal. *Dukakis: The Man Who Would Be President.* New York: Avon Books, 1988. Print.

Goldman, Peter, Tom Matthews et al. *Quest for the Presidency: The 1988 Campaign.* New York: Simon & Schuster Books, 1989. Print.

Naftali, Timothy. *George H. W. Bush: The American President Series: The 41st President, 1989-1993.* New York: Times Books, 2007. Print.

Schwartzapfel, Beth and Bill Keller. "Willie Horton Revisited." *The Marshall Project.* New York: The Marshall Project, 2015. Web. 26 March 2018.

Simon, Roger. "Simon Says: Questions that Kill Candidates' Careers." *Politico.* Arlington VA: Politico, 2007. Web. 27 March 2018.

■ Excerpts from the 1992 Presidential Debates

Date: October 15, 1992
Authors: George H.W. Bush; Bill Clinton; Ross Perot; with Carole Simpson
Genre: Debate

Summary Overview

The moderator played a less important role in this second 1992 presidential debate than in the other debates, as it had a different format. Members of the audience were selected to ask questions of the candidates. Although the questions covered the same range of topics that might have been covered by professional journalists, the questions were asked in a slightly different manner by "average voters" in the audience. All three of the candidates seem generally to have been straightforward in presenting their views to the audience, and to the larger audience watching on television. As in all debates, some questions were answered in a more direct fashion than were others, and some answers were better received than others. However, because of the manner in which Clinton related to the audience in the auditorium, he was perceived to have been the winner of the debate. Confirming this, the results of a poll conducted in the days following the poll, gave the outcome as follows: 58 percent said Clinton had won, 16 percent said the winner was Bush, and 15 percent said it was Perot. Leading going into the debate, Clinton was able to solidify his support, resulting in his election as president in November.

Defining Moment

This was the second of three presidential debates that were held from October 11 to 19. As a relatively popular incumbent, George Bush had been the leader in the polls early in the year. However, with the entry of an independent candidate, Ross Perot, Bush saw his lead shift to Perot. During the summer, Perot took a break from campaigning, and after the Democratic National Convention was held, Bill Clinton took the lead in the polls. Clinton's lead lasted for the remainder of the campaign. Bush knew that it was important for him to do well in the debates if he wanted to win. Clinton knew that he had to hold his own. The question surrounding Perot was, Which of the other candidates would he hurt most, by drawing away votes? In this second debate, Clinton's chemistry with the audience, as well as the style and content of his answers, carried the day. Although it did not guarantee victory, it made winning much more probable.

As with all presidential debates, the messages from the candidates were directed toward the voters. With three strong candidates—Perot ended up winning a larger share of the popular vote than any third-party candidate since 1912—the dynamics of the debate were somewhat unusual for the modern era. Although Perot had run commercials and half-hour infomercials, the debates were an important means of showing the average voter who he was. Bush's first-term record (with most of his major accomplishments being in the international arena) was known by virtually everyone. He had hoped that the debates would allow him to demonstrate how he could move his focus to domestic concerns to help more Americans. Clinton, running as an outsider at a time when many were dissatisfied with the status quo, hoped to use the debates to show voters how well he understood the country and how, as a small state governor, he was better able to create the changes necessary for improving the economy and society in general. Thus, not only did electoral victory in November hang in the balance, but the outcome of the debates stood to move the nation in a different direction, depending upon how well the participants responded. Clinton came through the debate with flying colors, and the other candidates performed reasonably well too.

Author Biographies

George H. W. Bush (born 1924) attended school in Connecticut and Massachusetts. After graduation became the youngest naval aviator in World War II, earning several medals. After the war, he attended Yale University, graduating in 1948. Moving to Texas, he became a millionaire in the oil industry. A Republican, in the 1960s he was twice elected to the House of Representatives from Houston. Nixon then appointed Bush Ambassador to the United Nations (1971-1973). Bush later served as Chairman of the Republican National Committee (1973-74), Envoy to China (1974-1975), and Director of the Central Intelligence Agency (1976-1977), before returning to private business. In 1981, he was elected vice president under Ronald Reagan, and then won the 1988 presidential election, serving until 1993.

William J. "Bill" Clinton (born 1946) a native of Arkansas graduated from Georgetown University and Yale Law School. A moderate Democrat, he was Arkansas' Attorney General, 1977-1979, and then served as governor from 1979-81 and 1983-1992. Clinton was president from 1993 to 2001. After the presidency, in addition to supporting many other Democratic candidates, Clinton supported his wife Hillary Clinton's successful senatorial efforts and her unsuccessful runs for the presidency. He also created the Clinton Foundation, which works on issues related to global interdependence.

Henry Ross Perot (born 1930) was raised in Texas and attended the U.S. Naval Academy. After his naval service, he worked for IBM, before creating Electronic Data Systems, and becoming a billionaire. Truly independent in most of his endeavors, he was socially somewhat liberal but fiscally relatively conservative. His 1992 campaign was best known for using infomercials with many charts and graphs.

Carole Simpson (born 1940) graduated from the University of Michigan and began work as a journalist in Chicago. She was the first African American woman to moderate a presidential debate, and previously the first to anchor a major network newscast.

HISTORICAL DOCUMENT

Q.: *I'd like to direct my question to Mr. Perot. What will you do as president to open foreign markets to fair competition from American business, and to stop unfair competition here at home from foreign countries so that we can bring jobs back to the United States?*

PEROT: That's right at the top of my agenda. We've shipped millions of jobs overseas and we have a strange situation because we have a process in Washington where after you've become a foreign lobbyist, make $30,000 a month; then take a leave, work on presidential campaigns, make sure you got good contacts, and then go back out. Now if you just want to get down to brass tacks, the first thing you ought to do is get all these folks who've got these one-way trade agreements that we've negotiated over the years and say, "Fellows, we'll take the same deal we gave you." And they'll gridlock right at that point because we've got international competitors who simply could not unload their cars off the ships if they had to comply.... We have got to stop sending jobs overseas.

To those of you in the audience who are business people, pretty simple: If you're paying $12, $13, $14 an hour for factory workers and you can move your factory south of the border, pay a dollar an hour labor, hire young— let's assume you've been in business for a long time and you've got a mature work force—pay a dollar an hour for your labor, have no health care, have no environmental controls, no pollution controls and no retirement, and you don't care about anything but making money, there will be a giant sucking sound going south....

Q.: *Thank you Mr. Perot. I see that the president has stood up so he must have something to say about this.*

BUSH: Well, Carole, the thing that saved us in this global economic slowdown is our exports. And what I'm trying to do is increase our exports. And if, indeed, all the jobs were going to move south because of lower wages, there are lower wages now and they haven't done that. And so I have just negotiated with the President of Mexico the North American Free Trade Agreement, and [with] the Prime Minister of Canada.... I want to have more of these free trade agreements. Because export jobs are increasing far faster than any jobs that may have moved overseas; that's a scare tactic because it's not that many. But anyone that's here, we want to have more jobs here and the way to do that is to increase our exports.

Some believe in protection. I don't. I believe in free fair trade and that's the thing that saved us, and so I will keep on as president trying to get a successful conclusion to the GATT round, the big Uruguay round of trade which will really open up markets for our agriculture particularly. I want to continue work after we get this NAFTA agreement ratified this coming year; I want to get one with Eastern Europe. I want to get one with Chile and free and fair trade is the answer, not protection. And, as I say, we've had tough economic times and it's exports that have saved us.

Q.: *Governor Clinton.*

CLINTON: I'd like to answer the question because I've actually been a governor for 12 years, so I've known a lot of people who've lost their jobs moving overseas and I know a lot of people whose plants have been strengthened by increasing exports. The trick is to expand our export base and to expand trade on terms that are fair to us. It is true that our exports to Mexico, for example, have gone up and our trade deficit's gone down. It's also true that just today a record high trade deficit was announced with Japan. So what is the answer?

Let me just mention three things very quickly.

Number 1, make sure that other countries are as open to our markets as our markets are to them. And if they're not, have measures on the books that don't take forever and a day to implement.

Number 2, change the tax code. There are more deductions in the tax code for shutting plants down and moving overseas than there are for modernizing plants and equipment here. Our competitors don't do that. Emphasize and subsidize modernizing plant equipment here, not moving plants overseas.

Number 3, stop the federal government's program that now gives low-interest loans and job training funds to companies that will actually shut down and move to other countries but we won't do the same thing for plants that stay here. So more trade, but on fairer terms and favor investments in America.

Q.: *This is for Governor Clinton. In the real world—that is, outside of Washington, D.C.—compensation and achievement are based on goals defined and achieved. Would you define in specific dollar goals how much you would reduce the deficit in each of the four years of a Clinton administration, and then enter into a legally binding contract with the American people that if you did not achieve those goals, that you would not seek a second term? Answer yes or no, and then comment on your answer please.*

CLINTON: No, and here's why. And I'll tell you exactly

why. Because the deficit now has been building up for 12 years. I'll tell you exactly what I think can be done. I think we can bring it down by 50 percent in four years and grow the economy. Now, I could get rid of it in four years in theory on the books now, but to do it, you'd have to raise taxes too much and cut benefits too much to people who need them. And it would even make the economy worse.

Mr. Perot will tell you, for example, that the expert he hired to analyze his plan said that it will bring the deficit down in five years, but it will make unemployment bad for four more years. So my view is, sir, you have to increase investment, grow the economy and reduce the deficit by controlling health care costs, prudent reductions in defense, cuts in domestic programs and asking the wealthiest Americans and foreign corporations to pay their fair share of taxes and investing in growing this economy....

Q.: *Mr. President.*

BUSH: I'm a little confused here because I don't see how you can grow the deficit down by raising people's taxes. You, see, I don't think the American people are taxed too little. I think they're taxed too much. I went for one tax increase. And when I make a mistake I admit it. Say that wasn't the right thing to do.

Governor Clinton's program wants to tax more and spend more. $150 billion in new taxes. Spend another 220. I don't believe that's the way to do it.

Here's some things that'll help. Give us a balanced budget amendment. He always talks about Arkansas having a balanced budget and they do. But he has a balanced budget amendment—[they] have to do it. I'd like the government to have that. And I think it would discipline not only the Congress, which needs it, but also the executive branch. I'd like to have what 43 governors have—the line item veto, so if the Congress can't cut, [if] we've got a reckless, spending Congress—let the president have a shot at it by wiping out things that are pork barrel or something of that nature....

Q.: *How about you, Mr. Perot?*

PEROT: Well we're $4 trillion in debt. We're going into debt an additional $1 billion—a little more than a billion dollars every working day of the year.

Now the things I love about it—I'm just a businessman. I was down in Texas taking care of business, tending to my family. This situation got so bad that I decided I'd better get into it. The American people asked me to get into it.

But I just find it fascinating that while we sit here tonight, we will go into debt an additional $50 million dollars in an hour and a half.

Now, it's not the Republicans' fault, of course. And it's not the Democrats' fault. And what I'm looking for is, who did it? Now, they're the two folks involved, so maybe if you put them together, they did it.

Now, the facts are we have to fix it. I'm here tonight for these young people up there in the balcony from this college. When I was a young man, when I got out of the Navy, I had multiple job offers. Young people [today] with high grades can't get a job. Now, whose fault is that? Not the Democrats, not the Republicans. Somewhere out there there's an extraterrestrial that's doing this to us, I guess. And everybody says they take responsibility. Somebody, somewhere has to take responsibility for this. [I'll] put it to you bluntly, American people. If you want me to be your president, we're going to face some problems, we'll deal with the problems, we'll solve our problems. We'll pay down our debt. We'll pass on the American dream to our children, and I will not leave our children a situation that they have today.

When I was a boy it took two generations to double the standard of living. Today, it will take 12 generations. Our children will not see the American dream because of this debt that somebody, somewhere dropped on us.

Q.: *Forgive the notes here, but I'm shy on camera. The focus of my work as a domestic mediator is meeting the needs of the children that I work with by way of their parents, and not the wants of their parents. And I ask the three of you, how can we, as symbolically the children of the future president, expect the two of you, the three of you, to meet our needs: the needs in housing and in crime and, you name it, as opposed to the wants of your political spin doctorism, and your political parties?*

PEROT: I agree with him.

Q.: *President Bush?*

BUSH: Let's do it. Let's talk about programs for children, [but] let's talk about these issues; let's talk about the programs, but in the presidency a lot goes into it. Caring goes into it; that's not particularly specific. Strength goes into it; that's not specific. Standing up against aggression; that's not specific in terms of a program. This is what a president has to do. So I, in principle, I'll take your point and think we ought to discuss child care, or whatever else it is.

Q.: *And you two?*

PEROT: No hedges, no ifs, ands and buts. I'll take the pledge. Because I know the American people want to talk about issues and not tabloid journalism. So I'll take the pledge and we'll stay on the issues.

Now, just for the record, I don't have any spin doctors. I don't have any speech writers. Probably shows. I make those charts you see on television.

But you don't have to wonder if it's me talking. What you see is what you get. And if you don't like it you got two other choices, right?

CLINTON: Now wait a minute. I want to say just one thing now, Ross, in fairness. The ideas I express are mine. I've worked on these things for 12 years and I'm the only person up here who hasn't been part of Washington in any way for the last 20 years. So I don't want any implication to be that somehow everything we say is just cooked up and put in our heads by somebody else. I worked 12 years very hard as a governor on the real problems of real people. I'm just as sick as you are of having to wake up and figure out how to defend myself every day.

Q.: *Yes, I would like to get a response from all three gentlemen, and the question is: What are your plans to improve the physical infrastructure of our nation, which includes the water system, the sewer system, our transportation systems, etc? Thank you.*

BUSH: I'm not sure that—and I can understand if you haven't seen this because there's been a lot of hue and cry—we passed, this year, the most far-reaching transportation bill in the history of this country, since Eisenhower started the interstate highways, $150 billion for improving the infrastructure. That happened when I was president and so I'm very proud of the way that came about and I think it's a very, very good beginning. Like Mr. Perot, I'm concerned about the money but it's awful hard to say we're going to spend more money when we're trying to get the deficit down. But I would cite that as a major accomplishment.

We hear all the negatives. When you're president you expect this, everybody's running against the incumbent, they can do better, everyone knows that. But here's something that we can take great pride in because it really does get to what you're talking about. Our home initiative—hope it'll pass the Congress—is a good start for having people own their homes instead of living in these deadly tenements. Our enterprise zones that we hear a lot of lip service about in Congress would bring jobs into the inner city. There's a good program and I need the help of everybody across this country to get it passed in a substantial way by the Congress....

Q.: *Mr. President, aren't you threatening to veto the bill, the Urban Aid bill that included enterprise zones?*

BUSH: Sure, but the problem is you get so many things included in a great big bill that you have to look at the overall good. That's the problem with our system; if you had a line-item veto you could knock out the tax increases, and you could do what the people want and that is create enterprise zones.

Q.: *Governor Clinton, you're champing at the bit.*

CLINTON: That bill pays for these urban enterprise zones by asking the wealthiest Americans to pay a little more, and that's why you want to veto it. Just like you vetoed an earlier bill this year; this is not mudslinging, this is fact-slinging. A bill early this year would have given investment tax credits and other incentives to reinvest in our cities, our country, but it asked the wealthiest Americans to pay a little more.

Let me tell you specifically what my plan does. My plan would dedicate $20 billion a year in each of the next four years for investment and new transportation, communications, environmental clean-up, and new technologies for the twenty-first century, and we would target it especially in areas that have been either depressed or which have lost a lot of defense-related jobs. There are 200,000 people in California, for example, who have lost their defense-related jobs. They ought to be engaged in making high-speed rail; they ought to be engaged in breaking ground in other technologies, doing waste recycling, clean water technology, and things of that kind.

We can create millions of jobs in these new technologies—more than we're going to lose in defense if we target it—but we're investing a much smaller percentage of our income in the things you just asked about than all of our major competitors, and our wealth growth is going down as a result of this, making the country poorer. We have to both bring down the deficit and get our economy going through these kinds of investments in order to get the kind of wealth and jobs and incomes we need in America.

Q.: *Mr. Perot, what about your plans for the cities?*

PEROT: First, you've got to have money to pay for these things. So, you've got to create jobs. There are all kinds of ways to create jobs in the inner city.

Now, I'm not a politician, but I think I could go to Washington in a week and get everybody holding hands and get this bill signed. Because I talked to the Democratic leaders and they want it; I talked to Republican leaders and they want it. But since they are bred from childhood to fight with one another rather than get results—you know, I would be glad to drop out and spend a little time and see if we couldn't build some bridges. Now, results is what count. The president can't order Congress around. Congress can't order the president around. That's not bad for a guy that's never been there, right? But you have to work together....

The facts are, the American people are hurting. These people are hurting in the inner cities. We're shipping the low-paying jobs—quote "low-paying jobs"—overseas. What are low-paying jobs? Textiles, shoes, things like that that we say are just yesterday's industries. They're tomorrow's industries in the inner cities.

Let me say in my case, if I'm out of work, I'll cut grass tomorrow to take care of my family. I'll be happy to make shoes, I'll be happy to make clothing, I'll make sausage. You just give me a job. Put those jobs in the inner cities instead of doing diplomatic deals and shipping them to China where prison labor does the work.

Q.: *Mr. Perot, everybody thought you won the first debate, because you were plain-speaking and you made it sound so simple: We'll just do it. What makes you think that you're going to be able to get the Democrats and Republicans together any better than these guys?*

PEROT: Well, I've listened to both sides and if they would talk to one another instead of throwing rocks, I think we could get a lot done. And among other things, I would say, O.K., over here in this Senate committee, to the chairman who is anxious—I'd say, rather than just yelling at one another, why don't we find out where we're apart, try to get together, get the bill passed and give the people the benefits and not play party politics right now?

And I would think the press would follow that so closely that probably they would get it done. That's the way I would do it. I doubt if they'll give me the chance but I will drop everything and go work on it.

Q.: *My question was originally for Governor Clinton but I think I would welcome a response from all three candidates. As you are aware, crime is rampant in our cities. And in the Richmond area, and I'm sure it's happening elsewhere, 12-year-olds are carrying guns to school. And I'm sure when our Founding Fathers wrote the Constitution they did not mean for the right to bear arms to apply to 12-year-olds. So I'm asking: Where do you stand on gun control and what do you plan to do about it?*

CLINTON: I support the right to keep and bear arms. I live in a state where over half the adults have hunting or fishing licenses or both. But I believe we have to have some way of checking handguns before they are sold—to check the criminal history, the mental health history and the age of people who are buying them. Therefore I support the Brady bill, which would impose a national waiting period unless and until a state did what only Virginia has done now, which is to automate its records. Once you automate your records then you don't have to have a waiting period. But at least you can check. I also think we should have, frankly, restrictions on assault weapons, whose only purpose is to kill. We need to give the police a fighting chance in our urban areas, where the gangs are building up.

The third thing I would say doesn't bear directly on gun control but it's very important. We need more police on the street. There is a crime bill which would put more police on the street which was killed for this session by a filibuster in the Senate, mostly by Republican Senators. And I think it's a shame it didn't pass. I think it should be made the law, but it had the Brady bill in it—the waiting period.

Q.: *Thank you. President Bush.*

BUSH: I think you put your finger on a major problem. I talked about strengthening the American family and it's very hard to strengthen the family and it's very hard to walk down to the corner store and you know send their kid down to get a loaf of bread, it's very hard. I have been fighting for very strong anti-crime legislation. Habeas corpus reform so you don't have these endless appeals, so when somebody gets sentenced, hey, this is for real. I've been fighting for changes in the exclusionary rule so if an honest cop stops somebody and makes a technical mistake, the criminal doesn't go away. I'll probably get into a fight in this room with some, but I happen to think that we need stronger death penalties for those that kill police officers. Virginia's on the lead in this, as Governor Clinton properly said on this identification system for firearms. I am not for national registration of firearms.

Some of the states that have the toughest anti-gun laws have the highest level of crime. I am for the right, as the Governor says, I'm a sportsman and I don't think you ought to eliminate all kinds of weapons. I was not for the bill that he was talking about because it was not tough enough on the criminal. I've very pleased that the fraternal order of police in Little Rock, Arkansas, endorsed me because I think they see I'm trying to strengthen the anti-crime legislation. We've got more money going out for local police than any previous administration. So we've got to get it under control and there is one last point I'd make. Drugs. We have got to win our national strategy against drugs, the fight against drugs. And we're making some progress. Doing a little better on interdiction. We're not doing as well amongst the people that get to be habitual users.

PEROT: On any program, and this includes crime, you'll find we have all kinds of great plans lying around that never get enacted into law and implemented. The Brady Bill—I agree that it's a tentative step in the right direction but it won't fix it. So why pass a law that won't fix it? Now, what it really boils down to is can you live— we have become so preoccupied with the rights of the criminal that we've forgotten the rights of the innocent. And in our country we have evolved to a point where we've put millions of innocent people in jail because you go to the poor neighborhoods and they put bars on their windows and bars on their doors and put themselves in jail to protect the things that they're acquired legitimately. That's where we are. We have got to become more concerned about people who play by the rules and get the balance we require. This is going to take first building consensus in grass-roots America; right from the bottom up the American people have got to say they want it. And at that point, we can pick from a variety of plans and develop new plans, and the way you get things done is bury yourselves in a room with one another, put together the best program, take it to the American people, use the electronic town hall—the kind of thing you're doing here tonight—build a consensus and then do it and then go on to the next one. But don't just sit here slow-dancing for four years doing nothing.

Q.: *Governor Clinton: Do you attribute the rising cost of health care to the medical profession itself? Or do you think the problem lies elsewhere, and what specific proposals do you have to tackle this problem?*

CLINTON: I've had more people talk to me about health care problems, I guess, than anything else. So let me try to answer you in this way. Let's start with a premise.

We spend 30 percent more of our income than any nation on earth on health care. And yet we insure fewer people. We have 35 million people without any insurance at all. I see them all the time. A hundred thousand Americans a month have lost their health insurance just in the last four years. So if you analyze where we're out of line with other countries, you come up with the following conclusions:

No. 1, we spend at least $60 billion a year on insurance, administrative costs, bureaucracy and government regulation that wouldn't be spent in any other nation. So we have to have, in my judgment, a drastic simplification of the basic health insurance policies of this country. Be very comprehensive for everybody. Employers would cover their employees. Government would cover the unemployed.

No. 2, I think you have to take on specifically the insurance companies and require them to make some significant change in the way they rate people into big community pools. I think you have to tell the pharmaceutical companies they can't keep raising drug prices at three times the rate of inflation. I think you have to take on medical fraud. I think you have to help doctors stop

practicing defensive medicine. I've recommended that our doctors be given a set of national practice guidelines and that if they follow those guidelines, that raises the presumption that they didn't do anything wrong. I think you have to have a system of primary and preventive clinics in our inner cities and our rural areas so people can have access to health care.

The key is to control the cost and maintain the quality. To do that you need a system of managed competition where all of us are covered in big groups and we can choose our doctors and our hospitals across a wide range, but there is an incentive to control costs. I think there has to be a national commission of health care providers and health care consumers that set ceilings to keep health costs in line with inflation plus population growth.

Now let me say, some people say we can't do this but Hawaii does it. They cover 98 percent of their people and their insurance premiums are much cheaper than the rest of America. And so does Rochester, New York. They now have a plan to cover everybody and their premiums are two-thirds of the rest of the country. This is very important. It's a big human problem for America. And I'm going to send a plan to do this within the first hundred days of my presidency.

BUSH: She asked the question, I think, if whether the health care profession was to blame.

No. One thing is to blame is these malpractice lawsuits. They are breaking the system. It costs 20 to 25 billion dollars a year and I want to see those outrageous claims capped. Doctors don't dare to deliver babies sometimes because they're afraid that somebody's going to sue them. Medical practitioners don't dare to help somebody along the highway that is hurt, because they're afraid that some lawyer's going to come along and get a big lawsuit. So you can't blame the practitioners for the health problem.

And my program is this. Keep the government as far out of it as possible. Make insurance available to the poorest of the poor through vouchers, in the next range in the income bracket through tax credits. And get on about the business of pooling insurance. A great big company can buy insurance cheaper than the mom and pop store on the corner. But if those mom and pop stores all get together and pool, they too can bring the cost of insurance down. So, I want to keep the quality of health care,

[and] that means keep government out of it. I don't like this idea of these boards. It all sounds to me like you're going to have some government settling price. I want competition and I want to pool the insurance and take care of it that way.

And here's another point. I think medical care should go with the person. If you leave a business, I think your insurance should go with you to some other business. If you're working for the Jones company, you go to the Smith company, you insurance goes with you. And I think it's a good program. I'm really excited about getting it done, too.

PEROT: We have the most expensive health-care system in the world; 12 percent of our gross national product goes to health care. Our industrial competitors who are beating us in competition spend less and have better health care. Japan spends a little over 6 percent of its gross national product. Germany spends 8 percent. It's fascinating. You bought a front row box seat and you're not happy with your health care, and you're saying we've got bad health care, but very expensive health care. Folks, here's why. Go home and look in the mirror. You own this country but you have no voice in it the way it's organized now. And if you want to have a high-risk experience comparable to bungee jumping, go into Congress some time when they're working on this kind of legislation, when the lobbyists are running up and down the halls. Wear your safety-toe shoes when you go. And as a private citizen, believe me, you are looked on as a major nuisance. The facts are, you now have a government that comes at you and you're supposed to have a government that comes from you. Now there are all kinds of good ideas, brilliant ideas, terrific ideas on health care. None of them ever get implemented because—let me give you an example. A senator runs every six years; he's got to raise 20,000 bucks a week to have enough money to run. Who's he going to listen to, us? Or the folks running up and down the aisles with money—the lobbyists, the PAC money. He listens to them. Who do they represent? The health-care industry. Not us.

Now you've got to have a government that comes from you again; you've got to reassert your ownership in this country and you've got to completely reform our government. And at that point they'll just be like apples falling out of a tree—the programs will be good because the

elected officials will be listening.

CLINTON: One brief point. We have elections so people can make decisions about this. The point I want to make to you is that a bipartisan commission reviewed my plan and the Bush plan and concluded—there were as many Republicans as Democratic health-care experts on it—they concluded that my plan would cover everybody and his would leave 27 million behind by the year 2000.

And that my plan in the next 12 years would save $2.2 trillion in public and private money to reinvest in this economy. And the average family would save $1,200 a year under the plan that I offered without any erosion in the quality of health care. So I ask you to look at that. And you have to vote for somebody with a plan. That's what you have elections for.

Q.: *How has the national debt personally affected each of your lives? And if it hasn't, how can you honestly find a cure for the economic problems of the common people if you have no experience in what's ailing them?*

PEROT: It caused me to disrupt my private life and my business to get involved in this activity. That's how much I care about it. And believe me, if you knew my family and if you knew the private life I have you would agree in a minute that that's a whole lot more fun than getting involved in politics.

But I have lived the American dream. I came from a very modest background; nobody's been luckier than I've been, all the way across the spectrum. And the greatest riches of all are my wife and children. Just as it's true of any family.

But, I want all the children—I want these young people up here to be able to start with nothing but an idea like I did and build a business. But they've got to have a strong basic economy. And if you're in debt, it's like having a ball and chain around you. I just figure as lucky as I've been, I owe it to them. And I owe it to the future generations. And on a very personal basis, I owe it to my children and grandchildren.

Q.: *Thank you Mr. Perot. Mr. President.*

BUSH: Well I think the national debt affects everybody. Obviously it has a lot to do with interest rates. It has—

Q.: *She's saying you personally. On a personal basis, has it affected you personally?*

BUSH: Well, I'm sure it has. I love my grandchildren and I want to think that—

Q.: *How?*

BUSH: I want to think that they're going to be able to afford an education. I think that that's an important part of being a parent. Maybe I get it wrong. Are you suggesting that if somebody has means that the national debt doesn't affect them? I'm not sure I get it. Help me with the question and I'll try and answer it.

Q.: *Well, I've had friends that have been laid off from jobs. I know people who cannot afford to pay the mortgage on their homes or their car payment. I have personal problems with the national debt. But how has it affected you? And if you have no experience in it, how can you help us if you don't know what we're feeling?*

BUSH: Well, you ought to be in the White House for a day and hear what I hear and see what I see and read the mail I read and touch the people that I touch from time to time. I was in the Lomax A.M.E. Church. It's a black church just outside of Washington, D.C. And I read in the bulletin about teenage pregnancies, about the difficulty that families are having to make ends meet. I talk to parents. I mean, you've got to care. Everybody cares if people aren't doing well. But I don't think it's fair to say, "You haven't had cancer, therefore you don't know what it's like." I don't think it's fair to say, you know whatever it is, that if you haven't been hit by it personally—but everybody's affected by the debt because of the tremendous interest that goes into paying on that debt, everything's more expensive. Everything comes out of your pocket and my pocket.

So it's sad, but I think in terms of the recession, of course you feel it when you're president of the United States. And that's why I'm trying to do something about it by stimulating the exports, investing more, better education system. Thank you, I'm glad to clarify it.

Q.: *Governor Clinton.*

CLINTON: Tell me how it's affected you again. You know people who've lost their jobs and lost their homes.

Q.: *Well, yeah, uh-huh.*

CLINTON: Well, I've been governor of a small state for 12 years. I'll tell you how it's affected me. Every year, Congress and the president sign laws that make us do more things and give us less money to do it with. I see people in my state, middle class people, their taxes have gone up in Washington and their services have gone down while the wealthy have gotten tax cuts. I have seen what's happened in this last four years. In my state, when people lose their jobs, there's a good chance I'll know them by their names. When a factory closes I know the people who ran it. When businesses go bankrupt, I know them. And I've been out here for 13 months meeting in meetings just like this ever since October with people like you all over America, people that have lost their jobs, lost their livelihood, lost their health insurance.

What I want you to understand is the national debt is not the only cause of that. It is because America has not invested in its people. It is because we've had 12 years of trickle-down economics. We've gone from first to 12th in the world in wages. We've had four years where we've produced no private-sector jobs. Most people are working harder for less money than they were making 10 years ago. It is because we are in the grip of a failed economic theory. And this decision you're about to make better be about what kind of economic theory you want. Not just people saying I want to go fix it, but what are we going to do. What I think we have to do is invest in American jobs, American education, control American health care costs and bring the American people together again.

Q.: *We've come to a position where we're in the new world order. And I'd like to know what the candidates feel our position is in this new world order and what our responsibilities are as a superpower.*

BUSH: Well, we have come to that position since I became president—43, 44 countries have gone democratic. No longer totalitarian, no longer living under dictatorship or Communist rule. This is exciting. This new world order to me means freedom and democracy. I think we will have a continuing responsibility as the only remaining superpower to stay involved. If we pull back into some isolation and say we don't have to do our share or more than our share anymore, I believe you can just ask for conflagration that we'll get involved in the future. NATO for example, has kept the peace for many, many years and I want to see us keep fully staffed in NATO so we'll continue to guarantee the peace in Europe.

But the exciting thing is the fear of nuclear war is down and—you hear all the bad stuff that's happened on my watch—I hope people will recognize that this is something pretty good for mankind. I hope they'll think it's good that democracy and freedom are on the move. And we're going to stay engaged, as long as I'm president, working to improve things. You know, it's so easy now to say, "Hey, cut out foreign aid, we got a problem at home." I think the United States has to still be having the Statue of Liberty as a symbol of caring for others. We're sending supplies in to help these little starving kids in Somalia. It's the United States that's taken the lead in, in humanitarian aid into Bosnia. We're doing this all around the world. Yes, we got problems at home and I think I got a good plan to help fix those problems at home. But because of our leadership, we didn't listen to the nuclear freeze group back in the late '70s. Freeze, they said. Don't touch it. We're going to lock it now or else we'll have war.

President Reagan said, "No, peace through strength." It worked. The Soviet Union is no more and now we're working to help them become totally democratic through the Freedom Support Act that I led on. A great democratic ambassador, Bob Strauss, is over there, and Jim Baker. All of us got this thing passed through cooperation, helping Russia become democratic. So the new world order, to me, means freedom and democracy, keep engaged. Do not pull back into isolation and we are the United States and we have a responsibility to lead and to guarantee the security. If it hadn't been for us, Saddam Hussein would be sitting on top of three-fifths of the oil supply of the world and he'd have nuclear weapons. And only the United States could do that.

PEROT: Well, it's cost effective to help Russia succeed in its revolution. Pennies on the dollar compared to going back to the Cold War. Russia's still very unstable; they could go back to square one and worse. Still, all the nuclear weapons are not dismantled. I'm particularly concerned about the intercontinental weapons, the ones that can hit us. We've got agreements but they're still there. With all this instability and breaking in the republics, and all the Middle Eastern countries going over there shopping for weapons, we've got our work cut out for us, so we need to stay right on top of that and constructively help

them move toward democracy and capitalism. We have to have money to do that. We have to have our people at work.

See, for 45 years we were preoccupied with the Red Army. I suggest now that our number 1 preoccupation is red ink in our country, and we've got to put our people back to work, so that we can afford to do these things we want to do in Russia. We cannot be the policeman for the world any longer. We spend $300 billion a year defending the world. Germany and Japan spend around $30 billion apiece. It's neat. If I can get you to defend me and I can spend all my money building industry, that's a homerun for me. Coming out of World War II it made sense. Now, the other superpowers need to do their part. I close on this point. You can't be a superpower unless you're an economic superpower [like] we used to be, then we will no longer be a force for good throughout the world. And if nothing else gets you excited about rebuilding our industrial base, maybe that will, because it's job one to put our people back to work.

Q.: *Governor Clinton, the president mentioned Saddam Hussein. Your vice president and you have had some words about the president and Saddam Hussein. Would you care to comment?*

CLINTON: I'd rather answer a question first, then I'll be glad to, 'cause the question you ask is important. The end of the Cold War brings an incredible opportunity for change. Winds of freedom blowing around the world. Russia demilitarizing. And it also requires us to maintain some continuity, some bipartisan American commitment to certain principles. And I would just say, there are three things that I would like to say.

Number 1, we do have to maintain the world's strongest defense. We may differ about what the elements of that are. I think the defense needs to be with fewer people and permanent armed services, but with greater mobility on the land, in the air, and on the sea. With a real dedication to continuing the development of high technology weaponry and well-trained people. I think we're going to have to work to stop the proliferation of weapons of mass destruction. Got to keep going until all the nuclear weapons in Russia are gone, and the other republics.

Number 2, if you don't rebuild the economic strength

of this country at home we won't be a superpower. We can't have any more instances like what happened when Mr. Bush went to Japan and the Japanese prime minister said he felt sympathy for our country. We have to be the strongest economic power in the world. That's what got me into this race. So we could rebuild the American economy.

And number 3, we need to be a force for freedom and democracy and we need to use our unique position to support freedom, whether it's in Haiti or in China or in any other place; wherever the seeds of freedom are sprouting. We can't impose it but we need to nourish it. And that's the kind of thing that I would do as president. Follow those three commitments into the future.

Q.: *What I'd like to know—and this is to any of the three of you—is, aside from the recent accomplishments of your party, aside from those accomplishments in racial representation, and without citing any of your current appointments or successful elections, when do you estimate your party will both nominate and elect an Afro-American and female ticket to the presidency of the United States?*

CLINTON: Well I don't have any idea, but I hope it will happen in my lifetime.

BUSH: I do, too.

CLINTON: I believe that this country is electing more and more African Americans who are representing districts that are themselves not necessarily of a majority of their race. The American people are beginning to bolt across racial lines and I hope it will happen more and more.

More and more women are being elected. Look at all these women Senate candidates we have here. And, you know, according to my mother and my wife and my daughter this world would be a lot better place if women were running it most of the time. I do think there are special experiences and judgments and backgrounds and understandings that women bring to this process, by the way. This lady said here, how have you been affected by the economy. I mean, women know what it is like to be paid an unequal amount for equal work. They know what it's like not to have flexible working hours. They know what it's like not to have family leave or child care. So I think it would be a good thing for America if it happened, and I think it will happen in my lifetime.

BUSH: If Barbara Bush were running this year, she'd be elected. But it's too late. You don't want us to mention appointees, but see the quality of people in our administration, see how Colin Powell performed....

PEROT: I have a fearless forecast. Unless he just won't do it, Colin Powell will be on somebody's ticket in four years from now, right? Right?

Q.: *Thank you. I want to apologize to our audience, because there were 209 people here and there were 209 questions. We only got a fraction of them, and I'm sorry to those of you that didn't get to ask your questions, but we must move to the conclusion of the program. It's time now for the two closing statements and, by our prior agreement, President Bush will go first.*

BUSH: Let me just say to the American people, in two and a half weeks we're going to choose who should sit in this Oval Office to lead the economic recovery, to be the leader of the free world, to get the deficit down.

Three ways to do that: One is to raise taxes; one is to reduce spending, controlling that mandatory spending; another one is to invest and save and to stimulate growth.

I don't want to raise taxes. I differ with the two here on that. I'm just not going to do that. I do believe that we need to control mandatory spending. I think we need to educate better and retrain better. I believe that we need to export more so I'll keep working for export agreements where we can sell more abroad. And I believe that we must strengthen the family. Now let me pose this question to America: If in the next five minutes, a television announcer came on and said there is a major international crisis—there is a major threat to the world or in this country—a major threat. My question is: Who, if you were appointed to name one of the three of us, who would you choose? Who has the perseverance, the character, the integrity, the maturity to get the job done? I hope I'm that person. Thank you very, very much.

Q.: *Thank you Mr. President. And now a closing statement from Mr. Perot.*

PEROT: If the American people . . . just want to keep slow-dancing and talk about it, and not do it, I'm not your man. I am results-oriented, I am action-oriented. I've built my businesses. Getting done in 3 months what my competitors took 18 months to do. Everybody says you can't do that in Congress; sure you can do that with Congress. Congress is—they're all good people. They're all patriots. But you've got to link arms and work with them. Sure, you'll have arguments; sure you'll have fights. We have them all day, every day. But we get the job done.

I have to come back in my close to one thing because I am passionate about education. I was talking about early childhood education for disadvantaged low-income children. And let me tell you one specific pilot program, where children who don't have a chance go to this program when they're three, and now we're going back to when the mother's pregnant. They'll start right after they're born. But going—starting when they're three and going to this school until they're nine, and then going into public schools, in the fourth grade? Ninety percent are on the honor roll. Now, that will change America. Those children will all go to college. They will live the American dream.

And I beg the American people any time they think about reforming education, to take this piece of society that doesn't have a chance and take these little pieces of clay that can be shaped and molded and give them the same love and nurture and affection and support you give your children, and teach them that they are unique and that they're precious and there's only one person in the world like them and you will see this nation bloom. And we will have so many people who are qualified for the top job that it will be terrific.

Finally, if you can't pay the bill you're dead in the water. And we have got to put our nation back to work. If you don't want to really do that, I'm not your man. I'd go crazy sitting up there slow-dancing that one; in other words, unless we're going to do it, then pick somebody who likes to talk about it. Now just remember, when you think about me, I didn't create this mess, I've been paying my share. Over a billion dollars in taxes.

Q.: *And finally, last but not least, Governor Clinton.*

CLINTON: Thank you, Carole. Thank you, ladies and gentlemen. Since I suggested this forum (and I hope it's been good for all of you). I've really tried to be faithful to your request that we answer the questions specifically and pointedly. I thought I owed that to you and I respect you for being here and for the impact you've had on making this a more positive experience. These problems are not easy and not going to be solved overnight. But I want you to think about just two or three things. First of all, the people of my state have let me be the governor for 12 years because I made commitments to two things: more jobs and better schools. Our schools are now better; our children get off to a better start from pre-school programs and smaller classes in the early grades, and we have one of the most aggressive adult education programs in the country. We talked about that. This year my state ranks first in the country in job growth, fourth in manufacturing job growth, fourth in income growth, fourth in the decline of poverty. I'm proud of that. It happened because I could work with people, Republicans and Democrats. That's why we've had 24 retired generals and admirals, hundreds of business people, many of them Republican, support this campaign.

You have to decide whether you want to change or not. We do not need four more years of an economic theory that doesn't work. We've had 12 years of trickle-down economics. It's time to put the American people first, to invest and grow this economy. I'm the only person here who's ever balanced a government budget and I've presented 12 of them and cut spending repeatedly, but you cannot just get there by balancing the budget. We've got to grow the economy by putting people first. Real people like you. I got into this race because I did not want my child to grow up to be part of the first generation of Americans doing worse than their parents. We're better than that. We can do better than that. I want to make America as great as it can be and I ask for your help in doing it. Thank you very much.

GLOSSARY

exclusionary rule: legal tenet holding that illegally obtained evidence cannot be used in court

habeas corpus: literally "to bring a person (to a court)," an appeals process designed to insure that a person is not illegally imprisoned

trickle-down economics: a theory that if corporations and the wealthy have more money, they will spend more and stimulate the rest of the economy

Document Analysis

Each presidential debate was unique, as the dynamics created opportunities for candidates to express their ideas in different ways than they had in their normal stump speeches or via sound bites. Clinton, knowing the strength of his interpersonal skills, had sought the "audience as questioner" format, and the results proved beneficial to him. The styles of the answers varied with the candidates. Bush relied on his record, as president and previously as vice-president, and the specific proposals for which he advocated. However, when the questioning moved outside these areas, he tended to falter. Somewhat more than the other two, Clinton often directly answered the question asked, rather than the question he desired to answer. He made extensive use of the benefits of having been an accessible governor in a small state in his responses to the people. Perot had a tendency to create answers/solutions phrased in monetary terms, rather than in broader social policy phraseology. In addition, he demonstrated that he wanted an all-or-nothing approach in crafting solutions. Additionally, his style of public speaking did not lend itself well to interaction with individual voters. The eight policy questions and two political party questions asked during the debate covered a wide range of topics. Among the policy questions, six were on domestic issues, only one on foreign policy, and one straddled both areas. This domestic emphasis hurt Bush, as the United States had major international successes during his administration which he was unable to include in his answers. Overall, Clinton's ability to relate to the people asking the questions, and Bush's major lapse in attempting to answer the "has it affected you personally" question, regarding the national debt, made Clinton the winner of the debate.

The domestic focus of the debate was perhaps not unexpected. Skyrocketing unemployment (a 50 percent increase in the unemployment rate) and a ballooning national debt, made many people feel unsecure about their future. Questions were asked about how the candidates would deal with the national debt during the next presidential term, how the debt was affecting them personally, and how the candidates proposed to meet the needs of the average voter. In response to the national debt question, only Clinton basically answered it with specific goals, as requested. However, Bush faltered on these. Bush, unfortunately for him, used the phrase "I'm confused," in answering the general debt question, seemed lost when asked how the debt affected him personally, and misunderstood the "helping people" question. Perot gave "trust me, I can do it" types of answers to each question.

The other issues, related to domestic concerns (health care, gun control, and infrastructure), had fewer disagreements on policies, although not unity in the answers. All agreed health care was too expensive, with Clinton blaming administrative costs; Bush, malpractice suits; and Perot, lobbying by the health-care industry.

All supported the Second Amendment, but Clinton wanted better, more efficient background checks combined with limits on certain types of weapons. Bush agreed with the background check proposal, with limiting certain weapons, and then moved beyond the question to mention programs to combat drug abuse. Perot accepted certain limits on gun ownership, and pushed for stronger punishment for criminals, while saying only that he could "build a consensus" for the steps necessary for gun control.

On infrastructure and development, Bush pointed out what he had signed into law and some hopes for the future. Clinton pushed taxing the wealthy to help those unemployed who needed to be retrained for jobs in new fields of technology. Perot argued that he could solve this in a week, and that the low paying jobs which were leaving for other countries, should be exported to the unemployed in urban areas, not overseas. This tied in with his answer to the first question (a mixture of international-domestic policies), regarding how to keep international trade fair and keep American jobs from moving overseas. In that answer, Perot used one of his well-known phrases from his campaign, regarding jobs moving to Mexico, saying, "there will be a giant sucking sound going south." He seemed to be in favor of allowing wages in the United States to decrease, while at the same time pushing for better trade agreements. Bush, who had just negotiated the North American Free Trade Agreement (NAFTA), believed that this would level the playing field, so that more American products could be sold in Mexico and Canada protecting American jobs. Clinton, who liked NAFTA, pushed for more open markets overseas and change to government programs to discourage the movement of American jobs to other countries.

As to the position of the United States in the "New World Order" created by the fall of communism, Bush responded to this first and touted what had happened during the last four years, asserting that the United States was the world leader and staying engaged was necessary. Perot argued that it would be "cost effective" to aid the transition to democracy around the world. Clinton wanted to encourage the "winds of freedom" to keep blowing around the world and pushed for continued American involvement. Thus, there was a general agreement among all three that the United States should remain involved internationally.

The two questions relating to the operations of political parties were answered optimistically by all. One was directed toward Perot, as to how he could work with the major parties, and his response was that, with help from the press, he could "probably get it done." The other question, dealing with African Americans and women being on the major parties' tickets, was given a hopeful "in my lifetime" answer by Bush and Clinton, with Perot affirming this by naming Colin Powell as a likely African American candidate.

The style of answers given by the candidates made it clear to the voters which approaches the various candidates were taking to the election and the problems confronting America. Perot's was a straightforward dollars-and-cents approach to everything. Bush seemed to focus only on the larger picture, leaving many feeling left out. Clinton carried the day, and ultimately the election, by blending a presentation of his proposed national policies with insights and empathy relating to the

challenges faced by individual voters. It was not that his proposals for the next four years were seen as far superior to Bush's proposals, although obviously people did make judgments about those proposals. Rather, it was Clinton's ability to better relate to the individual in the audience and at home that was key to his victory.

Essential Themes

In this debate, the three points of view presented by the three candidates clearly represented their positions. This was not a situation in which misstatements on policy were common or in which the participants tried to grossly distort the opponents' position. There were areas of agreement and disagreement. However, this debate was not won on substance (with the exception of Bush's response to one question); rather it was won on style, and the ability to answer the questions asked. How well the candidates were able to relate to the persons asking the questions was the key to victory. Bush seemed out of touch and Perot seemed too inflexible, while Clinton related well to people.

The one answer, or lack thereof, that stood out in the minds of most who watched the debate, was from President Bush. This was Bush's inability to state how the national debt affected him "personally." Whether or not it was true, his bumbling response made him seem removed from the concerns and lives of average voters. He seemed to be disconnected from the nation. This in conjunction with two earlier problematic responses (question two: "I'm a little confused here"; and question three, the family mediator's question) made Bush the loser for the evening.

Clinton's ability to relate to people was responsible for his success. His lack of clear misstatements, such as happened to Bush, and his direct responses to most questions, allowed his message on the economy to be more easily understood than was the case for either Bush or Perot. Clinton tried to relate to middle-class, or working-class voters, saving his strongest attacks for Bush's endorsement of trickle-down economics, which clearly helped the upper class. Clinton's ability to be personable while communicating his message was the key to his victory in the debate and in the election.

When voting day came in November, Bill Clinton carried most of the states, wining 370 electoral votes to Bush's 168. While Perot did well for a third-party candidate; his vote was spread among all the states, meaning he did not win any electoral votes. In the popular vote (rounded off), Clinton had 43 percent, Bush had

37 percent, and Perot had 19 percent. The victory was in large part due to Clinton's ability to relate to people, which resonated with the voters just as it had in this debate.

—*Donald A Watt, PhD*

Bibliography and Additional Reading

CNN. "1992 Presidential Debates." *All Politics: CNN, Time.* New York: AllPolitics, 1996. Web. 28 March 2018.

Commission on Presidential Debates. "1992 Debates." *Commission on Presidential Debates.* Washington: The Commission on Presidential Debates, 2018. Web. 28 March 2018

DeFrank, Thomas M., Mark Miller, Andrew Murr, and Tom Matthews. *Quest for the Presidency 1992.* College Station TX: Texas A&M University Press, 1994. Print.

Matalin, Mary and James Carville. *All's Fair: Love, War and Running for President.* New York: Simon & Schuster, 1995. Print.

Perot, Ross. *United We Stand: How We Can Take Back Our Country.* New York: Hyperion Books, 1992. Print.

Siddiqui, Sabrina. "Bill Clinton Won 1992 Town Hall Debate by Engaging with One Voter." *Huffpost.* New York: Huffpost, 2012. Web. 28 March 2018.

Toner, Robin. "The 1992 Elections: President—the Overview; Clinton Captures Presidency with Huge Electoral Margin; Wins a Democratic Congress." *The New York Times.* New York: The New York Times Company, 1992. Web. 28 March 2018.

■ *Bush v. Gore*

Date: December 12, 2000
Author: Per curiam
Genre: Court opinion

Summary Overview

In *Bush v. Gore* the Supreme Court of the United States reversed a Florida Supreme Court request for a selective manual recount of that state's U.S. presidential election ballots. The 5–4 decision effectively awarded Florida's 25 votes in the electoral college—and thus the presidential election itself—to Republican candidate George W. Bush.

Defining Moment

It was the evening of November 7, 2000, and a clear winner had yet to emerge in the United States presidential election between George W. Bush and Al Gore. Broadcast and print media supplied contradictor exit polling information and it became increasingly clear that races in Oregon and New Mexico would remain too close to call a clear winner for some days. The election ultimately came down to the voting results in Florida. Gore was initially projected to the winner in Florida but it was later reported that Bush had an insurmountable lead. Gore called Bush to concede the election. However, by early the following morning it was revealed that the vote count was much closer than Gore's staff had originally predicted. There were fewer than 600 votes separating the two candidates and the margin was narrowing. At approximately 3:00 a.m. Gore called Bush to retract his earlier concession. Pursuant to Florida election law, a machine recount of all votes cast was required when the margin of victory was less than 0.5%. Here the gap appeared to be approximately 0.01%, or less than 600 votes.

Both campaigns put a legal team in action in Florida, both filing lawsuits contending conflicts of interest. Notably, Bush's brother, Jeb Bush, was the governor of Florida and Florida secretary of state, Katherine Harris, was the co-chair of Bush's Florida campaign. Alternatively, Florida Attorney General Bob Butterworth, chaired Gore's campaign. A machine recount was completed on November 10, 2000, and the Bush campaign led by 327 votes out of the six million votes cast. Court challenges were filed regarding the legality of hand recounting ballots that was occurring in certain Florida counties. Meanwhile, the broadcast and print media nationally were running stories regarding voter fraud, and inaccurate tallying of votes. Issues with paper ballots including "hanging chads" (where paper ballots were not completely punched) and "pregnant chads" (where paper ballots had been dimpled but not pierced during voting) were issues in the forefront. There were also allegations of "overvoting," where an individual ballot recorded multiple votes for the same elected office as well as "undervoting", where a ballot contained no votes for a particular elected office. Palm Beach County had a particular problem with a butterfly ballot design which caused confusion with Gore voters, prompting an alleged 3,400 inadvertent votes for a third-party candidate because of the name layout on the ballot.

Harris initially sought to certify the state election results on November 14 but the Florida Supreme Court ruled that hand recounts of any questionable ballots should proceed in the four counties at issue and that those results should be included in the state's final count. There were approximately 50 individual lawsuits in the following month, all relating to the vote counting, recounting and certification deadlines.

On December 4, 2000, the Florida Supreme Court ruled that hand recounts should continue in all the counties where a statistically significant number of undervotes existed. The Bush campaign responded by filing a lawsuit in the United States Supreme Court.

The Court granted a writ of certiorari, agreeing to hear the matter. On December 9, 2000, in an unprecedented time period, the U S Supreme Court ruled in a 5-4 decision that the hand recounts must stop and it agreed to hear oral arguments from both parties. On December 11, 2000, the arguments took place and both sides presented their cases. The Bush team contended the Florida Supreme Court exceeded its authority by authorizing the hand recounts. The Gore team argued that the matter had been settled at the state level and it was not a matter for the federal courts to decide. The following day, the Court, in a 7-2 vote, overruled the Florida decision and held that the various methods and standards used for the recount process violated the Equal Protection clause of the U.S. Constitution. The court ruled 5-4 on the remedy that should be provided, with the majority holding that the Florida Supreme Court's decision had created new election law which was a right only for the Florida legislature and that no recount could be held in time to satisfy a federal deadline for the selection of state electors. The majority's opinion was heavily criticized by the minority justices. The dissent argued that, while the recount process was somewhat flawed, it should be permitted to proceed, ensuring the constitutional protection of each vote and should not be subjected to an arbitrary deadline. Notably, Justice Ruth Bader Ginsburg noted in her dissent, "I dissent" rather than the traditional "I respectfully dissent." As a result of the decision, the hand recounting process was terminated and Gore officially conceded the election on December 13, 2000, noting, "While I strongly disagree with the court's decision, I accept it."

Legal scholars believe that without the United States Supreme Court intervening, the Florida election decision would have most likely worked itself out on the floor of the Florida legislature and most likely with the election of Bush. The Supreme Court's decision to take part in the process has been seen by some as either the Supreme Court risking its reputation for being apolitical in order to avoid an election crisis and by others as overstepping its bounds by unnecessarily intervening and creating an equal protection right for essentially one individual as the court noted in its opinion, "[o]ur consideration is limited to our present circumstances." In any event, although the Court noted the limited precedential value of its decision, the effects of *Bush v. Gore* have been noted in several federal appellate court cases as having precedence in election law in issues from a challenge to voting systems in Ohio, to voting recount litigation in Minnesota.

Author Biography

Unlike most U.S. Supreme Court opinions, the ruling in *Bush v. Gore* was not signed by a single justice as author. Rather, the opinion was issued as a per curiam ruling, or an unsigned ruling—written by one or more justices but presented as merely being "from the court." Supreme Court justices often issue a per curiam ruling when they wish to express a result that enjoyed the full and total institutional support of all nine justices. At other times, they issue such a ruling when a case is so lacking in complexity that no member of the Court wishes to commit the time to draft and sign his or her own opinion. Per curiam rulings also can provide cover in politically sensitive cases, shielding the writing justice within the protecting arms of the whole Court. Last, a per curiam ruling, especially in a case featuring dissent among the nine justices, can be a means of expressing the barest measure of consensus.

Most likely, the Court adopted the per curiam approach to authorship in *Bush v. Gore* for all of these reasons. With little time to spare, the opinion was probably written in different chambers and later cobbled together to form a whole—n point of fact, the evidence that exists suggests that most of this ruling was written by Justices Anthony Kennedy and Sandra Day O'Connor working in tandem. The per curiam approach also served as a means to consensus, permitting the members of the 7-2 majority in agreement on equal protection to reach a rough accord on the basic proposition that the Florida recount was flawed and unconstitutional; with this accord expressed in the per curiam statement, the justices were free to write separate concurring and dissenting opinions further detailing their personal views. Of course, the per curiam ruling also spared one of the justices from having to sign his or her name to an opinion that, owing to severe time constraints, was less coherent than the authors might have wished. So, too, it provided protection from the ruling's politically explosive impact. Perhaps above all, the per curiam statement gave the Court's ruling an air of consensus that actually did not exist, implied that the ruling was of modest scope, and supported the assertion that the Court was only reluctantly entering the fray to fulfill its constitutional role.

HISTORICAL DOCUMENT

531 U.S. 98, 148 L. Ed. 2d 388, 121 S. Ct. 525 (2000)
Wednesday, Dec. 13, 2000
[Here are excerpts from the U.S. Supreme Court decision in *Bush v. Gore*, from the per curiam opinion of seven justices.]

The closeness of this election, and the multitude of legal challenges which have followed in its wake, have brought into sharp focus a common, if heretofore unnoticed, phenomenon. Nationwide statistics reveal that an estimated 2% of ballots cast do not register a vote for President for whatever reason, including deliberately choosing no candidate at all or some voter error, such as voting for two candidates or insufficiently marking a ballot… In certifying election results, the votes eligible for inclusion in the certification are the votes meeting the properly established legal requirements.

This case has shown that punch card balloting machines can produce an unfortunate number of ballots which are not punched in a clean, complete way by the voter. After the current counting, it is likely legislative bodies nationwide will examine ways to improve the mechanisms and machinery for voting…

The individual citizen has no federal constitutional right to vote for electors for the President of the United States unless and until the state legislature chooses a statewide election as the means to implement its power to appoint members of the Electoral College. U.S. Const., Art. II, §1. This is the source for the statement in McPherson v. Blacker, 146 U.S. 1, 35 (1892), that the State legislature's power to select the manner for appointing electors is plenary; it may, if it so chooses, select the electors itself, which indeed was the manner used by State legislatures in several States for many years after the Framing of our Constitution. Id., at 28-33. History has now favored the voter, and in each of the several States the citizens themselves vote for Presidential electors. When the state legislature vests the right to vote for President in its people, the right to vote as the legislature has prescribed is fundamental; and one source of its fundamental nature lies in the equal weight accorded to each vote and the equal dignity owed to each voter. The State, of course, after granting the franchise in the special context of Article II, can take back the power to appoint electors. See id., at 35 ("[T]here is no doubt of the right of the legislature to resume the power at any time, for it can neither be taken away nor abdicated") (quoting S. Rep. No. 395, 43d Cong., 1st Sess.).

The right to vote is protected in more than the initial allocation of the franchise. Equal protection applies as well to the manner of its exercise. Having once granted the right to vote on equal terms, the State may not, by later arbitrary and disparate treatment, value one person's vote over that of another. See, e.g., Harper v. Virginia Bd. of Elections, 383 U.S. 663, 665 (1966) ("[O]nce the franchise is granted to the electorate, lines may not be drawn which are inconsistent with the Equal Protection Clause of the Fourteenth Amendment"). It must be remembered that "the right of suffrage can be denied by a debasement or dilution of the weight of a citizen's vote just as effectively as by wholly prohibiting the free exercise of the franchise." Reynolds v. Sims, 377 U.S. 533, 555 (1964).

There is no difference between the two sides of the present controversy on these basic propositions. Respondents say that the very purpose of vindicating the right to vote justifies the recount procedures now at issue. The question before us, however, is whether the recount procedures the Florida Supreme Court has adopted are consistent with its obligation to avoid arbitrary and disparate treatment of the members of its electorate…

The Supreme Court of Florida has said that the legislature intended the State's electors to "participate fully in the federal electoral process" … as provided in 3 U.S.C. 5.

That statute, in turn, requires that any controversy or contest that is designed to lead to a conclusive selection of electors be completed by December 12. That date is upon us, and there is no recount procedure in place under the State Supreme Court's order that comports with minimal constitutional standards.

Because it is evident that any recount seeking to meet the December 12 date will be unconstitutional for the reasons we have discussed, we reverse the judgment of the Supreme Court of Florida ordering a recount to proceed. Seven Justices of the Court agree that there are constitutional problems with the recount ordered by the Florida Supreme Court that demand a remedy.... The only disagreement is as to the remedy.

Because the Florida Supreme Court has said that the Florida Legislature intended to obtain the safe-harbor benefits of 3 U. S. C. 5, Justice Breyer's proposed remedy remanding to the Florida Supreme Court for its ordering of a constitutionally proper contest until December 18—contemplates action in violation of the Florida election code, and hence could not be part of an "appropriate" order ....

None are more conscious of the vital limits on judicial authority than are the members of this Court, and none stand more in admiration of the Constitution's design to leave the selection of the President to the people, through their legislatures, and to the political sphere. When contending parties invoke the process of the courts, however, it becomes our unsought responsibility to resolve the federal and constitutional issues the judicial system has been forced to confront.

The judgment of the Supreme Court of Florida is reversed, and the case is remanded for further proceedings not inconsistent with this opinion.

= = =

From Chief Justice Rehnquist, with whom Justice Scalia and Justice Thomas join, concurring:

We join the per curiam opinion. We write separately because we believe there are additional grounds that require us to reverse the Florida Supreme Court's decision. We deal here not with an ordinary election, but with an election for the President of the United States ...

In most cases, comity and respect for federalism compel us to defer to the decisions of state courts on issues of state law. That practice reflects our understanding that the decisions of state courts are definitive pronouncements of the will of the States as sovereigns ... Of course, in ordinary cases, the distribution of powers among the branches of a State's government raises no questions of federal constitutional law, subject to the requirement that the government be republican in character.... But there are a few exceptional cases in which the Constitution imposes a duty or confers a power on a particular branch of a State's government. This is one of them.

= = =

From Justice Stevens, with whom Justice Ginsburg and Justice Breyer join, dissenting:

When questions arise about the meaning of state laws, including election laws, it is our settled practice to accept the opinions of the highest courts of the States as providing the final answers. On rare occasions, however, either federal statutes or the Federal Constitution may require federal judicial intervention in state elections. This is not such an occasion. The federal questions that ultimately emerged in this case are not substantial. ...

Nor are petitioners correct in asserting that the failure of the Florida Supreme Court to specify in detail the precise manner in which the intent of the voter, Fla. Stat. 101.5614(5) (Supp. 2001), is to be determined rises to the level of a constitutional violation. ...

The Florida statutory standard is consistent with the practice of the majority of States, which apply either an 'intent of the voter' standard or an impossible to determine the elector's choice standard in ballot recounts. ...

Admittedly, the use of differing substandards for determining voter intent in different counties employing similar voting systems may raise serious concerns. Those concerns are alleviated, if not eliminated, by the fact that a single impartial magistrate will ultimately adjudicate all objections arising from the recount process. ...

In the interest of finality, however, the majority effectively orders the disenfranchisement of an unknown number of voters whose ballots reveal their intent, and are therefore legal votes under state law, but were for some reason rejected by ballot-counting machines.

Finally, neither in this case, nor in its earlier opinion in *Palm Beach County Canvassing Bd. v. Harris* ... did the Florida Supreme Court make any substantive change in Florida electoral law. Its decisions were rooted in long-established precedent and were consistent with the relevant statutory provisions, taken as a whole. It did what courts do—it decided the case before it in light of the legislature's intent to leave no legally cast vote uncounted. ...

What must underlie petitioners' entire federal assault on the Florida election procedures is an unstated lack of confidence in the impartiality and capacity of the state judges who would make the critical decisions if the vote count were to proceed. Otherwise, their position is wholly without merit. The endorsement of that position by the majority of this Court can only lend credence to the most cynical appraisal of the work of judges throughout the land. It is confidence in the men and women who

administer the judicial system that is the true backbone of the rule of law. Time will one day heal the wound to that confidence that will be inflicted by today's decision.

GLOSSARY

judicial review: a constitutional doctrine which allows a court to review legislative or executive acts to

determine whether they are constitutional

Equal Protection: part of the Fourteenth Amendment of the U.S. Constitution which took effect in 1868 and provides that no state should deny any person within its jurisdiction "the equal protection of the laws."

Presidential Electors: when voting for a candidate on a presidential ballot, voters are actually choosing electors when they vote for a president and vice president. Those electors in turn cast votes for those respective offices.

Document Analysis

The United States Supreme Court granted certiorari in *Bush v. Gore* to address the argument that there had been a violation of the Fourteenth Amendment's equal protection clause in the manual recounts that had been ordered in Florida. It is undisputed that Art. II, § 1, cl. 2 of the U.S. Constitution clearly specifies that it is the sole right and responsibility of the state legislatures to provide for the selection of Presidential electors. Under Florida law, this had been accomplished by providing for a popular vote, the winner of which was to receive all of the state's electoral votes. Since this right had been extended to the people of Florida, the equal protection clause mandates that the right to vote not be infringed either by preventing the act of voting or by unequal treatment of votes after they have been cast. Regarding the Florida recount, the majority opinion concluded that equal protection was violated due to the lack of uniform standards on assessing voter intent on a ballot. The Court also concluded that there would not be enough time to conduct an acceptable recount before the "safe harbor" provision of the federal statute expired so that hand recount had to be terminated.

The Court was presented with several options for addressing an equal protection problem. It could have held that legal votes are defined as those that were marked correctly and counted mechanically which was the remedy argued for by Florida secretary of state Harris. However, the Florida election law as written did not support that solution. Therefore, the Court accepted the Florida

Supreme Court's definition of a legal vote being one that clearly shows the intention of the voter. Having accepted that a vote tabulation should seek out the intent of each voter, the court majority found that arbitrary and inconsistent state-wide standards for assessing voter intent constituted a violation of equal protection, making the Florida recount unconstitutional as it had been ordered.

In its decision, the majority did not deny that a legal recount was possible. However, it found that circumstances would not permit such a recount before the expiration of the "safe harbor" afforded by 3 U.S.C. § 5. This clause essentially guarantees that the electors selected in the general election to represent a state will be counted in the Electoral College so long as they are selected under legislation that predates the election and are chosen at least six days before the Electoral College convenes. Since Florida law is designed to take advantage of 3 U.S.C. § 5, the court majority ruled that the selection of electors could not extend past that safe harbor time without ignoring the Florida statutes, which in turn would violate Art. II, § 1, cl. 2 of the U.S. Constitution. By invoking this restricted time frame, the court majority made it infeasible to conduct a constitutional recount and concluded that it was appropriate to order the cessation of all recounts in Florida.

Several of the dissenting Justices argue persuasively that in this case, the safe harbor clause can be ignored without causing any harm. Justice Stevens noted in his dissent that the Hawaiian slate of electors counted in the 1960 election was not certified until January 4, 1961 but was still counted by Congress. This effectively refutes the argument that missing the safe harbor deadline would risk the disenfranchisement of millions of Florida voters who cast mechanically-recordable ballots. If, as the Court defined, the undervotes and overvotes in Florida represent potential legal votes, it is a violation of equal protection for these votes not to be counted. In the majority's own words, "Having once granted the right to vote on equal terms, the State may not, by later arbitrary and disparate treatment, value one person's vote over that of another." The largest criticism by the dissent was that counting only those legal votes that happen to be easily tabulated by mechanical equipment to fulfill an unnecessary time limit for vote certification is the very definition of arbitrary and disparate treatment and by refusing to allow a legal recount to go on for as long as possible, the court majority supported the very abuses that the equal protection clause is designed to prevent, even as it claimed to be ruling in the spirit of equal protection.

The Court found itself in a very difficult situation as it tried to reach a decision in *Bush v. Gore*. Regardless of the outcome, half the voting public was likely to come out feeling that their candidate had been treated unfairly. Disagreement over judicial interpretations of the law is to be expected, especially in a complicated case like *Bush v. Gore*. As the court noted it considered the case itself to be of limited precedential value based upon the facts of the particular case.

Essential Themes

In *Bush v. Gore* the Supreme Court of the United States reversed a Florida Supreme Court request for a selective manual recount of that state's U.S. presidential election ballots and ordered the hand recounting of the Florida to be halted. The Court concluded that no constitutionally adequate recount could take place prior to the safe harbor deadline set forth in federal election law. The 5–4 decision effectively awarded Florida's 25 votes in the electoral college to Republican candidate George W. Bush.

—*Michele McBride Simonelli, JD*

Bibliography and Additional Reading

Bush v. Gore, 121 S.Ct. 525 (2000). Justia: U.S. Supreme Court https://supreme.justia.com/cases/federal/us/531/98/ [accessed March 28, 2018].

Edward Foley, "Voting Rules and Constitutional Law," *George Washington Law Review,* 81 Geo. Wash. L. Rev. 1836, 2013.

Hasen, Richard L., *The Supreme Court and Election Law: Judging Equality from Baker v. Carr to Bush v. Gore.* New York: New York University Press, Inc., 2003.

Mark Tushnet, "Renormalizing *Bush v. Gore:* An Anticipatory Intellectual History", Georgetown Law Journal Association, 90 Geo. L.J. 113, 2001.

Patterson, James T., Restless Giant: The United States from Watergate to *Bush v. Gore.* New York: Oxford University Press. Inc., 2005.

Neighboring yard signs for Bush and Kerry in Grosse Pointe, Michigan.

■ "Bush Wins Second Term"

Date: November 2, 2004
Author: Dan Balz
Genre: News story; article

Summary Overview

After winning a landmark presidential election in 2000 that was decided by way of the Supreme Court case *Bush v. Gore*, President George W. Bush entered the presidential election fray once again and faced off against John Kerry and Howard Dean. Even though Bush held the highest public approval rating of any president ever in 2001, his popularity wavered between 2001 and 2004. The aftermath of 9/11 and the invasion of Iraq in 2003 gave the public a lot to judge Bush on in terms of his leadership style and ability to guide the country through significantly challenging times. As such, Bush was a polarizing figure and people tended to either favor him highly or hold him in extremely low regard. With Kerry's campaign efforts focused on the choices and the actions of Bush during his first term in office, combined with the fluctuating approval rating Bush experienced, it seemed possible Bush could fail to secure the win and forgo a second term in office. However, on Election Day any fears President Bush may have had of losing the election were vanquished, and Bush was the clear winner.

Defining Moment

The presidential election of 2004 was one the American public was highly engaged in. Button displays, bumper stickers, and yard signs touting one's preferred candidate were everywhere. The reason for this was the polarizing nature of incumbent president George W. Bush. The central issue of the 2004 campaign was the performance of President Bush's administration; in particular the response to 9/11 and the invasion of Iraq. Of course the president's competitors, John Kerry and Howard Dean, were central figures in the race, but heightened attention was given to scrutinizing Bush's actions during his first four years as president. After 9/11 Bush's approval ratings were extremely high, but they fluctuated significantly in the years that followed. Questions surrounding Bush's performance in office combined with the fact that he faced not one, but two serious contenders for the of-

fice would render the presidential election of 2004 exciting and unpredictable.

George W. Bush, a Yale and Harvard graduate, former Texas Governor, and sitting president, was naturally poised to have an advantage in the election due to his status as the incumbent. However, he squared off against John Kerry, a Democrat, also a Yale graduate, lawyer, and Senator from Massachusetts with a military background, including having served in the Vietnam War. Howard Dean (Democrat) was the third candidate who, despite his background as a physician and governor of Vermont from 1991-2003, was considered to be a longshot for the win. Because this election began just 18 months after the start of the Iraq War, terrorism was a major focus coming from the Bush camp. Kerry's strategy was to focus on domestic issues with a social and economic focus, but he did call into question whether or not Bush had effectively handled the aftermath of 9/11 and the Iraq War. After a media flub in which Howard Dean released a bizarre scream upon placing third in the Iowa Caucus, Dean was perceived as behaving in an un-presidential manner; he became fodder for late-night talk shows and programs like Saturday Night Live, and was no longer considered to be serious competition in the race.

While both Bush and Kerry were spending considerable amounts of money to have their message heard by voters, both candidates became the target of negative campaigning. Bush was criticized for the controversy over the existence of weapons of mass destruction and his leadership during a time of war, and Kerry was labelled a "flip-flopper" for changing his stance on certain policy matters. Additionally, Kerry's service in the Vietnam War was questioned, although it became clear that those allegations were largely false. After months of campaign stops, television appearances, and debates, it was time for the votes to be cast. In a race where 60 percent of eligible voters in America turned out to vote on Election Day, all eyes were watching to see if President Bush would remain in office. The win, albeit a narrow one, went to president, who received 286 Electoral College votes versus Kerry's 251 votes.

Author Biography

Dan Balz, the author of the news story reprinted here, is a chief correspondent at the *Washington Post*, where he has worked since 1978. Balz has authored four books, and has received numerous awards for his writing. He frequently serves as a panelist on PBS's "Washington Week" and various other programs.

HISTORICAL DOCUMENT

An elated President Bush claimed a reelection victory yesterday after a tumultuous night of vote counting and a gracious concession by challenger John F. Kerry, and he pledged that he would seek to earn the trust of those who did not back him during the long, contentious campaign.

In an explicit appeal to those Americans who voted for Kerry, Bush said: "To make this nation stronger and better, I will need your support, and I will work to earn it. I will do all I can do to deserve your trust. A new term is a new opportunity to reach out to the whole nation."

Bush spoke to jubilant supporters at the Ronald Reagan Building in Washington, where he had planned to go for a pre-dawn victory speech after he had won Florida's 27 electoral votes and appeared to have locked up Ohio's 20 votes. He postponed that event when Kerry declined to concede the election overnight and signaled a possible fight over the vote totals in Ohio.

But an hour before Bush's appearance, an emotional Kerry took the stage at Boston's historic Faneuil Hall to offer Bush his congratulations and a formal concession. The Massachusetts senator had called Bush earlier to convey the same message privately. Kerry snuffed out the hopes of many Democrats who were eager to keep the fight for the White House alive by declaring, "We cannot win this election."

Bush will begin his second term with strengthened majorities in the House and Senate. With GOP candidates picking off a string of Democratic open seats, Republicans expanded their Senate caucus from 51 to 55 members—a significant gain but still not a filibuster-proof margin. Senate Minority Leader Thomas A. Daschle (S.D.) lost his reelection bid to former congressman John Thune (R). In the House, the GOP added three seats and could emerge with a 29-seat majority once all the races are concluded.

With the second term that eluded his father secured, Bush pivoted to the task of trying to heal a nation that appeared on Tuesday as culturally and geographically divided as the country that produced the disputed presidential election in 2000. Vice President Cheney said that Bush had run on a clear agenda and that "the nation resounded by giving him a mandate."

Bush's speech offered an olive branch to the opposition, but he provided no hint of policy concessions to the Democrats. He outlined a domestic agenda that included broad tax reform and a proposal to allow younger workers to establish personal accounts with some of their Social Security payroll taxes. Many Democrats oppose his Social Security plans, and he may face partisan opposition on tax reform.

The president also vowed to continue to put the fight against terrorism at the forefront of his agenda, saying, "With good allies at our side, we will fight this war on terror with every resource of our national power so our children can live in freedom and in peace."

His stance on terrorism proved to be a significant political asset on Tuesday, but Bush faces enormous problems in trying to stabilize Iraq and pull off elections there scheduled for early next year. In his speech, the president did not mention the frayed international relationships that also will occupy him now that the election is over.

Bush claimed 51 percent of the popular vote to Kerry's 48 percent, with a margin of about 3.5 million votes, removing the label of minority president that he had carried since 2000. Four years ago, Bush lost the popular vote to Vice President Al Gore, but on Tuesday he became the first president since his father in 1988 to be elected with a majority of all votes cast. Independent Ralph Nader proved to be a non-factor, winning less than

1 percent.

With Ohio in his column, Bush won 30 states and 279 electoral votes. Kerry won 19 states and the District for 252 electoral votes. Iowa and its seven electoral votes remain in doubt. Bush was leading there with 100 percent of precincts reporting, and while counties were still tabulating absentee and provisional ballots, officials in the state said they did not expect a change in the lead.

Two states—New Hampshire, which went for Kerry, and New Mexico, which went for Bush—switched sides from 2000, despite efforts by both sides to take the campaigns into each other's territory.

Nearly 120 million Americans voted, or about 60 percent of those eligible, the highest number since 1968, according to the Associated Press. Many strategists believed an increase of that magnitude would favor Kerry, but the Bush campaign proved more than equal to the task of getting supporters to vote.

The swift and courteous end to the campaign came in marked contrast to the emotional roller coaster that played out overnight and that provided eerie similarities to the triggering events that produced the 36-day recount in Florida four years ago.

The battle for Ohio turned out to be short and conclusive. By the time more than 90 percent of the precincts there had reported, Bush strategists were certain there was no way for Kerry to win the state, and they chafed that the challenger would not concede.

Kerry aides originally believed there might be enough provisional ballots—those cast by voters whose eligibility was in doubt—to win Ohio. At that point, Kerry's running mate, Sen. John Edwards (N.C.), made a speech at Boston's Copley Plaza in which he vowed that "every vote would be counted," a thinly veiled warning that the Democrats were prepared to begin legal action to contest the state. At the time, Kerry aides said, there was pandemonium inside the campaign.

Overnight, the Kerry campaign's senior staff, in a series of calls with the boiler-room leadership in Washington and political and legal advisers in Ohio, analyzed the situation. They concluded that the estimated 150,000 provisional ballots were not enough to overcome Bush's margin of 136,000 votes in Ohio, even if Kerry were to win the lion's share of them.

Some lawyers argued that Kerry had a good legal argument to make and said that if the campaign was serious about a possible challenge, it needed to move immediately to force the state's counties to adopt uniform rules for counting the provisional ballots. Eventually, senior adviser Tad Devine said, the Kerry high command presented the candidate with a unanimous recommendation not to fight the count. "It's fair to say the unanimous recommendation was that this would not succeed," he said.

Kerry further discussed the situation with Edwards, Sen. Edward M. Kennedy (D-Mass.) and campaign manager Mary Beth Cahill, eventually agreeing that it was time to concede. At 11 a.m. yesterday, Kerry called Bush in the Oval Office to concede the election and pledge to bridge the nation's divisions. Three hours later, accompanied by his wife, Teresa Heinz Kerry, he left his home in Boston's Beacon Hill area for the short drive to Faneuil Hall.

There, he found a hall packed with campaign staff members and supporters, many of them trying to hold back tears over a loss that they never dreamed possible as they heard results of the first wave of exit polls Tuesday afternoon.

Kerry wasted no time in ending any talk of contesting the election. "In America, it is vital that every vote count and that every vote be counted," he said, in a nod to the exhortation that Edwards had invoked almost 12 hours earlier and that the two had used to rouse the Democratic base throughout the campaign. "But the outcome should be decided by voters, not a protracted legal process."

Kerry choked back tears and his voice broke as he recalled the experiences of his two-year campaign and talked about the need for unity in the election's aftermath, citing his conversation with the president. "We talked about the danger of division in our country and the need, the desperate need, for unity and for finding the common ground, coming together," he said.

Kerry advisers fully expected to win the election, based on their final polls, their analysis of Bush's weaknesses, their belief that the country hungered for change and their confidence that they would do a better job than the Republicans of getting their supporters to vote. Instead, they were swamped by a huge outpouring of votes in Republican-leaning areas of battleground states, particularly rural and small-town counties in Florida and the Midwest.

"We had [vote] goals that we set out that we thought were very realistic, that we thought could achieve victory," Devine said. "But a lot of people in rural areas participated in this process at levels that we have not seen before."

Another Kerry strategist said the campaign may have miscalculated the power of incumbency, especially during a time of heightened concern about terrorism. "It's easy to underestimate the reluctance in general that the American public would have in throwing out an incumbent president," the strategist said. "It's even more of a challenge when the country's perceived to be in some level of a war. That was an overriding backdrop that some of us tended to underestimate."

The Kerry camp also may have misjudged the power of Bush's appeal to social and cultural conservatives, even though White House senior adviser Karl Rove had explicitly set about to expand turnout among Christian conservatives.

Led by Rove, campaign manager Ken Mehlman, chief strategist Matthew Dowd and others, Bush's reelection team ran a disciplined operation that rarely deviated from the plan that was set from the start. Bush paid tribute to his team in his remarks yesterday, describing Rove, who has been at his side as he ascended through the Texas governorship to the presidency and now to a second term, as "the chief architect."

Bush's advisers, often second-guessed over their strategic decisions, took satisfaction not only from the victory but from the size of Bush's margin, which they said would end questions of legitimacy that had dogged him after 2000. Dowd, in a final strategy memo before returning to Texas, said the president had won more votes—more than 59 million—than any other candidate in history and that the campaign had succeeded in changing the shape of the electorate, raising Republicans to parity with Democrats.

"The other side did a very good job identifying their voters and getting them out to vote," Devine said. "It's just that simple."

Document Analysis

After fighting hard during the election, Kerry initially did not appear to want to concede the race on Election Night. There were questions surrounding the Ohio vote totals, and for a moment it looked as if the nation was going to revisit the drama of the 2000 presidential race. However, knowing there was not a fight to be had and perhaps to save face for his party, Kerry conceded the election to Bush. Since then, both Kerry and Dean have gone on record to state they do not believe voting in Ohio was conducted fairly, and had they pushed the issue the win could have gone to Kerry. This is speculative, of course, and regardless of those sentiments Bush was named the winner. While victory was his, Bush faced the extremely difficult task of attempting to unite a very divided nation.

The 2004 election was the closest election since 1916, and the political divisions throughout the country were palpable. The country was divided between conservative red states and more liberal leaning blue states. Issues surrounding the United States' decision to engage in a war, and major disagreements over social issues with moral foundations seemed to split the country. In addition to ideological differences, the country was also divided

among those who wholeheartedly supported George W. Bush and those who found him repugnant. Uniting a nation that held such strong feelings towards issues and towards Bush as a person would prove to be a challenge for the president himself, as he did not hint at policy concessions regardless of how divided the country was, nor did he seem concerned with appeasing those with whom he was not popular. In his victory speech, Bush made a promise to remain engaged in the war on terror, and emphasized peace and individual liberty—which is a typical type of message to include in a speech following a win. As victory euphoria waned, and Bush was tasked with bringing people back together, the burden of such a responsibility must have weighed heavily on him as he entered his second term.

Essential Themes

While President Bush will always be able to claim the highest approval rating of any president, he will also be known for seeing that approval plummet during his second term in office. Questions about the existence of weapons of mass destruction, economic downfalls, and criticisms regarding the administration's response during the aftermath of Hurricane Katrina plagued Bush's second term. Since leaving office, Bush has not been particularly prominent in the public eye, and, aside from penning a memoir, has kept a low profile. It is likely that history will remember Bush as an extremely polarizing president, regardless of any accomplishments he may be credited with.

—*Amber R. Dickinson, PhD*

Bibliography and Additional Reading

Abramowitz, Alan I., and Walter J. Stone. "The Bush Effect: Polarization, Turnout, and

Activism in the 2004 Presidential Election." *Presidential Studies Quarterly*, vol. 36, no. 2, 2006, pp. 141–154., doi:10.1111/j.1741-5705.2006.00295.x.

Balz, Dan. "Bush Wins Second Term." *The Washington Post*, WP Company, 4 Nov. 2004, www.washingtonpost.com/wp-dyn/articles/A19510-2004Nov2_2.html.

Crotty, William J. *A Defining Moment: the Presidential Election of 2004*. M.E. Sharpe, 2005.

Nelson, Michael. *The Elections of 2004*. CQ Press, 2005.

"Dan Balz." *The Washington Post*, WP Company, www.washingtonpost.com/people/dan-balz/?utm_term=.34804503d8c6.

Obama supporters gathered on Independence Mall before Obama's speech. By Tony Fischer – "She's Excited at Obama Rally."

◼ Barack Obama's "A More Perfect Union" Speech

Date: March 18, 2008
Author: Barack Obama
Genre: Speech

Summary Overview

Barack Obama's "A More Perfect Union" speech, also sometimes referred to as the "race" speech, was a direct and intentional attempt to focus attention on racial divisions and tensions within the United States. The forty-minute speech given at the Constitution Center in Philadelphia on March 18, 2008, was delivered in response to comments about race and the treatment of black people in America made by the Reverend Jeremiah Wright of the Trinity United Church of Christ located in Chicago's South Side. Because this was the church the Obamas had been attending for years, and because of the close relationship between Barack Obama and Wright, the Reverend's comments were particularly problematic for Obama's presidential campaign, which was reaching a critical point in the election cycle. As a Democratic Senator from Illinois, Barack Obama was fighting to earn the presidency, and it was crucial that he did not let these comments derail his campaign. Seeing an opportunity to encourage an open dialogue about racial tensions, Obama delivered a powerful message directed to the American public which candidly and honestly addressed tensions between white and black America. Drawing upon his own background as a man from a multi-racial background, Obama's speech urged Americans to come together, try to understand each other's perspectives, and make an attempt to move the country forward.

Defining Moment

As the presidential race of 2008 moved into the sixth week of the Democratic primary battle between Hillary Clinton and Barack Obama, the Obama campaign faced a challenge that almost completely disrupted the campaign efforts to date. Comments made by the Revered Jeremiah Wright of the Trinity United Church of Christ in Chicago began to make press headlines, and Obama found it increasingly difficult to field the persistent questions he was facing. Wright had made comments addressing the racial injustices black Americans face, and

had also stated that he believed the United States government was involved with events that occurred on 9/11. Some were calling the comments made in the church an attack on white America, and a media frenzy ensued. Initially, Obama attempted to downplay the comments by acknowledging the Reverend had a fiery presentation style, and admitted the Reverend sometimes made comments Obama did not agree with. But, as the press continued to focus on the story, and as the public became aware of just how close a relationship Rev. Wright and Obama shared, it became increasingly difficult for Obama to deflect scrutiny.

Obama had known the Reverend for over twenty years and was a regular church attendee. The Reverend had married Barack and Michelle Obama, and baptized their two daughters. Obama often credited the Revered as being his spiritual advisor and has cited the Reverend as inspiring the title of his book, *The Audacity of Hope*. It was this close relationship, and the offense and shock some felt in reaction to the comments made by the Reverend that made it necessary for the Obama campaign to seriously address the issue. Furthermore, the Reverend's message directly contradicted Obama's campaign slogan of "hope," and therefore needed to be dealt with before the campaign reached a point it could not recover from. In a move that would prove to propel the Obama campaign forward in the race, Obama delivered a speech on race that was called "A More Perfect Union." The speech plainly broke down the history of racial injustice in the nation, and urged people to come together to work towards making progress towards racial equality. The speech was personal, it was honest, and it garnered a significant amount of positive attention for Obama and his presidential campaign.

Author Biography

Barack Obama was born in Honolulu, Hawaii in 1961. He was raised by his mother and grandparents, and had no real relationship with his biological father who passed away when Obama was 21. Despite the difficulty of having an absent father, a subject he has discussed at great length both in the media and his writings, Obama attended Columbia University for his undergraduate studies where he graduated with a bachelor's degree in political science. In the early 1980s, Obama moved to Chicago where he worked as a community organizer. He went on to enroll in law school at Harvard University, where he served as the president of the Harvard Law Review. Obama began his political career by serving as an Illinois U.S. Senator before becoming the first African American president of the United States in 2008. He and his wife Michelle have two daughters. Obama has been regarded as one of the American public's most favored presidents, and since leaving office he has been traveling the world delivering speeches and formalizing plans to create the Obama Presidential Center in Chicago.

HISTORICAL DOCUMENT

"We the people, in order to form a more perfect union ..."—221 years ago, in a hall that still stands across the street, a group of men gathered and, with these simple words, launched America's improbable experiment in democracy. Farmers and scholars, statesmen and patriots who had traveled across an ocean to escape tyranny and persecution finally made real their declaration of independence at a Philadelphia convention that lasted through the spring of 1787.

The document they produced was eventually signed but ultimately unfinished. It was stained by this nation's original sin of slavery, a question that divided the colonies and brought the convention to a stalemate until the founders chose to allow the slave trade to continue for at least 20 more years, and to leave any final resolution to future generations.

Of course, the answer to the slavery question was already embedded within our Constitution—a Constitution that had at its very core the ideal of equal citizenship under the law; a Constitution that promised its people liberty and justice and a union that could be and should be perfected over time.

And yet words on a parchment would not be enough to deliver slaves from bondage, or provide men and women of every color and creed their full rights and obligations as citizens of the United States. What would be needed were Americans in successive generations who were willing to do their part—through protests and struggles, on the streets and in the courts, through a civil war and civil disobedience, and always at great risk—to narrow that gap between the promise of our ideals and the reality of their time.

This was one of the tasks we set forth at the beginning of this presidential campaign—to continue the long march of those who came before us, a march for a more just, more equal, more free, more caring and more prosperous America. I chose to run for president at this moment in history because I believe deeply that we cannot solve the challenges of our time unless we solve them together, unless we perfect our union by understanding that we may have different stories, but we hold common hopes; that we may not look the same and we may not have come from the same place, but we all want to move in the same direction—toward a better future for our children and our grandchildren.

This belief comes from my unyielding faith in the decency and generosity of the American people. But it also comes from my own story.

I am the son of a black man from Kenya and a white woman from Kansas. I was raised with the help of a white grandfather who survived a Depression to serve in Patton's Army during World War II and a white grandmother who worked on a bomber assembly line at Fort Leavenworth while he was overseas. I've gone to some of the best schools in America and lived in one of the world's poorest nations. I am married to a black American who carries within her the blood of slaves and slaveowners—an inheritance we pass on to our two precious daughters. I have brothers, sisters, nieces, nephews, uncles and cousins of every race and every hue, scattered across three continents, and for as long as I live, I will never forget that in no other country on Earth is my story even possible.

It's a story that hasn't made me the most conventional of candidates. But it is a story that has seared into my genetic makeup the idea that this nation is more than the sum of its parts—that out of many, we are truly one.

Throughout the first year of this campaign, against all predictions to the contrary, we saw how hungry the American people were for this message of unity. Despite the temptation to view my candidacy through a purely racial lens, we won commanding victories in states with some of the whitest populations in the country. In South Carolina, where the Confederate flag still flies, we built a powerful coalition of African-Americans and white Americans.

This is not to say that race has not been an issue in this campaign. At various stages in the campaign, some commentators have deemed me either "too black" or "not black enough." We saw racial tensions bubble to the surface during the week before the South Carolina primary. The press has scoured every single exit poll for the latest evidence of racial polarization, not just in terms of white and black, but black and brown as well.

And yet, it has only been in the last couple of weeks that the discussion of race in this campaign has taken a particularly divisive turn.

On one end of the spectrum, we've heard the implication that my candidacy is somehow an exercise in affirmative action; that it's based solely on the desire of wide-eyed liberals to purchase racial reconciliation on the cheap. On the other end, we've heard my former pastor, Jeremiah Wright, use incendiary language to express views that have the potential not only to widen the racial divide, but views that denigrate both the greatness and the goodness of our nation, and that rightly offend white and black alike.

I have already condemned, in unequivocal terms, the statements of Reverend Wright that have caused such controversy and, in some cases, pain. For some, nagging questions remain. Did I know him to be an occasionally fierce critic of American domestic and foreign policy? Of course. Did I ever hear him make remarks that could be considered controversial while I sat in the church? Yes. Did I strongly disagree with many of his political views? Absolutely—just as I'm sure many of you have heard remarks from your pastors, priests, or rabbis with which you strongly disagreed.

But the remarks that have caused this recent firestorm weren't simply controversial. They weren't simply a religious leader's efforts to speak out against perceived injustice. Instead, they expressed a profoundly distorted view of this country—a view that sees white racism as endemic, and that elevates what is wrong with America above all that we know is right with America; a view that sees the conflicts in the Middle East as rooted primarily in the actions of stalwart allies like Israel, instead of emanating from the perverse and hateful ideologies of radical Islam.

As such, Reverend Wright's comments were not only wrong but divisive, divisive at a time when we need unity; racially charged at a time when we need to come together to solve a set of monumental problems—two wars, a terrorist threat, a falling economy, a chronic health care crisis and potentially devastating climate change—problems that are neither black or white or Latino or Asian, but rather problems that confront us all.

Given my background, my politics, and my professed values and ideals, there will no doubt be those for whom my statements of condemnation are not enough. Why associate myself with Reverend Wright in the first place, they may ask? Why not join another church? And I confess that if all that I knew of Reverend Wright were the snippets of those sermons that have run in an endless loop on the television sets and YouTube, or if Trinity United Church of Christ conformed to the caricatures being peddled by some commentators, there is no doubt that I would react in much the same way.

But the truth is, that isn't all that I know of the man. The man I met more than 20 years ago is a man who helped introduce me to my Christian faith, a man who spoke to me about our obligations to love one another, to care for the sick and lift up the poor. He is a man who served his country as a United States Marine; who has studied and lectured at some of the finest universities and seminaries in the country, and who for over 30 years has led a church that serves the community by doing God's work here on Earth—by housing the homeless, ministering to the needy, providing day care services and scholarships and prison ministries, and reaching out to those suffering from HIV/AIDS.

In my first book, *Dreams From My Father*, I describe the experience of my first service at Trinity:

"People began to shout, to rise from their seats and clap and cry out, a forceful wind carrying the reverend's voice up into the rafters. And in that single note—hope!—I heard something else: At the foot of that cross, inside the thousands of churches across the city, I imagined the stories of ordinary black people merging with the stories of David and Goliath, Moses and Pharaoh, the Christians in the lion's den, Ezekiel's field of dry bones. Those stories—of survival and freedom and hope—became our stories, my story. The blood that spilled was our blood, the tears our tears, until this black church, on this bright day, seemed once more a vessel carrying the story of a people into future generations and into a larger world. Our trials and triumphs became at once unique and universal, black and more than black. In chronicling our journey, the stories and songs gave us a meaning to reclaim memories that we didn't need to feel shame about—memories that all people might study and cherish, and with which we could start to rebuild."

That has been my experience at Trinity. Like other predominantly black churches across the country, Trinity embodies the black community in its entirety—the doctor and the welfare mom, the model student and the former gang-banger. Like other black churches, Trinity's services are full of raucous laughter and sometimes bawdy humor. They are full of dancing and clapping and screaming and shouting that may seem jarring to the untrained ear. The church contains in full the kindness and cruelty, the fierce intelligence and the shocking ignorance, the struggles and successes, the love and, yes, the bitterness and biases that make up the black experience in America.

And this helps explain, perhaps, my relationship with Reverend Wright. As imperfect as he may be, he has been like family to me. He strengthened my faith, officiated my wedding, and baptized my children. Not once in my conversations with him have I heard him talk about any ethnic group in derogatory terms, or treat whites with whom he interacted with anything but courtesy and respect. He contains within him the contradictions—the good and the bad—of the community that he has served diligently for so many years.

I can no more disown him than I can disown the black community. I can no more disown him than I can disown my white grandmother—a woman who helped raise me, a woman who sacrificed again and again for me, a woman who loves me as much as she loves anything in this world, but a woman who once confessed her fear of black men who passed her by on the street, and who on more than one occasion has uttered racial or ethnic stereotypes that made me cringe.

These people are a part of me. And they are part of America, this country that I love.

Some will see this as an attempt to justify or excuse comments that are simply inexcusable. I can assure you it is not. I suppose the politically safe thing to do would be to move on from this episode and just hope that it fades into the woodwork. We can dismiss Reverend Wright as a crank or a demagogue, just as some have dismissed Geraldine Ferraro, in the aftermath of her recent statements, as harboring some deep-seated bias.

But race is an issue that I believe this nation cannot afford to ignore right now. We would be making the same mistake that Reverend Wright made in his offending sermons about America—to simplify and stereotype and amplify the negative to the point that it distorts reality.

The fact is that the comments that have been made and the issues that have surfaced over the last few weeks reflect the complexities of race in this country that we've never really worked through—a part of our union that we have not yet made perfect. And if we walk away now, if we simply retreat into our respective corners, we will never be able to come together and solve challenges like health care or education or the need to find good jobs for every American.

Understanding this reality requires a reminder of how we arrived at this point. As William Faulkner once wrote, "The past isn't dead and buried. In fact, it isn't even past." We do not need to recite here the history of racial injustice in this country. But we do need to remind ourselves that so many of the disparities that exist between the African-American community and the larger American community today can be traced directly to inequalities passed on from an earlier generation that suffered under the brutal legacy of slavery and Jim Crow.

Segregated schools were and are inferior schools; we still haven't fixed them, 50 years after Brown v. Board of Education. And the inferior education they provided, then and now, helps explain the pervasive achievement gap between today's black and white students.

Legalized discrimination—where blacks were prevented, often through violence, from owning property, or loans were not granted to African-American business owners, or black homeowners could not access FHA mortgages, or blacks were excluded from unions or the police force or the fire department—meant that black families could not amass any meaningful wealth to bequeath to future generations. That history helps explain the wealth and income gap between blacks and whites, and the concentrated pockets of poverty that persist in so many of today's urban and rural communities.

A lack of economic opportunity among black men, and the shame and frustration that came from not being able to provide for one's family contributed to the erosion of black families—a problem that welfare policies for many years may have worsened. And the lack of basic services in so many urban black neighborhoods—parks for kids to play in, police walking the beat, regular garbage pickup, building code enforcement—all helped create a cycle of violence, blight and neglect that continues to haunt us.

This is the reality in which Reverend Wright and other African-Americans of his generation grew up. They came of age in the late '50s and early '60s, a time when segregation was still the law of the land and opportunity was systematically constricted. What's remarkable is not how many failed in the face of discrimination, but how many men and women overcame the odds; how many were able to make a way out of no way, for those like me who would come after them.

For all those who scratched and clawed their way to get a piece of the American Dream, there were many who didn't make it—those who were ultimately defeated, in one way or another, by discrimination. That legacy of defeat was passed on to future generations—those young men and, increasingly, young women who we see standing on street corners or languishing in our prisons, without hope or prospects for the future. Even for those blacks who did make it, questions of race and racism continue to define their worldview in fundamental ways. For the men and women of Reverend Wright's generation, the memories of humiliation and doubt and fear have not gone away; nor has the anger and the bitterness of those years. That anger may not get expressed in public, in front of white co-workers or white friends. But it does find voice in the barbershop or the beauty shop or around the kitchen table. At times, that anger is exploited by politicians, to gin up votes along racial lines, or to make up for a politician's own failings.

And occasionally it finds voice in the church on Sunday morning, in the pulpit and in the pews. The fact that so many people are surprised to hear that anger in some of Reverend Wright's sermons simply reminds us of the old truism that the most segregated hour of American life occurs on Sunday morning. That anger is not always productive; indeed, all too often it distracts attention from solving real problems; it keeps us from squarely facing our own complicity within the African-American community in our condition, and prevents the African-American community from forging the alliances it needs to bring about real change. But the anger is real; it is powerful. And to simply wish it away, to condemn it without understanding its roots, only serves to widen the chasm of misunderstanding that exists between the races.

In fact, a similar anger exists within segments of the white community. Most working- and middle-class white Americans don't feel that they have been particularly privileged by their race. Their experience is the immigrant experience—as far as they're concerned, no one handed them anything. They built it from scratch. They've worked hard all their lives, many times only to see their jobs shipped overseas or their pensions dumped after a lifetime of labor. They are anxious about their futures, and they feel their dreams slipping away. And in an era of stagnant wages and global competition, opportunity comes to be seen as a zero sum game, in which your dreams come at my expense. So when they are told to bus their children to a school across town; when they hear an African-American is getting an advantage in landing a good job or a spot in a good college because of an injustice that they themselves never committed; when they're told that their fears about crime in urban neighborhoods are somehow prejudiced, resentment builds over time.

Like the anger within the black community, these resentments aren't always expressed in polite company. But they have helped shape the political landscape for at least a generation. Anger over welfare and affirmative action helped forge the Reagan Coalition. Politicians routinely exploited fears of crime for their own electoral ends. Talk show hosts and conservative commentators built entire careers unmasking bogus claims of racism while dismissing legitimate discussions of racial injustice and inequality as mere political correctness or reverse racism.

Just as black anger often proved counterproductive, so have these white resentments distracted attention from the real culprits of the middle class squeeze—a corporate culture rife with inside dealing, questionable accounting practices and short-term greed; a Washington dominated by lobbyists and special interests; economic policies that favor the few over the many. And yet, to wish away the resentments of white Americans, to label them as misguided or even racist, without recognizing they are grounded in legitimate concerns—this too widens the racial divide and blocks the path to understanding.

This is where we are right now. It's a racial stalemate we've been stuck in for years. Contrary to the claims of some of my critics, black and white, I have never been so naïve as to believe that we can get beyond our racial divisions in a single election cycle, or with a single candidacy—particularly a candidacy as imperfect as my own.

But I have asserted a firm conviction—a conviction rooted in my faith in God and my faith in the American people—that, working together, we can move beyond some of our old racial wounds, and that in fact we have no choice if we are to continue on the path of a more perfect union.

For the African-American community, that path means embracing the burdens of our past without becoming victims of our past. It means continuing to insist on a full measure of justice in every aspect of American life. But it also means binding our particular grievances—for better health care and better schools and better jobs—to the larger aspirations of all Americans: the white woman struggling to break the glass ceiling, the white man who has been laid off, the immigrant trying to feed his family. And it means taking full responsibility for our own lives—by demanding more from our fathers, and spending more time with our children, and reading to them, and teaching them that while they may face challenges and discrimination in their own lives, they must never succumb to despair or cynicism; they must always believe that they can write their own destiny.

Ironically, this quintessentially American—and yes,

conservative—notion of self-help found frequent expression in Reverend Wright's sermons. But what my former pastor too often failed to understand is that embarking on a program of self-help also requires a belief that society can change.

The profound mistake of Reverend Wright's sermons is not that he spoke about racism in our society. It's that he spoke as if our society was static; as if no progress had been made; as if this country—a country that has made it possible for one of his own members to run for the highest office in the land and build a coalition of white and black, Latino and Asian, rich and poor, young and old—is still irrevocably bound to a tragic past. But what we know—what we have seen—is that America can change. That is the true genius of this nation. What we have already achieved gives us hope—the audacity to hope—for what we can and must achieve tomorrow.

In the white community, the path to a more perfect union means acknowledging that what ails the African-American community does not just exist in the minds of black people; that the legacy of discrimination—and current incidents of discrimination, while less overt than in the past—are real and must be addressed, not just with words, but with deeds, by investing in our schools and our communities; by enforcing our civil rights laws and ensuring fairness in our criminal justice system; by providing this generation with ladders of opportunity that were unavailable for previous generations. It requires all Americans to realize that your dreams do not have to come at the expense of my dreams; that investing in the health, welfare and education of black and brown and white children will ultimately help all of America prosper.

In the end, then, what is called for is nothing more and nothing less than what all the world's great religions demand—that we do unto others as we would have them do unto us. Let us be our brother's keeper, scripture tells us. Let us be our sister's keeper. Let us find that common stake we all have in one another, and let our politics reflect that spirit as well.

For we have a choice in this country. We can accept a politics that breeds division and conflict and cynicism. We can tackle race only as spectacle—as we did in the O.J. trial—or in the wake of tragedy—as we did in the aftermath of Katrina—or as fodder for the nightly news. We can play Reverend Wright's sermons on every channel, every day and talk about them from now until the election, and make the only question in this campaign whether or not the American people think that I somehow believe or sympathize with his most offensive words. We can pounce on some gaffe by a Hillary supporter as evidence that she's playing the race card, or we can speculate on whether white men will all flock to John McCain in the general election regardless of his policies.

We can do that.

But if we do, I can tell you that in the next election, we'll be talking about some other distraction. And then another one. And then another one. And nothing will change.

That is one option. Or, at this moment, in this election, we can come together and say, "Not this time." This time, we want to talk about the crumbling schools that are stealing the future of black children and white children and Asian children and Hispanic children and Native American children. This time, we want to reject the cynicism that tells us that these kids can't learn; that those kids who don't look like us are somebody else's problem. The children of America are not those kids, they are our kids, and we will not let them fall behind in a twenty-first-century economy. Not this time.

This time we want to talk about how the lines in the emergency room are filled with whites and blacks and Hispanics who do not have health care, who don't have the power on their own to overcome the special interests in Washington, but who can take them on if we do it together.

This time, we want to talk about the shuttered mills that once provided a decent life for men and women of every race, and the homes for sale that once belonged to Americans from every religion, every region, every walk of life. This time, we want to talk about the fact that the real problem is not that someone who doesn't look like you might take your job; it's that the corporation you work for will ship it overseas for nothing more than a profit.

This time, we want to talk about the men and women of every color and creed who serve together and fight together and bleed together under the same proud flag. We want to talk about how to bring them home from a war that should have never been authorized and should have never been waged. And we want to talk about how we'll show our patriotism by caring for them and their

families, and giving them the benefits that they have earned.

I would not be running for President if I didn't believe with all my heart that this is what the vast majority of Americans want for this country. This union may never be perfect, but generation after generation has shown that it can always be perfected. And today, whenever I find myself feeling doubtful or cynical about this possibility, what gives me the most hope is the next generation—the young people whose attitudes and beliefs and openness to change have already made history in this election.

There is one story in particularly that I'd like to leave you with today—a story I told when I had the great honor of speaking on Dr. King's birthday at his home church, Ebenezer Baptist, in Atlanta.

There is a young, 23-year-old white woman named Ashley Baia who organized for our campaign in Florence, S.C. She had been working to organize a mostly African-American community since the beginning of this campaign, and one day she was at a roundtable discussion where everyone went around telling their story and why they were there.

And Ashley said that when she was 9 years old, her mother got cancer. And because she had to miss days of work, she was let go and lost her health care. They had to file for bankruptcy, and that's when Ashley decided that she had to do something to help her mom.

She knew that food was one of their most expensive costs, and so Ashley convinced her mother that what she really liked and really wanted to eat more than anything else was mustard and relish sandwiches—because that was the cheapest way to eat. That's the mind of a 9-year-old.

She did this for a year until her mom got better. So she told everyone at the roundtable that the reason she joined our campaign was so that she could help the millions of other children in the country who want and need to help their parents, too.

Now, Ashley might have made a different choice. Perhaps somebody told her along the way that the source of her mother's problems were blacks who were on welfare and too lazy to work, or Hispanics who were coming into the country illegally. But she didn't. She sought out allies in her fight against injustice.

They're supporting the campaign. They all have different stories and different reasons. Many bring up a specific issue. And finally they come to this elderly black man who's been sitting there quietly the entire time. And Ashley asks him why he's there. And he does not bring up a specific issue. He does not say health care or the economy. He does not say education or the war. He does not say that he was there because of Barack Obama. He simply says to everyone in the room, "I am here because of Ashley."

"I'm here because of Ashley." By itself, that single moment of recognition between that young white girl and that old black man is not enough. It is not enough to give health care to the sick, or jobs to the jobless, or education to our children.

But it is where we start. It is where our union grows stronger. And as so many generations have come to realize over the course of the 221 years since a band of patriots signed that document right here in Philadelphia, that is where the perfection begins.

GLOSSARY

Jim Crow: the former practice keeping black and white people separate in the United States

Document Analysis

In a speech that, at times, was highly personal in nature, then-Senator Barack Obama used his speech to invite Americans to join a productive conversation about the state of race relations in the United States. It was an urgent call to the public to stop avoiding or ignoring racial injustices and tensions still very much thriving in modern times. Obama used his own life story to emphasize his points and attempt to make the idea of discussing race accessible to those who felt it was a taboo subject. The speech addressed racial tensions, white privilege, anger felt by black Americans, and white resentment towards the black population. Essentially, the speech served to contextualize the comments that Rev. White had made, and structured those statements in a way that was not meant to offend but rather to enlighten.

The speech began by highlighting the "original sin of slavery" in this country, and reminded people that the Constitution was built on the principle of equality. Therefore, slavery itself was a direct contradiction to the supposed goals of our founding fathers. While generations of men and women, both black and white, worked towards making equality in America a real thing, Obama told his listeners there was more work to be done. In what would be a repetitive theme in the speech, Obama told people that they must work together for the common goal of equality to be achieved. The thesis of the speech served as a reminder of why he was running for president: he emphasized the idea of bringing people together to facilitate the goal of equality. In doing this, Obama

established himself as solid political candidate who understood the power of uniting people behind a common cause. Obama's choice to personalize the speech by drawing on his own life history only solidified his potential as a leader and made him relatable to voters.

Barack Obama's own personal background as a multiracial individual allowed him to examine the issue of race from both a white and black perspective. He talked about his own experiences in a way that made race and the idea of discussing race accessible for the average American. Obama did condemn the statements made by Rev. Wright, but found it important to support Wright as a person. The personal history Obama shared with Wright was too great for him to deny, and although the actual statements the Reverend had made were not supported by Obama, Obama did view the comments as an opportunity to open a racial dialogue which had been ignored in this country for years. While arguably it would have been more politically conventional to try to move forward without directly discussing race in America, Obama clearly felt that this was too important an issue to ignore for political purposes. To ignore the issue would be to allow Americans to remain in their own isolated racial corners of the country; and because Obama's central theme of the campaign was hope and unity, it was extremely important that he address the nation regarding this issue. However, discussing race candidly meant that listeners would have to face some unsavory and uncomfortable truths about race relations and injustices.

In his "A More Perfect Union" speech, Obama shone

a light on the reality that black people have been disproportionately impacted in a negative way in America simply because they are black. He cited things such as Jim Crow laws, the segregation of schools, unequal economic opportunities, and legalized discrimination prevalent throughout American history. Obama explained to his listeners that the type of treatment black people have been subjected to creates a festering anger, and to ignore those injustices and the anger they spawn is to allow for further divisions between white people and minorities. To truly begin to make the move towards actual equality, people would have to come together and discuss these types of problems, regardless of how uncomfortable or difficulty it could be. To discuss these issues across racial lines would have to be the first step in working together for true equality in America. Obama urged the general public to engage in these types of discussions, and reinforced the idea that he held out hope for the future if people would only work with, instead of against one another.

Essential Themes

Obama's race speech held both political and social ramifications. Just three weeks prior to delivering this speech, the Pew Research Center reported that people believed that both Hillary Clinton and Barack Obama were equally visible in the public eye. However, after the speech 70 percent of people reported that they heard more about Obama in the news media than any other candidate in the race. Furthermore, 85 percent of people questioned stated they had heard a little about the speech, and 54 percent had heard a lot. Reverend Wright had cast an initial shadow over the Obama campaign with his inflammatory remarks, but Obama's speech aided in the campaign's recovery and appeared to help Obama move forward—at least in terms of voter visibility. Clearly, the speech gave Obama an edge in the presidential race and helped him to progress towards winning the election. In that regard, the speech was a success.

It remains an open question, however, as to how far the speech actually advanced racial equality in America. If one considers the ills continuing to affect American society today, it appears that racial injustice is no closer to being eradicated than it was in 2008 or before. Debates rage on about unfair treatment of black people in America, interactions between police and African Americans are scrutinized and criticized, and movements such as Black Lives Matter are gaining in strength. While there are laws on the books guaranteeing the equal treatment of black people in this country, there are still credible stories of active and intentional race-based discrimination occurring on a daily basis in America. So while Obama's "A More Perfect Union" speech garnered major attention on the campaign trail, the lasting impact of the message is debatable, having been overrun by later political events. The call to come together and talk about, and combat, racial injustice has not as yet been answered by a majority of American citizens.

—*Amber R. Dickinson, PhD*

Bibliography and Additional Reading

Maraniss, David. *Barack Obama: the Story*. Simon & Schuster Paperbacks, 2012.

Fletcher, Michael. "The Speech on Race That Saved Obama's Candidacy." *The Washington Post*, WP Company, www.washingtonpost.com/graphics/national/obama-legacy/jeremiah-wright-2008-philadelphia-race-speech.html.

Ross, Brian, and Rehab El-buri. "Obama's Pastor: God Damn America, U.S. to Blame for 9/11." *ABC News*, ABC News Network, 13 Mar. 2008, abcnews.go.com/Blotter/DemocraticDebate/story?id=4443788&page=1.

Schwarz, Sam. "What Has Barack Obama Been up to since Leaving Office?" *Newsweek*, 28 Dec. 2017, www.newsweek.com/barack-obama-leaving-white-house-761504.

Sharpley-Whiting, T. Denean. 2009. *The Speech: Race and Barack Obama's "A More Perfect Union"*. Bloomsbury.

"Transcript: Barack Obama's Speech on Race." *NPR*, NPR, 18 Mar. 2008, www.npr.org/templates/story/story.php?storyId=88478467.

Pew Research Center. 2008. *"Obama Speech on Race Arguably Biggest Event of Campaign."*

The Palins and McCains in Fairfax, Virginia, September 2008. Left to right: Todd Palin, Sarah Palin, Cindy McCain, and John McCain. Rally in Fairfax, Virginia on September 10, 2008. Photo by Rachael Dickson.

Sarah Palin's Acceptance Speech at the 2008 Republican National Convention

Date: September 3, 2008
Author: Sarah Palin
Genre: Speech

Summary Overview

When Sarah Palin took the stage at the Republican National Convention in Saint Paul, Minnesota, to give this speech, she had much to prove. Although she had her ardent fans, many Americans—including some Republicans—were rooting for her to fail. She had begun her political career just a decade and a half earlier as city councilwoman in the small Alaskan city of Wasilla. Her rise to governor of Alaska and eventually to vice presidential nominee was remarkably steep. Her relative inexperience and brash style grated detractors and worried fans. The speech itself praises her running mate, John McCain, attacks their opponent, Barack Obama, and tells Palin's own narrative. It exceeded expectations and was largely viewed as a success. Palin's role as vice presidential candidate seemed, at the time, to be unprecedented. As a political outsider, she did not speak or act like candidates that most Americans were accustomed at the time. In the age of Trump, however, her performance as vice presidential candidate rings quite familiar. Palin, as witnessed in this speech, was a harbinger of American politics to come.

Defining Moment

The quick ascendence of Sarah Palin from a councilwoman in a small city in Alaska to the Republican candidate for vice president in a little over ten years foreshadowed the subsequent Tea Party movement and the political rise of Donald Trump.

George W. Bush's eight years in office saw a substantial decline in his approval ratings from a high in the mid-eighty percent following the September 11 attacks to a low in the mid-twenty percent at the time of the 2008 election. Such a swing is extraordinary during the era of hyper-partisanship that has marked the early twenty-first century. Various analysts point to various causes for the decline, but many point to the ongoing wars in Iraq and Afghanistan as well as the onset of the great recession for the Bush's loss in popularity. It was this political climate that John McCain faced as he ran for president in 2008. McCain had a storied history as a Navy veteran who bravely faced imprisonment and torture in Vietnam; however, he was very much a part of the same Republican establishment as George Bush. The two men were the final contenders for the Republican presidential nomination in 2000, which Bush eventually won. This, along with the unfavorable climate for Republicans, put McCain in a tough position facing off against the Democratic candidate, Barack Obama, and his calls for hope and change.

Depending upon whom you ask, the McCain campaign's choice of Sarah Palin as McCain's running mate was either a savvy, long-shot maneuver by a campaign already well behind in the polls or an impulsive gamble on a vice-presidential candidate untested at the national level. Supporters saw Palin's outsider status as a strength, while detractors painted it as a negative. Some minor episodes featuring her brought negative press to the Republican ticket. For example, Palin stumbled several times in her interviews with journalist Katie Couric in late September 2008, including when she was unable to name any periodicals or magazines that she reads to inform her worldview. Nevertheless, Palin mostly executed her duties as vice-presidential candidate effectively. She outperformed expectations in her two most important performances in the role of vice presidential candidate, the convention speech featured here and the vice presidential debate against Joe Biden. Ultimately, the political climate and the larger dynamics of the race played a more influential role in the Republicans' 2008 presidential loss than did the selection of Sarah Palin as vice presidential nominee.

Although Palin's role in the 2008 election was not decisive, her style and rapid rise offered a glimpse of things to come. During the presidency of Barack Obama, the Tea Party movement gained steam. This term is used to described a nebulous and multifarious political movement of the right that arose shortly after Obama took office. Tea partiers decried the rising budget deficit and what they considered a bloated federal government. The movement's claim to consist of "real Americans" and its disdain for the "Washington establishment" mirror Palin's own rhetoric from the 2008 campaign. She herself played a large role in shaping and directing the Tea Party movement. For example, she was the keynote speaker at the much ballyhooed Tea Party Convention on February 6, 2010 in Nashville, Tennessee. However, years later, when the Trump administration substantially increased the deficit, the movement did not react with the same furor—nor at all, really, revealing that much of its motivation came from cultural grievances and backlash against the election of the nation's first African American president.

The rise of Donald Trump from reality television celebrity to the forty-fifth president of the United States flabbergasted political analysts and pundits. However, Sarah Palin's previous rise showcased the possibility that a brash-talking political outsider could exceed expectations in the early twenty-first century American political landscape. Trump, like Palin before him, was accused by detractors of lacking the experience and intelligence to serve in the executive branch. Trump, like Palin before him, used these arguments against him to his advantage, painting himself as the outsiders' outsider willing to break the norms of Washington and depicting his detractors as out-of-touch elitists. Palin, like Trump after her, courted controversy to generate headlines. Her PAC, or political action committee, posted a picture on its website of a crosshair over the district of Democratic representative Gabrielle Giffords shortly after she had been shot and almost killed. The stunt received much criticism yet brought Palin back into the national conversation at a time when her influence was waning. The same forces that brought Palin to prominence allowed for Trump's subsequent success.

Author Biography

Sarah Louise Palin, née Sarah Louise Heath, was born on February 11, 1964 in Sandpoint, Idaho. When Palin was only a few month old, her family moved to Alaska and eventually settled in the city of Wasilla in 1972. She attended several different colleges en route to earning a Bachelor's degree in communications with an emphasis on journalism in 1987. Her political rise was meteoric: Elected to the Wasilla City Council in 1992, she was elected mayor of Wasilla in 1996. In 2003, she was appointed to oversee the Alaska Oil and Gas Conservation Commission, a powerful state agency of Alaska. Three years later, on November 7, 2006, she was the youngest person and first woman to be elected as Alaska's governor. John McCain, after winning the Republican nomination for president in 2008, selected Palin to be his running mate, making her the first female Republican vice-presidential candidate, and marking the apex of her political career. In this role, she gave the speech featured in this chapter at the Republican Nation Convention. McCain and Palin lost the 2008 election to the Democratic ticket, Barack Obama and Joe Biden; the following year, Palin resigned from the governorship, a year before her term was up. Since the resignation, Palin has formed a PAC (political action committee), written a book, and appeared frequently as a pundit on Fox News and the Sportsman Channel.

HISTORICAL DOCUMENT

Mr. Chairman, delegates, and fellow citizens: I am honored to be considered for the nomination for vice president of the United States.

I accept the call to help our nominee for president to serve and defend America.

I accept the challenge of a tough fight in this election against confident opponents at a crucial hour for our country.

And I accept the privilege of serving with a man who has come through much harder missions ... and met far graver challenges and knows how tough fights are won—the next president of the United States, John S. McCain.

It was just a year ago when all the experts in Washington counted out our nominee because he refused to hedge his commitment to the security of the country he loves.

With their usual certitude, they told us that all was lost—there was no hope for this candidate who said that he would rather lose an election than see his country lose a war.

But the pollsters and pundits overlooked just one thing when they wrote him off.

They overlooked the caliber of the man himself—the determination, resolve, and sheer guts of Sen. John McCain. The voters knew better.

And maybe that's because they realize there is a time for politics and a time for leadership ... a time to campaign and a time to put our country first.

Our nominee for president is a true profile in courage, and people like that are hard to come by.

He's a man who wore the uniform of this country for 22 years and refused to break faith with those troops in Iraq who have now brought victory within sight.

And as the mother of one of those troops, that is exactly the kind of man I want as commander in chief. I'm just one of many moms who'll say an extra prayer each night for our sons and daughters going into harm's way.

Our son Track is 19.

And one week from tomorrow—Sept. 11—he'll deploy to Iraq with the Army infantry in the service of his country.

My nephew Kasey also enlisted and serves on a carrier in the Persian Gulf.

My family is proud of both of them and of all the fine men and women serving the country in uniform. Track is the eldest of our five children.

In our family, it's two boys and three girls in between—my strong and kind-hearted daughters, Bristol, Willow and Piper.

And in April, my husband, Todd, and I welcomed our littlest one into the world, a perfectly beautiful baby boy named Trig. From the inside, no family ever seems typical.

That's how it is with us.

Our family has the same ups and downs as any other—the same challenges and the same joys.

Sometimes even the greatest joys bring challenge.

And children with special needs inspire a special love.

To the families of special-needs children all across this country, I have a message: For years, you sought to make America a more welcoming place for your sons and daughters.

I pledge to you that if we are elected, you will have a friend and advocate in the White House. Todd is a story all by himself.

He's a lifelong commercial fisherman ... a production operator in the oil fields of Alaska's North Slope ... a proud member of the United Steel Workers Union ... and world champion snow machine racer.

Throw in his Yup'ik Eskimo ancestry, and it all makes for quite a package.

We met in high school, and two decades and five children later he's still my guy. My mom and dad both worked at the elementary school in our small town.

And among the many things I owe them is one simple lesson: that this is America, and every woman can walk through every door of opportunity.

My parents are here tonight, and I am so proud to be the daughter of Chuck and Sally Heath. Long ago, a young farmer and haberdasher from Missouri followed an unlikely path to the vice presidency.

A writer observed: "We grow good people in our small towns, with honesty, sincerity, and dignity." I know just the kind of people that writer had in mind when he praised Harry Truman.

I grew up with those people.

They are the ones who do some of the hardest work in America who grow our food, run our factories and fight our wars.

They love their country, in good times and bad, and they're always proud of America. I had the privilege of living most of my life in a small town.

I was just your average hockey mom and signed up for the PTA because I wanted to make my kids' public education better.

When I ran for City Council, I didn't need focus groups and voter profiles because I knew those voters, and knew their families, too.

Before I became governor of the great state of Alaska, I was mayor of my hometown.

And since our opponents in this presidential election seem to look down on that experience, let me explain to them what the job involves.

I guess a small-town mayor is sort of like a "community organizer," except that you have actual responsibilities. I might add that in small towns, we don't quite know what to make of a candidate who lavishes praise on working people when they are listening, and then talks about how bitterly they cling to their religion and guns when those people aren't listening.

We tend to prefer candidates who don't talk about us one way in Scranton and another way in San Francisco.

As for my running mate, you can be certain that wherever he goes, and whoever is listening, John McCain is the same man. I'm not a member of the permanent political establishment. And I've learned quickly, these past few days, that if you're not a member in good standing of the Washington elite, then some in the media consider a candidate unqualified for that reason alone.

But here's a little news flash for all those reporters and commentators: I'm not going to Washington to seek their good opinion. I'm going to Washington to serve the people of this country. Americans expect us to go to Washington for the right reasons, and not just to mingle with the right people.

Politics isn't just a game of clashing parties and competing interests.

The right reason is to challenge the status quo, to serve the common good, and to leave this nation better than we found it.

No one expects us to agree on everything.

But we are expected to govern with integrity, good will, clear convictions, and ... a servant's heart.

I pledge to all Americans that I will carry myself in this spirit as vice president of the United States. This was the spirit that brought me to the governor's office, when I took on the old politics as usual in Juneau ... when I stood up to the special interests, the lobbyists, big oil companies, and the good-ol' boys network.

Sudden and relentless reform never sits well with entrenched interests and power brokers. That's why true reform is so hard to achieve.

But with the support of the citizens of Alaska, we shook things up.

And in short order we put the government of our state back on the side of the people.

I came to office promising major ethics reform, to end the culture of self-dealing. And today, that ethics reform is the law.

While I was at it, I got rid of a few things in the governor's office that I didn't believe our citizens should have to pay for.

That luxury jet was over the top. I put it on eBay.

I also drive myself to work.

And I thought we could muddle through without the governor's personal chef—although I've got to admit that sometimes my kids sure miss her. I came to office promising to control spending—by request if possible and by veto if necessary.

Sen. McCain also promises to use the power of veto in defense of the public interest—and as a chief executive, I can assure you it works.

Our state budget is under control.

We have a surplus.

And I have protected the taxpayers by vetoing wasteful spending: nearly half a billion dollars in vetoes.

I suspended the state fuel tax and championed reform to end the abuses of earmark spending by Congress.

I told the Congress "thanks, but no thanks," for that Bridge to Nowhere.

If our state wanted a bridge, we'd build it ourselves. When oil and gas prices went up dramatically, and filled up the state treasury, I sent a large share of that revenue back where it belonged—directly to the people of Alaska.

And despite fierce opposition from oil company lobbyists, who kind of liked things the way they were, we broke their monopoly on power and resources.

As governor, I insisted on competition and basic fairness to end their control of our state and return it to the people.

I fought to bring about the largest private-sector infrastructure project in North American history.

And when that deal was struck, we began a nearly 40 billion-dollar natural gas pipeline to help lead America to energy independence.

That pipeline, when the last section is laid and its valves are opened, will lead America one step farther away from dependence on dangerous foreign powers that do not have our interests at heart.

The stakes for our nation could not be higher.

When a hurricane strikes in the Gulf of Mexico, this country should not be so dependent on imported oil that we are forced to draw from our Strategic Petroleum

Reserve.

And families cannot throw away more and more of their paychecks on gas and heating oil.

With Russia wanting to control a vital pipeline in the Caucasus, and to divide and intimidate our European allies by using energy as a weapon, we cannot leave ourselves at the mercy of foreign suppliers.

To confront the threat that Iran might seek to cut off nearly a fifth of world energy supplies ... or that terrorists might strike again at the Abqaiq facility in Saudi Arabia ... or that Venezuela might shut off its oil deliveries ... we Americans need to produce more of our own oil and gas.

And take it from a gal who knows the North Slope of Alaska: We've got lots of both.

Our opponents say, again and again, that drilling will not solve all of America's energy problems—as if we all didn't know that already.

But the fact that drilling won't solve every problem is no excuse to do nothing at all.

Starting in January, in a McCain-Palin administration, we're going to lay more pipelines ... build more nuclear plants ... create jobs with clean coal ... and move forward on solar, wind, geothermal and other alternative sources.

We need American energy resources, brought to you by American ingenuity, and produced by American workers. I've noticed a pattern with our opponent.

Maybe you have, too.

We've all heard his dramatic speeches before devoted followers.

And there is much to like and admire about our opponent.

But listening to him speak, it's easy to forget that this is a man who has authored two memoirs but not a single major law or reform—not even in the state Senate.

This is a man who can give an entire speech about the wars America is fighting and never use the word "victory" except when he's talking about his own campaign. But when the cloud of rhetoric has passed ... when the roar of the crowd fades away ... when the stadium lights go out, and those Styrofoam Greek columns are hauled back to some studio lot—what exactly is our opponent's plan? What does he actually seek to accomplish, after he's done turning back the waters and healing the planet? The answer is to make government bigger ... take more of your money ... give you more orders from Washington

... and to reduce the strength of America in a dangerous world. America needs more energy ... our opponent is against producing it.

Victory in Iraq is finally in sight ... he wants to forfeit.

Terrorist states are seeking nuclear weapons without delay ... he wants to meet them without preconditions.

Al-Qaida terrorists still plot to inflict catastrophic harm on America ... he's worried that someone won't read them their rights? Government is too big ... he wants to grow it.

Congress spends too much ... he promises more.

Taxes are too high ... he wants to raise them. His tax increases are the fine print in his economic plan, and let me be specific.

The Democratic nominee for president supports plans to raise income taxes ... raise payroll taxes ... raise investment income taxes ... raise the death tax ... raise business taxes ... and increase the tax burden on the American people by hundreds of billions of dollars.

My sister Heather and her husband have just built a service station that's now opened for business—like millions of others who run small businesses. How are they going to be any better off if taxes go up? Or maybe you're trying to keep your job at a plant in Michigan or Ohio ... or create jobs with clean coal from Pennsylvania or West Virginia ... or keep a small farm in the family right here in Minnesota.

How are you going to be better off if our opponent adds a massive tax burden to the American economy? Here's how I look at the choice Americans face in this election.

In politics, there are some candidates who use change to promote their careers.

And then there are those, like John McCain, who use their careers to promote change.

They're the ones whose names appear on laws and landmark reforms, not just on buttons and banners, or on self-designed presidential seals.

Among politicians, there is the idealism of high-flown speechmaking, in which crowds are stirringly summoned to support great things.

And then there is the idealism of those leaders, like John McCain, who actually do great things. They're the ones who are good for more than talk ... the ones we have always been able to count on to serve and defend America. Sen. McCain's record of actual achievement and reform helps explain why so many special interests, lobbyists and comfortable committee chairmen in Congress have fought the prospect of a McCain presidency—from the primary election of 2000 to this very day.

Our nominee doesn't run with the Washington herd.

He's a man who's there to serve his country, and not just his party.

A leader who's not looking for a fight, but is not afraid of one either. Harry Reid, the majority leader of the current do-nothing Senate, not long ago summed up his feelings about our nominee.

He said, quote, "I can't stand John McCain." Ladies and gentlemen, perhaps no accolade we hear this week is better proof that we've chosen the right man. Clearly what the majority leader was driving at is that he can't stand up to John McCain. That is only one more reason to take the maverick of the Senate and put him in the White House. My fellow citizens, the American presidency is not supposed to be a journey of "personal discovery." This world of threats and dangers is not just a community, and it doesn't just need an organizer.

And though both Sen. Obama and Sen. Biden have been going on lately about how they are always, quote, "fighting for you," let us face the matter squarely.

There is only one man in this election who has ever really fought for you ... in places where winning means survival and defeat means death ... and that man is John McCain. In our day, politicians have readily shared much lesser tales of adversity than the nightmare world in which this man, and others equally brave, served and suffered for their country.

It's a long way from the fear and pain and squalor of a 6-by-4 cell in Hanoi to the Oval Office.

But if Sen. McCain is elected president, that is the journey he will have made.

It's the journey of an upright and honorable man—the kind of fellow whose name you will find on war memorials in small towns across this country, only he was among those who came home.

To the most powerful office on Earth, he would bring the compassion that comes from having once been powerless ... the wisdom that comes even to the captives, by the grace of God ... the special confidence of those who have seen evil, and seen how evil is overcome. A fellow prisoner of war, a man named Tom Moe of Lancaster, Ohio, recalls looking through a pinhole in his cell door as Lt. Cmdr. John McCain was led down the hallway, by the guards, day after day.

As the story is told, "When McCain shuffled back from torturous interrogations, he would turn toward Moe's door and flash a grin and thumbs up"—as if to say, "We're going to pull through this." My fellow Americans, that is the kind of man America needs to see us through these next four years.

For a season, a gifted speaker can inspire with his words.

For a lifetime, John McCain has inspired with his deeds.

If character is the measure in this election ... and hope the theme ... and change the goal we share, then I ask you to join our cause. Join our cause and help America elect a great man as the next president of the United States.

Thank you all, and may God bless America.

Document Analysis

Political speechwriters often point to convention speeches—for both presidential and vice presidential nominees—as among the most difficult to write. Not only are the stakes very high, but instead of tailoring one's message to a given community, one must hit upon every single major issue that faces the nation and tie them all together into a coherent message. (Mitt Romney was disparaged four years later for failing to mention the troops in his convention speech.) The stakes were particularly high for Sarah Palin as she was largely expected to fail in this major test as a vice presidential nominee. She exceeded those expectations, touching all the necessary bases, telling her own narrative, attacking her opponent, and building up her running mate.

The fact that Palin is able to wrap so many topics into a coherent narrative is a testament to her hard work as well as that of her speech writers. Palin begins and ends with her running mate John McCain. The presidential nominee also frequently comes up in the middle portions of her speech. It is Palin's job, as vice presidential nominee, to direct the audience's attention back to the presidential candidate frequently. She also builds her own narrative, starting with her family and moving on to her political career. She praises her "small town" values and identifies herself as a "hockey mom." As for the issues, she focuses particularly on energy independence and the importance of the military. With the former, she as governor of Alaska has much experience; the latter represents the major issue with which the Republicans tried to distinguish themselves from their opponents in this election cycle. In the beginning of the speech, Palin discusses the service of her son and nephew. However, this fact does not separate Palin or the Republicans from her opposition; Joe Biden, the Democratic vice presidential candidate, also had a son serving in the military. Therefore, Palin returns the theme of her running mate's distinguished service record: "There is only one man in this election who has ever really fought for you ... in places where winning means survival and defeat means death ... and that man is John McCain." Americans were very impressed with McCain's bravery and service, and the Republican strategists were attempting to stress this theme as much as possible

One small misstep comes when Palin briefly discusses the so-called bridge to nowhere. Before Palin became governor of Alaska, the U.S. Congress allocated $233 million dollars for the state of Alaska to build a bridge connecting the airport on Gravina Island to the nearby city of Ketchikan. However, this city was inhabited by only fifty people, and the project got dubbed the "bridge to nowhere," becoming an example of unnecessary federal spending. In her successful campaign for governor, Palin supported the construction of the bridge and said that the term bridge to nowhere was disrespectful to the inhabitants of Ketchikan. As governor, she cancelled the project, but her state retained the transportation funding. Therefore, it came as a surprise to people familiar with the project when she said in this speech that "I told the Congress 'thanks, but no thanks,' for that Bridge to Nowhere. If our state wanted a bridge, we'd build it ourselves." Some criticized Palin's misleading portrayal of the event. This puts her in a long line of politicians accused of changing their positions as they move from state to national politics. The different stages pull politicians in different directions, so the shift can force a politician to change positions. This particular instance did not register with much of the audience and proved overall inconsequential in decreasing the approval that Palin won for the speech.

One of Palin's major duties in this speech was to attack her and McCain's opponent, Democratic presidential nominee Barack Obama. Campaigns often task vice-presidential candidates with spearheading these attacks on the opponents to allow the presidential candidate to appear magnanimous, transcend the mudslinging, and focus on their own agenda. In this speech and throughout the campaign, Palin leaned into this role. She consistently mocks Obama's former role as a community organizer. In relaying her own narrative, she says that "I guess a small-town mayor is sort of like a 'community organizer,' except that you have actual responsibilities." Later in the speech, she adds, "This world of threats and dangers is not just a community, and it doesn't just need an organizer." She seems to concede that Obama is an eloquent orator, but she attempts to contrast this negatively with her running mate's record: "For a season, a gifted speaker can inspire with his words. For a lifetime, John McCain has inspired with his deeds." Despite her dismissal of the efficacy of words, this speech of hers won her praise at a time when many Republicans were regretting her role as vice presidential nominee.

Essential Themes

Sarah Palin emphasizes her outsider status throughout this speech, as she has done consistently throughout her political and journalistic careers. At several points in the speech, she disparagingly insults the perspective of what she would dub the Washington establishment. In discussing John McCain's winning of the Republican nomination, she states: "It was just a year ago when all the experts in Washington counted out our nominee because he refused to hedge his commitment to the security of the country he loves." She continues a few lines later, "But the pollsters and pundits overlooked just one thing when they wrote him off. They overlooked the caliber of the man himself—the determination, resolve, and sheer guts of Sen. John McCain." In constructing her own narrative, she continues her rejection of Washington's status quo: "I'm not a member of the permanent political establishment." When discussing her tenure as governor of Alaska, she adds, "Sudden and relentless reform never sits well with entrenched interests and power brokers." She concludes by attempting to twist the Obama campaign's calls for hope and change into a message for her and her running mate: "If character is the measure in this election ... and hope the theme ... and change the goal we share, then I ask you to join our cause." While Palin was a genuine outsider, true to her rhetoric, her running mate had been a member of congress for three and a half decades and was a part of the same Republican establishment as concurrent president George W. Bush. The

2008 election occurred when the American citizenry was fed up with Washington, so one can see why both Democratic and Republican strategists constructed narratives in which their candidates were outsiders who would bring change to Washington. However, this was a tougher sell in the case of John McCain. Analysts have often asked if Palin's unpredictable style cost McCain the election. However, given the subsequent success of Donald Trump with the Republican base and in the 2016 election, perhaps we should be asking if McCain cost Palin the election.

—*Anthony Vivian, MA*

Bibliography and Additional Reading

Benet, Lorenzo. *Trailblazer: An Intimate Biography of Sarah Palin*. New York: Threshold Editions, 2009. Print.

Heilemann, John & Mark Halperin. *Game Change: Obama and the Clintons, McCain and Palin, and the Race of a Lifetime*. New York: HarperCollins, 2010. Print.

McCain, John & Mark Salter. *The Restless Wave: Good Times, Just Causes, Great Fights, and Other Appreciations*. New York: Simon & Schuster, 2018. Print.

Palin, Sarah. *Going Rogue: An American Life*. New York: HarperCollins, 2009. Print

■ *Citizens United v. Federal Election Commission*

Date: January 21, 2010
Author: Anthony Kennedy
Genre: Court opinion

Summary Overview

Citizens United v. Federal Election Commission transformed the electoral landscape, as well as strengthening organizations standing as regards the First Amendment. Justice Anthony Kennedy, considered a moderate on the Supreme Court, wrote a lengthy opinion which overturned portions of the 2002 Bipartisan Campaign Reform Act (BCRA), as well as portions of two earlier Supreme Court rulings. While the Court had treated organizations as persons, for certain legal purposes, since 1853, it was not until the 1970s that it ruled on campaign finance regulations for organizations. In *Buckley v. Valeo* the Court ruled that money is speech and as such its use in the political forum was protected by the First Amendment. However, even though the Watergate inspired campaign finance reform was limited by this ruling, Congress continued to seek ways to regulate campaign fundraising and expenditures. One result was the BCRA, which established a prohibition on soft money (money given to a party but not for direct campaign expenses), a limitation on electioneering communication, a prohibition on using general funds from a for-profit corporation or a labor union for campaign donations, and a ban on contributions by minors.

When *Citizens United* came before the Supreme Court, it used this case to examine all of the BCRA, not just those provisions which Citizens United claimed were unconstitutional. In its ruling, the Court held that most of the BCRA was unconstitutional and put forward the assertion that all organizations had total freedom of speech in the electoral process.

Citizens United is a conservative non-profit organization which has produced a substantial number of documentary, and documentary style, films. It was a controversy with the Federal Election Commission (FEC) over a film critical of Hillary Clinton, prior to the 2008 election, which led to the court case. Citizens United wanted the freedom to distribute and promote the film without interference from the FEC. Ultimately, the ruling by the Supreme Court went far beyond what might have been necessary to deal with the specific case. The Court not only ruled that films such as this were protected under the First Amendment, it ruled that all campaign expenditures by organizations were also protected. Thus, *Citizens United* allowed the expansion of campaign spending for, or against, candidates or initiatives, as long as the organization clearly stated that it was the source of the campaign ad, the candidate, or side, which the ad supported.

Defining Moment

Throughout the history of the United States, free speech has been one aspect of life which has been held in high esteem. While those involved with the adoption of the Bill of Rights may have had people in mind when it was written, the rights granted through freedom of speech and of the press were not specified as applying only to citizens, or even to people. While mega-corporations did not exist at that time, newspapers, and similar publications, were businesses, even if wholly owned by one person. Thus, the right of expression was broadly conferred to people and companies within the American society. The type of speech historically most protected was politically-oriented assertions and discussions.

In the slightly more than two hundred and twenty years between when the First Amendment was written and the *Citizens United v. Federal Election Commission* ruling was made, the technology available for communicating ideas, including political ideas, changed tremendously. However, it was the changes which had been made in the fifty years prior to the ruling which created the circumstances from which the case was derived. While in the mid-twentieth century electronic communication, radio or television, was only offered through a few networks and local channels, by the first decade of the twenty-first century, audio and video communications could be "broadcast" by almost anyone. The technology to create and "transmit" ideas and information of all types was relatively inexpensive and available to the public. Thus, when individuals or organizations wanted to support, or hinder, a political campaign, it could be done relatively easily via the internet or a cable company, and the potential audience for each "broadcast" could be in the millions.

Concern over groups, or rich individuals, having too much power within the political system had developed throughout the history of the United States. In 1907, the Tillman Act outlawed corporations giving money to individuals running for federal office. In 1947, a similar law was passed outlawing contributions by labor unions. At the end of the twentieth century, many rich individuals and interest groups (including corporations and unions) started greatly increasing the amount they were spending in support of their preferred candidates through unregulated support. As a result, in 2002, the BCRA was passed which made campaign contribution and expenditure regulations more restrictive for individuals and organizations. Another provision outlawed electronic "electioneering" by corporations in the period of 60 days prior to a general election, or 30 days prior to a primary election. Citizens United had produced a video critical of Senator Hillary Clinton, which it wanted to distribute during the prohibited period around the 2008 primaries, when Clinton was running for the Democratic nomination for president. Because the FEC was charged with overseeing the regulations established by the BCRA, Citizens United filed a suit against it to block enforcement of the law.

The Court, with the majority opinion written by Justice Kennedy, took a broad view of the issue and the ruling it made went far beyond the specifics of the case or what was needed to remedy the issue. Thus, the ruling did away with the ban on "broadcasting" political message by corporations and much more. It went beyond BCRA to the law which had established the FEC, doing away with restrictions that had been in place since 1971. The Court ruled that while the government had a need to inhibit corruption, the BCRA, and other laws and previous rulings, were too broad, so they were mainly overturned. However, the part of the BCRA which mandated identifying which group created the electronic communication was held as constitutional. Thus, beginning in 2010, all types of corporations were free to independently engage in political campaigning for, or against, a specific candidate or cause. Some have seen this as a disaster for American democracy, while others believe it has given all legal entities, individuals or corporations, the same right to fully participate in the electoral process through the free speech guaranteed in the First Amendment.

Author Biography

Born July 23, 1936, Anthony McLeod Kennedy became a member of the Supreme Court in 1988. Having been raised in Sacramento, California, by politically active parents, Anthony J. and Gladys Kennedy, he attended Stanford University and then Harvard Law School. Following in his father's footsteps, Kennedy went into private practice in 1961, and then returned to Sacramento in 1963, when his father died. During that time he also joined the law school faculty at the University of the Pacific's McGeorge School of Law, serving until 1988. During the 1970s, while working in Sacramento, Kennedy helped Gov. Ronald Reagan rewrite the California tax code.

In 1975, President Gerald Ford nominated Kennedy to a position on the Ninth Circuit of the Court of Appeals. Confirmed in this position, Kennedy ended his private practice. During 1987, a vacancy occurred on the Supreme Court and President Reagan nominated two individuals, Robert Bork and Douglas Ginsburg, who failed to be confirmed. In November, Kennedy was nominated by Reagan for that position and in February, 1988, Kennedy was confirmed by a vote of 97-0. Since joining the court, he has often been seen as a moderate, the swing vote on many cases. In 2017, rumors of a pending retirement have circulated although have not been confirmed. However, given his age and length of service it can be anticipated that a retirement in the near future is not out of the realm of possibility.

HISTORICAL DOCUMENT

Justice Kennedy delivered the opinion of the Court.

Federal law prohibits corporations and unions from using their general treasury funds to make independent expenditures for speech defined as an "electioneering communication" or for speech expressly advocating the election or defeat of a candidate....

I

A

Citizens United is a nonprofit corporation. It brought this action in the United States District Court for the District of Columbia. A three-judge court later convened to hear the cause. The resulting judgment gives rise to this appeal.

Citizens United has an annual budget of about $12 million. Most of its funds are from donations by individuals; but, in addition, it accepts a small portion of its funds from for-profit corporations.

In January 2008, Citizens United released a film entitled *Hillary: The Movie....* It is a 90-minute documentary about then-Senator Hillary Clinton, who was a candidate in the Democratic Party's 2008 Presidential primary elections. *Hillary* mentions Senator Clinton by name and depicts interviews with political commentators and other persons, most of them quite critical of Senator Clinton. *Hillary* was released in theaters and on DVD, but Citizens United wanted to increase distribution by making it available through video-on-demand.

... In December 2007, a cable company offered, for a payment of $1.2 million, to make *Hillary* available on a video-on-demand channel called "Elections '08." Some video-on-demand services require viewers to pay a small fee to view a selected program, but here the proposal was to make *Hillary* available to viewers free of charge.

To implement the proposal, Citizens United was prepared to pay for the video-on-demand; and to promote the film, it produced two 10-second ads and one 30-second ad for *Hillary*. Each ad includes a short (and, in our view, pejorative) statement about Senator Clinton, followed by the name of the movie and the movie's Website address. Citizens United desired to promote the video-on-demand offering by running advertisements on broadcast and cable television.

B

Before the Bipartisan Campaign Reform Act of 2002 (BCRA), federal law prohibited—and still does prohibit—corporations and unions from using general treasury funds to make direct contributions to candidates or independent expenditures that expressly advocate the election or defeat of a candidate, through any form of media, in connection with certain qualified federal elections.... An electioneering communication is defined as "any broadcast, cable, or satellite communication" that "refers to a clearly identified candidate for Federal office" and is made within 30 days of a primary or 60 days of a general election. The Federal Election Commission's (FEC) regulations further define an electioneering communication as a communication that is "publicly distributed."... Corporations and unions are barred from using their general treasury funds for express advocacy or electioneering communications. They may establish, however, a "separate segregated fund" (known as a political action committee, or PAC) for these purposes. The moneys received by the segregated fund are limited to donations from stockholders and employees of the corporation or, in the case of unions, members of the union.

C

Citizens United wanted to make *Hillary* available through video-on-demand within 30 days of the 2008 primary elections. It feared, however, that both the film and the ads would be covered by §441b's ban on corporate-funded independent expenditures, thus subjecting the corporation to civil and criminal penalties under §437g. In December 2007, Citizens United sought declaratory and injunctive relief against the FEC. It argued that (1) §441b is unconstitutional as applied to *Hillary*; and (2) BCRA's disclaimer and disclosure requirements, BCRA §§201 and 311, are unconstitutional as applied to *Hillary* and to the three ads for the movie.

The District Court denied Citizens United's motion for a preliminary injunction... and then granted the FEC's motion for summary judgment.... The court held that §441b was facially constitutional under *McConnell*, and that §441b was constitutional as applied to *Hillary* because it was "susceptible of no other interpretation than to inform the electorate that Senator Clinton is unfit for office, that the United States would be a dangerous place in a President Hillary Clinton world, and that viewers should vote against her." The court also rejected Citizens United's challenge to BCRA's disclaimer and disclosure requirements. It noted that "the Supreme Court has written approvingly of disclosure provisions triggered by political speech even though the speech itself was constitutionally protected under the First Amendment."

We noted probable jurisdiction. 555 U. S. ___ (2008). The case was reargued in this Court after the Court asked the parties to file supplemental briefs addressing whether we should overrule either or both *Austin* and the part of *McConnell* which addresses the facial validity of 2 U. S. C. §441b.

II

Before considering whether *Austin* should be overruled, we first address whether Citizens United's claim that §441b cannot be applied to *Hillary* may be resolved on other, narrower grounds.

A

Citizens United contends that §441b does not cover *Hillary*, as a matter of statutory interpretation, because the film does not qualify as an "electioneering communication."… Under the definition of electioneering communication, the video-on-demand showing of *Hillary* on cable television would have been a "cable… communication" that "refer[red] to a clearly identified candidate for Federal office" and that was made within 30 days of a primary election. Citizens United, however, argues that *Hillary* was not "publicly distributed," because a single video-on-demand transmission is sent only to a requesting cable converter box and each separate transmission, in most instances, will be seen by just one household—not 50,000 or more persons.

This argument ignores the regulation's instruction on how to determine whether a cable transmission "[c]an be received by 50,000 or more persons." The regulation provides that the number of people who can receive a cable transmission is determined by the number of cable subscribers in the relevant area. Here, Citizens United wanted to use a cable video-on-demand system that had 34.5 million subscribers nationwide. Thus, *Hillary* could

have been received by 50,000 persons or more.

One *amici* brief asks us, alternatively, to construe the condition that the communication "[c]an be received by 50,000 or more persons," to require "a plausible likelihood that the communication will be viewed by 50,000 or more potential voters"—as opposed to requiring only that the communication is "technologically capable" of being seen by that many people. Whether the population and demographic statistics in a proposed viewing area consisted of 50,000 registered voters—but not "infants, pre-teens, or otherwise electorally ineligible recipients"—would be a required determination, subject to judicial challenge and review, in any case where the issue was in doubt.

In our view the statute cannot be saved by limiting the reach of 2 U. S. C. §441b through this suggested interpretation. In addition to the costs and burdens of litigation, this result would require a calculation as to the number of people a particular communication is likely to reach, with an inaccurate estimate potentially subjecting the speaker to criminal sanctions. The First Amendment does not permit laws that force speakers to retain a campaign finance attorney, conduct demographic marketing research, or seek declaratory rulings before discussing the most salient political issues of our day. Prolix laws chill speech for the same reason that vague laws chill speech: People "of common intelligence must necessarily guess at [the law's] meaning and differ as to its application."… The Government may not render a ban on political speech constitutional by carving out a limited exemption through an amorphous regulatory interpretation.…

B

Citizens United next argues that §441b may not be applied to *Hillary* under the approach taken in WRTL. *McConnell* decided that §441b(b)(2)'s definition of an "electioneering communication" was facially constitutional insofar as it restricted speech that was "the functional equivalent of express advocacy" for or against a specific candidate. WRTL then found an unconstitutional application of §441b where the speech was not "express advocacy or its functional equivalent." As explained by The Chief Justice's controlling opinion in *WRTL*, the functional-equivalent test is objective: "a court should find that [a communication] is the functional equivalent of express advocacy only if [it] is susceptible of no reasonable interpretation other than as an appeal to vote for or against a specific candidate."

Under this test, *Hillary* is equivalent to express advocacy. The movie, in essence, is a feature-length negative advertisement that urges viewers to vote against Senator Clinton for President. In light of historical footage, interviews with persons critical of her, and voiceover narration, the film would be understood by most viewers as an extended criticism of Senator Clinton's character and her fitness for the office of the Presidency....

Citizens United argues that *Hillary* is just "a documentary film that examines certain historical events." We disagree. The movie's consistent emphasis is on the relevance of these events to Senator Clinton's candidacy for President....

As the District Court found, there is no reasonable interpretation of *Hillary* other than as an appeal to vote against Senator Clinton. Under the standard stated in *McConnell* and further elaborated in *WRTL*, the film qualifies as the functional equivalent of express advocacy.

C

Citizens United further contends that §441b should be invalidated as applied to movies shown through video-on-demand, arguing that this delivery system has a lower risk of distorting the political process than do television ads. On what we might call conventional television, advertising spots reach viewers who have chosen a channel or a program for reasons unrelated to the advertising. With video-on-demand, by contrast, the viewer selects a program after taking "a series of affirmative steps": subscribing to cable; navigating through various menus; and selecting the program....

While some means of communication may be less effective than others at influencing the public in different contexts, any effort by the Judiciary to decide which means of communications are to be preferred for the particular type of message and speaker would raise questions as to the courts' own lawful authority. Substantial questions would arise if courts were to begin saying what means of speech should be preferred or disfavored. And in all events, those differentiations might soon prove to be irrelevant or outdated by technologies that are in rapid flux....

Courts, too, are bound by the First Amendment. We must decline to draw, and then redraw, constitutional lines based on the particular media or technology used to disseminate political speech from a particular speaker.... The interpretive process itself would create an inevitable, pervasive, and serious risk of chilling protected speech pending the drawing of fine distinctions that, in the end, would themselves be questionable. First Amendment standards, however, "must give the benefit of any doubt to protecting rather than stifling speech."...

D

Citizens United also asks us to carve out an exception to §441b's expenditure ban for nonprofit corporate political speech funded overwhelmingly by individuals. As an alternative to reconsidering *Austin*, the Government also seems to prefer this approach. This line of analysis, however, would be unavailing.

In *MCFL*, the Court found unconstitutional §441b's restrictions on corporate expenditures as applied to nonprofit corporations that were formed for the sole purpose of promoting political ideas, did not engage in business activities, and did not accept contributions from for-profit corporations or labor unions.... Citizens United does not qualify for the *MCFL* exemption, however, since some funds used to make the movie were donations from for-profit corporations.

The Government suggests we could find BCRA's Wellstone Amendment unconstitutional, sever it from the statute, and hold that Citizens United's speech is exempt from §441b's ban under BCRA's Snowe-Jeffords Amendment.... Citizens United would not qualify for the Snowe-Jeffords exemption, under its terms as written, because *Hillary* was funded in part with donations from for-profit corporations.

Consequently, to hold for Citizens United on this argument, the Court would be required to revise the text of MCFL, sever BCRA's Wellstone Amendment, §441b(c)(6), and ignore the plain text of BCRA's Snowe-Jeffords Amendment.... There is no principled basis for doing this without rewriting Austin's holding that the Government can restrict corporate independent expenditures for political speech.

...

E

As the foregoing analysis confirms, the Court cannot resolve this case on a narrower ground without chilling political speech, speech that is central to the meaning and purpose of the First Amendment....

Citizens United has preserved its First Amendment challenge to §441b as applied to the facts of its case; and given all the circumstances, we cannot easily address that issue without assuming a premise—the permissibility of restricting corporate political speech—that is itself in doubt....

As noted above, Citizens United's narrower arguments are not sustainable under a fair reading of the statute. In the exercise of its judicial responsibility, it is necessary then for the Court to consider the facial validity of §441b. Any other course of decision would prolong the substantial, nation-wide chilling effect caused by §441b's prohibitions on corporate expenditures....

The ongoing chill upon speech that is beyond all doubt protected makes it necessary in this case to invoke the earlier precedents that a statute which chills speech can and must be invalidated where its facial invalidity has been demonstrated....

III

The First Amendment provides that "Congress shall make no law... abridging the freedom of speech."...

The law before us is an outright ban, backed by criminal sanctions. Section 441b makes it a felony for all corporations—including nonprofit advocacy corporations—either to expressly advocate the election or defeat of candidates or to broadcast electioneering communications within 30 days of a primary election and 60 days of a general election. Thus, the following acts would all be felonies under §441b: The Sierra Club runs an ad, within the crucial phase of 60 days before the general election, that exhorts the public to disapprove of a Congressman who favors logging in national forests; the National Rifle Association publishes a book urging the public to vote for the challenger because the incumbent U.S. Senator supports a handgun ban; and the American Civil Liberties Union creates a Web site telling the public to vote for a Presidential candidate in light of that candidate's defense of free speech. These prohibitions are classic examples of censorship.

Section 441b is a ban on corporate speech notwithstanding the fact that a PAC created by a corporation can still speak.... So the PAC exemption from §441b's expenditure ban, §441b(b)(2), does not allow corporations to speak. Even if a PAC could somehow allow a corporation to speak—and it does not—the option to form PACs does not alleviate the First Amendment problems with §441b....

Given the onerous restrictions, a corporation may not be able to establish a PAC in time to make its views known regarding candidates and issues in a current campaign.

Section 441b's prohibition on corporate independent expenditures is thus a ban on speech....

Speech is an essential mechanism of democracy, for it is the means to hold officials accountable to the people....

For these reasons, political speech must prevail against laws that would suppress it, whether by design or inadvertence. Laws that burden political speech are "subject to strict scrutiny," which requires the Government to prove that the restriction "furthers a compelling interest and is narrowly tailored to achieve that interest."...

Premised on mistrust of governmental power, the First Amendment stands against attempts to disfavor certain subjects or viewpoints.... As instruments to censor, these categories are interrelated: Speech restrictions based on the identity of the speaker are all too often simply a means to control content.

Quite apart from the purpose or effect of regulating content, moreover, the Government may commit a constitutional wrong when by law it identifies certain preferred speakers. By taking the right to speak from some and giving it to others, the Government deprives the disadvantaged person or class of the right to use speech to strive to establish worth, standing, and respect for the speaker's voice. The Government may not by these means deprive the public of the right and privilege to determine for itself what speech and speakers are worthy of consideration. The First Amendment protects speech and speaker, and the ideas that flow from each.

...

We find no basis for the proposition that, in the context of political speech, the Government may impose restrictions on certain disfavored speakers. Both history and logic lead us to this conclusion.

A
1

...

At least since the latter part of the nineteenth century, the laws of some States and of the United States imposed a ban on corporate direct contributions to candidates.... Yet not until 1947 did Congress first prohibit independent expenditures by corporations and labor unions in §304 of the Labor Management Relations Act 1947....

For almost three decades thereafter, the Court did not reach the question whether restrictions on corporate and union expenditures are constitutional....

2

In *Buckley*, the Court addressed various challenges to the Federal Election Campaign Act of 1971 (FECA) as amended in 1974....

The *Buckley* Court recognized a "sufficiently important" governmental interest in "the prevention of corruption and the appearance of corruption." This followed from the Court's concern that large contributions could be given "to secure a political *quid pro quo*."

The *Buckley* Court explained that the potential for *quid pro quo* corruption distinguished direct contributions to candidates from independent expenditures. The Court emphasized that "the independent expenditure ceiling... fails to serve any substantial governmental interest in stemming the reality or appearance of corruption in the electoral process," because "[t]he absence of prearrangement and coordination... alleviates the danger that expenditures will be given as a *quid pro quo* for improper commitments from the candidate.".....

3

Thus the law stood until *Austin. Austin* "uph[eld] a direct restriction on the independent expenditure of funds for political speech for the first time in [this Court's] history." There, the Michigan Chamber of Commerce sought to use general treasury funds to run a newspaper ad supporting a specific candidate. Michigan law, however, prohibited corporate independent expenditures that supported or opposed any candidate for state office. A viola-

tion of the law was punishable as a felony. The Court sustained the speech prohibition.

...

B

The Court is thus confronted with conflicting lines of precedent: a pre-*Austin* line that forbids restrictions on political speech based on the speaker's corporate identity and a post-*Austin* line that permits them. No case before *Austin* had held that Congress could prohibit independent expenditures for political speech based on the speaker's corporate identity.

...

1

...

Austin's antidistortion rationale would produce the dangerous, and unacceptable, consequence that Congress could ban political speech of media corporations....

Media corporations are now exempt from §441b's ban on corporate expenditures.... Yet media corporations accumulate wealth with the help of the corporate form, the largest media corporations have "immense aggregations of wealth," and the views expressed by media corporations often "have little or no correlation to the public's support" for those views. Thus, under the Government's reasoning, wealthy media corporations could have their voices diminished to put them on par with other media entities. There is no precedent for permitting this under the First Amendment.

The media exemption discloses further difficulties with the law now under consideration. There is no precedent supporting laws that attempt to distinguish between corporations which are deemed to be exempt as media corporations and those which are not.... With the advent of the Internet and the decline of print and broadcast media, moreover, the line between the media and others who wish to comment on political and social issues becomes far more blurred.

The law's exception for media corporations is, on its own terms, all but an admission of the invalidity of the antidistortion rationale. And the exemption results in a further, separate reason for finding this law invalid: Again by its own terms, the law exempts some corporations but covers others, even though both have the need or the motive to communicate their views. The exemption applies to media corporations owned or controlled by corporations that have diverse and substantial investments and participate in endeavors other than news. So even assuming the most doubtful proposition that a news organization has a right to speak when others do not, the exemption would allow a conglomerate that owns both a media business and an unrelated business to influence or control the media in order to advance its overall business interest. At the same time, some other corporation, with an identical business interest but no media outlet in its ownership structure, would be forbidden to speak or inform the public about the same issue. This differential treatment cannot be squared with the First Amendment.

There is simply no support for the view that the First Amendment, as originally understood, would permit the suppression of political speech by media corporations. The Framers may not have anticipated modern business and media corporations....

The great debates between the Federalists and the Anti-Federalists over our founding document were published and expressed in the most important means of mass communication of that era—newspapers owned by individuals.... At the founding, speech was open, comprehensive, and vital to society's definition of itself; there were no limits on the sources of speech and knowledge.... The Framers may have been unaware of certain types of speakers or forms of communication, but that does not mean that those speakers and media are entitled to less First Amendment protection than those types of speakers and media that provided the means of communicating political ideas when the Bill of Rights was adopted.

...

The censorship we now confront is vast in its reach. The Government has "muffle[d] the voices that best represent the most significant segments of the economy."... And "the electorate [has been] deprived of information, knowledge and opinion vital to its function."... By suppressing the speech of manifold corporations, both for-profit and nonprofit, the Government prevents their voices and viewpoints from reaching the public and advising voters on which persons or entities are hostile to their interests. Factions will necessarily form in our Republic, but the remedy of "destroying the liberty" of some factions is "worse than the disease."...

The purpose and effect of this law is to prevent corporations, including small and nonprofit corporations, from presenting both facts and opinions to the public. This makes *Austin*'s antidistortion rationale all the more an aberration....

When Government seeks to use its full power, including the criminal law, to command where a person may get his or her information or what distrusted source he or she may not hear, it uses censorship to control thought. This is unlawful. The First Amendment confirms the freedom to think for ourselves.

...

C

...

Austin is undermined by experience since its announcement. Political speech is so ingrained in our culture that speakers find ways to circumvent campaign finance laws.... Our Nation's speech dynamic is changing, and informative voices should not have to circumvent onerous restrictions to exercise their First Amendment rights. Speakers have become adept at presenting citizens with sound bites, talking points, and scripted messages that dominate the 24-hour news cycle. Corporations, like individuals, do not have monolithic views. On certain topics corporations may possess valuable expertise, leaving them the best equipped to point out errors or fallacies in speech of all sorts, including the speech of candidates and elected officials.

Rapid changes in technology—and the creative dynamic inherent in the concept of free expression—counsel against upholding a law that restricts political speech in certain media or by certain speakers.... The First Amendment does not permit Congress to make these categorical distinctions based on the corporate identity of the speaker and the content of the political speech.

...

Due consideration leads to this conclusion: *Austin* should be and now is overruled. We return to the principle established in *Buckley* and *Bellotti* that the Government may not suppress political speech on the basis of the speaker's corporate identity. No sufficient governmental interest justifies limits on the political speech of nonprofit or for-profit corporations.

D

Austin is overruled, so it provides no basis for allowing the Government to limit corporate independent expenditures....

IV
A

Citizens United next challenges BCRA's disclaimer and disclosure provisions as applied to *Hillary* and the three advertisements for the movie. Under BCRA §311, televised electioneering communications funded by anyone other than a candidate must include a disclaimer that "'_____ is responsible for the content of this advertising.'" The required statement must be made in a "clearly spoken manner," and displayed on the screen in a "clearly readable manner" for at least four seconds. It must state that the communication "is not authorized by any candidate or candidate's committee"; it must also display the name and address (or Web site address) of the person or group that funded the advertisement. Under BCRA §201, any person who spends more than $10,000 on electioneering communications within a calendar year must file a disclosure statement with the FEC. 2 U. S. C. §434(f)(1). That statement must identify the person making the expenditure, the amount of the expenditure, the election to which the communication was directed, and the names of certain contributors. §434(f)(2).

Disclaimer and disclosure requirements may burden the ability to speak, but they "impose no ceiling on campaign-related activities" and "do not prevent anyone from speaking."...

B

Citizens United sought to broadcast one 30-second and two 10-second ads to promote *Hillary*. Under FEC regulations, a communication that "[p]roposes a commercial transaction" was not subject to 2 U. S. C. §441b's restrictions on corporate or union funding of electioneering communications. The regulations, however, do not exempt those communications from the disclaimer and disclosure requirements in BCRA §§201 and 311....

Citizens United argues that the disclaimer requirements in §311 are unconstitutional as applied to its ads.

It contends that the governmental interest in providing information to the electorate does not justify requiring disclaimers for any commercial advertisements, including the ones at issue here. We disagree. The ads fall within BCRA's definition of an "electioneering communication": They referred to then-Senator Clinton by name shortly before a primary and contained pejorative references to her candidacy.... The disclaimers required by §311 "provid[e] the electorate with information" and "insure that the voters are fully informed" about the person or group who is speaking.... At the very least, the disclaimers avoid confusion by making clear that the ads are not funded by a candidate or political party....

The First Amendment protects political speech; and disclosure permits citizens and shareholders to react to the speech of corporate entities in a proper way. This transparency enables the electorate to make informed decisions and give proper weight to different speakers and messages.

C

For the same reasons we uphold the application of BCRA §§201 and 311 to the ads, we affirm their application to *Hillary*. We find no constitutional impediment to the application of BCRA's disclaimer and disclosure requirements to a movie broadcast via video-on-demand. And there has been no showing that, as applied in this case, these requirements would impose a chill on speech or expression.

V

...

Modern day movies, television comedies, or skits on *Youtube.com* might portray public officials or public policies in unflattering ways. Yet if a covered transmission during the blackout period creates the background for candidate endorsement or opposition, a felony occurs solely because a corporation, other than an exempt media corporation, has made the "purchase, payment, distribution, loan, advance, deposit, or gift of money or anything of value" in order to engage in political speech. Speech would be suppressed in the realm where its necessity is most evident: in the public dialogue preceding a real election. Governments are often hostile to speech, but under our law and our tradition it seems stranger than fiction for our Government to make this political speech a crime. Yet this is the statute's purpose and design.

Some members of the public might consider *Hillary* to be insightful and instructive; some might find it to be neither high art nor a fair discussion on how to set the Nation's course; still others simply might suspend judgment on these points but decide to think more about issues and candidates. Those choices and assessments, however, are not for the Government to make. "The First Amendment underwrites the freedom to experiment and to create in the realm of thought and speech. Citizens must be free to use new forms, and new forums, for the expression of ideas. The civic discourse belongs to the people, and the Government may not prescribe the means used to conduct it."...

The judgment of the District Court is reversed with respect to the constitutionality of 2 U. S. C. §441b's restrictions on corporate independent expenditures. The judgment is affirmed with respect to BCRA's disclaimer and disclosure requirements. The case is remanded for further proceedings consistent with this opinion.

It is so ordered.

GLOSSARY

Austin: *Austin v. Michigan Chamber of Commerce*, a case in which the Court upheld a prohibition against corporations spending funds to support a candidate or issue.

Bipartisan Campaign Reform Act of 2002: Also known as the McCain-Feingold Act, which sought to regulate the financing of political campaigns, passed in response to a rapid increase in the use of soft money, money raised outside previously regulated times and sources.

facial validity: valid on the surface

McConnell: *McConnell v. Federal Election Commission*, a previous case in which the BCRA was upheld as constitutional.

prolix laws: wordy, written in an extended length which confuses, causing un-clarity rather than clarity.

Document Analysis

Writing for the five member majority of the Court, Justice Kennedy ruled that limitations on the speech of corporations in order to decrease the chance of corruption, or the perception of corruption, was an overly broad remedy for the problem. Without a compelling interest, he wrote, the government should refrain from attempting to create boundaries on what corporations (and individuals) can say about an election or a candidate and when they can say it. For Kennedy, anything short of total freedom in this area would be too burdensome upon the groups, as these entities tried to ascertain what were, and what were not legally made statements about a candidate or issue. However, by an 8 – 1 vote, the Court did keep intact the provision requiring the group, or individual, doing the speaking to be identified. Otherwise, the major provisions of the BCRA were ruled unconstitutional, as were certain provisions of the 1971 law which created the FEC.

Citizens United, having previously distributed the film *Hillary: The Movie*, wanted to show it through a pay-per-view system into 2008, an election year. Knowing that this anti-Clinton film would be seen as electoral-related communications, Citizens United filed suit to keep the FEC from fining them. They sought to either have the film confirmed as not related to the election, because it did not express a view on the election, or to have a determination that the film fell outside the "electioneering communication" section of the BCRA. The logic behind this was the fact that to see it on a pay-per-view system, an individual had to request it be sent to their cable box. In the initial sections of his opinion, Kennedy made it clear that neither of these assertions by Citizens United could be upheld. Kennedy stated that the film focused on a "clearly identified candidate." In addition, he interpreted the content as a "feature-length negative advertisement" about Senator Clinton. For Kennedy, and the others on the Court, it was definitely "electioneering communication."

Kennedy also rejected the concept that an offer for a pay-per-view showing of the film did not constitute a public showing, because it was for one person at a time, not a large group. While Kennedy understood the difference between a regular, over the air or cable, broadcast and pay-per-view, this was not significant in terms of the number of people who could be reached. As he noted, the system being used had the potential for up to 34.5 million viewers of the film. As a result, Kennedy rejected the Citizens United claim that the breadth of distribution caused this film to not be covered by the BCRA.

However, after rejecting the narrow arguments presented by Citizens United, Kennedy and others on the majority moved to the broader issue regarding regulating political speech. Here they went far beyond what Citizens United was asking, although giving Citizens United the victory which it sought. Further examining the BCRA, Kennedy wrote that "Section 441b's prohibition on corporate independent expenditures is thus a ban on speech." He went on to assert, "political speech must prevail against laws that would suppress it," as he ruled that the limitations put in place by the BCRA were unconstitutional. In his examination of the BCRA, Kennedy presented hypothetical situations in which it might be unclear whether or not an organization was violating the law by its activities. Uncertainty, in his eyes, created a burden upon an individual or organization which decreased the ability and likelihood of their participation in the electoral system. This was unacceptable for him.

Kennedy and the Court's majority understood that their action would overturn precedents which had guided the lower courts, as well as parts of two laws. *Austin v. Michigan Chamber of Commerce* had guided lower courts since 1990 when the Court had accepted a Michigan law prohibiting the use of general funds in a corporation's treasury for political purposes. Within that ruling, and within the BCRA itself, an exception had been created for media companies, since the distribution of news was a part of the reason these corporations existed. In addition, the Court had ruled in *McConnell v. Federal Election Commission*, 2003, stating that the law creating the BCRA was constitutional, as the focus of the law was on money not directly used in campaigning, but on auxiliary activities. In *Citizens United v. Federal Election Commission,* the heart of these two rulings were overturned for the broader interpretation of free speech in the electoral process put forward by Kennedy. In *Austin*, it was, in Kennedy's mind, too great a limit upon the free speech of the corporation. In addition, with innovations such as

the internet, a media company, according to his thought process, could no longer be defined. As regarded the *McConnell* case, Kennedy asserted that the need for free speech overrode the logic which had led to that decision.

The major point of the BCRA which was upheld was the need for corporations to identify themselves, within the piece being distributed, as the producers/speakers of the material which was being distributed. These organizations must also make regular reports regarding donors to the organizations. This, Kennedy and the others believed, would act as a check on the power of the corporations when they entered the electoral process. Admitting that the requirements of publicly stating who was responsible for the ad and compiling a list of donors, were a type of burden, the majority of justices did not see them as being arduous enough to be a limiting factor on what was said, or the means by which it was communicated to the public.

Toward the end of his opinion, Kennedy wrote, "The civic discourse belongs to the people, and the Government may not prescribe the means used to conduct it." This was the majority view of the situation and the foundation of why they voted to extend the right of corporate free speech to all issues, and to all days on the calendar. However, for those who believed unfettered money (represented by corporate interests) was a corrupting influence on the electoral process, this ruling was major tragedy for the democratic system.

Essential Themes

When the Supreme Court rules on cases, there are times when it takes a narrow approach to the appeal with which it is dealing, while at others the justices take the opportunity to explore the possible broad ramifications of the case before them. In *Citizens United v. Federal Election Commission* they took the latter approach. They chose to examine the implications of limitations upon the speech of corporations in the electoral process. Since corporations, whether for-profit or non-profit, are composed of and owned by people, the majority of the justices believed that by limiting the speech of corporations, the government was limiting the speech of a particular group of people. They ruled this to be unconstitutional, by allowing any corporation to express the political views of its members via any means and at any time in the electoral process. The only boundary on the free expression of the "corporation's" ideas, was that, within the electoral related message, the corporation, or organization, must identify itself as the source of the material. This is true no matter what format is used to communicate the opinion or facts to the general public. Secondary requirements were that the corporation must identify the source of its funds and must act independently from the official campaign of the candidate or political party.

In the *Citizens United* ruling, the Court did not do away with limits on campaign contributions to the official campaign funds of the various candidates by individuals, nor the prohibition against corporations or unions make contributions to official campaign committees. Thus, it could be argued that for the official campaigns, the ruling had no effect. However, it allowed many more unofficial, non-affiliated campaign organizations to emerge with the potential to have a great impact upon the races.

In light of the *Citizens United* ruling, SpeechNOW. org expanded a suit it had filed against the FEC, hoping to do away with the contribution limits and the reporting requirements which the FEC had instructed them to follow prior to the *Citizens United* ruling. The United States Court of Appeals for the District of Columbia Circuit upheld the reporting requirement mandated by the FEC, just as the reporting requirements remained in *Citizens United*. However, following the logic of *Citizens United* the appeals court did away with any limitations on the amount of money individuals or groups could give to political groups not formally affiliated with political candidates or parties. The Supreme Court refused to hear the case, leaving the appeals court's *SpeechNOW.org* ruling as the precedent for other groups. This resulted in these independent political action committees' income growing from $62 million, in 2010, to $1.1 billion in 2016.

As a result of *Citizens United*, and the case filed by SpeechNOW.org, there has been a substantial increase in the amount of money pumped into political campaigns. In accordance with the rulings, this has not been money donated to the formal political party or candidate organizations; rather these are donations given to what are supposed to be independent advocates for or against candidates. The ruling has resulted in much more information being shared with the general public, and many more opinions being expressed. However, the quality and veracity of the independently-sponsored ads have not generally been held to the same standards as the official ads, and for some this is troubling. It is unclear whether in the long run, the optimistic view of the majority of the Court justices, that more ideas and greater freedom of speech will be better for the nation, or the pessimistic view of the minority, that a few rich individuals and groups will dominate the political system, will be upheld.

In addition, this ruling, granting corporations a fuller type of personhood, through the First Amendment rights of speech, has been used by other corporations to seek other rights. Thus, when Hobby Lobby refused to abide by all the provisions of Obamacare, which ended up as *Burwell v. Hobby Lobby Stores,* Hobby Lobby cited the *Citizens United* case as Hobby Lobby successfully sought protection from certain provisions of the Affordable Care Act on the basis of the closely held corporation's religious freedom. This has raised questions in many people's minds, regarding how far a corporation's legal personhood will extend.

—*Donald A. Watt, Ph.D.*

Bibliography and Additional Reading

Barnes, Robert and Dan Eggen. "Supreme Court rejects limits on corporate spending on political campaigns." *Washingtonpost.com.* Washington: The Washington Post Company, 2010. Web. 3 September 2017.

Clements, Jeffrey D. with Bill Moyers. *Corporations Are Not People: Reclaiming Democracy from Big Money and Global Corporations.* (2nd ed.) San Francisco: Berett-Koehler Publishers, 2014. Print.

Moyers, Bill with Floyd Abrams and Trevor Potter. ""Citizens United v. FEC." *Bill Moyers Journal.* (including *Frontline* September 4, 2009 broadcast) Washington: Public Affairs Television, 2017. Web 3 September 2017.

Oyez. "Citizens United v. Federal Election Commission." *Oyez.* Chicago: Kent College of Law at Illinois Tech, 2017. Web. 1 September 2017.

Post, Robert C. with Pamela S. Karlan, Lawrence Lessing, Frank I. Michelman, and Nadia Urbinati. *Citizens Divided: Campaign Finance Reform and the Constitution.* (The Tanner Lectures on Human Values) Cambridge: Harvard University Press, 2014. Print.

Spakovsky, Hans von. "Citizens United and the Restoration of the First Amendment." *The Heritage Foundation.* Washington: The Heritage Foundation, 2010. Web. 3 September 2017.

Youn, Monica (ed.) *Money, Politics, and the Constitution: Beyond Citizens United.* New York: The Century Foundation, 2011. Print.

THE SEVENTH PARTY SYSTEM? 2016-

In 2016, the results of the presidential election caused some observers to wonder whether a new, seventh party system might be taking shape. A complete political outsider, Donald Trump, won on the Republican ticket, gaining enough electoral votes to secure a victory yet falling short in the popular vote, which went to his opponent, Hillary Clinton. Moreover, Trump proceeded to change the nature of the Republican Party, or at least the nature of its political platform. He tossed out long-standing principles of fiscal conservatism, free trade, international security, trust in the federal justice system, individual moral responsibility, and, indeed, the very character of the presidency. Although during the election Trump won in all the usual Republican strongholds, during his first year in office he began, according to polls and some of the early state and district races, to turn off suburban voters and, especially, women voters. Trump also consistently polled in historically low numbers for a first-year president: his "favorability" ratings stayed at between 33 percent and 43 percent. The new president, in addition to not fitting the traditional mold, was dogged by investigations into Russia's involvement in distorting the campaign through the use of fake news and data hacks, and by various sexual allegations by women.

Some observers have argued that the seeds of the Trump presidency may have first been planted by the nomination, in 2008, of Governor Sarah Palin of Alaska as John McCain's running mate. For Palin, too, was an unconventional politician who eschewed "experts" and establishment norms in favor of homegrown wisdom. Although the McCain-Palin ticket did not do well, in 2010 the so-called Tea Party revolt inside the Republican Party echoed some of Palin's anti-establishment themes—although the Tea Partiers had their own, largely fiscal, agenda. Many of those Tea Partiers, nevertheless, are now avowed Trumpites.

The two parties in 2018 never seemed so far apart, as the Republicans under Trump continued to shift rightward and the Democrats in reaction to Trump began to shift leftward and to return to an earlier successful strategy—mass protests.

Hillary Clinton's Acceptance Speech at the 2016 Democratic National Convention

Date: July 28, 2016
Author: Hillary Rodham Clinton
Genre: Speech

Summary Overview

On the last night of the Democratic National Convention, Hillary Rodham Clinton finally took the stage to accept formally her nomination as the Democratic candidate for the United States presidential election in 2016. After a tense primary campaign between herself and challenger Senator Bernie Sanders, as well as a previous presidential run in 2008, this moment represented a culmination of many years of work by Clinton and her supporters. This moment also represented the first time a major national political party in the United States nominated a woman to be its presidential candidate, and was an important milestone for many women who had anticipated seeing a woman run for the highest office in the country. Clinton's speech shows a candidate ready to approach the next phase of the election cycle by establishing her vision for the United States and uniting her party and other supporters against her opponent, Republican Donald J. Trump.

Defining Moment

Speculation swirled for months around whether Hillary Clinton would run for president again before she officially announced her campaign in April 2015. She was one of the most notable and experienced women in politics in addition to the fact that she had run a formidable earlier campaign for the presidency during the 2008 Democratic primaries against President Obama. When she formally suspended her presidential campaign in 2008, she said to a crowd of supporters: "I am a woman and, like millions of women, I know there are still barriers and biases out there, often unconscious, and I want to build an America that respects and embraces the potential of every last one of us." After she stepped down from her role as President Obama's secretary of state in 2013, many suspected that she was preparing to capitalize on this earlier assertion and build a new campaign for 2016.

Hillary Clinton's second presidential campaign was not just a result of her deciding that she finally had the right support and sufficient experience to run successfully. The 2008 Democratic primary election between a woman and an African-American man was a radical moment in American history, which had largely been a narrative of white male political actors. The 2008 primaries, and Obama's successful presidential campaigns in 2008 and 2012, redefined who could plausibly run for and be elected to the highest political offices.

However, Clinton's path to the Democratic nomination was not a certainty despite her political experience and number of connections. Independent Senator Bernie Sanders of Vermont ran a competitive campaign against the former Secretary of State during the primaries between 2015 and 2016. Compared to the perspective of Clinton as an "establishment" politician," the Sanders campaign particularly excited young voters, utilized grassroots organizing, and raised millions through small donations. Although there were fears of widening internal divisions between progressive voters, ultimately Sanders suspended his campaign after it was clear that Clinton received more votes. Although Clinton practically clinched her nomination by June 2016, the Democratic National Convention at the end of July 2016 was the official venue for recognizing this feat and strengthening party bonds around the contender whom it would send to fight against the Republicans in the main presidential election in November of the same year.

Author Biography

Hillary Rodham was born in Chicago on October 26, 1947. She was politically active from an early age and continued to have an active political career over the years. She gained renown for her commencement ceremony speech as valedictorian at Wellesley College in 1969, in which she eloquently supported the student activist movements. As a student at Yale Law School, she not only met her future husband, Bill Clinton, who was then a student from Arkansas with a similar dedication to liberal politics; she also worked for the Children's Defense Fund and participated on the staff for the House Judiciary Committee investigating the Watergate scandal.

After she married Bill Clinton in 1975 and moved to Arkansas, Hillary Rodham, who had not yet taken her husband's last name, agreed to subordinate her own political ambitions for his in a southern state with conservative norms. Still, she continued to pursue her career and the policy goals that interested her. She became the first female partner at Rose Law Firm and actively advocated for children's health, education, and better medical care for poor people. After Bill Clinton was elected president of the United States in 1992 and 1996, she, now as Hillary Rodham Clinton, continued to take a more active political role than previous political spouses; she continued in this capacity to pursue the same interests that motivated her as a student and as First Lady of Arkansas. Although her efforts to pass universal healthcare reform were not successful, she did play a critical role in passing the Children's Healthcare Initiative Program.

After her husband's two terms, she began a political career in her own name. She was elected senator of New York in 2000. While senator, she was conspicuously present at the World Trade Center site after the terrorist attack of September 11, comforting victims and praising clean-up efforts. On the other hand, she voted in 2002 to give the Bush administration the prerogative to invade Iraq, a vote she later came to regret. In 2008 she decided to run for president, but was outpolled by fellow senator Barack Obama. Upon Obama's election to the presidency, she agreed to become his Secretary of State. As diplomat, she continued her active work, which included disaster relief efforts in Haiti and helping the president to send a Navy SEAL team to kill the terrorist leader Osama bin Laden, as well as continuing to pursue issues related to women and children.

However, political opponents have often capitalized on her and her husband's personal lives and professional careers to foment controversy. Her husband's infidelity, her use of a private e-mail server, and the attack at a U.S. embassy in Benghazi while she was Secretary of State are a few of the most notable scandals that threatened to derail her second presidential run in 2016. Despite a hard-fought primary battle with Senator Bernie Sanders of Vermont, she won the Democratic nomination and excited many Americans with the possibility that she might become the United States' first female president, but she was still dogged by controversy, which only intensified in the media as hacked e-mails were published online by internet vigilante group Wikileaks. This speculation over e-mails may have cost her the general election of November 2016, in which she won the popular vote but was still defeated based on electoral college votes by Republican Donald Trump in one of the most stunning upsets in American electoral history.

HISTORICAL DOCUMENT

Thank you! Thank you for that amazing welcome. And Chelsea, thank you. I'm so proud to be your mother and so proud of the woman you've become. Thanks for bringing Marc into our family, and Charlotte and Aidan into the world. And Bill, that conversation we started in the law library 45 years ago is still going strong. It's lasted through good times that filled us with joy, and hard times that tested us. And I've even gotten a few words in along the way. On Tuesday night, I was so happy to see that my Explainer-in-Chief is still on the job. I'm also grateful to the rest of my family and the friends of a lifetime.

To all of you whose hard work brought us here tonight.

And to those of you who joined our campaign this week. And what a remarkable week it's been.

We heard the man from Hope, Bill Clinton. And the man of Hope, Barack Obama. America is stronger because of President Obama's leadership, and I'm better because of his friendship.

We heard from our terrific vice president, the one-and-only Joe Biden, who spoke from his big heart about our party's commitment to working people.

First Lady Michelle Obama reminded us that our children are watching, and the president we elect is going to be their president, too.

And for those of you out there who are just getting to know Tim Kaine—you're soon going to understand why the people of Virginia keep promoting him: from City Council and mayor, to Governor, and now Senator. He'll make the whole country proud as our Vice President.

And…I want to thank Bernie Sanders. Bernie, your campaign inspired millions of Americans, particularly the young people who threw their hearts and souls into our primary. You've put economic and social justice issues front and center, where they belong. And to all of your supporters here and around the country: I want you to know, I've heard you. Your cause is our cause.

Our country needs your ideas, energy, and passion. That's the only way we can turn our progressive platform into real change for America. We wrote it together—now let's go out there and make it happen together.

My friends, we've come to Philadelphia—the birthplace of our nation—because what happened in this city 240 years ago still has something to teach us today. We all know the story. But we usually focus on how it turned out—and not enough on how close that story came to never being written at all.

When representatives from 13 unruly colonies met just down the road from here, some wanted to stick with the King. Some wanted to stick it to the king, and go their own way. The revolution hung in the balance. Then somehow they began listening to each other … compromising … finding common purpose. And by the time they left Philadelphia, they had begun to see themselves as one nation. That's what made it possible to stand up to a King.

That took courage. They had courage.

Our Founders embraced the enduring truth that we are stronger together. America is once again at a moment of reckoning. Powerful forces are threatening to pull us apart. Bonds of trust and respect are fraying. And just as with our founders, there are no guarantees. It truly is up to us. We have to decide whether we all will work together so we all can rise together.

Our country's motto is *e pluribus unum*: out of many, we are one. Will we stay true to that motto? Well, we heard Donald Trump's answer last week at his convention. He wants to divide us—from the rest of the world, and from each other. He's betting that the perils of today's world will blind us to its unlimited promise. He's

taken the Republican Party a long way … from "Morning in America" to "Midnight in America." He wants us to fear the future and fear each other.

Well, a great Democratic President, Franklin Delano Roosevelt, came up with the perfect rebuke to Trump more than eighty years ago, during a much more perilous time. "The only thing we have to fear is fear itself."

Now we are clear-eyed about what our country is up against. But we are not afraid. We will rise to the challenge, just as we always have. We will not build a wall. Instead, we will build an economy where everyone who wants a good paying job can get one. And we'll build a path to citizenship for millions of immigrants who are already contributing to our economy! We will not ban a religion. We will work with all Americans and our allies to fight terrorism.

There's a lot of work to do. Too many people haven't had a pay raise since the crash. There's too much inequality. Too little social mobility. Too much paralysis in Washington. Too many threats at home and abroad.

But just look at the strengths we bring to meet these challenges. We have the most dynamic and diverse people in the world. We have the most tolerant and generous young people we've ever had. We have the most powerful military. The most innovative entrepreneurs. The most enduring values. Freedom and equality, justice and opportunity.

We should be so proud that these words are associated with us. That when people hear them—they hear …America.

So don't let anyone tell you that our country is weak. We're not.

Don't let anyone tell you we don't have what it takes. We do.

And most of all, don't believe anyone who says: "I alone can fix it."

Those were actually Donald Trump's words in Cleveland. And they should set off alarm bells for all of us. Really? I alone can fix it? Isn't he forgetting? Troops on the front lines. Police officers and fire fighters who run toward danger. Doctors and nurses who care for us. Teachers who change lives. Entrepreneurs who see possibilities in every problem. Mothers who lost children to violence and are building a movement to keep other kids safe.

He's forgetting every last one of us.

Americans don't say: "I alone can fix it." We say: "We'll fix it together."

Remember: Our Founders fought a revolution and wrote a Constitution so America would never be a nation where one person had all the power. Two hundred and forty years later, we still put our faith in each other.

Look at what happened in Dallas after the assassinations of five brave police officers. Chief David Brown asked the community to support his force, maybe even join them. And you know how the community responded? Nearly 500 people applied in just 12 days. That's how Americans answer when the call for help goes out.

20 years ago I wrote a book called "It Takes a Village." A lot of people looked at the title and asked, what the heck do you mean by that? This is what I mean. None of us can raise a family, build a business, heal a community or lift a country totally alone. America needs every one of us to lend our energy, our talents, our ambition to making our nation better and stronger. I believe that with all my heart.

That's why "Stronger Together" is not just a lesson from our history. It's not just a slogan for our campaign. It's a guiding principle for the country we've always been and the future we're going to build. A country where the economy works for everyone, not just those at the top. Where you can get a good job and send your kids to a good school, no matter what ZIP code you live in. A country where all our children can dream, and those dreams are within reach. Where families are strong … communities are safe. And yes, love trumps hate.

That's the country we're fighting for. That's the future we're working toward. And so it is with humility … determination … and boundless confidence in America's promise … that I accept your nomination for President of the United States!

Now, sometimes the people at this podium are new to the national stage. As you know, I'm not one of those people. I've been your first lady. Served 8 years as a Senator from the great state of New York. I ran for President and lost. Then I represented all of you as Secretary of State.

But my job titles only tell you what I've done. They don't tell you why. The truth is, through all these years of public service, the "service" part has always come easier to me than the "public" part. I get it that some people just don't know what to make of me. So let me tell you.

The family I'm from … well, no one had their name on big buildings. My family were builders of a different kind. Builders in the way most American families are. They used whatever tools they had—whatever God gave them—and whatever life in America provided—and built better lives and better futures for their kids. My grandfather worked in the same Scranton lace mill for 50 years. Because he believed that if he gave everything he had, his children would have a better life than he did. And he was right.

My dad, Hugh, made it to college. He played football at Penn State and enlisted in the Navy after Pearl Harbor. When the war was over he started his own small business, printing fabric for draperies. I remember watching him stand for hours over silk screens. He wanted to give my brothers and me opportunities he never had. And he did.

My mother, Dorothy, was abandoned by her parents as a young girl. She ended up on her own at 14, working as a house maid. She was saved by the kindness of others. Her first grade teacher saw she had nothing to eat at lunch, and brought extra food to share. The lesson she passed on to me years later stuck with me: No one gets through life alone. We have to look out for each other and lift each other up. She made sure I learned the words of our Methodist faith: "Do all the good you can, for all the people you can, in all the ways you can, as long as ever you can."

I went to work for the Children's Defense Fund, going door-to-door in New Bedford, Massachusetts on behalf of children with disabilities who were denied the chance to go to school. I remember meeting a young girl in a wheelchair on the small back porch of her house. She told me how badly she wanted to go to school—it just didn't seem possible. And I couldn't stop thinking of my mother and what she went through as a child. It became clear to me that simply caring is not enough.

To drive real progress, you have to change both hearts and laws. You need both understanding and action. So we gathered facts. We built a coalition. And our work helped convince Congress to ensure access to education for all students with disabilities. It's a big idea, isn't it? Every kid with a disability has the right to go to school. But how do you make an idea like that real? You do it step-by-step, year-by-year … sometimes even door-by-door.

And my heart just swelled when I saw Anastasia Somoza on this stage, representing millions of young people who—because of those changes to our laws—are able to get an education. It's true … I sweat the details of policy—whether we're talking about the exact level of lead in the drinking water in Flint, Michigan, the number of mental health facilities in Iowa, or the cost of your prescription drugs.

Because it's not just a detail if it's your kid—if it's your family. It's a big deal. And it should be a big deal to your president.

Over the last three days, you've seen some of the people who've inspired me. People who let me into their lives, and became a part of mine. People like Ryan Moore and Lauren Manning. They told their stories Tuesday night. I first met Ryan as a seven-year old. He was wearing a full body brace that must have weighed forty pounds. Children like Ryan kept me going when our plan for universal health care failed … and kept me working with leaders of both parties to help create the Children's Health Insurance Program that covers 8 million kids every year.

Lauren was gravely injured on 9/11. It was the thought of her, and Debbie St. John, and John Dolan and Joe Sweeney, and all the victims and survivors, that kept me working as hard as I could in the Senate on behalf of 9/11 families, and our first responders who got sick from their time at Ground Zero.

I was still thinking of Lauren, Debbie and all the others ten years later in the White House Situation Room when President Obama made the courageous decision that finally brought Osama bin Laden to justice.

In this campaign, I've met so many people who motivate me to keep fighting for change. And, with your help, I will carry all of your voices and stories with me to the White House. I will be a President for Democrats, Republicans, and Independents. For the struggling, the striving and the successful. For those who vote for me and those who don't. For all Americans.

Tonight, we've reached a milestone in our nation's march toward a more perfect union: the first time that a major party has nominated a woman for President. Standing here as my mother's daughter, and my daughter's mother, I'm so happy this day has come. Happy for grandmothers and little girls and everyone in between.

Happy for boys and men, too—because when any barrier falls in America, for anyone, it clears the way for everyone. When there are no ceilings, the sky's the limit.

So let's keep going, until every one of the 161 million women and girls across America has the opportunity she deserves. Because even more important than the history we make tonight, is the history we will write together in the years ahead.

Let's begin with what we're going to do to help working people in our country get ahead and stay ahead.

Now, I don't think President Obama and Vice President Biden get the credit they deserve for saving us from the worst economic crisis of our lifetimes. Our economy is so much stronger than when they took office. Nearly 15 million new private-sector jobs. Twenty million more Americans with health insurance. And an auto industry that just had its best year ever. That's real progress. But none of us can be satisfied with the status quo. Not by a long shot.

We're still facing deep-seated problems that developed long before the recession and have stayed with us through the recovery. I've gone around our country talking to working families. And I've heard from so many of you who feel like the economy just isn't working. Some of you are frustrated—even furious. And you know what? You're right. It's not yet working the way it should. Americans are willing to work—and work hard. But right now, an awful lot of people feel there is less and less respect for the work they do. And less respect for them, period.

Democrats are the party of working people. But we haven't done a good enough job showing that we get what you're going through, and that we're going to do something about it. So I want to tell you tonight how we will empower Americans to live better lives.

My primary mission as President will be to create more opportunity and more good jobs with rising wages right here in the United States. From my first day in office to my last! Especially in places that for too long have been left out and left behind. From our inner cities to our small towns, from Indian Country to Coal Country. From communities ravaged by addiction to regions hollowed out by plant closures.

And here's what I believe.

I believe America thrives when the middle class thrives. I believe that our economy isn't working the way it should because our democracy isn't working the way it should. That's why we need to appoint Supreme Court justices who will get money out of politics and expand voting rights, not restrict them. And we'll pass a constitutional amendment to overturn Citizens United!

I believe American corporations that have gotten so much from our country should be just as patriotic in return. Many of them are. But too many aren't. It's wrong to take tax breaks with one hand and give out pink slips with the other. And I believe Wall Street can never, ever be allowed to wreck Main Street again.

I believe in science. I believe that climate change is real and that we can save our planet while creating millions of good-paying clean energy jobs.

I believe that when we have millions of hardworking immigrants contributing to our economy, it would be self-defeating and inhumane to kick them out. Comprehensive immigration reform will grow our economy and keep families together—and it's the right thing to do.

Whatever party you belong to, or if you belong to no party at all, if you share these beliefs, this is your campaign. If you believe that companies should share profits with their workers, not pad executive bonuses, join us.

If you believe the minimum wage should be a living wage … and no one working full time should have to raise their children in poverty … join us.

If you believe that every man, woman, and child in America has the right to affordable health care … join us.

If you believe that we should say "no" to unfair trade deals … that we should stand up to China … that we should support our steelworkers and autoworkers and homegrown manufacturers … join us.

If you believe we should expand Social Security and protect a woman's right to make her own health care decisions … join us.

And yes, if you believe that your working mother, wife, sister, or daughter deserves equal pay … join us.

Let's make sure this economy works for everyone, not just those at the top. Now, you didn't hear any of this from Donald Trump at his convention. He spoke for 70-odd minutes—and I do mean odd. And he offered zero solutions. But we already know he doesn't believe these things. No wonder he doesn't like talking about his plans. You might have noticed, I love talking about mine.

In my first 100 days, we will work with both parties to pass the biggest investment in new, good-paying jobs since World War II. Jobs in manufacturing, clean energy, technology and innovation, small business, and infrastructure. If we invest in infrastructure now, we'll not only create jobs today, but lay the foundation for the jobs of the future. And we will transform the way we prepare our young people for those jobs.

Bernie Sanders and I will work together to make college tuition-free for the middle class and debt-free for all! We will also liberate millions of people who already have student debt. It's just not right that Donald Trump can ignore his debts, but students and families can't refinance theirs.

And here's something we don't say often enough: College is crucial, but a four-year degree should not be the only path to a good job. We're going to help more people learn a skill or practice a trade and make a good living doing it.

We're going to give small businesses a boost. Make it easier to get credit. Way too many dreams die in the parking lots of banks. In America, if you can dream it, you should be able to build it.

We're going to help you balance family and work. And you know what, if fighting for affordable child care and paid family leave is playing the "woman card," then Deal Me In!

(Oh, you've heard that one?)

Now, here's the thing, we're not only going to make all these investments, we're going to pay for every single one of them. And here's how: Wall Street, corporations, and the super rich are going to start paying their fair share of taxes. Not because we resent success. Because when more than 90 percent of the gains have gone to the top 1 percent, that's where the money is. And if companies take tax breaks and then ship jobs overseas, we'll make them pay us back. And we'll put that money to work where it belongs … creating jobs here at home!

Now I know some of you are sitting at home thinking, well that all sounds pretty good. But how are you going to get it done? How are you going to break through the gridlock in Washington? Look at my record. I've worked across the aisle to pass laws and treaties and to launch new programs that help millions of people. And if you give me the chance, that's what I'll do as President. But Trump, he's a businessman. He must know something about the economy.

Well, let's take a closer look. In Atlantic City, 60 miles from here, you'll find contractors and small businesses who lost everything because Donald Trump refused to pay his bills. People who did the work and needed the money, and didn't get it—not because he couldn't pay them, but because he wouldn't pay them.

That sales pitch he's making to be your president? Put your faith in him—and you'll win big? That's the same sales pitch he made to all those small businesses. Then Trump walked away, and left working people holding the bag. He also talks a big game about putting America First. Please explain to me what part of America First leads him to make Trump ties in China, not Colorado. Trump suits in Mexico, not Michigan. Trump furniture in Turkey, not Ohio. Trump picture frames in India, not Wisconsin. Donald Trump says he wants to make America great again—well, he could start by actually making things in America again.

The choice we face is just as stark when it comes to our national security. Anyone reading the news can see the threats and turbulence we face. From Baghdad and Kabul, to Nice and Paris and Brussels, to San Bernardino and Orlando, we're dealing with determined enemies that must be defeated. No wonder people are anxious and looking for reassurance. Looking for steady leadership.

You want a leader who understands we are stronger when we work with our allies around the world and care for our veterans here at home. Keeping our nation safe and honoring the people who do it will be my highest priority. I'm proud that we put a lid on Iran's nuclear program without firing a single shot—now we have to enforce it, and keep supporting Israel's security. I'm proud that we shaped a global climate agreement—now we have to hold every country accountable to their commitments, including ourselves. I'm proud to stand by our allies in NATO against any threat they face, including from Russia.

I've laid out my strategy for defeating ISIS. We will strike their sanctuaries from the air, and support local forces taking them out on the ground. We will surge our intelligence so that we detect and prevent attacks before they happen. We will disrupt their efforts online to reach and radicalize young people in our country. It won't be easy or quick, but make no mistake—we will prevail.

Now Donald Trump says, and this is a quote, "I know more about ISIS than the generals do." No, Donald, you don't.

He thinks that he knows more than our military because he claimed our armed forces are "a disaster." Well, I've had the privilege to work closely with our troops and our veterans for many years, including as a senator on the Armed Services Committee. I know how wrong he is. Our military is a national treasure.

We entrust our commander-in-chief to make the hardest decisions our nation faces. Decisions about war and peace. Life and death. A president should respect the men and women who risk their lives to serve our country—including the sons of Tim Kaine and Mike Pence, both Marines.

Ask yourself: Does Donald Trump have the temperament to be Commander-in-Chief? Donald Trump can't even handle the rough-and-tumble of a presidential campaign. He loses his cool at the slightest provocation. When he's gotten a tough question from a reporter. When he's challenged in a debate. When he sees a protester at a rally. Imagine him in the Oval Office facing a real crisis. A man you can bait with a tweet is not a man we can trust with nuclear weapons.

I can't put it any better than Jackie Kennedy did after the Cuban Missile Crisis. She said that what worried President Kennedy during that very dangerous time was that a war might be started—not by big men with self-control and restraint, but by little men—the ones moved by fear and pride.

America's strength doesn't come from lashing out. Strength relies on smarts, judgment, cool resolve, and the precise and strategic application of power. That's the kind of Commander-in-Chief I pledge to be.

And if we're serious about keeping our country safe, we also can't afford to have a President who's in the pocket of the gun lobby. I'm not here to repeal the Second Amendment. I'm not here to take away your guns. I just don't want you to be shot by someone who shouldn't have a gun in the first place. We should be working with responsible gun owners to pass common-sense reforms and keep guns out of the hands of criminals, terrorists and all others who would do us harm.

For decades, people have said this issue was too hard

to solve and the politics were too hot to touch. But I ask you: How can we just stand by and do nothing? You heard, you saw, family members of people killed by gun violence. You heard, you saw, family members of police officers killed in the line of duty because they were out-gunned by criminals. I refuse to believe we can't find common ground here.

We have to heal the divides in our country. Not just on guns. But on race. Immigration. And more. That starts with listening to each other. Hearing each other. Trying, as best we can, to walk in each other's shoes. So let's put ourselves in the shoes of young black and Latino men and women who face the effects of systemic racism, and are made to feel like their lives are disposable. Let's put ourselves in the shoes of police officers, kissing their kids and spouses goodbye every day and heading off to do a dangerous and necessary job.

We will reform our criminal justice system from end-to-end, and rebuild trust between law enforcement and the communities they serve. We will defend all our rights—civil rights, human rights and voting rights … women's rights and workers' rights … LGBT rights and the rights of people with disabilities! And we will stand up against mean and divisive rhetoric wherever it comes from.

For the past year, many people made the mistake of laughing off Donald Trump's comments—excusing him as an entertainer just putting on a show. They think he couldn't possibly mean all the horrible things he says—like when he called women "pigs." Or said that an American judge couldn't be fair because of his Mexican heritage. Or when he mocks and mimics a reporter with a disability. Or insults prisoners of war like John McCain—a true hero and patriot who deserves our respect.

At first, I admit, I couldn't believe he meant it either. It was just too hard to fathom—that someone who wants to lead our nation could say those things. Could be like that. But here's the sad truth: There is no other Donald Trump … This is it. And in the end, it comes down to what Donald Trump doesn't get: that America is great—because America is good.

So enough with the bigotry and bombast. Donald Trump's not offering real change. He's offering empty promises. What are we offering? A bold agenda to improve the lives of people across our country—to keep you safe, to get you good jobs, and to give your kids the opportunities they deserve.

The choice is clear. Every generation of Americans has come together to make our country freer, fairer, and stronger. None of us can do it alone. I know that at a time when so much seems to be pulling us apart, it can be hard to imagine how we'll ever pull together again. But I'm here to tell you tonight—progress is possible. I know because I've seen it in the lives of people across America who get knocked down and get right back up. And I know it from my own life. More than a few times, I've had to pick myself up and get back in the game.

Like so much else, I got this from my mother. She never let me back down from any challenge. When I tried to hide from a neighborhood bully, she literally blocked the door. "Go back out there," she said. And she was right. You have to stand up to bullies. You have to keep working to make things better, even when the odds are long and the opposition is fierce. We lost my mother a few years ago. I miss her every day. And I still hear her voice urging me to keep working, keep fighting for right, no matter what.

That's what we need to do together as a nation. Though "we may not live to see the glory," as the song from the musical Hamilton goes, "let us gladly join the fight." Let our legacy be about "planting seeds in a garden you never get to see." That's why we're here … not just in this hall, but on this Earth. The Founders showed us that. And so have many others since. They were drawn together by love of country, and the selfless passion to build something better for all who follow.

That is the story of America. And we begin a new chapter tonight. Yes, the world is watching what we do. Yes, America's destiny is ours to choose. So let's be stronger together. Looking to the future with courage and confidence. Building a better tomorrow for our beloved children and our beloved country. When we do, America will be greater than ever.

Thank you and may God bless the United States of America!

Document Analysis

During important occasions in the 2016 presidential election, Hillary Rodham Clinton often wore outfits specifically designed to communicate a message. As she delivered her speech to a large crowd on July 28, 2016, she was dressed in a white pantsuit in homage to the color suffragettes in the early twentieth century commonly wore. In her convention speech, however, Clinton devotes only a few sentences to the historical gravity of the moment, as she was the first woman nominated by a major party as their presidential candidate. Instead, she focuses her speech much more on her campaign's motto, "Stronger Together," than on the gendered implications of her nomination. The theme of unity emphasizes that Clinton is a candidate who represents the core principles of the country, as well as it implies that Trump represents the direct opposite.

Clinton begins her speech by framing it around people other than herself who have worked together to accomplish a great feat. She first thanks many of the previous speakers and supporters at the convention, and then transitions into an overview of American history. Her review focuses on the collaborative efforts of the thirteen original colonies against one British king. Since she describes their fight against a king, Clinton is clearly describing the Founders as they came together to write the Declaration of Independence rather than another moment, like the Constitutional Convention, when she says: "somehow they began listening to each other … compromising … finding common purpose. And by the time they left Philadelphia, they had begun to see themselves as one nation." She continues to reinforce the ideals of compromise and collaboration as defining characteristics of the United States by citing the country's motto, *e pluribus unum*. Clinton translates this as "out of many, we are one," but she has included "we" into the translation where it does not exist in the Latin. This slight addition contributes to Clinton's depiction of the United States as a unified community built on cooperation.

After she transitions to introduce herself, Clinton similarly presents herself as practicing the same values as the Founders. Her family instilled in her the idea of service on behalf of others, and her career reflects the subordination of the self for a greater community good. After meeting one girl who was unable to go to school, she says that she was determined to change this. She does not put the emphasis on herself, but includes herself in a larger process: "We built a coalition. And our work helped convince Congress to ensure access to education for all students with disabilities." She completes this characterization of herself by saying finally: "I will be a President for Democrats, Republicans, and Independents. For the struggling, the striving and the successful. For those who vote for me and those who don't. For all Americans." Her opponent, on the other hand, she characterizes as more self-centered. Donald Trump uses the pronoun "I," as in "I alone can fix it," compared to Clinton, who repeatedly stresses the pronoun "we." Donald Trump, as she explains, mocks and attacks people for their identities, rather than working together with different people. He, she says, does not represent the "story of America," but she does.

This "story of America," of course, leaves out the many examples of hardship and division in the country's history. Clinton focuses on the positive aspects of American history, instead of, for example, on the great obstacles the women's rights movement had to combat to make her speech even conceivable. Clinton's focus on unity and history shows a politician hoping to present herself as a traditional candidate as well as a politician pivoting away from interparty divisions and towards a harder fight ahead.

Essential Themes

In her concession speech on November 9, 2016, Hillary Clinton alluded to her 2008 concession speech and said: "Now, I know we have still not shattered that highest and hardest glass ceiling, but someday someone will—and hopefully sooner than we might think right now." Although Hillary Clinton's stunning defeat meant that she would not be the first female president of the United States, her electoral college loss to Donald Trump inspired many women to follow her lead in running for office. Groups like Emerge America and Ready to Run which train women to run for office noticed a surge of women signing up and expressing interest in seeking political office in the wake of Clinton's defeat. Some of these new potential political candidates expressed that they were driven by Donald Trump's sexism, others by Clinton's loss. This surge in women running for political office may start to resolve eventually the imbalance in gender representation in U.S. politics. In 2017 women represented roughly twenty percent of the U.S. Congress; only six women held governorships out of fifty states; and women held only twenty five percent of the seats in state legislatures.

Increased female representation in positions of political power is not just a matter of symbolic importance. Research shows that women govern differently than men. In Congress, women sponsor and co-sponsor more bills, they bring more federal money to their districts, and they drive policies that support women, children, social welfare, and national security. Female politicians also tend to be more bipartisan and build coalitions, both of which qualities can be essential behind the scenes tactics to getting bills passed. Female legislators tend to bring both their experience as women to the bills they write and they tend to work in collaborative ways to pass those bills. Hillary Clinton's acceptance speech and her career as a whole support this model of female governing. A firm believer that "women's rights are human rights," she advocated for children and women from the time she was a student at Yale Law, and she ran her presidential campaign on the idea that the country was stronger working together than divided by partisan rhetoric.

—*Ashleigh Fata, MA*

Bibliography and Additional Reading

Clinton, Hillary Rodham. *What Happened*. New York: Simon & Schuster, 2017.

Center for American Women and Politics. Eagleton Institute of Politics at Rutgers U, 2017, http://www.cawp.rutgers.edu/. Accessed Nov. 1. 2017.

Miller, Claire Cain. "Women Actually Do Govern Differently." *The New York Times*, 10 Nov. 2016, https://www.nytimes.com/2016/11/10/upshot/women-actually-do-govern-differently.html.

Orr, Katie and Megan Kamerick. "Trump's Election Drives More Women to Consider Running for Office." *NPR*, 23 Feb. 2017, http://www.npr.org/2017/02/23/515438978/trumps-election-drives-more-women-to-consider-running-for-office.

■ Fake News—Pope Francis' Alleged Endorsement of Donald Trump

Date: July, 2016
Author: Unknown
Genre: Speech; article

Summary Overview

Misleading, even purposefully misleading, news stories are by no means new. However, given the advent of the Internet and the particular dynamics of the 2016 presidential election, fake news played a unprecedented role in that election. Entrepreneurial Americans trying to make money, and foreign powers trying to influence United States politics, published a wide array of fake news articles in the lead up to the 2016 vote. Unlike in the past when most Americans got their news primarily from reputable journalistic sources, many Americans in the 2010s began to rely on their social media networks to receive news shared by friends and acquaintances. The document reprinted here is the core of a fake news article allegedly quoting Pope Francis on his decision to endorse Donald Trump over Hillary Clinton in the 2016 race; it was widely shared on social media at the time.

Defining Moment

Deception, falsehoods, and lies, constants of human life as old as communication itself, have taken on a new life in American politics in the 2010s.

Deception plays a central role in many origin stories, such as the *Book of Genesis* and Hesiod's *Theogony*, as various cultures work their way through reconciling the central role that deception plays in human society. The innovation of writing only made deception easier. In the dialogue *Phaedrus*, Plato's character of Socrates discusses how the spoken word is more amenable to truth than the written word because a speaker must declare himself openly while a writer can remain anonymous. The framers of the U.S. Constitution understood that deceptiveness could hinder a fully functioning democracy. Their prescribed antidote was an informed citizenry, capable of distinguishing truth from falsehoods. Thomas Jefferson, author of the Declaration of Independence and third U.S. president, said, "An educated citizenry is a vital requisite for our survival as a free people." He believed education could act as a bulwark against the deceptiveness that would eventually threaten Americans' freedom. The First Amendment to the Constitution enshrined the freedom of the press to allow journalists to seek the truth unhindered and to prevent them from being forced to print falsehoods on behalf of the state.

And, indeed, an educated citizenry and the First Amendment have been necessary in fending off constant attacks on truth in the American democracy. While the First Amendment remains in place, the state of journalism in America has undergone its ups and downs. A particularly trying period came at the end of the nineteenth century when yellow journalism came into vogue, especially in New York City. Yellow journalism is a term, coined in that era, to refer to a sensationalist type of journalism that often completely fabricated quotations or interviews and cared more about newspaper sales than truth. An alternate term for yellow journalism is tabloid journalism. Although the prominence of yellow journalism waned after this era, it remained present in American journalism through the present day. Another low point in journalism came in a different form during the early 2000s. In the lead up to the United States' invasion of Iraq, the vast majority of American news outlets uncritically regurgitated the Bush Administration's false talking points regarding weapons of mass destruction in Iraq. Many journalists have since voiced regrets for their roles in the press' abdication of its duty as a critical assessor of state propaganda.

These prior eras pale in comparison to the crisis in American journalism occurring during the 2016 election cycle and the Trump presidency. Like the advent of writing, the Internet has made mass communication easier and faster; however, also like the advent of writing, the Internet has abetted deception by making anonymity easier. Communications experts had long noted how journalism on the web was more susceptible to sensationalism, yet it was not until the 2016 election that the Internet became a space for an all-out assault on the truth. With many people getting their news from friends and acquaintances on social media as opposed to traditional news sources, fake news stories, such as the one featured here, flourished. This story about alleged statements by Pope Francis first premiered on a fake news website, WTOE5News.com. Like other, similar fake new websites, this site uses a domain name that makes it appear to be a legitimate source—in this case, a local news station. BuzzFeed News discovered that this site was linked to a dozen other similar fake news sites run by the same person or group of people. Another such site, Ending the Fed, subsequently ran the same story. According to *BuzzFeed News*, by the time of election night 2016 this story had nearly one million engagements (i.e., looks or other actions) on Facebook.

Beyond the story discussed here, other widely shared fake news stories included: "Donald Trump sent his own plane to transport 200 stranded marines," "WikiLeaks confirms Hillary sold weapons to ISIS ... Then drops another bombshell," "FBI agent suspected in Hillary email leaks found dead in apartment murder-suicide," "ISIS leader calls for American Muslim voters to support Hillary Clinton," "FBI director received millions from Clinton Foundation, his brother's law firm does Clinton's taxes," and "Hillary Clinton in 2013: 'I would like to see people like Donald Trump run for office; they're honest and can't be bought.'" The fake news stories primarily targeted and circulated among Clinton bashers and Trump supporters, but some fake news stories also targeted and were circulated on the left of the political spectrum, such as "Ireland is now officially accepting Trump refugees from America." A story modeled after the one featured in this chapter, but claiming that Pope Francis endorsed Hillary Clinton, was circulated yet not nearly as widely as this one. Fake news stories claimed that Comet Ping Pong, a pizzeria in Washington DC, was running an underground child sex slavery ring somehow affiliated with Hillary Clinton. Employees of the pizzeria faced repeated harassment stemming from the fake stories, and then on December 4, 2016, a man entered the pizzeria with an assault rifle and fired three shots while attempting to "self-investigate" the conspiracy.

The rise in fake news stories bolstered the success of an unusually misleading politician. All politicians bend the truth to fit their needs; however, some do so more than others. An analysis by the *Washington Post* discovered that in his first 406 days in office, Donald Trump made 2,436 false or misleading claims, which averages out to six per day. More jarring than the lies—because, again, all politicians twist the truth—are Trump's assaults on the institution of American journalism and the freedom of the press. He does not only push back against stories that he thinks are unfair (a common practice among politicians), but he attacks the American press as a whole, unlike any major national politician since Richard Nixon. He has promised to "open up libel laws" to make it easier to sue journalists, thereby eliminating the freedom of the press. His tactics mirror those of strongmen from across the globe who have trampled upon or eliminated the local press' freedom; they also signal to concurrent strongmen that America is okay with this type of behavior. The term fake news itself, originally used to denote fabricated and purposefully misleading stories, has been transformed by Trump and other politicians. Trump uses it to denote any story or media outlet that does not depict him favorably. For instance, on February 17, 2017, he tweeted: "The FAKE NEWS media (failing @nytimes, @NBCNews, @ABC, @CBS, @CNN) is not my enemy, it is the enemy of the American People!"

It is possible that the era of fake news will wane just as the era of yellow journalism ultimately waned. Americans may become more discerning in the reading of news shared on social media and elsewhere. However, with new technologies allowing people to replicate someone's voice or seamlessly photoshop them into pictures and videos, new assaults on truth lie on the horizon.

Author Biography

The author of this fake news story is unknown. The story was first published on the website *WTOE5News. com*. *BuzzFeed News* has used the site's Google AdSense Id (which is used to post and collect money from advertisements on websites) to identify the owner of this and a network of other similar sites. BuzzFeed claims that a man named Justin Smithson owned these sites and, therefore, is the probable author of the content in this story. In his response to the BuzzFeed News article, Smithson denied ownership of the websites in question.

Reporters with various forms of "fake news" from an 1894 illustration by Frederick Burr Opper. (Library of Congress)

HISTORICAL DOCUMENT

Pope Francis Shocks World, Endorses Donald Trump for President
VATICAN CITY
… [statements attributed to Pope Francis]…

"I have been hesitant to offer any kind of support for either candidate in the U.S. presidential election but I now feel that to not voice my concern would be a dereliction of my duty as the Holy See. A strong and free America is vitally important in maintaining a strong and free world and in that sense what happens in American elections affects us all. The Rule of Law is the backbone of the American government as it is in any nation that strives for freedom and I now fear that the Rule of Law in America has been dealt a dangerous blow. The FBI, in refusing to recommend prosecution after admitting that the law had been broken on multiple occasions by Secretary Clinton, has exposed itself as corrupted by political forces that have become far too powerful. Though I don't agree with Mr. Trump on some issues, I feel that voting against the powerful political forces that have corrupted the entire American federal government is the only option for a nation that desires a government that is truly for the people and by the people. For this primary reason I ask, not as the Holy Father, but as a concerned citizen of the world that Americans vote for Donald Trump for President of the United States."

…

Document Analysis

This document represents the crux of a fake news article that first appeared on *WTOE5News.com*. The short article has a quick introduction and conclusion but primarily consists of this fake quotation attributed to Pope Francis. A comparison between the historical Pope Francis and the construction within this document will help make sense of the divide between fact and fiction in this era when the terms seem ever more muddled.

The fictionalized Pope Francis that speaks in the document has an uncharacteristically opinionated and specific perspective on American politics. The second sentence of the speech reads: "A strong and free America is vitally important in maintaining a strong and free world and in that sense what happens in American elections affects us all." The ideal America being "strong and free" is more of an American interpretation than a Vatican one, although the end of the sentence, "us all," does try to broaden the perspective. The following sentence is where the fictional Pope Francis starts to significantly depart from the historical one: "The Rule of Law is the backbone of the American government as it is in any nation that strives for freedom and I now fear that the Rule of Law in America has been dealt a dangerous blow." The phrase "Rule of Law" eludes to a theme with a long history in American politics (see the Essential Themes section below); however, the sentiment within this sentence has no real precedent in Vatican rhetoric. The next sentence offers further departures from a Vatican point of view: "The FBI, in refusing to recommend prosecution after admitting that the law had been broken on multiple occasions by Secretary Clinton, has exposed itself as corrupted by political forces that have become far too powerful." This view has been long developed in Republican and anti-Clinton circles within American politics. However, to suggest that this view comes from the pope reveals a misreading of non-Americans' priorities regarding American politics as well as a deep misunderstanding of the types of statements that the pope makes.

The historical Pope Francis was born in 1936 in Buenos Aires, Argentina. He himself is a norm-shattering figure as the first Jesuit pope, the first pope from the Southern hemisphere, and the first pope from the Americas. In the Middle Ages, popes used to be infamous for meddling in nations' political affairs, primarily on the European continent. However, those days are long gone. The popes of the twentieth and twenty-first centuries do meet with world leaders and offer statements that encourage specific agendas that align with their respective worldviews. They have been loath, however, to get down into the muck of any country's political battles. The statement from the fictionalized Pope Francis that most resembles something that the historical Pope Francis might say—perhaps the *only* statement that resembles something that the real Pope Francis might say—is the first half of the first sentence: "I have been hesitant to offer any kind of support for either candidate in the U.S. presidential election." If the alleged speech had cut off there it may have been credible; however, it immediately devolves into the fictionalized Pope Francis analyzed above. The historical Pope Francis has since discussed the problem of fake news. In an interview on December 7, 2016, he called fake news a "sickness." He does not name this or other fake news articles that reference him directly, but one can imagine him considering them as he speaks against fake news in general.

Essential Themes

It is impossible to tell from the document itself if the author who constructs the fictionalized Pope Francis is a political supporter of Trump or not. The author does, however, intend for this story to be shared among Trump supporters, so the fictional Pope Francis ends up sound much like a Trump supporter himself. In doing so, one of the themes he develops is that of law and order. In one of the sentences that sounds least like the historical Pope Francis, the fictional pope states: "The Rule of Law is the backbone of the American government as it is in any nation that strives for freedom and I now fear that the Rule of Law in America has been dealt a dangerous blow." The phrase "Rule of Law," emphasized with capital letters, echoes the Trump campaign's efforts to depict their candidate as an advocate of law and order. This, in turn, looks back to Richard Nixon's portrayal of himself as an advocate of law and order. Then, as now, the calls for law and order specifically play to white grievance and attempt to stir up white fear. For instance, in late November, 2015, Candidate Trump retweeted a false graphic that, among other falsehoods, vastly inflated the amount of crimes committed by "blacks." In another example, during a speech to police officers on July 28, 2017, Trump, by this time president, endorsed police brutality, saying, "When you guys put somebody in the car and you're protecting their head, you know, the way you put their hand over? Like, don't hit their head, and they just killed somebody—don't hit their head. I said, you can take the hand away, okay?" Multiple exhaustive analyses have shown that police brutality makes neighborhoods less safe; however, the specific kind of law and order espoused by Trump attempts to look tough and to blame political correctness for complicated societal issues. It is this narrow understanding of law and order that the document attempts to evoke, and the narrowness is seen in the document as well. The fictional Pope Francis focuses on Secretary Hillary Clinton, a favorite target of conservative media even before the 2016 election, when discussing the "Rule of Law," leaving aside the many systemic and individual challenges to the American criminal justice system.

—*Anthony Vivian, MA*

Bibliography and Additional Reading

Bartlett, Bruce. *The Truth Matters: A Citizen's Guide to Separating Facts from Lies and Stopping Fake News in Its Tracks*. Emeryville, CA: Ten Speed Press, 2017. Print.

Forgette, Richard. *News Grazers: Media, Politics, and Trust in an Information Age*. Washington: CQ Press, 2018. Print.

McIntyre, Lee. *Post-Truth*. Cambridge, MA: The MIT Press, 2018. Print.

McNair, Brian. *Fake News: Falsehood, Fabrication and Fantasy in Journalism*. London: Routledge, 2017. Print.

Preparations at the United States Capitol in Washington, D.C. as the sun begins to rise on the morning of the inauguration. (National Guard photo by Tech. Jonathan Young, JTF-DC)

■ Donald Trump's Inaugural Address

Date: January 20, 2017
Author: Donald J. Trump
Genre: Speech; address

Summary Overview

Donald J. Trump became the 45th president of the United States on January 20, 2017. In his inaugural speech, as had already become typical during his campaign, Trump broke with both expectations and precedent. Rather than the soaring oratory that had characterized prior inaugural speeches by both Republican and Democratic presidents, Trump painted a dystopian picture of the United States, directing attention to problems he would go on to attribute to the "traditional politicians" who had governed before him, and that he had already long claimed the unique ability to solve. Rather than daring Americans to dream, Trump chose to repeat many of the themes of his candidacy—the feeling of powerlessness among many of his working-class supporters, the feeling of vulnerability among the working class in the face of both immigration in the United States and terrorism around the world, the desire for isolationism in the face of these global threats, and the desire for a return to a past characterized by working-class opportunity in heavy industry. For Americans who considered the greatness of America to have diminished during prior administrations, Trump spoke directly to their fears when he promised to "make American great again."

Defining Moment

Trump's improbable road to the presidency involved, first, outlasting some thirteen Republican rivals in the primary campaign cycle. Though the repeated scandals caused many political commentators to predict the imminent end of his campaign, Trump seemingly reveled in both the scandals themselves and the predictions of his demise. Whether the scandals had to do with his personal conduct and comments regarding women, his political statements regarding Muslims, Mexicans, and other minority groups, or his mocking of a physically-challenged reporter, the scandals that were predicted to end his candidacy only reinforced his popularity among his supporters.

After winning the presidency by defeating Hillary Clinton in the Electoral College vote, many on the Right predicted that Trump would adopt a more conciliatory tone and govern as a traditional president. For many who thought this way, the words of his inaugural address spoke the opposite—that Trump would continue to be the politician he had become during his candidacy.

Author Biography

Donald Trump, born (1946) and raised in Queens, New York, entered politics as an outsider, which attracted many who were discontented with "traditional" politicians, but also as a well-known public figure, as a businessman, celebrity, and reality television star. Though he had written and spoken about politics much during the 1980s-2000s, giving sizable donations to many politicians of both parties, Trump's own political ambitions came to the fore during the presidency of Barack Obama (2009-17). One of the most persistent conspiracies of the Obama years was the so-called Birther idea, that Obama had not been born in Hawaii, despite much testimony and evidence, but rather had been born in Kenya, making him ineligible for the presidency. Though most "birthers" were fringe characters, Trump became the public face of the conspiracy, making claims (without providing any evidence) and keeping it in the news. Whereas baseless conspiracies would have likely scuttled other candidates, to some segments of the American population, Trump's actions endeared him to them.

Another part of the zeitgeist on which Trump drew heavily during the 2016 presidential campaign was the desire for much of the American public for a more populist tone from politicians. Characterized on the Democratic side by the unsuccessful primary campaign of Senator Bernie Sanders, Trump hit upon many of the same themes—the uneven distribution of the benefits of American society and a feeling of helplessness among some members of the American working class.

HISTORICAL DOCUMENT

Chief Justice Roberts, President Carter, President Clinton, President Bush, President Obama, fellow Americans, and people of the world: thank you.

We, the citizens of America, are now joined in a great national effort to rebuild our country and to restore its promise for all of our people.

Together, we will determine the course of America and the world for years to come.

We will face challenges. We will confront hardships. But we will get the job done.

Every four years, we gather on these steps to carry out the orderly and peaceful transfer of power, and we are grateful to President Obama and First Lady Michelle Obama for their gracious aid throughout this transition. They have been magnificent.

Today's ceremony, however, has very special meaning. Because today we are not merely transferring power from one Administration to another, or from one party to another—but we are transferring power from Washington, D.C. and giving it back to you, the American People.

For too long, a small group in our nation's Capital has reaped the rewards of government while the people have borne the cost.

Washington flourished—but the people did not share in its wealth.

Politicians prospered—but the jobs left, and the factories closed.

The establishment protected itself, but not the citizens of our country.

Their victories have not been your victories; their triumphs have not been your triumphs; and while they celebrated in our nation's Capital, there was little to celebrate for struggling families all across our land.

That all changes—starting right here, and right now, because this moment is your moment: it belongs to you.

It belongs to everyone gathered here today and everyone watching all across America.

This is your day. This is your celebration.

And this, the United States of America, is your country.

What truly matters is not which party controls our government, but whether our government is controlled by the people.

January 20th 2017, will be remembered as the day the people became the rulers of this nation again.

The forgotten men and women of our country will be forgotten no longer.

Everyone is listening to you now.

You came by the tens of millions to become part of a historic movement the likes of which the world has never seen before.

At the center of this movement is a crucial conviction: that a nation exists to serve its citizens.

Americans want great schools for their children, safe neighborhoods for their families, and good jobs for themselves.

These are the just and reasonable demands of a righteous public.

But for too many of our citizens, a different reality exists: Mothers and children trapped in poverty in our inner cities; rusted-out factories scattered like tombstones across the landscape of our nation; an education system, flush with cash, but which leaves our young and beautiful students deprived of knowledge; and the crime and gangs and drugs that have stolen too many lives and robbed our country of so much unrealized potential.

This American carnage stops right here and stops right now.

We are one nation—and their pain is our pain. Their dreams are our dreams; and their success will be our success. We share one heart, one home, and one glorious destiny.

The oath of office I take today is an oath of allegiance to all Americans.

For many decades, we've enriched foreign industry at the expense of American industry;

Subsidized the armies of other countries while allowing for the very sad depletion of our military;

We've defended other nation's borders while refusing to defend our own;

And spent trillions of dollars overseas while America's infrastructure has fallen into disrepair and decay.

We've made other countries rich while the wealth, strength, and confidence of our country has disappeared over the horizon.

One by one, the factories shuttered and left our

Donald Trump's Inaugural Address • 499

shores, with not even a thought about the millions upon millions of American workers left behind.

The wealth of our middle class has been ripped from their homes and then redistributed across the entire world.

But that is the past. And now we are looking only to the future.

We assembled here today are issuing a new decree to be heard in every city, in every foreign capital, and in every hall of power.

From this day forward, a new vision will govern our land.

From this moment on, it's going to be America First.

Every decision on trade, on taxes, on immigration, on foreign affairs, will be made to benefit American workers and American families.

We must protect our borders from the ravages of other countries making our products, stealing our companies, and destroying our jobs. Protection will lead to great prosperity and strength.

I will fight for you with every breath in my body—and I will never, ever let you down.

America will start winning again, winning like never before.

We will bring back our jobs. We will bring back our borders. We will bring back our wealth. And we will bring back our dreams.

We will build new roads, and highways, and bridges, and airports, and tunnels, and railways all across our wonderful nation.

We will get our people off of welfare and back to work—rebuilding our country with American hands and American labor.

We will follow two simple rules: Buy American and Hire American.

We will seek friendship and goodwill with the nations of the world—but we do so with the understanding that it is the right of all nations to put their own interests first.

We do not seek to impose our way of life on anyone, but rather to let it shine as an example for everyone to follow.

We will reinforce old alliances and form new ones— and unite the civilized world against Radical Islamic Terrorism, which we will eradicate completely from the face of the Earth.

At the bedrock of our politics will be a total allegiance to the United States of America, and through our loyalty to our country, we will rediscover our loyalty to each other.

When you open your heart to patriotism, there is no room for prejudice.

The Bible tells us, "how good and pleasant it is when God's people live together in unity."

We must speak our minds openly, debate our disagreements honestly, but always pursue solidarity.

When America is united, America is totally unstoppable.

There should be no fear—we are protected, and we will always be protected.

We will be protected by the great men and women of our military and law enforcement and, most importantly, we are protected by God.

Finally, we must think big and dream even bigger.

In America, we understand that a nation is only living as long as it is striving.

We will no longer accept politicians who are all talk and no action—constantly complaining but never doing anything about it.

The time for empty talk is over.

Now arrives the hour of action.

Do not let anyone tell you it cannot be done. No challenge can match the heart and fight and spirit of America.

We will not fail. Our country will thrive and prosper again.

We stand at the birth of a new millennium, ready to unlock the mysteries of space, to free the Earth from the miseries of disease, and to harness the energies, industries and technologies of tomorrow.

A new national pride will stir our souls, lift our sights, and heal our divisions.

It is time to remember that old wisdom our soldiers will never forget: that whether we are black or brown or white, we all bleed the same red blood of patriots, we all enjoy the same glorious freedoms, and we all salute the same great American Flag.

And whether a child is born in the urban sprawl of Detroit or the windswept plains of Nebraska, they look up at the same night sky, they fill their heart with the same dreams, and they are infused with the breath of life by the same almighty Creator.

So to all Americans, in every city near and far, small and large, from mountain to mountain, and from ocean to ocean, hear these words:

You will never be ignored again.

Your voice, your hopes, and your dreams, will define our American destiny. And your courage and goodness and love will forever guide us along the way.

Together, We Will Make America Strong Again. We Will Make America Wealthy Again. We Will Make America Proud Again. We Will Make America Safe Again. And, Yes, Together, We Will Make America Great Again. Thank you, God Bless You, And God Bless America.

Document Analysis

Donald Trump's January 20, 2017 inaugural speech was remarkably brief, coming in at only 1,400 words. But though shorter by far than the nine that preceded it, Trump's made more of an impression than most of those prior addresses. Trump began the speech, as so many of his predecessors had, by striking a conciliatory note. He spoke of the promise of America. He spoke of the graciousness demonstrated by the prior president, Barack Obama, and his wife Michelle Obama during the transition months between the election in November 2016 and the inauguration some two months later.

However, early on in the speech, Trump began to focus on the themes that had characterized his campaign during the prior year. He spoke in populist terms, stating that he was "transferring power from Washington, D.C. and giving it back to you, the people." He spoke of the fact that so many of the economic gains of prior administrations had gone to the few (who Trump characterized as "the politicians"), while the jobs that had given the working class a measure of prosperity during the late twentieth century had been exported to other countries. Without going into specifics on any of his plans, which had also been a characteristic of his presidential campaign, Trump promised to reverse all of those losses experienced by the working class, stating, "[t]hat all changes starting right here and right now because this moment is your moment, it belongs to you."

Though they may have disagreed about some of the ways to achieve them, both presidents Barack Obama and George W. Bush often articulated a broader vision of prosperity and peace for the entire world in their rhetoric. Trump, however, focused almost exclusively on the United States. Striking a heavily nationalist tone, Trump promised that the overriding rules of his administration would be to "buy American and hire American." Even when speaking of international threats, such as that posed by terrorism around the world, Trump couched it in bellicose, nationalistic terms.

Trump departed from the policy invectives of prior Republican administrations in a number of ways during his inaugural address. He promised a large program of spending to rebuild infrastructure in the United States, without delving into the details of how it would be paid for or how he would get it through a Congress led by Republicans who had long records of opposing such large-scale spending programs.

In the context of the history of presidential addresses, Trump's inaugural address will likely be remembered as one of the darkest. Throughout the speech, Trump presented a dystopian vision of America, talking about inner-city poverty, idle industrial factories, a broken education system, and violent crime. His campaign slogan, after all, was to "Make America Great Again," which was to infer that it was no longer great. This slight to many of the political figures present at the inauguration had been a characteristic of Trump's campaign, and carried through the transition period to his inauguration.

Though largely defined by Trump's antagonism to the politics of prior decades—an antagonism shared by most of his supporters—Trump finished his speech by framing his vision of a dystopian America in terms of the ability of he and his supporters' unique ability to overcome the past, stating "[y]our voice, your hopes, and your dreams, will define our American destiny. And your courage and goodness and love will forever guide us along the way."

Essential Themes

Much of Donald Trump's inaugural speech could be characterized as presenting a vision of a broken American that only he and those who support him can fix. And though this has remained a theme throughout the first portion of his presidency, delivering on the ideas he spoke of in his inaugural speech has proven incomplete. Some of this was due to the typical grandiosity of presidential inaugural speeches, which often set goals that are—at least in the short term—unreachable. Some of this was due to the political tenor of the times—dealing with a Congress, which, although led by Republican majorities in both houses, has proven alternately unwilling and incapable of fulfilling Trump's visions. And, some of this was due to the scandals that continued to plague Trump, which took a much higher toll on president Trump than they did on candidate Trump.

The first signs of opposition to Trump and his agenda came very quickly. On January 21, 2017—the very day after the inauguration—the Women's March took place on the National Mall in Washington, D.C., as well as in cities across the United States. Drawing between 500,000 and one million attendees across the nation, many in attendance focused on opposition to Trump personally, as well as to his stated policies. Opposition continued throughout the first portion of Trump's presidency, coming to various crescendos with the nominations of polarizing cabinet secretaries, such as Secretary of Education Betsy DeVos, Attorney General Jeff Sessions, and Secretary of the Interior Ryan Zinke. Opposition also arose in opposition to the attempted implementation of many of the policies on which Trump had campaigned, such as the Muslim Travel Ban, which twice was struck down by the federal courts. Personal and political scandal has played a very large part in the continuing opposition to Trump and his administration.

Though the lurid claims of an affair with adult film actress Stormy Daniels stole headlines, the longer lasting scandal had to do with actions and investigations relating to possible collusion between the Trump campaign and Russian efforts to influence the 2016 election. The interference of Russia with the election has had numerous ramifications for Trump and produced numerous casualties within his administration. Less than a month after his inauguration, Trump's first National Security Advisor, Michael Flynn was forced to resign due to his ties with Russians. On May 9, 2017, Trump fired FBI Director James Comey for what he admitted were the FBI's efforts to investigate his ties to Russia. By late 2017, both Flynn and Trump Campaign Chair Paul Manafort had been indicted by Special Prosecutor Robert Mueller for their actions in relation to the Russian scandal. By early 2018, the continuing investigation of Special Prosecutor Robert Mueller into Russian collusion was showing no signs of slowing, despite consistent pressure from Trump to end the investigation.

In his inaugural address, Trump claimed that "America will start winning again, winning like never before...[w]e will bring back our jobs. We will bring back our borders. We will bring back our wealth. And we will bring back our dreams." By early 2018 there was little evidence to show that any of those industrial jobs would be coming back (despite Trump's imposition of tariffs on imported steel in March 2018). While they claimed that the tax plan passed by Trump and congressional Republicans in December 2017 would benefit the working and middle classes, most analysis has shown that the vast majority of the benefit from the tax plan, which would raise the federal budget deficit dramatically, would go to the wealthy—a reality in stark opposition to Trump's campaign rhetoric. Though these incongruities between campaign rhetoric and the political realities of governing are by no means unique to Trump, they have seemed to be even more dramatic during Trump's first year in office than for past administrations.

The populism of Trump's campaign rhetoric, which carried through to his inaugural address, seemed hollow to many, as Trump's approval ratings hovered in the 30-40 percent range—the lowest of any president during his first year in office. Time will tell if Trump will be able to fulfill the promises made to America's working class in his inaugural address. But if he is not able to do so, the signs of his inability to follow through were sewn very early in his presidency, and even before.

—*Steven L. Danver, PhD*

Bibliography and Additional Reading

Kingsbury, Alex. "An analysis of Donald Trump's inaugural speech." *Boston Globe*. January 20, 2017. https://www.bostonglobe.com/news/politics/2017/01/20/analysis-donald-trump-inaugural-speech/

Morgan, Nick. "The Astonishing Rhetoric of President Trump's Inaugural Address." *Forbes*. January 20, 2017. https://www.forbes.com/sites/nickmorgan/2017/01/20/the-astonishing-rhetoric-of-president-trumps-inaugural-address/

Stahl, Jessica. "Trump's inauguration speech, one year later." *Washington Post*. January 19, 2018. https://www.washingtonpost.com/news/post-politics/wp/2018/01/19/trumps-inauguration-speech-one-year-later/

Trump, Donald J. *The America We Deserve*. New York: St. Martin's Press, 2000.

Vilade, C. Edwin. *President's Speech: The Stories Behind the Most Memorable Presidential Addresses*. Guilford, CT: Lyons Press, 2012.

Printed in March 1812, this political cartoon was drawn in reaction to the newly drawn state senate election district of South Essex created by the Massachusetts legislature to favor the Democratic-Republican Party candidates of Governor Elbridge Gerry over the Federalists. Elkanah Tisdale (1771-1835) (often falsely attributed to Gilbert Stuart) Originally published in the Boston Centinel, 1812.

■ Cooper v. Harris

Date: May 22, 2017
Author: Elena Kagan
Genre: Court opinion

Summary Overview

On May 22, 2017 the Supreme Court of the United States issued its opinion in *Cooper v. Harris*, a suit involving a challenge to the redrawing of voting districts in North Carolina on the basis of a violation of the Voting Rights Act of 1965. The Court upheld the lower Federal court's ruling that the North Carolina state legislators had illegally packed districts with African-American voters, which in turn reduced the influence of African-American voters in other North Carolina districts.

Defining Moment

A number of redistricting cases have come before the United States Supreme Court alleging violations of the Voting Rights Act. The majority of the cases have involved states in the southern United States, including Alabama, Virginia and North Carolina, which have a long history of voter suppression and utilizing redistricting (gerrymandering) as a means of diluting and minimizing the impact of African-American and Latino votes. *Cooper v. Harris* is the latest gerrymandering case heard by the Supreme Court in an attempt to provide guidance and to further shape federal law under the Voting Rights Act.

In 1993 the Supreme Court enumerated a general rule in another North Carolina gerrymandering case, *State v. Reno*, in which it held that race could not normally be the predominant factor considered in redistricting, as that would be a violation of the Equal Protection Clause of the U.S. Constitution. However, the Court concluded that race could be one of many factors considered in order to ensure compliance with the Voting Rights Act. If race was deemed to be a predominant factor in the redistricting, then a stringent level of review called strict scrutiny was applied which then required the state in question to show that the redistricting plan served a "compelling interest" and was "narrowly tailored" to meet that interest. *Shaw v. Reno* came before the Supreme Court in 1996 and in that case the Court established that the Voting Rights Act was considered to be a "compelling interest"

under the strict scrutiny standard.

In this latest challenge to a redistricting plan by the North Carolina legislature, Justice Elena Kagan, writing for the Court majority, held that race was a predominant factor in drawing the districts. However, North Carolina lacked a strong basis in evidence for believing that it needed a minority-dominated district in order to avoid any liability under Section 2 of the Voting Rights Act. Rather, Kagan's opinion held that racial gerrymandering, rather than political gerrymandering, was the predominant factor in drawing the other district as a minority-dominated district.

The case arises from two North Carolina congressional districts, District 1 and District 12 which have a long legislative history before the Supreme Court. The two districts have been the basis of four earlier racial gerrymandering cases at the Court. In 2016 a three-judge federal district court in North Carolina invalidated both districts, holding that the state legislators had illegally packed the districts with African-American voters, which had the effect of reducing the influence of African-American voters in other districts. District 1 has been likened to an octopus in its geographical shape, with a body that starts at the North Carolina/Virginia border with tentacles that stretch out west, south and east. District 12 is more serpentine in shape; as the court noted it "begins in the south-central part of the State (where it takes in a large part of Charlotte) and then travels northeast, zigzagging much of the way to the State's northern border."

The Supreme Court granted certiorari to hear the matter and upheld the district court decision by a 5-3 decision, in a major ruling on racial gerrymandering. Justice Kagan wrote for the majority. Justice Clarence Thomas wrote a concurring opinion. Justice Samuel Alito filed an opinion concurring in the judgment in part and dissenting in part, in which Chief Justice John Roberts and Justice Anthony Kennedy joined. Justice Gorsuch took no part in the consideration or decision of the case.

Author Biography

Elena Kagan is an Associate Justice on the Supreme Court. She was born on April 28, 1960 in New York City. Kagan studied history at Princeton before attending Harvard Law School, where she was supervising editor of the *Harvard Law Review*. Kagan was a law clerk for Judge Abner Mikva of the U.S. Court of Appeals for the District of Columbia Circuit after which she served as a law clerk for Justice Thurgood Marshall. She moved into the private sector working as an associate for the Washington D.C. law firm Williams & Connolly.

In 1991 Kagan began teaching at the University of Chicago Law School and by 1995 was a tenured professor of law. Kagan began working as associate counsel for President Bill Clinton later that year and spent four years working in the White House, first as Deputy Assistant to the President for Domestic Policy before taking the role of Deputy Director of the Domestic Policy Council.

President Clinton nominated Kagan to serve on the U.S. Court of Appeals D.C. Circuit. Her nomination languished in the Senate Judiciary Committee and, in 1999 Kagan returned to academia, beginning as a visiting professor at Harvard Law before eventually becoming Dean of Harvard Law in 2003. When President Barack Obama, a fellow Harvard alumnus, won the 2008 presidential election, Kagan was selected as solicitor general. She was confirmed in that position by the Senate on March 19, 2009, becoming the first woman to serve as solicitor general of the United States. Two months after being confirmed, President Obama nominated Kagan to replace Justice John Paul Stevens on the Supreme Court after his retirement. Kagan was confirmed by the Senate in a 63-37 vote, making her the fourth woman to sit on the Supreme Court. Kagan was also the youngest Justice at 50 years old and the only one without previous experience as a sitting judge.

During her tenure on the Supreme Court, Kagan sided with the majority on two landmark Supreme Court rulings. First, she was one of six justices to uphold a critical component of the 2010 Affordable Care Act (Obamacare) in *King v. Burwell*. That decision allowed the federal government to keep providing subsidies to Americans who purchased healthcare insurance through exchanges regardless of whether they were operated by state or federal government. Second, Kagan again joined the majority in a 5-4 ruling in *Obergefell v. Hodges* that made same sex marriage legal in all 50 states.

HISTORICAL DOCUMENT

ROY COOPER, GOVERNOR OF NORTH CAROLINA, ET AL., APPELLANTS *v.* DAVID HARRIS, ET AL. ON APPEAL FROM THE UNITED STATES DISTRICT COURT FOR THE MIDDLE DISTRICT OF NORTH CAROLINA

[May 22, 2017]

JUSTICE KAGAN delivered the opinion of the Court.

The Constitution entrusts States with the job of designing congressional districts. But it also imposes an important constraint: A State may not use race as the predominant factor in drawing district lines unless it has a compelling reason. In this case, a three-judge District Court ruled that North Carolina officials violated that bar when they created two districts whose voting-age populations were majority black. Applying a deferential standard of review to the factual findings underlying that decision, we affirm.

I

A

The Equal Protection Clause of the Fourteenth Amendment limits racial gerrymanders in legislative districting plans. It prevents a State, in the absence of "sufficient justification," from "separating its citizens into different voting districts on the basis of race." .... When a voter sues state officials for drawing such race-based lines, our decisions call for a two-step analysis.

First, the plaintiff must prove that "race was the predominant factor motivating the legislature's decision to place a significant number of voters within or without a particular district." ...

Second, if racial considerations predominated over others, the design of the district must withstand strict scrutiny. ...The burden thus shifts to the State to prove that its race-based sorting of voters serves a "compelling interest" and is "narrowly tailored" to that end. ...

Two provisions of the VRA—§2 and §5—are involved in this case. ... Section 2 prohibits any "standard, practice, or procedure" that "results in a denial or abridgement of the right . . . to vote on account of race." §10301(a). .... Section 5, at the time of the districting in dispute, worked through a different mechanism. Before this Court invalidated its coverage formula, see *Shelby County* v. *Holder*, ... that section required certain jurisdictions (including various North Carolina counties) to pre-clear voting changes with the Department of Justice, so as to forestall "retrogression" in the ability of racial minorities to elect their preferred candidates, *Beer* v. *United States*....

When a State invokes the VRA to justify race-based districting, it must show (to meet the "narrow tailoring" requirement) that it had "a strong basis in evidence" for concluding that the statute required its action. ... Or said otherwise, the State must establish that it had "good reasons" to think that it would transgress the Act if it did *not* draw race-based district lines. .... That "strong basis" (or "good reasons") standard gives States "breathing room" to adopt reasonable compliance measures that may prove, in perfect hindsight, not to have been needed. ...

B

This case concerns North Carolina's most recent redrawing of two congressional districts, both of which have long included substantial populations of black voters. In its current incarnation, District 1 is anchored in the northeastern part of the State, with appendages stretching both south and west (the latter into Durham). District 12 begins in the south-central part of the State (where it takes in a large part of Charlotte) and then travels northeast, zig-zagging much of the way to the State's northern border. ... The design of that "serpentine" district, we held, was nothing if not race-centric, and could not be justified as a reasonable attempt to comply with the VRA.

The next year, the State responded with a new districting plan, including a new District 12—and residents of that district brought another lawsuit alleging an imper-

missible racial gerrymander. A District Court sustained the claim twice, but both times this Court reversed. ... Racial considerations, we held, did not predominate in designing the revised District 12. Rather, that district was the result of a *political* gerrymander—an effort to engineer, mostly "without regard to race," a safe Democratic seat. ...

The State redrew its congressional districts again in 2001, to account for population changes revealed in the prior year's census. Under the 2001 map, which went unchallenged in court, neither District 1 nor District 12 had a black voting-age population (called a "BVAP") that was a majority of the whole: The former had a BVAP of around 48%, the latter a BVAP of around 43%. .... Nonetheless, in five successive general elections conducted in those reconfigured districts, all the candidates preferred by most African-American voters won their contests—and by some handy margins. In District 1, black voters' candidates of choice garnered as much as 70% of the total vote, and never less than 59%. ...

Another census, in 2010, necessitated yet another congressional map—(finally) the one at issue in this case. ...

The new map (among other things) significantly altered both District 1 and District 12. The 2010 census had revealed District 1 to be substantially underpopulated: To comply with the Constitution's one-person-one-vote principle, the State needed to place almost 100,000 new people within the district's boundaries. ... Rucho, Lewis, and Hofeller chose to take most of those people from heavily black areas of Durham, requiring a finger-like extension of the district's western line. ... With that addition, District 1's BVAP rose from 48.6% to 52.7%. ... District 12, for its part, had no need for significant total-population changes: It was overpopulated by fewer than 3,000 people out of over 730,000. ... Still, Rucho, Lewis, and Hofeller decided to reconfigure the district, further narrowing its already snakelike body while adding areas at either end—most relevantly here, in Guilford County. ...Those changes appreciably shifted the racial composition of District 12: As the district gained some 35,000 African-Americans of voting age and lost some 50,000 whites of that age, its BVAP increased from 43.8% to 50.7%. ...

... a three-judge District Court held both districts

unconstitutional. All the judges agreed that racial considerations predominated in the design of District 1... all rejected the State's argument that it had a "strong basis" for thinking that the VRA compelled such a race-based drawing of District 1's lines. ... the court explained that the State had failed to put forward any reason, compelling or otherwise, for its attention to race in designing that district.

The State filed a notice of appeal, and we noted probable jurisdiction. *McCrory* v. *Harris*, 579 U. S. ___ (2016).

II

We address at the outset North Carolina's contention that a victory it won in a very similar state-court lawsuit should dictate (or at least influence) our disposition of this case. As the State explains, the North Carolina NAACP and several other civil rights groups challenged Districts 1 and 12 in state court immediately after their enactment, charging that they were unlawful racial gerrymanders. ... By the time the plaintiffs before us filed this action, the state trial court, in *Dickson* v. *Rucho*, had rejected those claims... The North Carolina Supreme Court then affirmed that decision by a 4–3 vote, applying the state-court equivalent of clear error review. ...In this Court, North Carolina makes two related arguments based on the *Dickson* litigation: first, that the state trial court's judgment should have barred this case altogether, under familiar principles of claim and issue preclusion; and second, that the state court's conclusions should cause us to conduct a "searching review" of the decision below, rather than deferring (as usual) to its factual findings. ....

The State's preclusion theory rests on an assertion about how the plaintiffs in the two cases are affiliated. ...

But North Carolina never satisfied the District Court that the alleged affiliation really existed. ... Because of those unresolved "factual disputes," the District Court denied North Carolina's motion for summary judgment. ...

That conclusion defeats North Carolina's attempt to argue for claim or issue preclusion here. We have no basis for assessing the factual assertions underlying the State's argument any differently than the District Court did. Nothing in the State's evidence clearly rebuts Harris's and Bowser's testimony that they never joined any of the *Dickson* groups. We need not decide whether the alleged memberships would have supported preclusion if they had been proved. It is enough that the District Court reasonably thought they had not.

...

III

With that out of the way, we turn to the merits of this case, ... We uphold both conclusions.

A

Uncontested evidence in the record shows that the State's mapmakers, in considering District 1, purposefully established a racial target: African-Americans should make up no less than a majority of the voting-age population. ... Senator Rucho and Representative Lewis were not coy in expressing that goal. They repeatedly told their colleagues that District 1 had to be majority-minority, so as to comply with the VRA. ... Dr. Hofeller testified multiple times at trial that Rucho and Lewis instructed him "to draw [District 1] with a [BVAP] in excess of 50 percent." ...

Hofeller followed those directions to the letter, such that the 50%-plus racial target "had a direct and significant impact" on District 1's configuration. ...

Faced with this body of evidence...the District Court did not clearly err in finding that race predominated in drawing District 1. Indeed, as all three judges recognized, the court could hardly have concluded anything but. ...

B

The more substantial question is whether District 1 can survive the strict scrutiny applied to racial gerrymanders. ...

This Court identified, in *Thornburg* v. *Gingles*, three threshold conditions for proving vote dilution under §2 of the VRA...First, a "minority group" must be "sufficiently large and geographically compact to constitute a majority" in some reasonably configured legislative district. ... Second, the minority group must be "politically cohesive." ... And third, a district's white majority must "vote sufficiently as a bloc" to usually "defeat the minority's preferred candidate." ... ...If a State has good reason to think that all the "*Gingles* preconditions" are met, then so too it has good reason to believe that §2 requires drawing a majority-minority district. …But if not, then not.

Here, electoral history provided no evidence that a §2 plaintiff could demonstrate the third *Gingles* prerequisite—effective white bloc-voting. … In the lingo of voting law, District 1 functioned, election year in and election year out, as a "crossover" district, in which members of the majority help a "large enough" minority to elect its candidate of choice. …

The State counters that, in this context, past performance is no guarantee of future results… So, North Carolina contends, the question facing the state mapmakers was not whether the *then-existing* District 1 violated §2. Rather, the question was whether the *future* District 1 would do so if drawn without regard to race. And that issue, the State claims, could not be resolved by "focusing myopically on past elections."

… The prospect of a significant population increase in a district only raises—it does not answer—the question whether §2 requires deliberate measures to augment the district's BVAP. (…State must carefully evaluate whether a plaintiff could establish the *Gingles* preconditions—including effective white bloc-voting—in a new district created without those measures. We see nothing in the legislative record that fits that description.

…Over and over in the legislative record, Rucho and Lewis cited *Strickland* as mandating a 50%-plus BVAP in District 1. … In effect, they concluded, whenever a legislature *can* draw a majority-minority district, it *must* do so— even if a crossover district would also allow the minority group to elect its favored candidates. …

That idea, though, is at war with our §2 jurisprudence— *Strickland* included. Under the State's view, the third *Gingles* condition is no condition at all, because even in the absence of effective white bloc-voting, a §2 claim could succeed in a district (like the old District 1) with an under 50% BVAP. But this Court has made clear that unless *each* of the three *Gingles* prerequisites is established, "there neither has been a wrong nor can be a remedy." …

In sum: Although States enjoy leeway to take race-based actions reasonably judged necessary under a proper interpretation of the VRA, that latitude cannot rescue District 1. … But neither will we approve a racial gerrymander whose necessity is supported by no evidence and whose *raison d'être* is a legal mistake. Accordingly, we uphold the District Court's conclusion that North Carolina's use of race as the predominant factor in designing District 1 does not withstand strict scrutiny.

IV

We now look west to District 12, making its fifth (!) appearance before this Court. This time, the district's legality turns, and turns solely, on which of two possible reasons predominantly explains its most recent reconfiguration. The plaintiffs contended at trial that the General Assembly chose voters for District 12, as for District 1, because of their race; more particularly, they urged that the Assembly intentionally increased District 12's BVAP in the name of ensuring preclearance under the VRA's §5. But North Carolina declined to mount any defense …The mapmakers drew their lines, in other words, to "pack" District 12 with Democrats, not African-Americans. After hearing evidence supporting both parties' accounts, the District Court accepted the plaintiffs'.

… In *Shaw II*, for example, this Court emphasized the "highly irregular" shape of then-District 12 in concluding that race predominated in its design. … But such evidence loses much of its value when the State asserts partisanship as a defense, because a bizarre shape—as of the new District 12—can arise from a "political motivation" as well as a racial one…

…

… we uphold the District Court's finding of racial predominance respecting District 12. The evidence offered at trial, including live witness testimony subject to credibility determinations, adequately supports the conclusion that race, not politics, accounted for the district's reconfiguration. And no error of law infected that judgment…the District Court had no call to dismiss this challenge just because the plaintiffs did not proffer an alternative design for District 12 as circumstantial evidence of the legislature's intent.

A

Begin with some facts and figures, showing how the redistricting of District 12 affected its racial composition. …

As the plaintiffs pointed out at trial, Rucho and Lewis had publicly stated that racial considerations lay behind District 12's augmented BVAP. ... Thus, the District Court found, Rucho's and Lewis's own account "evince[d] intentionality" as to District 12's racial composition: *Because of* the VRA, they increased the number of African-Americans. ....

Hofeller confirmed that intent ...Before the redistricting, Hofeller testified, some black residents of Guilford County fell within District 12 while others fell within neighboring District 13. The legislators, he continued, "decided to reunite the black community in Guilford County into the Twelfth." ..."[M]indful that Guilford County was covered" by §5, Hofeller explained, the legislature "determined that it was prudent to reunify [the county's] African-American community" into District 12. ... It would "avoid the possibility of a [VRA]charge" that would "inhibit preclearance." ...

...

... Congressman Mel Watt ...recounted a conversation he had with Rucho in 2011 ..., Rucho said that "his leadership had told him that he had to ramp the minority percentage in [District 12] up to over 50 percent to comply with the Voting Rights Law." ...In the court's view, Watt's account was of a piece with all the other evidence—including the redistricters' on-the-nose attainment of a 50% BVAP—indicating that the General Assembly, in the name of VRA compliance, deliberately redrew District 12 as a majority-minority district. ...

The State's contrary story—that politics alone drove decision making—came into the trial mostly through Hofeller's testimony. Hofeller explained that Rucho and Lewis instructed him, first and foremost, to make the map as a whole "more favorable to Republican candidates." ...In part of his testimony, Hofeller further stated that the Obama-McCain election data explained (among other things) his incorporation of the black, but not the white, parts of Guilford County then located in District 13. ...

The District Court, however, disbelieved Hofeller's asserted indifference to the new district's racial composition. The court recalled Hofeller's contrary deposition testimony—his statement (repeated in only slightly different words in his expert report) that Rucho and Lewis "decided" to shift African-American voters into District 12 "in order to" ensure preclearance under §5...Right after asserting that Rucho and Lewis had told him "[not]

to use race" in designing District 12, Hofeller added a qualification: "except perhaps with regard to Guilford County." ...As the District Court understood, that is the kind of "exception" that goes pretty far toward swallowing the rule. ...

Finally, an expert report by Dr. Stephen ... looked at the six counties overlapping with District 12.... The question he asked was: Who from those counties actually ended up in District 12? The answer he found was: Only 16% of the region's white registered voters, but 64% of the black ones. ... Those stark disparities led Ansolabehere to conclude that "race, and not party," was "the dominant factor" ....

The District Court's assessment that all this evidence proved racial predominance clears the bar of clear error review. The court emphasized that the districting plan's own architects had repeatedly described the influx of African-Americans into District 12 as a §5 compliance measure, not a side-effect of political gerrymandering...—that Watt told the truth when he recounted Rucho's resolve to hit a majority-BVAP target; and conversely that Hofeller skirted the truth (especially as to Guilford County) when he claimed to have followed only race-blind criteria in drawing district lines. We cannot disrespect such credibility judgments. ...

B

The State mounts a final, legal rather than factual, attack on the District Court's finding of racial predominance. When race and politics are competing explanations of a district's lines, argues North Carolina, the party challenging the district must introduce a particular kind of circumstantial evidence: "an alternative [map] that achieves the legislature's political objectives while improving racial balance." ...

....

A plaintiff 's task... is simply to persuade the trial court—without any special evidentiary prerequisite—that race (not politics) was the "predominant consideration in deciding to place a significant number of voters within or without a particular district." ...that burden of proof, we have often held, is "demanding." ... And because that is so, a plaintiff will sometimes need an alternative map, as a practical matter, to make his case. But in no area of our equal protection law have we forced plaintiffs to submit one particular form of proof to prevail. ...Nor would it make sense to do so here. ...

...

V

Applying a clear error standard, we uphold the District Court's conclusions that racial considerations predominated in designing both District 1 and District 12. For District 12, that is all we must do, because North Caro-

lina has made no attempt to justify race-based districting there. For District 1, we further uphold the District Court's decision that §2 of the VRA gave North Carolina no good reason to reshuffle voters because of their race. We accordingly affirm the judgment of the District Court.

It is so ordered.

JUSTICE GORSUCH took no part in the consideration or decision of this case.

GLOSSARY

gerrymandering: purposefully dividing a geographical region into electoral districts with intent to allow one political party to have a majority of sympathetic voters

judicial review: a constitutional doctrine which allows a court to review legislative or executive acts to determine whether they are constitutional

strict scrutiny: the highest level of judicial review, applied by the Supreme Court to a law that is alleged to violate equal protection rights under the U.S. Constitution and to determine if the law is narrowly tailored to serve a compelling state interest

Voting Rights Act of 1965: a landmark federal law that seeks to prohibit racial discrimination in voting

Document Analysis

In the majority opinion, Justice Kagan noted that the crux of a racial gerrymandering case amounts to answering two questions. The first is whether race was the predominant factor behind the state legislature's decision to move particular voters in or out of a particular district. The second question is, if race was the predominant factor, can the state show that it had "good reasons" to believe that the Voting Rights Act would be violated if the legislature did not use race to draw the districts?

The Supreme Court's inquiry into the first question is limited because it can only review the district court's findings of fact to determine if they are clearly wrong, a very high threshold. Thus, a district court's factual findings on whether race was the predominant factor will not be overturned if the findings are "plausible," even if the justices might reach a different conclusion. In analyzing the first question, Kagan noted that before drawing the boundary lines for District 1, the gerrymandering map "purposefully established a racial target: African-Americans should make up no less than a majority of the voting-age population." Kagan noted that in fulfilling

this goal, the gerrymandering plan resulted in a "district with stark racial borders. Within the same counties, the portions that fall inside District 1 have black populations two to three times larger than the portions placed in neighboring districts." Kagan concluded that the federal district court was not clearly wrong in finding that "race predominated in drawing District 1."

Regarding the second question in the analysis, Kagan found the state did not have "good reasons" to believe that it had to either consider race or risk violating the Voting Rights Act with its redistricting plan. To the contrary, the opinion concludes that the state provided "no reason" to show that it needed to increase the number of African-American voters in District 1 because the district had consistently been electing minority members of Congress.

The state attempted to argue that race wasn't a factor but, rather, that party affiliation was a predominant factor and many Democrats happened to be African-American. The district court had concluded that although race and party affiliation were closely aligned, it was race that was the predominant factor. Kagan's opinion acknowledged it was not an easy task for the district court to make the determination on whether race was a predominant factor in drawing the redistricting maps but that the Supreme Court had to find the district court's determination to be "clearly wrong" in its determination, and that in the instant case it was not.

Thus, the majority concluded that race was a predominant factor; that the district wrong was not "clearly wrong" in making that finding; and, that the state failed to make any showing of a "good reason" demonstrating the Voting Rights Act would be violated if race had not been used to draw the redistricting map.

Justices Alito, Chief Justice Roberts, and Justice Kennedy disagreed with the majority opinion about District 12 being invalidated. Justice Thomas provided the needed fifth vote to uphold the district court's invalidating of District 12, somewhat surprising as he traditionally is regarded as a more conservative jurist.

In his opinion, Justice Alito concurred in part with Kagan's opinion, and dissented in part as well. He believed that the challengers to the racial gerrymandering should have been required to provide their own redistricting map, stating that an alternative map "is a logical response to the difficult problem of distinguishing between racial and political motivations when race and political party preference closely correlate." Alito further asserted that the majority opinion risked confusing "a political gerrymander for a racial gerrymander" and that the opinion "invades a traditional domain of state authority."

Essential Themes

Although *Cooper v. Harris* did not definitively create new law on the issue, its interpretation of state legislature motives in drawing up redistricting maps in coordination with the Voting Rights Act was regarded as a major ruling on racial gerrymandering. Particularly, *Cooper* made clear that the Supreme Court took a common-sense approach to the idea that legislatures that utilize race in drawing districts, even if race is used as a proxy for political affiliation, would be seen as highly suspect. It provided guidance and a road map for what challengers to redistricting needed to prove in order to establish that race was a predominant factor in the drawing of districts.

—*Michele McBride Simonelli, JD*

Bibliography and Additional Reading

Cooper v. Harris, 137 S.Ct. 1455 (2017). Justia: US Supreme Court https://supreme.justia.com/cases/ federal/us/581/15-1262/ [accessed August 3, 2017].

Daley, David. *Ratf**ked : The True Story Behind the Secret Plan to Steal America's Democracy*. New York: Liveright Publishing Corp., 2016.

Grofman, Bernard, editor. *Race and Redistricting in the 1990s*. New York: Agathon Press, 1998.

Michael Kent Curtis, "Using the Voting Rights Act to Discriminate: North Carolina's Use of Racial Gerrymanders, Two Racial Quotas, Safe Harbors, Shields, and Inoculations to Undermine Multiracial Coalitions and Black Political Power," *Wake Forest Law Review*, 51 (2016): 421-492.

Shaw v. Reno, 113 S.Ct. 2816 (1993). Justia: US Supreme Court https://supreme.justia.com/cases/ federal/us/509/630/ [accessed August 3, 2017].

"The Future of Majority-Minority Districts in Light of Declining Racially Polarized Voting," *Harvard Law Review*, 116 (2003): 2208-2229.

■ Danica Roem's Election Victory Speech

Date: November 7, 2017
Author: Danica Roem
Genre: Address; speech

Summary Overview

The document reproduced here is the victory speech of Danica Roem in the November 2017 election for a seat in the Virginia Statehouse. With this victory, Roem became the first openly transgender elected official in United States history. It was a momentous occasion for several reasons. The first was that, previously, this particular seat had been held for over 20 years by a very socially conservative Republican and is now held by a much more liberal Democrat. Second, the victory would seem to be part of a larger, nation-wide response to the election of Donald J. Trump as president in 2016 and the far-right policies he has espoused. It likely also was a reaction to the increasingly unpopular Republicans in government who support Trump. Finally, Roem was one of several transgender individuals to win elected positions, although her victory was for an office higher than the rest. This possibly signals a turn toward less discriminatory practices vis-à-vis the transgender community at large. Roem's campaign was based on policy issues, such as improvements to infrastructure, and on holding out against the discriminatory remarks of her opponent. She did not make the issue of sexual identity her defining message, nor did she shy away from the topic.

Defining Moment

After eight years of presidential leadership by the modestly liberal Democrat Barack Obama, the U.S. electorate swung in the direction of far-right conservatism with the election of Republican Donald Trump. The Republican-dominated Congress moved rightward as well in the wake of the election. Thus, replacing liberal policies of inclusivity and civil rights protections were, now, Trumpist policies of immigration restriction, ultra-nationalism (including white nationalism), denigration of women, hostility toward various ethnic groups and followers of non-Christian religions, and the mocking of persons with disabilities (as Trump famously did on the campaign trail). Exclusionary politics, fear-mongering,

and, in the case of a violent incident in Charlottesville, VA, in the summer of 2017, white-supremacist hatred, came to dominate political rhetoric in or associated with the White House. Trump's popularity remained historically low (between 30 and 40 percent), and from the moment of his inauguration his presidency was the subject of protests (including a massive women's march in Washington, D.C., the day after the inauguration). Democrats across the nation were motivated to oppose Trump and the Republicans politically; new candidates for office, many of them women, entered the ring in unprecedented numbers. The midterm elections in 2017 saw several significant wins by Democratic candidates, including the one by Danica Roem.

Roem's victory, moreover, is part of a small but noticeable increase in the participation of transgender individuals in the electoral process, even though they face discrimination from the U.S. Congress itself. Since the early 1990s, transgender officials have been elected to various offices. However, they were generally not open about their gender identity or had not begun or completed their transitions; one or two such individuals were elected or re-elected each year. In 2017, nine transgender persons were elected. While this may not be a large number, for a seriously unreported and massively under-represented portion of the populace, the increase is a big deal.

Author Biography

Danica Roem was born in Prince William County, near Manassas, Virginia, on September 30, 1984. She attended St. Bonaventure University in western New York before becoming an award-winning journalist and editor for the Gainesville Times and, then, the Prince William Times. Roem came to national attention when she won the Democratic primary for Virginia's 13th District and then went on to win the general election on November 7, 2017. Roem based her political campaign on local issues, specifically the traffic congestion on Route 28, which had plagued Manassas for decades; but her gender was also put on center stage. As an openly transgender woman, Roem never hid from the complex social dynamics at play in her bid for office. The incumbent official, Robert Marshall, refused to hold debates with Roem or to address her by means of feminine pronouns (a serious insult and breach of social norms). As such, the issue became a key element in the campaign—on both political sides, both locally and nationally. With Roem's victory, the LGBTQ community nationwide celebrated.

HISTORICAL DOCUMENT

To every person who's ever been singled out, who's ever been stigmatized, who's ever been the misfit, who's ever been the kid in the corner, who's ever needed someone to stand up for them when they didn't have a voice of their own, because there was no one else who was with them – this one's for you….

I'm a reporter. I believe in accountability…The people of the 13th District are tired of all the stoplights in Centerville, they've got to go and I've proposed a way to get it through. This is the time for leadership to get it done. We need to fix the existing problems we have instead of creating new ones.

I know that all sounds like policy stuff. I know it sounds like boring stuff. That's why I got in this race because I'm fed up with the … road over in my hometown. And, yeah, I'm a lifelong Manassas resident. Yeah, I'm a reporter. And, yeah, I'm a trans woman too. And I have ideas for how to deal with our public policy issues. I have ideas for what we can do to improve our infrastructure. Because I believe in building up our infrastructure instead of tearing down each other.

When the negative ads started coming out, attacking transgender kids … when those came out, we stayed on our message while decrying discrimination. This election has to prove nationwide that discrimination is a disqualifier. And when you champion inclusion, when you champion equality, when you champion equity, and you focus on the issues that unite us—like building up our infrastructure, taking care of our roads, making sure that our teacher pay isn't the lowest in northern Virginia … like expanding Medicaid … —that's the sort of stuff, those are the issues that you gotta focus on as a delegate, that you gotta focus on as a candidate, because that's what directly affects everyone's life, every single day. This is the important stuff.

We can't get lost in discrimination, we can't get lost in B.S., we can't get lost tearing each other down. I want to make a point here: that no matter what you look like, where you come from, how you worship, who you love, how you identify—and yeah, how you rock—if you have good public policy ideas, if you're well-qualified for office, bring those ideas to the table, because this is your America too, this is our Commonwealth of Virginia too… and we are stronger together.

GLOSSARY

stigmatized: to be marked with some kind of disgrace, shame, or infamy

decry: to denounce as faulty or worthless; express censure of; condemn

delegate: a person designated to act for or represent another or others

DANICA 2017
Virginia House of Delegates - District 13

Document Analysis

The document represents a moment after Danica Roem's victory in the November 7, 2017, race for Virginia's 13th District seat. In it, Roem thanks her constituents, reminds the under-represented that she stands for them, takes pride in herself and the work that she has been doing, and reiterates her promise to better Virginia's 13th District and continue to promote inclusivity through her policies. Though Roem did not win by a landslide, she attempts to draw in those who voted against her by arguing that they too face common problems for which she sees a solution. Her attention to policy details (the "boring stuff"), as well as her fight against discrimination, are strong themes throughout the speech.

Unlike her opponent, Roem spent a large part of her campaign dealing specifically with the issues that most affected the citizens of the 13th District. In the political atmosphere of today, where polarization runs strong, this is a significant fact in itself. Roem openly states that she got into the race, not for particular social issues or to act as an activist for the transgender community, but to deal with the shared problems of all members of her district, such as the traffic conditions on Route 28. In her victory speech, she acknowledges that policy can sometimes be "boring," but it is nevertheless important and she has tried to make policy the most substantive part of her political campaign. Her focus on policy brought her many voters who were tired of the political mud-slinging and personality competitions that make up much of today's polarized politics. As Roem puts it, "I believe in building up our infrastructure instead of tearing down each other." She wants to focus on building a better community, beginning with the roads, rather than on making identity politics the central issue of her forthcoming tenure in office.

But her identity, of course, is a factor, especially as many people, both in the political arena and in society generally, are still adjusting to the idea of "transgender." Both because of that and for traditional political reasons, Roem also addresses her detractors in the speech. She does not attack anyone for disagreeing with her; she does not specifically call out her now-defeated opponent, even though he and his supporters ran some hateful ads in opposition to her. Rather, she refers to "the issues that unite us," thereby subtly paying attention to everyone who did not vote for her and indicating that she will do her best for them as well. Her speech is an example of how politics can be an inclusive, positive, hopeful, and caring phenomenon.

One of the most prominent messages in the speech is the idea that through her position she will promote unity and inclusion going forward. This is evident in her opening lines, giving hope to anyone who has ever felt marginalized or overlooked. It is especially evident when she declares, "This election has to prove nationwide that discrimination is a disqualifier"—and calls for everyone to "champion equality." It is evident when she wants people to come together and not lose themselves in the differences between people. In the end, she says, "that no matter what you look like, where you come from, how you worship, who you love, how you identify … if you have good public policy ideas, if you're well-qualified for office, bring those ideas to the table, because this is your America too, this is our Commonwealth of Virginia too…and we are stronger together." This is not always an easy view to take. It takes work to be truly accepting of different points of view, different creeds, and different cultures. It is not easy to unite people who are set in their own ways. Yet, to build a better society, all types of people have to be involved. Everyone needs to have a voice. And everyone needs to work together.

Essential Themes

The basic needs of modern society is one topic at work here. Roem deals with this when she says, "building up our infrastructure, taking care of our roads, making sure that our teacher pay isn't the lowest in northern Virginia…like expanding Medicaid…" These are references to political issues and policies that have a long history of debate in this country, and that matter both locally and nationally. At the same time, infrastructure and the like are not exactly hot-button issues for the bulk of voters. They lack political "sex appeal," and people do not ordinarily donate money to candidates who focus on such causes. Roem, though, is trying to redirect the conversation to the basic needs of her district and her people. Much of the political machination in this country comes down to cultural wars or moral and ethical debates based on religious belief systems. Campaigns run in the style of Roem's, however, deal with common issues and try not to be distracted by broader moral concerns. In this case, the distractions were present and were highlighted by her opponent, despite Roem's best efforts at focusing on the dull stuff of policy.

Roem does not dwell on the negative impact of discrimination and marginalization on the transgender community, but instead only mentions it in passing and argues for inclusivity and unity generally. The reality of the situation, though, is that the transgender individuals can face serious hardship, especially during their early years. A report composed by the Williams Institute found that transgendered individuals attempt suicide in 41 percent of cases, while the number for the LGB community is 10 to 20 percent. This compares to 4.6 percent for the general population. In cases where families disown an individual or withdraw their support, the suicide rate is 57 percent—the highest of nearly any group in the United States. Figures such as Danica Roem may serve to inspire others and turn them away from inflicting harm on themselves while helping non-transgender persons to better understand and accept the reality of being transgender.

Over the centuries since the founding of the United States, there has always been tension between various groups, whether they be religious, ethnic, or cultural. In the last fifty years, sexual orientation and gender identity have been added to the list of ways in which people differentiate between one another—ways that people find to alienate one another. While one might say that it is "human nature" to fear something that is new or different, the last century has shown us that identity politics can play a positive role in educating people and expanding their outlook. Politicians like Danica Roem, who break out of the standard mold and try to lead by example, try to find ways to lessen the differences between people through their words and actions. They seek ways for people of different backgrounds to find common ground in order to build a better life for everyone.

—*Anna Accettola, MA*

Bibliography and Additional Reading

D'Emilio, John, and Estelle B. Freedman. *Intimate Matters: a History of Sexuality in America.* University of Chicago Press, 2012.

Haas, Ann P., et al. *Suicide Attempts among Transgender and Gender Non-Conforming Adults: Findings of the National Transgender Discrimination Survey.* Williams Institute, University of California, Los Angeles, 2014.

Meyerowitz, Joanne J. *How Sex Changed: a History of Transsexuality in the United States.* Harvard University Press, 2009.

Olivo, Antonio. "Danica Roem of Virginia to Be First Openly Transgender Person Elected, Seated in a U.S. Statehouse." *The Washington Post,* 8 Nov. 2017, www.washingtonpost.com/local/virginia-politics/danica-roem-will-be-vas-first-openly-transgender-elected-official-after-unseating-conservative-robert-g-marshall-in-house-race/2017/11/07/d534bdde-c0af-11e7-959c-fe2b598d8c00_story.html?utm_term=.c94839bb27bf.

Stryker, Susan. *Transgender History: The Roots of Today's Revolution.* Seal Press, 2017.

Chronological List

Web Resources

presidency.ucsb.edu/

The American Presidency Project provides online access to thousands of documents related to the study of the U.S. presidency; also has selected audio recordings.

millercenter.org/

The Miller Center provides a comprehensive collection of material about the presidents and the history of the presidency, including essays about the presidents' lives before, during, and after each presidential term.

pbs.org/wgbh/americanexperience/collections/presidents/

PBS offers streaming documentaries on ten American presidents in its *American Experience* history series. The site includes a summary page for each chief executive, provides Featured Presidents, an in-depth look at the presidents in the broadcast series, and links to presidential sites and more.

whitehouse.gov/

This official government White House website features factual information for all the presidents (including their official White House portraits) and the first ladies, as well as information about the vice president's residence, the Eisenhower Executive Office building, and more.

americanantiquarian.org/

The American Antiquarian Society's (AAS) collections cover topics from the Colonial Era through the Civil War and Reconstruction. Collections include books, pamphlets, newspapers, periodicals, broadsides, manuscripts, music, graphic arts, and local histories. The website also has online exhibits related to the study of early American history and culture.

gilderlehrman.org/

The Gilder Lehrman Institute of American History maintains this website to serve as a portal for American history on the Web; to offer high-quality educational material for teachers, students, historians, and the public; and to provide up-to-date information about the Institute's programs and activities.

digitalhistory.uh.edu/

Digital History, maintained by the University of Houston, offers numerous documents, most of them primary sources, relating to U.S. history, including political history and other topics.

loc.gov

The home page of the Library of Congress provides direct access to thousands of resources devoted to topics and exhibits related to American history.

archives.gov

The National Archives has a useful website that highlights valuable historical documents like the Declaration of Independence, the Constitution, the Bill of Rights and much more. It also has many important presidential papers, primary source materials, war records, etc.

sourcebooks.fordham.edu/mod/modsbook.asp

The Internet Modern History Sourcebook (Fordham University) is intended to serve the needs of teachers and students in college survey courses in modern European history and American history, as well as well as other areas.

historyexplorer.si.edu/

The Smithsonian National Museum of American History is a gateway to useful, standards-based online resources for teaching and learning American history.

Bibliography

1888 Democratic Party Platform, June 5, 1888. The American Presidency Project, http://www.presidency.ucsb.edu/ws/index.php?pid=29584.

1888 Republican Party Platform, June 19, 1888. The American Presidency Project, http://www.presidency.ucsb.edu/ws/index.php?pid=29627.

Abraham Lincoln Online. *House Divided Speech*. Abraham Lincoln Online, 2013. Web. 6 Oct. 2013.

Abramowitz, Alan I., and Walter J. Stone. "The Bush Effect: Polarization, Turnout, and

Activism in the 2004 Presidential Election." *Presidential Studies Quarterly*, vol. 36, no. 2, 2006, pp. 141–154., doi:10.1111/j.1741-5705.2006.00295.x.

Alexander, Thomas B. *Political Reconstruction in Tennessee*. Nashville: Vanderbilt UP, 1950. Print.

"Alien and Sedition Acts." *Library of Congress*. Library of Congress, 2010. Web. 6 June 2012.

Allen, Frederick Lewis. Only *Yesterday: An Informal History of the 1920's*. Marblehead: Wiley, 1931. Print.

Ambrose, Stephen E. *Eisenhower, Vol. II: The President*. New York: Simon, 1984. Print.

———. *Nixon: Ruin and Recovery, 1973–1990*. New York: Simon, 1991. Print.

———. *Nixon: The Education of a Politician 1913-1962*. New York: Simon and Schuster, 1987. Print.

"American President: Abraham Lincoln (1809–1865)." *The Miller Center*. U of Virginia, 2013. Web. 24 Apr. 2013.

"American President: Herbert Hoover (1874–1964)." *The Miller Center*. U of Virginia, n.d. Web. 17 June 2014.

"American Presidents Life Portraits: Abraham Lincoln." *AH: American History TV*. National Cable Satellite Corporation, 2013. Web. 24 Apr. 2013.

"Americans Call for Term Limits, End to Electoral College." *Gallup.com*. Gallup, Inc., 18 Jan. 2013. Web. 12 Dec. 2014.

Andrew, John A. *Lyndon Johnson and the Great Society*. Chicago: Dee, 1998. Print.

Balz, Dan. "Bush Wins Second Term." *The Washington Post*, WP Company, 4 Nov. 2004, www.washington-post.com/wp-dyn/articles/A19510-2004Nov2_2.html.

Bancroft, Frederic. *The Life of William Henry Seward*. Vol. 1. New York: Harper, 1900. Print.

Barnes, Robert and Dan Eggen. "Supreme Court rejects limits on corporate spending on political campaigns." *Washingtonpost.com*. Washington: The Washington Post Company, 2010. Web. 3 September 2017.

Bartlett, Bruce. *The Truth Matters: A Citizen's Guide to Separating Facts from Lies and Stopping Fake News in Its Tracks*. Emeryville, CA: Ten Speed Press, 2017. Print.

Baylor, Christopher. *First to the Party: The Group Origins of Party Transformation*. Philadelphia: University of Pennsylvania Press, 2018.

Benet, Lorenzo. *Trailblazer: An Intimate Biography of Sarah Palin*. New York: Threshold Editions, 2009. Print.

Bensel, Richard Franklin. *Passion and Preferences: William Jennings Bryan and the 1896 Democratic National Convention*. New York: Cambridge UP, 2008. Print.

Berg, A. Scott. *Wilson*. New York: G. Putnam's Sons, 2013.

Bergeron, Paul H., Stephen V. Ash, and Jeanette Keith. *Tennesseans and Their History*. Knoxville: U of Tennessee P, 1999. Print.

Berman, Larry. Lyndon Johnson's War: The Road to Stalemate in Vietnam. New York: W. W. Norton, 1989. Print.

Beschloss, Michael, and Hugh Sidey. *The Presidents of the United States of America*. Washington: White House Historical Assn., 2009. Print.

Borneman, Walter R. *Polk: The Man Who Transformed the Presidency and America*. New York: Random House, 2009.

Braeman, John. *Albert J. Beveridge: American Nationalist*. Chicago: U of Chicago P, 1971. Print.

Brands, H.W. *Andrew Jackson: His Life and Times*. New York: Doubleday, 2005.

———. *Reagan: The Life*. New York: Doubleday, 2015. Print.

———. *Traitor to His Class: The Privileged Life and Radical Presidency of Franklin Delano Roosevelt*. Anchor, 2009.

———. *T.R.: The Last Romantic*. Basic Books, 1998.

———. *Woodrow Wilson*. New York: Times Books, 2003.

Brass, Chelsea. "The Life and Work of Barbara Jordan: Remembering a Legacy." Lyndon B. Johnson School of Public Affairs. U of Texas, 2011. Web. 15 Apr. 2016.

Brennan, Mary. *Turning Right in the Sixties: The Conservative Capture of the GOP*. Chapel Hill: U of North Carolina P, 1995. Print.

"Brief Biography of Thomas Jefferson". *The Jefferson Monticello*. Thomas Jefferson Foundation, 2012. Web. 1 June 2012.

Brookhiser, Richard. *Founding Father: Rediscovering George Washington*. New York: Free Press, 1996. Print.

———. *James Madison*. New York: Basic, 2011. Print.

Bryan, Steven. *The Gold Standard at the Turn of the Twentieth Century: Rising Powers, Global Money and the Age of Empire*. New York: Columbia UP, 2010. Print.

Budiansky, Stephen. *The Bloody Shirt: Terror after Appomattox*. New York: Viking, 2008. Print.

Busby, Horace. The Thirty-First of March: Lyndon Johnson's Final Days in Office. New York: Farrar, Straus, and Giroux, 2005. Print.

Bush v. Gore, 121 S.Ct. 525 (2000). Justia: U.S. Supreme Court https://supreme.justia.com/cases/federal/us/531/98/ [accessed March 28, 2018].

Calhoun, Charles W. *Minority Victory: Gilded Age Politics and the Front Porch Campaign of 1888*. Lawrence, Kansas: University Press of Kansas, 2008.

Califano, Joseph A., Jr. *The Triumph and Tragedy of Lyndon Johnson: The White House Years*. New York: Simon, 1991. Print.

Caress, Stanley M., & Todd T. Kunioka. *Term Limits and Their Consequences: The Aftermath of Legislative Reform*. Albany: State U of New York P, 2012. Print.

Carroll, Sarah. "Causes of the Great Depression". *OK Economics*. Boston U, 2002. Web. 17 June 2014.

Edsforth, Ronald. *The New Deal: America's Response to the Great Depression*. Hoboken: Wiley, 2000. Print.

Carter, Jimmy. *White House Diary*. New York: Farrar, 2010. Print.

Carwardine, Richard. *Lincoln: A Life of Purpose and Power*. New York: Vintage, 2006. Print.

Center for American Women and Politics. Eagleton Institute of Politics at Rutgers U, 2017, http://www.cawp.rutgers.edu/. Accessed Nov. 1. 2017.

Cerulo, Karen. "Symbols and the World System: National Anthems and Flags." *Sociological Forum 8.2* (1993): 243–71. *Print.*

Chambers II, John Whiteclay. *The Tyranny of Change: America in the Progressive Era, 1900-1917*. New York: St. Martins, 1980.

Cheathem, Mark R. *Andrew Jackson and the Rise of the Democrats: A Reference Guide*. Santa Barbara: ABC-CLIO, 2015.

Chernow, Ron. *Grant*. New York: Penguin Press, 2017. Print.

———. *Washington: A Life*. New York: Penguin, 2010. Print.

Cherny, Robert W. *A Righteous Cause: The Life of William Jennings Bryan*. Norman: U of Oklahoma P, 1994. Print.

Civil War Research Engine. *House Divided: Lincoln-Douglas Debates Digital Classroom*. Carlisle, Penn.: Dickinson College, 2010. Web. 6 Oct. 2013.

Clarke, Thurston. *The Last Campaign: Robert F. Kennedy and 82 Days That Inspired America*. New York: Henry Holt and Company, 2008. Print.

Clements, Jeffrey D. with Bill Moyers. *Corporations Are Not People: Reclaiming Democracy from Big Money and Global Corporations*. (2nd ed.) San Francisco: Berett-Koehler Publishers, 2014. Print.

Clements, Kendrick A. *The Presidency of Woodrow Wilson*. Lawrence: University Press of Kansas, 1992.

Clines, Francis X. "Barbara Jordan Dies at 59; Her Voice Stirred the Nation." *New York Times*. New York Times, 18 Jan. 1996. Web. 15 Apr. 2016

Clinton, Hillary Rodham. *What Happened*. New York: Simon & Schuster, 2017.

CNN. "1992 Presidential Debates." *All Politics: CNN, Time.* New York: AllPolitics, 1996. Web. 28 March 2018.

Cohen, Michael A. *American Maelstrom: The 1968 Election and the Politics of Division.* New York: Oxford University Press, 2016.

Commission on Presidential Debates. "1988 Debates." *Commission on Presidential Debates.* Washington: The Commission on Presidential Debates, 2018. Web. 27 March 2018.

Commission on Presidential Debates. "1992 Debates." *Commission on Presidential Debates.* Washington: The Commission on Presidential Debates, 2018. Web. 28 March 2018

Constitutioncenter.org, constitutioncenter.org/blog/behind-the-biggest-upset-in-presidential-history-truman-beats-dewey.

Cooke, Alistair. *Six Men.* Rev. ed. New York: Penguin, 2008. Print.

Cooper, John Milton. *Breaking the Heart of the World: Woodrow Wilson and the Fight for the League of Nations.* New York: Cambridge University Press, 2001.

———. *Woodrow Wilson: A Biography.* New York: Alfred A. Knopf, 2009.

Cooper v. Harris, 137 S.Ct. 1455 (2017). Justia: US Supreme Court https://supreme.justia.com/cases/federal/us/581/15-1262/ [accessed August 3, 2017].

Corry, John. *Lincoln at Cooper Union.* New York: Xlibris, 2003. Print.

Coulter, E. Merton. *William G. Brownlow: Fighting Parson of the Southern Highlands.* Chapel Hill: U of North Carolina P, 1937. Print.

Critchlow, Donald. *American Political History: A Very Short Introduction.* New York: Oxford University Press, 2015.

Crotty, William J. *A Defining Moment: the Presidential Election of 2004.* M.E. Sharpe, 2005.

C-SPAN American History TV. *Lincoln-Douglas Debate Reenactment.* Washington, D.C.: National Cable Satellite Corporation, 2011. Web.

C-SPAN. *American Presidents: Life Portraits: Abraham Lincoln.* Washington: National Cable Satellite Corporation, 2012. Web. 6 Oct 2013.

C-SPAN with Theodore Olson and J. Douglas Smith. "Baker v. Carr, 1962." *Landmark Cases.* Washington: National Cable Satellite Corporation, 2017. Web. 3 August 2017.

Daley, David. *Ratf**ked : The True Story Behind the Secret Plan to Steal America's Democracy.* New York: Liveright Publishing Corp., 2016.

"Dan Balz." *The Washington Post,* WP Company, www.washingtonpost.com/people/dan-balz/?utm_term=.34804503d8c6.

DeFrank, Thomas M., Mark Miller, Andrew Murr, and Tom Matthews. *Quest for the Presidency 1992.* College Station TX: Texas A&M University Press, 1994. Print.

———. *Write It When I'm Gone: Remarkable Off-the-Record Conversations with Gerald R. Ford.* New York: Putnam's, 2007. Print.

Delaplaine, Edward Schley. *Francis Scott Key: Life and Times.* Biography Press, 1937. Print.

D'Emilio, John, and Estelle B. Freedman. *Intimate Matters: a History of Sexuality in America.* University of Chicago Press, 2012.

Diggins, John Patrick. *Ronald Reagan: Fate, Freedom, and the Making of History.* New York: Norton, 2007. Print.

Digital History. "Baker v. Carr." *Digital History.* Houston: Digital History, 2016. Web. 3 August 2017.

Donaldson, Gary A. *Truman Defeats Dewey.* The University Press of Kentucky, 2015.

Douglas, Joshua, and Eugene Mazeo. *Election Law Stories.* Foundation Press, 2016. Print.

Drew, Elizabeth. *Richard M. Nixon.* New York: Times, 2007. Print.

D'Souza, Dinesh. 1997. *Ronald Reagan: How an Ordinary Man Became an Extraordinary Leader.* Simon & Schuster: New York, NY.

Du Bois, W. E. B. *Black Reconstruction in America: Toward a History of the Part of Which Black Folk Played in the Attempt to Reconstruct Democracy in America, 1860–1880.* Rev. ed. New Brunswick: Transaction, 2012.

Ecelbarger, Gary. *The Great Comeback: How Abraham Lincoln Beat the Odds to Win the 1860 Republican Nomination.* New York: Dunne, 2008. Print.

Edward Foley, "Voting Rules and Constitutional Law," *George Washington Law Review,* 81 Geo. Wash. L. Rev. 1836, 2013.

Egerton, Douglas. *Year of Meteors: Stephen Douglas, Abraham Lincoln, and the Election That Brought On the Civil War.* New York: Bloomsbury, 2010. Print.

Eisenhower, Susan. "Fifty Years Later, We're Still Ignoring Ike's Warning." *Washington Post.* Washington Post, 16 Jan. 2011. Web.

Ellis, Joseph J. *American Sphinx: The Character of Thomas Jefferson.* New York: Vintage, 1998. Print.

———. *His Excellency: George Washington.* New York: Vintage, 2005. Print.

Ellis, Sylvia. *Freedom's Pragmatist: Lyndon Johnson and Civil Rights.* Gainesville: University of Florida Press, 2013. Print.

Etcheson, Nicole. *Bleeding Kansas: Contested Liberty in the Civil War Era.* Lawrence: UP of Kansas, 2004. Print.

Farrell, John A. *Richard Nixon: The Life.* New York: Doubleday, 2017.

Ferling, John. *Adams vs. Jefferson: The Tumultuous Election of 1800.* Oxford: Oxford UP, 2005. Print.

Ferrell, Robert H. *The Presidency of Calvin Coolidge.* Lawrence: UP of Kansas, 1998. Print.

———. "Woodrow Wilson: Man and Statesman. *Review of Politics* 18, no. 2 (April 1956): 131–145.

Fletcher, Michael. "The Speech on Race That Saved Obama's Candidacy." *The Washington Post,* WP Company, www.washingtonpost.com/graphics/national/obama-legacy/jeremiah-wright-2008-philadelphia-race-speech.html.

Flexner, James Thomas. *Washington: The Indispensable Man.* Boston: Little, 1974. Print.

Foner, Eric. *Free Soil, Free Labor, Free Men: The Ideology of the Republican Party before the Civil War.* New York: Oxford UP, 1995. Print.

———. *Reconstruction: America's Unfinished Revolution, 1863–1877.* New York: Harper, 1988. Print.

———. *The Fiery Trial: Abraham Lincoln and American Slavery.* New York: Norton, 2010. Print.

Ford, Gerald R. *A Time to Heal: The Autobiography of Gerald R. Ford.* New York: Harper, 1979. Print.

Forgette, Richard. *News Grazers: Media, Politics, and Trust in an Information Age.* Washington: CQ Press, 2018. Print.

Gains, Richard and Michael Segal. *Dukakis: The Man Who Would Be President.* New York: Avon Books, 1988. Print.

Goldberg, David J. *Discontented America: The United States of the 1920s.* Baltimore: Johns Hopkins UP, 1999. Print.

Goldberg, Robert Alan. *Barry Goldwater.* New Haven: Yale UP, 1995. Print.

Goldman, Peter, Tom Matthews et al. *Quest for the Presidency: The 1988 Campaign.* New York: Simon & Schuster Books, 1989. Print.

Goodwin, Doris Kearns. *Team of Rivals: The Political Genius of Abraham Lincoln.* New York: Simon, 2005. Print.

———. *The Bully Pulpit: Theodore Roosevelt, William Howard Taft, and the Golden Age of Journalism.* Simon and Schuster, 2014.

Greene, John Robert. *The Presidency of Gerald R. Ford.* Lawrence: UP of Kansas, 1995. Print.

Grofman, Bernard, editor. *Race and Redistricting in the 1990s.* New York: Agathon Press, 1998.

Guelzo, Allen. *Abraham Lincoln as a Man of Ideas.* Carbondale: Southern Illinois UP, 2009. Print.

———. *Abraham Lincoln: Redeemer President.* Grand Rapids: Eerdmans, 1999. Print.

———. *Fateful Lightning: A New History of the Civil War and Reconstruction.* New York: Oxford UP, 2012. Print.

———. *Lincoln and Douglas: The Debates that Defined America.* New York: Simon & Schuster, 2008. Print.

Gutzman, Kevin R. C. *James Madison and the Making of America.* New York: St. Martin's, 2012. Print.

Haas, Ann P., et al. *Suicide Attempts among Transgender and Gender Non-Conforming Adults: Findings of the National Transgender Discrimination Survey.* Williams Institute, University of California, Los Angeles, 2014.

Hansen, Bradley A. *The National Economy.* Westport: Greenwood, 2006. Print

Hansen, Richard. *The Supreme Court and Election Law: Judging from Baker v. Carr to Bush v. Gore.* New edition. New York: New York University Press, 2006. Print.

Heckscher, August. *Woodrow Wilson*. New York: Scribners, 1991.

Heilemann, John & Mark Halperin. *Game Change: Obama and the Clintons, McCain and Palin, and the Race of a Lifetime*. New York: HarperCollins, 2010. Print.

"Herbert Clark Hoover: A Biographical Sketch." *Herbert Hoover Presidential Library and Museum*. National Archives, n.d. Web. 17 June 2014.

"Herbert Clark Hoover." Herbert Hoover Presidential Library and Museum. National Archives and Records Administration, 2014. Web. 20 May 2014.

"Herbert Clark Hoover." Miller Center. University of Virginia, 2013. Web. 20 May 2014.

Herring, George C. *From Colony to Superpower: US Foreign Relations since 1776*. New York: Oxford UP, 2008. Print.

———. *LBJ and Vietnam: A Different Kind of War*. Austin, TX: University of Texas Press, 1994. Print.

Himmelberg, Robert F., ed. *Antitrust and Regulation during World War I and the Republican Era, 1917–1932*. New York: Routledge, 1994. Print.

Hitchens, Christopher. *Thomas Jefferson: Author of America*. Atlas & Co./Harper Perennial, 2009.

Hoff, Joan. *Nixon Reconsidered*. New York: Basic, 1994. Print.

Holt, Michael F. *By One Vote: The Disputed Presidential Election of 1876* (American Presidential Elections). Lawrence, Kansas: University Press of Kansas, 2008.

———. *The Rise and Fall of the American Whig Party: Jacksonian Politics and the Onset of Civil War*. Oxford: Oxford University Press, 1999.

Holzer, Harold, ed. *The Lincoln-Douglas Debates: The First Complete, Unexpurgated Text*. New York: Fordham UP, 2004. Print.

———. *Lincoln at Cooper Union: The Speech That Made Abraham Lincoln President*. New York: Simon, 2004. Print.

Hoogenboom, Ari. *Rutherford B. Hayes: Warrior and President*. Lawrence, Kansas: University Press of Kansas, 1995

Horn, Stanley F. *Invisible Empire: The Story of the Ku Klux Klan, 1866–1871*. Cos Cob: Edwards, 1969. Print.

Howe, Daniel Walker. *What Hath God Wrought: The Transformation of America, 1815–1848*. New York: Oxford UP, 2007. Print.

Huston, James L. *Stephen A. Douglas and the Dilemmas of Democratic Equality*. Lanham: Rowman, 2007. Print.

Irons, Peter. *A People's History of the Supreme Court*. New York, NY: Penguin, 1999. Print.

Jaffa, Harry, and Robert Johannsen, eds. *In the Name of the People: Speeches and Writings of Lincoln and Douglas in the Ohio Campaign of 1859*. Columbus: Ohio State UP, 1959. Print.

———. *A New Birth of Freedom: Abraham Lincoln and the Coming of the Civil War*. Lanham: Rowman, 2000. Print.

Jamieson, Patrick E. "Seeing the Lyndon B. Johnson Presidency through the March 31, 1968, Withdrawal Speech." Presidential Studies Quarterly 29.1 (March 1999): 134–49. Print.

Jensen, Richard. The Winning of the Midwest: Social and Political Conflict, 1888-1896. Chicago: University of Chicago Press, 1971.

"Jimmy Carter: Life before the Presidency." Miller Center. University of Virginia, 2016. Web. 5 Apr. 2016.

"Jimmy Carter: Thirty-Ninth President of the United States and Founder of the Carter Center." Carter Center. Carter Center, 2016. Web. 5 Apr. 2016.

Johannsen, Robert Walter. *Stephen A. Douglas*. New York: Oxford UP, 1997 ed. Print.

Johnson, Robert David. *All the Way with LBJ: The 1964 Presidential Election*. New York: Cambridge UP, 2009. Print.

"Jordan, Barbara Charline." U.S. House of Representatives: History, Art & Archives. Office of the Historian, n.d. Web. 15 Apr. 2016.

Karabell, Zachary. *The Last Campaign: How Harry Truman Won the 1948 Election*. Vintage

Katznelson, Ira. *Fear Itself: The New Deal and the Origins of Our Time*. New York: Liveright, 2013. Print.

Katz, William L. *The Invisible Empire: The Ku Klux Klan Impact on History*. Washington: Open Hand,

1986. Print.

Kearns, Doris. *Lyndon Johnson and the American Dream.* New York: St. Martins Griffin, 1991. Print.

Kesler, Charles R., ed. *Saving the Revolution: The Federalist Papers and the American Founding.* New York: Free, 1987. Print.

Ketcham, Ralph, ed. *The Anti-Federalist Papers and the Constitutional Convention Debates.* New York: Signet, 2003. Print.

Kingsbury, Alex. "An analysis of Donald Trump's inaugural speech." *Boston Globe.* January 20, 2017. https://www.bostonglobe.com/news/politics/2017/01/20/analysis-donald-trump-inaugural-speech/

Kinzer, Stephen. *Overthrow: America's Century of Regime Change from Hawaii to Iraq.* New York: Time Books, 2006. Print.

Knock, Thomas. *To End All Wars: Woodrow Wilson and the Quest for a New World Order.* New York: Oxford University Press, 1992.

Knott, Stephen F., and Jeffrey L. Chidester. *Presidential Profiles: The Reagan Years.* New York: Facts on File, 2005. Print.

Korzi, Michael J. *Presidential Term Limits in American History: Power, Principles, and Politics.* College Station: Texas A&M U Press, 2013. Print.

Kreitner, Richard. "July 13, 1960: John F. Kennedy Secures the Democratic Presidential Nomination." *Nation.* Nation, 13 July 2015. Web. 11 Feb. 2016.

Larson, Edward J. *A Magnificent Catastrophe: The Tumultuous Election of 1800, America's First Presidential Campaign.* New York: Simon, 2007. Print.

LBJ Presidential Library. "LBJ and Civil Rights." Austin: Lyndon Baines Johnson Library and Museum, 2015. Web 10 September 2015.

Legal Information Institute. "*Baker v. Carr.*" Cornell: Cornell Law School, 2017. Web. 3 August 2017.

LeMay, Michael C. *The American Political Party System: A Reference Handbook.* Santa Barbara, CA: ABC-CLIO, 2017.

Lepore, Jill. "Party Time for a Young America." *The New Yorker,* The New Yorker, 18 June 2017, www.newyorker.com/magazine/2007/0d9/17/party-time.

Lincoln, Abraham. "First Inaugural Address—Final Text." *The Collected Works of Abraham Lincoln.* Ed.

Roy Prentice Basler. Vol. 4. New Brunswick: Rutgers UP, 1953. Print. 262–71.

LincolnNet. *The Lincoln/Douglas Debates of 1858.* Lincoln Library, Northern Illinois U, 2002. Web. 6 Oct. 2013.

"Lincoln's First Inaugural Address." *American Treasures of the Library of Congress.* Lib. of Cong., 27 July 2010. Web. 24 Apr. 2013.

Link, Arthur S., ed. *Woodrow Wilson and a Revolutionary World.* Chapel Hill: University of North Carolina Press, 1982.

———. *Woodrow Wilson and the Progressive Era 1910-1917.* New York: Harper & Row, 1954.

Lowi, Theodore J. *The End of the Republican Era.* Norman: U of Oklahoma P, 1996. Print.

Madison, James, et al. *The Federalist Papers.* Lib. of Cong., n.d. Web. 25 May 2012.

———. "The James Madison Papers." *American Memory.* Lib. of Cong., n.d. Web. 23 May 2012.

Maraniss, David. *Barack Obama: the Story.* Simon & Schuster Paperbacks, 2012.

Martin, Daniel W. "The Fading Legacy of Woodrow Wilson. *Public Administration Review* 48, no. 2 (March–April 1988): 631–636.

Martinez, J. Michael. *Carpetbaggers, Cavalry, and the Ku Klux Klan: Exposing the Invisible Empire during Reconstruction.* Lanham: Rowman, 2007. Print.

Matalin, Mary and James Carville. *All's Fair: Love, War and Running for President.* New York: Simon & Schuster, 1995. Print.

Matthews, Christopher. *Kennedy and Nixon: The Rivalry That Shaped Postwar America.* New York: Simon and Schuster, 1996. Print.

McBride, Alex. "Landmark Cases: *Reynolds V. Sims.*" *PBS,* Public Broadcasting Services, www.pbs.org/wnet/supremecourt/rights/landmark_reynolds.html. Accessed 24 Aug. 2017.

McCain, John & Mark Salter. *The Restless Wave: Good Times, Just Causes, Great Fights, and Other Appreciations.* New York: Simon & Schuster, 2018. Print.

McClosky, Robert G. *The American Supreme Court: Fourth Edition.* University of Chicago Press, 2005. Print.

McCullough, David. *Truman*. New York: Simon, 1992. Print.

McElvaine, Robert S. *The Great Depression: America, 1929–1941*. 25ᵗʰ anniv. ed. New York: Three Rivers, 2009. Print.

McFeely, William S. *Grant: A Biography*. New York: W. W. Norton, 1981. Print.

McIntyre, Lee. *Post-Truth*. Cambridge, MA: The MIT Press, 2018. Print.

McKeever, Porter. *Adlai Stevenson: His Life and Legacy*. New York: Quill, 1989. Print.

McNair, Brian. *Fake News: Falsehood, Fabrication and Fantasy in Journalism*. London: Routledge, 2017. Print.

McPherson, James M. *Battle Cry of Freedom: The Civil War Era*. New York: Ballantine, 1989. Print.

Meyerowitz, Joanne J. *How Sex Changed: a History of Transsexuality in the United States*. Harvard University Press, 2009.

Meyerson, Michael. *Liberty's Blueprint: How Madison and Hamilton Wrote the Federalist Papers, Defined the Constitution, and Made Democracy Safe for the World*. New York: Basic, 2008. Print.

Michael Kent Curtis, "Using the Voting Rights Act to Discriminate: North Carolina's Use of Racial Gerrymanders, Two Racial Quotas, Safe Harbors, Shields, and Inoculations to Undermine Multiracial Coalitions and Black Political Power," *Wake Forest Law Review*, 51 (2016): 421-492.

Middendorf, John William. *A Glorious Disaster: Barry Goldwater's Presidential Campaign and the Origins of the Conservative Movement*. New York: Basic, 2006. Print.

Mikis, Sydney M. *Theodore Roosevelt, the Progressive Party, and the Transformation of American Democracy (American Political Thought)*. University Press of Kansas, 2009.

Miller Center of Public Affairs. *American President: Abraham Lincoln (1809-1865)*. Charlottesville: U of Virginia, 2012. Web. 15 Oct 2012.

Miller, Claire Cain. "Women Actually Do Govern Differently." *The New York Times*, 10 Nov. 2016, https://www.nytimes.com/2016/11/10/upshot/women-actually-do-govern-differently.html.

Morgan, Nick. The Astonishing Rhetoric of President Trump's Inaugural Address. *Forbes*. January 20, 2017. https://www.forbes.com/sites/nickmorgan/2017/01/20/the-astonishing-rhetoric-of-president-trumps-inaugural-address/

Morgan, Robert. *Lions of the West*. Chapel Hill: Algonquin Books, 2012. Print.

Morris, Edmund. *Colonel Roosevelt (Theodore Roosevelt Series Book 3)*. Random House, 2010.

Morris, Kenneth E. *Jimmy Carter, American Moralist*. Athens: U of Georgia P, 1997. Print.

Morrison, Michael A. *Slavery and the American West: The Eclipse of Manifest Destiny and the Coming of the Civil War*. Chapel Hill: U of North Carolina P, 1997. Print.

Moss, George Donelson. *Vietnam: An American Ordeal*. Upper Saddle River, New Jersey: Pearson Prentice Hall, 2006. Print.

Moyers, Bill with Floyd Abrams and Trevor Potter. "*Citizens United v. FEC*." *Bill Moyers Journal*. (including *Frontline* September 4, 2009 broadcast) Washington: Public Affairs Television, 2017. Web 3 September 2017.

Muller, Joseph. *The Star Spangled Banner; Words and Music Issued between 1814–1864; an Annotated Bibliographical List with Notices of the Different Versions, Texts, Variants, Musical Arrangements, and Notes on Music Publishers in the United States*. New York: Da Capo, 1973. Print.

Murray, Robert K. *The Harding Era: Warren G. Harding and His Administration*. Minneapolis: U of Minnesota P, 1969. Print.

Naftali, Timothy. *George H. W. Bush: The American President Series: The 41st President, 1989-1993*. New York: Times Books, 2007. Print.

"National Constitution Center." *National Constitution Center – Constitutioncenter.org*,

National Park Service. *House Divided Speech*. Springfield: Lincoln National Historic Site, 2013. Web. 30 Sept. 2013.

———. *The Lincoln-Douglas Debates of 1858*. Washington: Department of the Interior, 2013. Web. 30 Sept. 2013.

National Voting Rights Museum and Institute. "Selma Movement." Selma, Alabama: National Voting Rights

Museum and Institute, 2015. Web.

NCC Staff. "Looking Back at the Truman Beats Dewey Upset." *National Constitution Center –*

Nelson, Michael. *The Elections of 2004.* CQ Press, 2005.

Networks, 1 Nov. 2013, www.history.com/news/the-truman-dewey-election-65-years-ago.

Newton, Michael. *The Ku Klux Klan: History, Organization, Language, Influence, and Activities of America's Most Notorious Secret Society.* Jefferson: McFarland, 2007. Print.

Nix, Elizabeth. "The Truman-Dewey Election, 65 Years Ago." *History.com,* A&E Television

Nixon, Richard M. *RN: The Memoirs of Richard Nixon.* New York: Grosset and Dunlap, 1978. Print.

Oakes, James. *The Radical and the Republican: Frederick Douglass, Abraham Lincoln, and the Triumph of Antislavery Politics.* New York: Norton, 2007. Print.

Oberdorfer, Don. *Tet!: The Turning Point in the Vietnam War.* Baltimore, MD: Johns Hopkins UP, 2001. Print.

O'Donnell, Lawrence. *Playing with Fire: 1968 and the Transformation of American Politics.* New York: Penguin House, 2017.

Oliphant, Thomas, and Wilkie, Curtis. *The Road to Camelot: Inside JFK's Five-Year Campaign.* New York: Simon and Schuster, 2017. Print.

Olivo, Antonio. "Danica Roem of Virginia to Be First Openly Transgender Person Elected, Seated in a U.S. Statehouse." *The Washington Post,* 8 Nov. 2017, www.washingtonpost.com/local/virginia-politics/danica-roem-will-be-vas-first-openly-transgender-elected-official-after-unseating-conservative-robert-g-marshall-in-house-race/2017/11/07/d534bdde-c0af-11e7-959c-fe2b598d8c00_story.html?utm_term=.c94839bb27bf.

Orr, Katie and Megan Kamerick. "Trump's Election Drives More Women to Consider Running for Office." *NPR,* 23 Feb. 2017, http://www.npr.org/2017/02/23/515438978/trumps-election-drives-more-women-to-consider-running-for-office.

Our Documents.Gov. "100 Milestone Documents: Voting Rights Act (1965)." Washington, D.C.: *National Archives and Records Administration,* 2015. Web.

Oyez. "Citizens United v. Federal Election Commission." *Oyez.* Chicago: Kent College of Law at Illinois Tech, 2017. Web. 1 September 2017.

Palin, Sarah. *Going Rogue: An American Life.* New York: HarperCollins, 2009. Print

Parrish, Michael E. *Anxious Decades: American in Prosperity and Depression 1920–1941.* New York: Norton, 1992. Print.

Patterson, James T., *Restless Giant: The United States from Watergate to Bush v. Gore.* New York: Oxford University Press. Inc., 2005.

Patton, James Welch. *Unionism and Reconstruction in Tennessee 1860–1869.* Chapel Hill: U of North Carolina P, 1980. Print.

Pear, Robin Toner and Robert. "THE 40TH PRESIDENT: THE OPPONENTS; Critics See a Reagan Legacy Tainted by AIDS, Civil Rights and Union Policies." *The New York Times,* The New York Times, 9 June 2004, www.nytimes.com/2004/06/09/us/40th-president-opponents-critics-see-reagan-legacy-tainted-aids-civil-rights.html.

Perlstein, Rick. *Nixonland: The Rise of a President and the Fracturing of America.* New York: Scribner, 2008. Print.

Perot, Ross. *United We Stand: How We Can Take Back Our Country.* New York: Hyperion Books, 1992. Print.

Pew Research Center. 2008. "*Obama Speech on Race Arguably Biggest Event of Campaign.*"

Polakoff, Keith Ian. *The Politics of Inertia: The Election of 1876 and the End of Reconstruction.* Baton Rouge: Louisiana State University Press, 1973.

Post, Robert C. with Pamela S. Karlan, Lawrence Lessing, Frank I. Michelman, and Nadia Urbinati. *Citizens Divided: Campaign Finance Reform and the Constitution.* (The Tanner Lectures on Human Values) Cambridge: Harvard University Press, 2014. Print.

Potter, David M., and Don E. Fehrenbacher. *The Impending Crisis, 1848–1861.* New York: Harper Perennial, 2011. Print.

Potter, David. *The Impending Crisis, 1848–1861.* New York: Harper, 1977. Print.

Presidential Election of 1824: A Resource Guide. The Library of Congress. https://www.loc.gov/rr/program/

bib/elections/election1824.html

Presidential Election of 1844, A Resource Guide. Library of Congress, https://www.loc.gov/rr/program/bib/elections/election1844.html.

Presidential Election of 1876: A Resource Guide. https://www.loc.gov/rr/program/bib/elections/election1876.html.

"Presidential Election of 1888: A Resource Guide," Library of Congress. https://www.loc.gov/rr/program/bib/elections/election1888.html.

Queener, Verton M. "A Decade of East Tennessee Republicanism, 1867–1876." *East Tennessee Historical Society's Publications* 14 (1942): 59–85. Print.

Rable, George C. *But There Was No Peace: The Role of Violence in the Politics of Reconstruction*. Athens: U of Georgia P, 2007. Print.

Randel, William P. *The Ku Klux Klan: A Century of Infamy*. Philadelphia: Chilton, 1965. Print.

Ratcliffe, Donald J. *The One-Party Presidential Contest: Adams, Jackson, and 1824's Five-Horse Race*. Lawrence, Kansas: University Press of Kansas, 2015.

Reagan, Ronald. *An American Life: The Autobiography*. New York: Simon, 2011. Print.

Remini, Robert. *Henry Clay: A Statesman for the Union*. New York: WW Norton, 1991.

Ritter, Kurt W. "Ronald Reagan and 'The Speech': The Rhetoric of Public Relations Politics." *Western Speech* 32.1 (1968): 50–58. Print.

"Ronald Reagan: Inaugural Address - January 20, 1981." *The American Presidency Project*, www.presidency.ucsb.edu/ws/?pid=43130.

Roosevelt, Franklin D. "Statement on Signing the Social Security Act." August 14, 1935. The American Presidency Project, University of California Santa Barbara, http://www.presidency.ucsb.edu/ws/?pid=14916.

Rorabaugh, W. J. *The Real Making of the President: Kennedy, Nixon, and the 1960 Election*. Lawrence: UP of Kansas, 2009. Print.

Ross, Brian, and Rehab El-buri. "Obama's Pastor: God Damn America, U.S. to Blame for 9/11." *ABC News*, ABC News Network, 13 Mar. 2008, abcnews.go.com/Blotter/DemocraticDebate/story?id=4443788&page=1.

Rothman, Lily, and Arpita Aneja. "President Ronald

Reagan Elected: Remembering That Day." *Time*, Time, 4 Nov. 2015, time.com/4090907/time-remembers-ronald-reagan-1980/.

Rozwenc, Edwin C. *The Causes of the American Civil War*. 2nd ed. Lexington, MA: Heath, 1972. Print.

Sandbrook, Dominic. *Eugene McCarthy: The Rise and Fall of Postwar American Liberalism*. New York: Alfred A. Knopf, 2004.

Sandburg, Carl. *Abraham Lincoln: The Prairie Years and the War Years*. New York: Harcourt Brace, 1954. Print.

Scaturro, Frank J. *President Grant Reconsidered*. Latham, MD: Rowman & Littlefield, 1999. Print.

Schlesinger, Arthur M. *A Thousand Days: John F. Kennedy in the White House*. Boston: Houghton, 1965. Print.

Schwartzapfel, Beth and Bill Keller. "Willie Horton Revisited." *The Marshall Project*. New York: The Marshall Project, 2015. Web. 26 March 2018.

Schwarz, Sam. "What Has Barack Obama Been up to since Leaving Office?" *Newsweek*, 28 Dec. 2017, www.newsweek.com/barack-obama-leaving-white-house-761504.

Sellers, Charles S. *The Market Revolution: Jacksonian America, 1815–1846*. New York: Oxford UP, 1991. Print.

Severance, Ben H. *Tennessee's Radical Army: The State Guard and Its Role in Reconstruction, 1867–1869*. Knoxville: U of Tennessee P, 2005. Print.

Sharp, James Robert. *The Deadlocked Election of 1800: Jefferson, Burr, and the Union in the Balance*. Lawrence: UP of Kansas, 2010. Print.

Sharpley-Whiting, T. Denean. 2009. *The Speech: Race and Barack Obama's "A More Perfect Union"*. Bloomsbury.

Shaw v. Reno, 113 S.Ct. 2816 (1993). Justia: US Supreme Court https://supreme.justia.com/cases/federal/us/509/630/ [accessed August 3, 2017].

Shlaes, Amity. *The Forgotten Man: A New History of the Great Depression*. New York: HarperCollins, 2007. Print.

Siddiqui, Sabrina. "Bill Clinton Won 1992 Town Hall Debate by Engaging with One Voter." *Huffpost*. New York: Huffpost, 2012. Web. 28 March 2018.

Silbey, Joel H. *Storm over Texas: The Annexation Controversy and the Road to Civil War*. Oxford: Oxford University Press, 2005.

Silkett, John T. *Francis Scott Key and the History of the Star Spangled Banner*. Washington: Vintage America Pub., 1978. Print.

Simon, Roger. "Simon Says: Questions that Kill Candidates' Careers." *Politico*. Arlington VA: Politico, 2007. Web. 27 March 2018.

Sitkoff, Harvard. "Harry Truman and the Election of 1948: The Coming of Age of Civil Rights in American Politics." *The Journal of Southern History*, vol. 37, no. 4, 1971, p. 597., doi:10.2307/2206548.

Skipper, John C. *The 1964 Republican Convention: Barry Goldwater and the Beginning of the Conservative Movement*. Jefferson: McFarland, 2016. Print.

Small, Melvin. Antiwarriors: *The Vietnam War and the Battle for America's Hearts and Minds*. Lanham, MD: Rowman & Littlefield Publishers, 2002. Vietnam: America in the War Years Ser. Print.

Smith, Jean Edward. *FDR*. New York: Random, 2007. Print.

————. *Grant*. New York: Simon and Schuster, 2001. Print.

Spakovsky, Hans von. "Citizens United and the Restoration of the First Amendment." *The Heritage Foundation*. Washington: The Heritage Foundation, 2010. Web. 3 September 2017.

Stahl, Jessica. Trump's inauguration speech, one year later. *Washington Post*. January 19, 2018. https://www.washingtonpost.com/news/post-politics/wp/2018/01/19/trumps-inauguration-speech-one-year-later/

Stampp, Kenneth M. *And the War Came: The North and the Secession Crisis, 1860–61*. Chicago: U of Chicago P, 1964. Print.

————. *The Imperiled Union: Essays on the Background of the Civil War*. New York: Oxford UP, 1980. Print.

Stern, Seth and Stephen Wermiel. *Justice Brenan*. New York: Houghton Mifflin Harcourt Publishing Company, 2010. Print.

Stid, Daniel D. "Woodrow Wilson and the Problem of Party Government. *Polity* 26, no. 4 (Summer 1994): 553–578.

Stryker, Susan. *Transgender History: The Roots of Today's Revolution*. Seal Press, 2017.

Summers, Mark W. *A Dangerous Stir: Fear, Paranoia, and the Making of Reconstruction*. Chapel Hill: U of North Carolina P, 2009. Print.

————. *Party Games: Getting, Keeping, and Using Power in Gilded Age Politics*. Chapel Hill: University of North Carolina Press, 2004.

Swint, Kerwin. "Founding Fathers' Dirty." *CNN*, Cable News Network, www.cnn.com/2008/LIVING/wayoflife/08/22/mf.campaign.slurs.slogans/.

Thomas, Evans. *Ike's Bluff: President Eisenhower's Secret Battle to Save the World*. New York: Little, 2012. Print.

"Thomas Jefferson." *Biography.com*, A&E Networks Television, 7 Feb. 2018, www.biography.com/people/thomas-jefferson-9353715.

"Thomas Jefferson: The Revolution of 1800" *PBS*. Public Broadcasting Service, 2012. Web. 10 June 2012. Bernstein, R. B. *Thomas Jefferson*. Oxford: Oxford UP, 2005. Print.

Thompson, Kenneth W. *The Carter Presidency: Fourteen Intimate Perspectives of Jimmy Carter*. Lanham: UP of America, 1990. Print.

Toner, Robin. "The 1992 Elections: President—the Overview; Clinton Captures Presidency with Huge Electoral Margin; Wins a Democratic Congress." *The New York Times*. New York: The New York Times Company, 1992. Web. 28 March 2018.

Trani, Eugene P., and David L. Wilson. *The Presidency of Warren G. Harding*. Lawrence: Regents P of Kansas, 1977. Print.

"Transcript: Barack Obama's Speech on Race." *NPR*, NPR, 18 Mar. 2008, www.npr.org/templates/story/story.php?storyId=88478467.

Trelease, Allen W. *White Terror: The Ku Klux Klan Conspiracy and Southern Reconstruction*. New York: Harper, 1971. Print.

Trump, Donald J. *The America We Deserve*. New York: St. Martin's Press, 2000.

Van Deusen, Glyndon G. *Horace Greeley: Nineteenth-Century Crusader*. New York: Hill and Wang, 1964. Print.

Vilade, C. Edwin. *President's Speech: The Stories Behind the Most Memorable Presidential Addresses.* Guilford, CT: Lyons Press, 2012.

Walker, Larry. "Woodrow Wilson, Progressive Reform, and Public Administration. *Political Science Quarterly* 104, no. 3 (Autumn 1989): 509–525.

Walker, Martin. *The Cold War: A History.* New York: Holt, 1993. Print.

Walsh, Kenneth T. "The Most Consequential Elections in History: Ronald Reagan and the Election of 1980." *U.S. News & World Report*, U.S. News & World Report, www.usnews.com/news/articles/2008/09/25/the-most-consequential-elections-in-history-ronald-reagan-and-the-election-of-1980.

Warner, Geoffrey. "Lyndon Johnson's War? Part 2: From Escalation to Negotiation." International Affairs 81.1 (January 2005): 187–215. Print.

Washington, George, and Howard F. Bremer. *George Washington, 1732–1799; Chronology, Documents, Bibliographical Aids.* Dobbs Ferry, NY: Oceana, 1967. Print.

Washington, George, and John H. Rhodehamel. *Writings.* New York: Lib. of America/Penguin, 1997. Print.

Washington Secretary of State. "*Baker v. Carr* et al., March 2, 1962." *Shifting Boundaries: Redistricting in Washington State.* Olympia: Office of the Secretary of State, 2017. Web. 7 August 2017.

Weiner, Tim. *One Man against the World: The Tragedy of Richard Nixon.* New York: Holt, 2015. Print.

Whisenhunt, *Donald W. President Herbert Hoover.* Hauppauge: Nova, 2007. Print.

White, Ronald C. *Abraham Lincoln: A Biography.* New York: Random House, 2009. Print.

———. *American Ulysses: A Life of U.S. Grant.* New York: Random House, 2016. Print.

———, Jr. *Lincoln's Greatest Speech: The Second Inaugural.* New York: Simon, 2002. Print.

White, Theodore H. White. *The Making of the President: 1968.* New York: Atheneum House, 1969.

Wilentz, Sean. *The Politicians & The Egalitarians: The Hidden History of American Politics.* New York: W.W. Norton & Co., 2016.

———. *The Rise of American Democracy: Jefferson to Lincoln.* New York: Horton, 2008.

Williams, R. Hal. *Realigning America: McKinley, Bryan and the Remarkable Election of 1896.* Lawrence: UP of Kansas, 2010. Print.

Williams, Robert Chadwell. *Horace Greeley: Champion of American Freedom.* New York: New York University Press, 2006. Print.

Wills, Garry. *Negro President: Jefferson and the Slave Power.* Houghton Mifflin, 2005.

———. *Nixon Agonistes: The Crisis of the Self-Made Man.* New York: First Mariner Books, 2002.

Wilson, Woodrow. *The New Freedom: A Call for the Emancipation of the Generous Energies of a People.* New York: Doubleday, Page & Company, 1918.

Winkle, Kenneth J. *The Young Eagle: The Rise of Abraham Lincoln.* Dallas: Taylor, 2001. Print.

Wolraich, Michael. *Unreasonable Men: Theodore Roosevelt and the Republican Rebels Who Created Progressive Politics.* St. Martin's Press, 2014.

Youn, Monica (ed.) *Money, Politics, and the Constitution: Beyond Citizens United.* New York: The Century Foundation, 2011. Print.

Zelizer, Julian E. *The Fierce Urgency of Now: Lyndon Johnson*, Congress, and the Battle for the Great Society. New York: Penguin, 2015. Print.

Index